What people are saying
Relaxing into Clear S...

"This book offers deep insight and understanding of the human process that must be entered into and transformed before humanity can advance to it's next stage in evolution. This book is a living process— one that will help us get there."

—**Jacquelyn Small,**
Founding Director of the Eupsychia Institute.
Author of *Transformers, Embodying Spirit* **and** *Rising to the Call.*

"I love this book. It offers all, not just some, a simple and fundamental opportunity to find the only thing really wanted: Truth and Peace —our True Nature. Thank you, Arjuna, for showing us one more time that heaven is earth."

—**Byron Katie Rolle,**
Founder of The Center for The Work, Barstow, California.
Author of *What to Do When Nothing Else Works.*

"Relaxing into Clear Seeing inspires the very experience of its title. In it, Arjuna offers a wide-ranging, contemporary description of the non-dual view, as well as pragmatic exercises which dissolve one into that always-shining vision. Homegrown in the West, here is a clear seeing of the eternal truth in our own time. An excellent book."

—**Catherine Ingram,**
President of the Living Dharma Foundation.
Author of *In the Footsteps of Gandhi.*

"Arjuna comes down through the line of Ramana Maharshi and Poonjaji, threading that core of silence with his own playful, garrulous practical crazy-wisdom. He is widely read and yet liberated from books; he is centered in the essence of the Self and yet generously anecdotal, deeply grounded in daily experience. This book is something new."

—**Coleman Barks,**
Professor of Poetry, University of Georgia.
Translator of Rumi: *Open Secret, This Longing, Unseen Rain,*
We Are Three, Delicious Laughter.

"The wisdom of the East is profound—but often too different from us to grasp and benefit from. I am very impressed by this book's exercises for making the wisdom more available to us Westerners, especially the use of partner exercises."

—**Charles T. Tart, Ph.D.,**
Professor Emeritus of Psychology, U.C. Davis.
Author of *Altered States of Consciousness,*
Waking Up,* and *Living the Mindful Life.

"*Relaxing Into Clear Seeing* helps us do just that. Arjuna knows the way, and has a way with words about it. Bringing together the non-dual teachings of Vedantic Self inquiry with the Buddhist tools of awakening and with Western psychology, he puts forward the radiant essence of the perennial philosophy. I recommend it to anyone interested in awakening the mind, knowing and opening the Heart, and living with wisdom and ease today."

—**Lama Surya Das,**
Western Tibetan Teacher.
Founder of the Dzogchen Foundation, Boston MA.
Author of *Awakening the Buddha Within.*

"Arjuna has accomplished a clear, heartfelt invitation that heralds a turning point in the availability of awakening to mankind. The text is easy to read and comprehend, allowing for direct experience. A beautiful contribution."

—**Isaac Shapiro,**
International Spiritual teacher.
Author of *Outbreak of Peace.*

"For far too long, awakening has been considered the exclusive domain of Saints and sages far removed from conventional life. This book contributes significantly to exploding that myth, showing that teachings of liberation can be made accessible to people from all walks of life. Drawing extensively on different spiritual traditions, the book points to freedom from clinging and anguish born from lack of clarity.

This book also contains practical exercises and skillful teaching to enable readers to discover That which is beyond all measure. *Clear Seeing* is suitable for anyone genuinely interested in discovering the true expression of a realized life."

—**Christopher Titmuss,**
Co-founder of Gaia House, Devon, U.K.
Author of *The Profane and the Sacred, Freedom of the Spirit,* and
Spirit of Change.

"*Relaxing into Clear Seeing* is a master work. There is an ancient script which states from out of the wisdom of the East will come that which will bring sunshine to the wisdom of the West. When the two combine will come brightness to the world. Brightness = light. Light to mind = enlightenment. With enlightenment will come man's evolutionary advancement from homosapien to homosuperior. Homosuperior is holistic man ("holy"—if you can assimilate that word) who is both a mystic and scientist. This book by Arjuna Nick Ardagh leads the reader down a path in which sunshine brightens."

—**Ormond McGill,**
Dean of American Hypnotists.
Author of *Hypnotism and Meditation,* **and**
Hypnotism and Mysticism of India.

"I found the tools offered in this book allow my clients to recognize through immediate, direct experience the beauty, power and simplicity of their own natural state. With this recognition all suffering dissolves. The Living Essence approach cuts through all other systems of healing, all stories, all creations of the mind, all identification with the past and suffering, and takes you directly to the source of healing, joy and creation: your own natural state, which has only been covered over. Through the tools in this book the natural state is restored."

—**Donna Hamilton M.S. M.A.,**
Health Educator, Hypnotherapist.
Founder of the Institute for Natural Discovery.

"Many books about awakening are long on philosophy but short on practicality. In this groundbreaking new book, Arjuna brings the powerful technology of his Living Essence work to bear on the mystic's journey with considerable power and effect. I recommend this book to anyone serious about their quest for enlightenment."

—**David Quigley,**
Developer of Alchemical Hypnotherapy.

"Insightful help to those on a spiritual pathway."

—**Gerald G. Jampolsky,**
Founder of the Center for Attitudinal Healing.
Author of *Love is Letting go of Fear.*

Relaxing Into Clear Seeing

interactive tools in the service of
Self-awakening

Arjuna Nick Ardagh

edited by Stephan Bodian

illustrated by Jaclyne Scardova

First Edition
1998

SELF X PRESS
San Rafael, California

Relaxing Into Clear Seeing
interactive tools in the service of Self-awakening

by Arjuna Nick Ardagh

Published by

SELF X PRESS

454 Las Gallinas Avenue, #308
San Rafael, California, 94903
tel: (415) 492-1186
fax:(415) 491-1085
e-mail: books@livingessence.com
world wide web: http://www.livingessence.com

Cover Design and Digital Manipulation by Lightbourne Images.
Original cover photograph by Trinette Reed.
Illustrations by Jaclyne Scardova.

Printed in the United States of America on acid-free recycled paper using soy-based inks.

Grateful acknowledgment is made for permission to reprint previously published materials. Details are on pages 339-348.

All photographs within the book are by Arjuna Nick Ardagh, except page x, used with permission of Sri Ramanasramam, and pages 116, 160, 216 and 359, by Trinette Reed, and page 195 by Tony Ise.

ISBN   1-890909-15-7 (pbk.)
Library of Congress Catalog Card Number: 97-91936

CONTENTS

DEDICATION

This book is laid with gratitude and humility at the feet of the nameless and formless Benevolence which guides us home to ourselves again and again.

It is dedicated to you, to You, to the One which is everywhere.

It is dedicated to the myriad embodiments of that One loving intelligence, which have materialized at every step of the way in response to the calling of the Heart to itself.

To my beloved Master and eternal friend, H.W.L. Poonjaji, for the ruthless rubbing of my nose in my own nature, till it would not rub off again.

To the incomparable Ramana Maharshi, for stealing my heart, and for being the Heart which is everywhere.

And to every other mirror who has shown up along the way to dance the eternal dance of awakening with me.

To all my countless friends and dharma brothers and sisters, for providing a sangha without walls or dogma.

To Subhadra, my wife, for endless patience and sweetness of heart.

And above all to Abhi and Shuba, for demonstrating to me constantly how to live in spontaneity and beyond the mind, every moment of every day: and for being my greatest Gurus, at the ages of four and two respectively.

Bhagavan Shri Ramana Maharshi (1879–1950)

Shri H.W.L. Poonjaji (1910–1997)

IMPORTANT NOTE

This book describes a number of interactive sessions which you can give and receive with your friends, to facilitate the relaxing of consciousness into direct recognition of its own nature. They require no special psychological training or academic study.

These sessions have been tested on hundreds of people, both in trainings and in individual sessions given by many different practitioners. The processes have been demonstrated to work in a predictable and repeatable way, and are determined to be safe and beneficial.

If you are already a certified hypnotherapist, licensed psychologist or counselor, you can incorporate the technologies described here into your professional practice, within the scope that you are qualified to address within State and Federal laws.

Please be aware that these processes have been designed for and are to be used with people in a state of normal mental and physical health and functioning, to help them to relax more deeply into awakening and Self-awareness. They are not designed to treat, diagnose, cure or alleviate symptoms of any kind of mental or physical or illness. If you suspect that the friend or client you are working with may be experiencing symptoms of mental or physical illness or disturbance, either short- or long-term, please refer them immediately to a licensed health care professional trained to address such issues.

Neither the author, publisher nor any of their associates can accept liability for the use of these processes. If you are not willing to exercise the vigilance and responsibility requested here, please return this book to the place of purchase for a prompt refund.

For information about our training programs which leads to certification specializing in this approach, see the information at the end of the book.

HOW TO USE THIS BOOK

This is a handbook of applied mysticism. You can use it in many different ways according to your taste.

If you are interested only in deeper understanding and the provocative assimilation of new ideas, read chapters 1, 2 and the discursive introductions of chapters 5 through 14.

If you are also interested in using the tools here on your own for self exploration, you can put the exercises in chapters 3 to 14 onto tape, or purchase ready made guided tapes from the Living Essence Foundation (see page 358).

If you are also interested in experimenting with friends to mutually deepen your relaxation into Clear Seeing, read the whole book at least once, and then experiment with the interactive exercises. If you are qualified to work with people as a counsellor, psychologist or as another professional, please feel free to use these tools in a way that may enhance your practice. If you desire more in-depth support, please contact us for training.

This book uses natural states of deep relaxation to wake up more completely to what the Heart already knows to be true. Such induced states of relaxation have also sometimes been called 'hypnosis' or 'trance.' Although the technology used to create relaxation may be similar, in other respects this book has very little to do with conventional hypnosis or hypnotherapy. Instead, you will find here a set of tools to guide awareness back to itself, to a state of Peace, Silence, Love and innate Wisdom. This we call Clear Seeing.

The English language is, in many ways, inadequate to describe states of consciousness because of its agricultural origins. For this reason you will find that I have made up many words in the book that do not appear in your dictionary. Also, whereever a word is being used to refer to your absolute unchanging nature, rather than the relative shifting of the mind, I have used a capital letter. Hence Truth (absolute, unchanging, beyond the mind, Sanskrit *Sat*) is distinguished from truth (shifting opinions and perceptions), Love from love, and Self from self.

The state of Clear Seeing described here in this book is familiar to everyone. It is who you are. It is frequently revealed in meditative experience, sometimes in love making or in nature. It is that which is revealed when the mind is not interfering with things. You will find here a methodology to make the realization and embodiment of your True nature more accessible, reliable and stable.

This book invites you to call off the search for anything outside of your True nature. It promises that if you are willing to stop, even for a moment, to find out who you already are, rather than to fixate on who you wish to become, you will rest in complete fulfillment.

Relaxing
Into
Clear Seeing

Come, come
Whosoever you are!
Wanderer, Worshiper, Lover of Leaving,
It doesn't matter if you have broken your vows
A thousand times or more.
This is not a caravanserai of despair.
Come and yet again come.

JELALUDDIN RUMI

CHAPTER 1

THE ROAD TO HERE

I have lived on the lip
Of insanity, wanting to know reasons
Knocking on a door. The door opens.
I've been knocking from the inside![1]

JELALUDDIN RUMI

ere is a book about you. This book is about who you really are,
prior to the habits of identification with thought, feeling and
physical sensation. This book is about awakening from the illusion of separation and the dream of the person you have taken yourself to
be, and how this awakening can become more and more stable in your
life. The suchness of things revealed in this awakening is not a truth that
belongs to me, or to my teacher, or to my teacher's teacher. It is what your
Heart already knows to be true. It is not something that needs to be remembered or forgotten. It is what has been wisely called the "natural state,"
which can be directly seen and realized by every human being as soon as
we cease to pay attention, even for one moment, to the eternally changing
whirlpool of thoughts and emotions. The testimony to this realization has
been at the core of all mystical teachings throughout recorded history.

This is not one of those books that is guaranteed to solve all of your problems (although it well may!). It will probably not fulfill the mind's desire to manipulate reality and give it what it says "I want." You will not find here a set of tools to make more money, have better sex with more people, or heal every disease known to man. This will not teach you how to channel ascended masters, or even promise you advancement along your spiritual path. To the person you have taken yourself to be, this book promises no gold at the end of the rainbow.

Instead here is an invitation, right now, to recognize the Heart's one and true longing: to come home to Peace, Silence, Love, and an acceptance of the perfection already inherent within life. This book invites you to sit down, right where you are in the midst of your path, to look up at the trees, feel the sunshine on your face, and ask yourself, perhaps for the first time, "What's wrong with this moment right here? Where do I feel I need to go? What proof do I really have that anything is wrong with me or this life as it is?" And most important, "Who is this person advancing down a path and dreaming of a spiritual goal in an imagined future?"

A PERSONAL PREAMBLE

For several decades, I was an inveterate seeker. Born into a highly dysfunctional family, I watched my parents undergo a violent divorce when I was four. Neither of them, nor indeed anyone in my life as a child, provided a model of happiness or love. By the age of fourteen, I had become obsessed with the idea that there must be more to life than that which met my immediate perception. It was either suicide, a mental hospital, or divine intervention.

At fourteen I learned meditation and yoga and began to sniff the possibility that there might be a way of life more real, more loving, and more meaningful than the one I saw around me. Over the years that followed, I tried every approach I could find to move forward along "the path." I learned bodywork, participated in therapy groups, and spent extended periods with a number of different teachers from India and Tibet. I attended retreats, traveled many times to Asia, and maintained an unbroken spiritual practice for more than 23 years.

Based on my reading and my imagination, I had created a goal for myself called "enlightenment." I imagined it to be a state with no unwanted thoughts or emotions, one in which there was never disharmony or conflict with another human being and everything worked perfectly. Most of the time, I was unaware that my search was motivated primarily by a need to escape from emotional pain. I was too busy driving myself crazy chasing the ever-elusive carrot of liberation.

At the same time, I acquired an extensive toolbox of skills to help others on their journey of healing, releasing the past, and discovering their "higher selves." After leaving Cambridge University in 1979, I studied hypnotherapy and a variety of other therapeutic models, and during the 1980s I taught in a number of different schools on the West Coast of America. I also published a series of hypnosis tapes which sold well throughout the United States.

By the summer of 1990, I could no longer deny that something essential was missing. Despite the seeming efficacy of the tools I used and taught, and the many students who were attending our trainings, something in my heart knew that there was a state of perfection and love where seeking would come to an end. But this state remained out of reach. I sold my house, abandoned my work, and went back to India, where I'd already spent considerable time.

In 1991, while in India, I heard of a little-known teacher named H.W.L. Poonja. He was a disciple of the renowned Indian sage Ramana Maharshi, who had been an important influence on me since I first developed a passion for spiritual inquiry. I had encountered a few Westerners, people just like me, who had visited Poonjaji and undergone an irreversible transformation in consciousness. By this point I was so desperate to be through with the whole torturous path of seeking that I was ready to try anything. I took a train to Lucknow without knowing exactly where Poonjaji lived. After checking into a hotel, surrounded by rickshaws and buses and the thickest pollution I had ever seen, I looked up "Poonja" in the phone book. There was only one listed in Lucknow. A man answered, sounding much younger than I expected, and told me to meet him outside my hotel the following morning. I went to bed filled with anticipation.

The next morning, a plump Indian man arrived on a moped, about 45 minutes late, and urged me to jump on the back. He introduced himself as Poonjaji's son. We weaved through endless traffic snares and finally arrived in a distant suburb of the city, outside a modest house. I was ushered into a simple, sparsely-furnished living room where about a dozen Westerners sat at the feet of a big, elderly Indian man who gazed into space with an amused and detached expression on his face.

Something in me knew that I had found what I was looking for. In some way I could not define, this man held the answer to my unspoken prayers. After some time, he left the gathering, and I was called in to his bedroom to meet with him. The room contained two plain, unpainted single beds. Plaster was crumbling from the walls in a number of places. I had already become disenchanted with teachers who flaunt their wealth and draw thousands of adoring followers, and I was surprised by Poonjaji's minimalist style.

In our first conversation, alone together in his room, I asked him in deadly seriousness, "I feel like I've been seeking as long as I can remember. What is in the way of finding?" Knitting his eyebrows, he looked back at me as though it was the stupidest question he'd ever heard. "What is in the way of finding?" he replied. "Why, seeking, of course!"

When I returned to my hotel room, his answer ricocheted deeper into my mind. I came to realize the truth of what he was saying: all my efforts—to be free of the past, to heal, to be liberated—were in some way counter-productive. In fact, the very restlessness and discontent of the mind was at once the problem and the only tool available to solve it.

Over the next six days, thoughts flew off in every direction without any coherence or logic to them. Memories that did not even belong to this life would flash up and disappear as it became clear that nothing within the control of an individual could help free me of the knot of illusion. I would meet with Poonjaji in the morning, together with a dozen others, then spend the rest of the day studying the ceiling of my hotel room. A tremendous fire was raging inside me; I did not sleep at night, and during the day I was in a state of complete disorientation.

On the sixth night in Lucknow, I went to bed feeling like I was ready to die if that's what it would take to be liberated from duality, from the feeling of bondage and separation, from the "core suffering" that we experience as human beings. Before going to sleep, I wrote a note to give to Poonjaji the next morning, begging him to destroy the binding quality of the egoic identity. Again that night I did not sleep, but entered instead into a light hypnotic state, in which I remained aware of the sounds around me.

At six the next morning I arose with the sense that there was something important I needed to do. "Now what was it?" I wondered. "Oh, that's right, I have to kill the ego!"

In that moment, feeling rested after the night, I looked within with the innocence of a child, seeking the ego that had to be killed. Suddenly, in an instant out of time, reality turned inside out. I burst out laughing, and continued for twenty minutes, unabated, alone in my hotel room. It became suddenly obvious that there is no such entity as "ego" or "mind"—it is only an appearance. It became irrefutably clear that the person I had taken myself to be, with all his problems, concepts and memories, does not actually exist at all, and never has. What remained untouched was a vastness of consciousness in which thoughts arise and fall, happening of themselves to nobody in particular. In this Clear Seeing, time disappeared, along with the belief in the solidity of past and future. Although external circumstances remained exactly as they had been the night before, no "problem" could be found anywhere. A self-perfected state of life opened up that had exactly the same content as a world full of problems, but without the feeling of time and pressure and the need to change things. Everything was drenched in silence and immense love.

I watched this human body, which now seemed something like a horse, eat an enormous breakfast in the hotel's restaurant, unable to restrain the overwhelming affection it felt for the waiters. Life was unfolding perfectly, without the sense of there being anyone there to interfere with it. The feeling of being a seeker on a path had evaporated completely—there was no one to be found to walk the path anyway! The processes of thought died down and became silent.

It was rather like discovering that you've just had a major robbery in your home. You call 911; the police come with fingerprint experts and criminologists. But the moment you recognize that you made a mistake and the jewels were in the drawer all the time, the problem dissolves. In the same way, once you realize that there is no seeker and nothing to seek, the urge to search for something external completely disappears.

This awareness lasted completely undisturbed for about three weeks. Life was lived with a sense of moment-to-moment perfection, without the imposition of any individual identity. Slowly the habits of a "normal" life also began to return in the form of likes and dislikes and conditioned responses, and with them came a subtle sense of separation. But the underlying vastness and silence remained.

I continued to live in Lucknow for about a year after this. My girlfriend came to join me, and in November Poonjaji suggested that we marry and settle down. He presided over a full Vedic wedding complete

The wedding: November 11th, 1991.

with fire, rose petals, and chanting. He became our father, teacher, mirror, and the Beloved the Heart had always longed for. In the fall of 1991, he became much more widely known, and the morning Satsangs[2] grew from a handful of friends to two or three hundred people. Over this period I saw thousands of people come to be with him and fall into this same awakening. For some, the realization was so deep and the "fed-up-ness" with their previous condition so strong that the awakening was irreversible and became their ground of being. For others, there was a dramatic experience of seeing that was quickly overshadowed again by old tendencies of the mind; as a result, the awakening became more of an "experience" in memory than an irreversible shift in perception. And still others came, met a sweet old man, wondered what all the fuss was about, and left a few days later.

The year passed quickly. Our days were simple. We attended Satsang in the morning, ate lunch, had a nap, and then read or took a walk. Most of the usual stimuli that challenge and stress us had been removed. Then my wife became pregnant with our first child. Agreeing that India was not the ideal place to give birth to a baby, we made arrangements to return to America. About two weeks before it was time to leave, Poonjaji asked me to "share this secret" with my friends by giving Satsang in America. As you can perhaps imagine, I was more than a little shocked by his suggestion. I had assumed not only that enlightenment or awakening was the unquestioned domain of Indian sages, but that I was not even remotely qualified to pass this teaching on to others. We returned to Seattle in May, a time when the trees are full of blossoms and the city is caught by a spirit of exuberance as it emerges from its long winter malaise.

In fact, Satsang started to happen quite by itself. First one friend and then another called to ask where I had been and what had occurred. One Sunday, a few friends came over and I switched on a tape of Poonjaji, hoping that it would give them a taste of what had happened for me. But the audio quality was so bad that they were forced to sit uncomfortably near to the tape player, craning their necks and knitting their brows, trying to figure out what was being said on the tape. After fifteen minutes, I switched the machine off and attempted to explain to them what he was saying. Then a strange thing happened. As soon as I began speaking myself, as soon as life pushed me to represent the nameless and the formless to others, an extraordinary presence filled the room. My friends felt that it was coming from me, but that was not really true, for I was as affected by it as they were. During that first Satsang, to my astonishment, three or four people experienced the same kind of awakening that I had in India. If anything, their awakening was easier and more spontaneous than mine. Pretty soon, Satsangs were drawing seventy or eighty people several times a week.

I continued to share this open secret with my friends in this way for almost two years. During that time, I saw hundreds of people recognize the false assumptions they had made in believing in the existence of a separate self. Hundreds of waves recognizing, "Aha! I am actually the ocean itself, not separate from other waves in my essence." Also during this time, I met many other people who had experienced a similar realization, either with a different Indian guru or with a Buddhist or Western teacher. For one, it occurred through reading *A Course in Miracles*; for others, it happened all by itself. But the essence of the realization was unmistakably the same. It became clear to me that labels like "enlightenment," "self-realization," "awakening," or "liberation" are misleading. It is really more of a state of normal sanity. In Clear Seeing, that which exists in this moment is, and that which does not exist in this moment simply is not. A flower is a flower, a tree is a tree, but as hard as we look, we cannot find a separate person to whom we can refer as "I" or "me."

As I took the teacher seat, I saw the whole affair to be much simpler and easier than we had made it out to be. Only our belief that it was difficult made it so, and only our belief that it was the sole domain of Eastern sages kept it out of our reach. The most common response people had to seeing the truth of things was to burst out laughing and say, "It can't be this simple!"

Since the tenacious habits of thought that obscure the simplicity of things are strong, however, this realization was extremely unstable for most people. Despite a profound perception of the emptiness of awareness, of the absence of an individual doer, there was still the familiar tendency to believe in a separate "I" who is called upon to do things. People would testify that the sense of separation, post-realization, was immensely more painful and frustrating than it had ever been before the secret was revealed. Once you know what it's like to experience the warmth and light of a bright sunny day, it becomes even more difficult to live in a perpetual fog. Once you have experienced love and intimacy, it becomes even more difficult to live apart from your beloved.

About two and a half years after my first meeting with Poonjaji, I received a crash course in *samsara*.[3] Life was unfolding quite magically.

A visit to Papaji in 1992

I had a beautiful wife and child, Satsangs kept expanding; the feeling of being absorbed in the mystery grew stronger every day, for me as well as for most of the people who attended, and I was surrounded by deep and dedicated *dharma* friends. However, there was also a subtle complacency creeping into the situation, although I did not recognize it at the time—not, that is, until some unseen force pulled the plug.

I had some money left over from the days when I was teaching hypnotherapy, and I had invested it in what seemed, at least to my untrained eye, to be reliable places. One fateful November morning I discovered that one of the two companies I had invested in had gone bankrupt. Soon I learned that the other one had as well. My complacency gave way to amazement that I could have been so naive. A few other situations, including a severe attack of parasitis from recent visits to India, threw me back into all the human emotions to which I thought I had become immune. If you have ever lost a lot of money or been through a severe disappointment, you no doubt know the feelings of depression and panic that arise. As a result, I was forced to look more deeply into the emotions and mind-states that can seem to overshadow the self-perfected state.

I found myself and my friends in an interesting predicament. Having seen the perfection underlying all apparent imperfection, there is no turning back. You cannot unsee what has been seen. It's like those computer-generated 3-D images. Once you see the three-dimensional figure embedded in that mass of colored dots and squiggly lines, you can't forget what you have seen. You know that the figure is there, and it becomes progressively easier to find it. Similarly, once the illusion has been penetrated and the truth of things has been seen, there is no turning back. Yet for almost everyone I know there has appeared to be some coming and going, some deep, invisible mechanism that pulls consciousness back into separation, desire, suffering, and time.

In the summer of 1994, I was in India on one of my many visits to Poonjaji. When it came time to go home I went to the railway station to book my ticket, only to be told that there were no seats to New Delhi for another two days. I was astonished, since there are usually tickets available last minute on the Tourist Quota, and that is one of India's most frequently traveled routes. Instead, the man offered me a ticket to Varanasi on the next train. From there I could fly to Katmandu to catch a plane home. Once arrived in Nepal, however, I was stranded for two weeks, because the only person who could authorize a change in my ticket was away on vacation. I was obliged to wait. I spent long periods in my little room in the Lotus Guest House, writing, reading, and escaping the monsoon rains.

It was there that most of the processes outlined in this book appeared, like a fax out of nowhere. I simply wrote them down, and little has been changed since that time. Over the following months I was able to try them out with many people, and I was amazed at how simply and effectively they could bring transparency to a problem state that seemed to obscure Clear Seeing, and return awareness to resting in itself. Later, I discovered a striking similarity to many of the practices of the Dzogchen tradition of Tibetan Buddhism, which is interesting since they all came to me in a guest-house surrounded on every side by Tibetan monasteries.

Ever since then, a mysterious synchronicity has surrounded these simple tools. When I was traveling to London, the perfect person appeared to host a weekend workshop there. The same thing happened in Boston and Seattle. When I started to work on a book, the ideal editor immediately showed up, without any effort on my part. And when I returned to California, the school where I had been Director of Hypnosis Training in the 1980s was ready to integrate this work as its hypnotherapy training. We have also established a foundation[4] to share these tools wherever they may be helpful, to integrate the timeless realizations of freedom into the context of life in uncertain times.

THE BIGGER PICTURE

We are at a critical juncture in human history. This beautiful planet offers the possibility of fulfilling lives for us all, yet we are destroying it, and we are creating endless unnecessary suffering in the process. I feel passionately that only by awakening from the dream of separation can we eliminate the root causes of conflict and greed. The situation is urgent; we cannot wait any longer. In order for a wakeful and sane view of reality to become more commonplace, we must thoroughly re-examine the context in which such a view has been held. Most of the historical models for abiding in this state of clear perception and wakefulness have lived lives very different from our own.

Ramana Maharshi, Poonjaji's teacher, is revered by many as the greatest sage of this century. He awakened at the age of 16, when his body spontaneously began to go through the stages of dying. Instead of resisting the process, he lay down and welcomed it, looking to find out to whom this death was occurring. Through this inquiry, the eternal

Self was revealed to him. A few weeks after his awakening, he left home with almost no money and just a few possessions, traveling south to a holy mountain called Arunachala.

Because he lived in a culture that supported renunciation, Ramana was able to sit silently by the mountain for years, without speaking to a soul or moving his body. People brought him food and took care of him, and he was not called upon to perform any activity. Not only did outward circumstances support him, we also have to assume from the fact that he was able to remain silent for so long that he did not carry within him the karmic tendencies that would lead him to participate in a more conventional life, such as having a family and making money. Ramana Maharshi lived mostly in silence for several decades until a small group of people gathered around him. He began giving his teachings on scraps of paper, gradually began to teach aloud, and finally an ashram was built around him.

Ramana has been the inspiration and awakening catalyst for many in this century, including myself. Yet the circumstances of his life are radically different from ours. Unless you have considerable private means, you are obliged to work and to undergo the stresses that work entails. Unless you have no pull towards human relationships, you will have to live with the all-too-human tendencies that these situations evoke. And unless you have none of the usual restlessness that characterizes the Western personality, you will probably find that your life inevitably involves activity, beginnings and endings in time.

There are other cultures that have supported the enlightened view. Tibet has a rich history of unbroken lineages that preserve non-dual awareness, and the Zen tradition, which took Buddhism to Japan by way of China, also bears testimony to Clear Seeing. However, in both these cultures, awakening became associated with a monastic or reclusive life and generally excluded women. The recognition of this original ground of being has been something very unusual. In fact, when this awakening took place, the apparent individual for whom it occurred often has been revered as a saint or a mystic.

In the past few years, there has been a dramatic increase in the ease with which Self-realization can occur. Indeed, a kind of "epidemic" has begun in the West whereby the awakened view is becoming increasingly available. It's like the four-minute mile. For decades it was considered impossible for a human being to run a mile in four minutes, so nobody did, though many came close. The four-minute barrier seemed impenetrable until May 1954, when it was broken by Roger Bannister at Oxford. Not only have many others broken the barrier since, but the current record is nearly 20 seconds better than Roger Bannister's historic time of 3:59.4. The four-minute mile is now a standard training mark for the majority of Olympic-caliber athletes. Similarly, as more and more ordinary Westerners speak out in their testimony to the nature of realization, it becomes easier for others to realize the same thing, sometimes without any preparation at all.

Padmasambhava, who brought Buddhism to Tibet in the 8th century AD, gave teachings to his disciples about the essentially free nature of consciousness. He told them that the teachings should be hidden in specific remote places in Tibet and that they would be discovered in "degenerate times when the capacity of humankind is more ready to recognize it." These hidden teachings are known as *termas:*

> It is for the benefit of those sentient beings belonging to the
> Later generations of those future degenerate times
> That all of my Tantras, Agamas, and Upadesas,
> Though necessarily brief and concise, have been composed.
> And even though I have disseminated them at the present time,
> Yet they shall be concealed as precious treasures.[5]

Perhaps we are living right now in those degenerate times, when the awakened view is a real and immediate possibility for just about everyone. In fact, it is only today that the Dzogchen teachings are being freely given in the West, often with startling results. What used to take decades, if not lifetimes, has for whatever reasons become more commonplace and accessible, often after little formal practice or preparation.

In many cases this is met with a spirit of cynicism or disbelief among practitioners of discipline and a gradual path who claim, "It is just not that easy." Yet often the very masters these devotees of discipline follow are saying that the realization of the truth of things is easier than falling off a log. What is difficult is letting go of attachment to effort and spiritual struggle.

Our circumstances today are calling forth something quite new. Just among the people I know, I can think of hundreds for whom the unchanging Truth has become irreversibly clear. Twenty or thirty years ago, that was not the case. At that time, anyone who was interested in spiritual matters was a seeker on a path, turning toward a Guru to learn the Truth, because there was no direct experience of it available. Now, more and more people are relaxing into this awareness with greater stability, or have enough familiarity with the awakened view that they can never fall into identification again in the same way.

A completely new kind of integration and permeation is called for. What does it mean to be in relationship with another while seeing that you and the other are expressions of the same Self? How is it to operate from this view in an economic model that is based in competition and separation? What relationship do we have to a personal history and past when we can see that time does not exist? We are entering a new era where new paradigms of realization and stabilization are being called forth. As more people are coming to realize that they are not really individual people at all, as more waves are beginning to recognize their common "ocean-ness," a new context for the process of awakening is being created, based on friendship and equality rather than hierarchy and competition.

The hierarchical structures that have monopolized the Truth have often kept people trapped in the role of student and seeker rather than bringing them to the realization that "I am the One." We have been dependent on an "other" on a throne or a podium to supply the answers, while we have stayed identified with questions and confusion. I feel confident that we are seeing a democratization of this process in the 1990s and beyond.

A completely new and unprecedented way of approaching awakening and spiritual values is called for today. Anything that smells of hierarchy and dualism, of teacher/taught, enlightened/unenlightened, better than/less than, arrived at a goal/still on a path, is being challenged and broken down, if not by individuals then by the force of life itself. We are entering a new phase where realization is being stripped of its elitist trappings and embraced in an ordinary, friendly way. The Heart itself is demanding this; it cannot be resisted.

The historical Buddha is reputed to have prophesied that when the wheel of dharma would next be turned, the Buddha to come and turn it would be known as Maitreya, "the Friend." The traditional interpretation is that a person called Maitreya would be born, walk the earth, and give teachings. But we could also interpret his statement to mean that when the wheel of dharma is turned again, it would be between friends, free of a hierarchical context. It may well be that the massive arising and subsequent self-destruction of certain guru-centered spiritual organizations in the past few decades were the death throes of a model that we have outgrown.[6]

A "new view" is clearly being called forth, a new embodiment of the awakened view which includes the willingness to embrace every aspect of the human condition, especially what has been thought of as the "shadow." A new manifestation is emerging which can include being sexual, being in relationship and all that it entails, being a parent and having a family, and dealing with money and survival in the world. This view can embrace both the transcendental Source of ourselves and our incarnateness.

This new view with the honesty and ordinariness it implies, can only happen in a fresh context where friend meets friend, and where the Teacher is discovered to be neither of them and both of them simultaneously. In this way we can together lay all our cards on the table and discover that we are truly One, not only in the Unmanifest ground of being, but also in our emotions, our challenges, and our humanness. It is through this willingness to face and integrate every aspect of human life that awakening may be stabilized and brought to include the entire range of our experience.

STABILIZING THE VIEW

Many means have been tested throughout history to stabilize this awakened view. The most traditional approach is to hang out with a teacher who is more deeply established in the view than you are, so the teacher's state of perception rubs off and becomes yours also. According to this model, it is the *darshan*, the look or the gaze of the teacher, that brings you to the realization of your own Being. Although this approach has the most reliable track record, it has been called into question by the recent consequences of the guru setup. There is growing awareness of the perils of setting up another human being as the source of what is in fact your own true nature.

Patrul Rimpoche, who lived in Tibet in the 19th century, had this to say about the present age:

> *Alas! How depressing to see the beings of this degenerate age!*
> *Alas! Can anyone trust what anyone says?*
> *It's like living in a land of vicious, man-eating demons—*
> *Think about it, and do yourself a big favor.[7]*

He goes on to advise us to flee to the mountains and be a "hidden yogi."

Another method of stabilization with a venerable history is consistent spiritual practice. This practice can be highly formalized or it can be so transparent that it hardly seems like a practice at all. A detached use of practice may be an important part of stabilizing this view, but the danger of practice, of which I am sure you are aware, is that more attachment and importance may be given to the practice than to the

Truth of things itself. The practitioner may be led to believe that awakening only occurs in certain circumstances as the result of efforts of a certain kind.

The Buddha tells a story about a group of friends who were stranded on a desert island. They were finally able to liberate themselves from imprisonment by cutting down a tree, hollowing it out, and using it as a boat to navigate across the sea to the mainland. Once they arrived, they were so grateful to their boat that they walked around everywhere carrying it on their heads. People would see a row of feet walking along capped by an enormous hollowed-out tree trunk. If anyone asked, "Why are you carrying this tree?" the friends would say, "This tree set us free, and therefore we are obliged for the rest of our lives to pay obeisance to it." Buddha likened this to the way we relate to spiritual practice or any tool that can provoke liberation. We can become so attached to the form of the practice or the right way of doing it that we forget the reason for which we adopted it in the first place.

Perhaps the most rigorous set of spiritual practices is the *gnondro* in the Vajrayana tradition of Tibetan Buddhism. *Gnondro* involves, for example, a hundred thousand prostrations to an image, a hundred thousand devotional offerings to the guru, and a hundred thousand repetitions of a hundred-syllable mantra. But Dilgo Khyentse Rimpoche, one of the greatest exponents of *gnondro,* who did the entire cycle himself six times, pointed out that the reason for doing a hundred-thousand prostrations is the hope that just one of those prostrations might be done in a spirit of real selflessness and devotion.[8] In other words, the purpose of the practice is more important than the specifics of its execution.

Another time-tested way of stabilizing awakening is to be of service, thereby transcending the limiting needs of the person we took ourselves to be and giving our life to something vaster and more important. But again we can get so caught up in the practical aspects of our service that we become more identified with being a person who is of service than in losing our sense of personal identity.

This book offers another way of stabilizing awakening through a simple set of tools for returning to what we call "Clear Seeing," a state in which no individual identity is to be found, in which there is no time, no mind, no ego, and no problem. It is not intended to replace the relationship you may have with a spiritual teacher or to be a substitute for whatever spiritual practice you find works for you. Nor is it intended to be a substitute for whatever way you feel called upon to be of service in life. And nothing in this book is intended as a substitute for the services of a licensed therapist or medical practitioner.

The processes described here are simple ways in which seeming obscurations can be returned to transparency or clarity through deeply relaxed states of body and mind. We will work directly with the very situations that appear to be the biggest obstacles to wakefulness, such as relationships, money, and obsessive memories. We will discover how these very situations themselves, as well as the emotions and patterns of thought they evoke, can become invitations back to an even deeper immersion in the mystery of our original nature.

These processes require no previous training in hypnosis or therapy. Anyone with a spiritual dimension to their life and an open heart will find them easy to use.

This book is dedicated to a state of perception that has sometimes been called the "self-perfected state," in which the underlying perfection of things is revered irrespective of the particular content of life at that time. Like many things in life, the realization of this is self-justifying. Those who have known this state of being, prior to thought, prior to any sense of identity, say that it is the ultimate intrinsically fulfilling state. It requires no external justification. It needs no specific benefits outside of itself. Nisargadatta Maharaj, when asked how this realization might be of benefit to one's life, replied, "In no way whatsoever."

In the same way, this book promises no benefits to the egoic habits of control with which we are familiar, but a seeing through their apparent existence. Here instead is an invitation to recognize what you truly are, prior to defining yourself as a person—that which is unborn and undying, and that which is and always has been the source of all Beauty, Love, and meaning. It is dedicated to who you really are, the one and only true divinity.

CHAPTER 2

THE VIEW

There is no goal to be reached. There is nothing to be attained.
You are the Self. You exist always. Seeing God or the Self is
only being the Self or yourself. Seeing is being.[1]

RAMANA MAHARSHI

The view to which the processes in this book aim to return us is the same one expressed in every mystical tradition. In Tibetan Buddhism it is referred to as *Dzogchen*, the Great Perfection; in Advaita Vedanta it is called Self-realization; in Zen, *Satori*. We find it in the poetry of Rumi and Kabir, as well as among the Christian mystics. It is found in the Hindu Upanishads as well as in the work of Plato and Lao-Tzu. Yet this natural state of the unconditioned mind does not properly belong within the confines of any particular tradition; rather, it is our natural state, the source of all thought and apparent duality, and the state to which every individual must eventually return.

All rivers have the ocean as their final destination, yet one could not claim "ocean-ness" as the unique property of the Ganges in India, the Mississippi in America, or the Thames in England. While each river flows through different terrain and may serve different kinds of people, all have the same salty, vast, deep ocean as their final goal. And once they have discharged themselves, one can no longer differentiate between one part of the ocean and another.

In the same way, Clear Seeing of the way things are when not obscured by thought, belief, or concept cannot be confined to a particular tradition or body of teaching. These traditions can be thought of as the banks of a river through which the water flows, but not as the water itself.

This chapter is a brief introduction, in words and concepts, to a state of knowing which is at once silent and non-conceptual. If you have no interest in conceptual understanding, you might want to skip ahead to a later chapter. Since almost all the mystical texts and poetry of every culture have tried to describe this mystery, these few pages can only aim to bring us to a place where we speak a common language. You have undoubtedly already tasted this natural state of primordial awareness. Perhaps you have lingered in it for long periods of time; perhaps it has even become the abiding substratum of all else that arises in your awareness. Although the natural state cannot be encapsulated in language, we can use words to share a mutual recognition, a common vision. Padmasambhava, who introduced Buddhism to Tibet in the eighth century, uses tasting sugar as an analogy.[2] Once sugar has been tasted, a word like "sweet" takes on meaning. Without direct experience, however, the description means nothing, like describing color to someone born without eyesight. Whatever is described in this chapter in words merely points attention back to the wordlessness that has already been recognized.

While this chapter presents a conceptual understanding of our original nature and points to the essential similarity of the descriptions of this realization that exist in every tradition, Chapter Five and subsequent chapters explain simple interactive exercises to take the recognition of Self beyond words and ideas and into direct realization. They cannot *create* this state—that would be like trying to create the sky by painting the ceiling blue. Rather they are intended to draw attention back to that which is common to all experiences—awareness itself—and to stabilize this recognition within the context of our ordinary lives.

The state of consciousness prior to the arising of thoughts and concepts is obviously beyond the capacity of the mind to understand, or of language to communicate. How could that which is silent be expressed through sound? How could that which is infinite be expressed through boundaries and limitations? As Lao-Tzu says in the opening stanzas of the *Tao Te Ching*:

The Tao that can be told is not the eternal Tao.
The name that can be spoken is not the eternal Name.
The nameless is the unchanging reality.
Naming is the mother of all form.[3]

Or, as Wittgenstein puts it, "The essence of all religion can have nothing to do with what is sayable."[4] Nevertheless, from the oldest records of human communication, we find attempts in words to bring the beyond back into the finite world of words. Although that which is seen in the moment of realization cannot be fully described in words, there are certain common elements to all testimonies of awakening. We will describe these elements one by one.

THERE IS NO "I"

The first and most important element, the one upon which all else rests, is the realization that there is no separate entity to which the pronoun "I" refers. This seeing—this looking back into consciousness in search of the individuality and the discovery of its nonexistence— has been at the heart of every testimony to awakening throughout mystical literature. It was this that the Buddha realized, sitting under the bodhi tree.

This does not mean that through rigorous practice the ego is destroyed or subjugated or brought under control. Most spiritual practices from both East and West have attempted to wear down or eliminate the sense of individual identity. Thus many contemporary schools and teachers justify harsh and even seemingly cruel treatment of practitioners with the argument that it is "good for the death of the ego." Spiritual inquiry has been dominated by the male psyche, which wants to go to war, do battle, and overcome. That is not what we are speaking of here. As long as there is the belief that "I" am somebody, and this "I" that I am has a thing called "my ego" which needs to be worn down and destroyed, we are willing to tolerate all kinds of hardship to help us achieve our elusive goal. The feminine approach is much softer and more relaxed, as Rumi gently reminds us when he says, "There's no need to go outside. Be melting snow. Wash yourself of yourself."[5]

Our assumptions have rarely been examined. We have not stopped long enough to ask ourselves who is this "I" that is concerned with spiritual progress. Upon vigilant examination, we can have no direct experience of any such thing called ego, mind, or soul. They exist only as ideas and, like any idea, they cannot be eliminated, only seen through. Trying to kill the ego is like trying to drain a mirage of its water. The essential point has been missed. In Gautama Buddha's words, "No bodhisattva who is a real bodhisattva cherishes the idea of an ego entity, a personality, a being, or a separated individuality."[6]

Realization, awakening, *Satori*—or simple sanity—is to recognize that there is no ego, no mind, no individual soul. There is not now, nor has there ever been, nor will there ever be. This is not the achievement of a higher state or the end of a long and arduous journey, but rather the recognition of what has always been the case. The ego has not been eliminated; it has been recognized as never existing in the first place.

This realization may come as a momentary glimpse, followed by a return to clinging to the idea of "me" and "mine." It may come in such a way that it becomes impossible to get caught in the idea of separation again. Ultimately, however, it makes no difference to the very nature of things. Whether we imagine a ghost in the closet or not is immaterial; any time we open the door, we find nothing there.

There is all the difference in the world between understanding this as an intellectual concept and experiencing it directly. Imagine a frightened young man running down the road as fast as he can from what he sincerely believes is a robber with a gun. It seems he has been running for ages, in a desperate attempt to save his own life. His whole body is affected by his immense effort to save himself: he is sweating profusely; his heart is beating fast; his body is contracted in fear. All his physiological and psychological symptoms bear testimony to the fact that the robber is real. Eventually he passes an old man sitting quietly by the side of the road. Curious about why the younger man looks so frightened, the old man looks down the road behind him. "What are you running from?" he shouts. "I am running from the robber with the gun," the fugitive yells back. "But I see no one following you!" the quiet old man retorts. And in fact there is no one there. The robber was a figment of the tortured young man's imagination.

Only when the terrified fugitive realizes that there is no robber, and in fact that there never has been, will he stop running. Only then will his body relax, his heartbeat slow down again, and his thoughts become quiet. However much others may have reasoned with him along the way, it is only his own direct looking that frees him of the torment he had invented in his imagination. In the recognition that no one is following him, the problem has not been solved—it has disappeared without a trace. It has been recognized never to have existed.

Ramana Maharshi captures the simplicity of the situation like this: "Reality is simply the loss of the ego. Destroy the ego by seeking its identity. It will automatically vanish and reality will shine forth by itself. This is the direct method. There is no greater mystery than this, that we keep seeking reality though in fact we are reality. We think that there is something hiding reality and that this must be destroyed before reality is gained. How ridiculous! A day will dawn when you will laugh at all your past efforts. That which will be on the day you laugh is also here and now." [7]

WHO IS AWARE OF THIS MOMENT?

In the recognition that there is no individual identity to eliminate, there still remains that which is experiencing this moment, reading these words, hearing sounds, registering sensations, being aware of thoughts arising and falling and emotions passing. Padmasambhava puts it in this way:

> Even though activities exist, there is no awareness of an agent who is the actor.
> Even though they are without any inherent nature, experiences are actually experienced. [8]

Devoid of any individual characteristics, that which remains outside of time, unchanging and without any limitation is the natural state, your true identity. Being that which is aware of thought and identity arising, it is in itself silent and without identity. It is revealed instantaneously in the moment when the individual "I" ceases to be grasped at in belief.

> The blessedness of love and joy
> Are present everywhere,
> But none of this can fill your heart
> Till you're no longer there,

says Angelus Selesius. [9] Douglas Harding describes his realization of his real nature in this way: "It was all, quite literally, breathtaking. I seemed to stop breathing altogether, absorbed in the Given. Here it was, this superb scene, brightly shining in the clear air, alone and unsupported, mysteriously suspended in the void, and (and this was the real miracle, the wonder and delight) utterly free of 'me,' unstained by any observer. Its total presence was my total absence, body and soul. Lighter than air, clearer than glass, altogether released from myself, I was nowhere around." [10]

You are revealed to be the consciousness in which all thoughts and emotions arise, out of which all sentient and insentient beings are born, through which they move and back into which they must return. In the full realization that your true nature is this consciousness, all sense of duality between "I" and "God," "divinity" and "life" disappears.

That which remains in the absence of any individual identity is unerasable. "When you realize this point, you can try to destroy it, but you will find nothing," the Dzogchen teachings explain. "Whatever you do, it is not possible to do anything with this empty nature. Even when all thoughts are stopped, there is still a very bright and clear presence that is empty. That is called Clear Natural Mind." [11] In fact it can be called by a variety of names. Ramana Maharshi calls the mystery that is revealed in the abandonment of individuality the Self *(Atman)*. Buddha calls it no-self *(Anatta)*. In Tibet, it is referred to as *Rigpa,* and a distinction is made between the unborn nature of mind and mind in activity which is individualized. Many interpreters of Jesus' words feel that this is what he referred to as "the Kingdom of Heaven within." Lao-Tzu calls it the Tao. Many esoteric traditions of Christianity refer to this nameless formless omniscience when they use the word "God." [12] It has been characterized as Beingness, No-mind, Emptiness, Fullness, Source, Truth, Sat, Chit, Ananda, Consciousness, and Awareness. "However many names may be applied to it," says Padmasambhava, "even though they are well conceived and fancy sounding, with regard to its real meaning, it is just this immediate present awareness and nothing else." [13]

The bibliography provides extensive references to expressions of this recognition which you can explore at your own leisure. The academic mind might want to debate whether all these words refer to the same thing, or "no-thing," but such a question becomes irrelevant in a single instant of direct experience. When no thought is stirring, when there is no content, no concept, and no understanding in the conventional sense, what possibility of comparison between "this" and "that" remains?

While the words used to refer to our original nature may vary from one tradition to another, the qualities used to describe it are identical. It is said to be infinite, without the imposed limitations of thought and mind. It is timeless, for without content there can be no past or future. It is empty of content, yet full, for it is both the source and destination of every form that is born and dies. It is beyond the capacity of the mind to grasp, being the source from which all thought, whether spiritual or mundane, arises. Throughout this book, I will refer to this ocean of consciousness prior to individuality as the "Self," and I will refer to the perception of reality arising from this recognition as the "View" or as "Clear Seeing." Please feel free to translate these terms into those that might feel more comfortable to you.

THIS HAS NO LIMITS

In a sense, the nature of the Self has always been immediate and obvious. You have only to step outside and look up into the sky to see infinity staring you in the face. There is no limit. You have only to look into a mirror to see the mystery of an object which has no content but is capable of reflecting all content. And yet, because of the addiction to looking outward, and because of the tendency of thought to deal only in that which has limitation and can be measured, the obvious has been overlooked. When we look back into the one who is experiencing this moment, no limitation can be found. Take a tape measure now and stretch it all the way to the left, all the way to the right, all the way up and down, forward and back, and see if there is any place where consciousness ends and something else begins. Although we can call this "space," it is actually the immeasurable infinity in which space exists; it is simultaneously infinite and without location. Like a circle with no circumference and no center, it defies conceptual understanding.

Of course, the more we try to speak about it, the clearer it becomes that the Self cannot be contained in any mental constructs. Yet how wonderful it is to see that, despite the fact that the mind cannot grasp it, still *it is*. In this moment, as these words are written, and as you read them, *it is*. It is the one who writes and the one who reads.

IT HAS NO BIRTH AND DEATH

Because it is limitless and free of content, the Self cannot possibly have a beginning or an ending. It is uncreated. There is nothing prior to it. In fact, out of it arises all that has beginning, all that has perpetuity, and all that has an end. The Self does not begin with its recognition. A moment of realization of the true nature of things is not a creation of something new, but a recognition of that which has never for one moment been absent. But just as the Self is not "space," but that in which space arises, so it is not "eternity" in the sense of a continuum in time. It is the timeless substratum out of which time arises. Likewise, the "unified field theory" envisioned by quantum physics also postulates an uncreated, unchanging field out of which all energy and material objects are created.

IT IS BOTH EMPTY AND ALWAYS FULL

The Self is empty of content and yet infinitely full of all possible phenomena. "Like an empty vessel," says Lao Tzu, "it is used but never exhausted."[14] "Our 'original mind' includes everything within itself," says Shunryu Suzuki. "It is always rich and sufficient within itself....This does not mean a closed mind, but actually an empty mind and a ready mind. If your mind is empty, it is always ready for anything; it is open to everything."[15]

Look back, even in this moment as you read, into that which is behind the eyes, into that which receives these words and their meaning. What content does that awareness have in itself? It is free of all content, yet it perceives all content. It is rather like a white canvas that is capable of reflecting any movie but free of any fixed images itself. No movie can demonstrate the canvas. Only the cessation of projected images will reveal it, and once it has been revealed, it is seen to be always there whether images are projected or not.

In the same way, consciousness itself, the Self, is empty, and yet pregnant with all possibility.

The Tao remains beyond description.
Although infinitely small,
It contains the whole universe,[16]

says Lao Tzu. Where else can phenomena arise but out of that? In this sense, it is not separate from phenomena, because all things have this no-thing-ness as their source. "Nothing exists beyond the natural state," says Shardza Gyaltsen. "Earth is not independent of the natural state, stone is not independent of the natural state, visions are not independent visions. Everything is a vision of the natural state. The natural state is like a single point. The natural state is like where birds fly—behind there is no trace. If you understand this point you will realize that the natural state is the creator of all things—the king of creators."[17]

Look into a thought as it arises. Now the thought is there; a second ago it was not there. Where did the thought come from? It must arise from somewhere and return to somewhere. It is a movement in something, a wave in otherwise unmoving water. What is the medium in which the wave moves? All thought, emotion, identity, and manifestation must be arising out of this Self, which is also perceiving it. What else is available? In this sense "the view" is non-dual. There is no duality remaining between "Self" and "no-self," for everything that could arise is none other than a manifestation of this Self that you are. This is not just empty philosophy. Look into your own mind now, as you read these words, and find out if this is true or not.

Initially, the realization that "all I see is part of me" may be difficult to grasp as a direct experience. But these days the same discovery which has been the basis of all non-dual mystical realization is being corroborated by quantum physics. When we investigate matter we find molecules, within molecules we find atoms, and within atoms are subatomic particles with strange names like quarks and bozons. When we look into these subatomic particles—the smallest constituents of what we call matter—we find only waves, which behave like particles when consciousness is brought to bear upon them. But waves in what? At this level of manifestation, there is no matter left to act as a medium. Ultimately, then, all matter is revealed to be a wave in, or a contraction of, nothingness itself, just as all thought is revealed to be a wave in consciousness.

NOTHING TO ATTAIN

In the Diamond Sutra, Subhuti asks the Buddha about his awakening under the bodhi tree. The Buddha's response is significant: "Through the consummation of incomparable enlightenment, I acquired not even the least thing; wherefore it is called 'the consummation of incomparable enlightenment.'"[18] Although realization often comes after a long period of striving, inquiry, and discipline, all who awaken, either in a sudden glimpse or a stable state, nevertheless say that it was not the fruit of the practice, but the fruit of stopping the practice! "This thing we tell of can never be found by seeking, yet only seekers find it," says al-Bistami. It is that which is revealed when all striving ends. "Realization is nothing to be gained afresh," says Ramana Maharshi, "it is already there. All that is necessary is to get rid of the thought 'I have not realized.'"[19] The final revelation of the Truth comes through divine Grace, rather than through any individual effort.

Someone once asked Poonjaji whether effort was needed to wake up to the Self. He told a story about a crow which comes to rest on the branch of a coconut tree and, at the same moment, a coconut falls. The synchronicity of the two events gives the appearance that the coconut's fall was caused by the crow's landing, but the coconut would have fallen anyway. "You may attribute freedom to meditation, *sadhanas*, and effort," he added, "but when the coconut fell, it fell of its own accord, not because the crow sat on the tree. When you get it, you may attribute it to some *sadhana*, to staying with the teacher, to going to the Himalayas for years of contemplation, or to long austerities and meditations, but it has nothing to do with these things: it is simply a question of keeping quiet. Keep quiet just for a moment, for this instant of time, and allow it to happen. Don't interfere, just keep quiet and watch what happens."[20]

In the stories of awakening in the Zen tradition, when the monk finally solves the koan or comes to direct recognition of unborn awareness, the most common response is to burst out laughing. "I've been looking for my nose everywhere, but forgot to look on my own face," said one Zen monk at the moment of awakening. In Lucknow, where I watched hundreds of Westerners brought to this realization by my teacher, the most common response was, "But I have been this all the time!" Hence, the moment of realization is not perceived to be the fruit of a long process of striving, but the cessation, temporarily or permanently, of the attempt to become something other than what one already is. It is the abandonment of effort, not the fruit of effort. Angelus Selesius puts it so succinctly:

> God is pure no-thing-ness
> Outside of time and space.
> The more you try to reach for him
> The more he will escape.[21]

Imagine a man who finds himself locked inside a prison cell. Over the years, he despairs at his bad luck and sorrowful state. He gazes through the bars of his window and longs to be free. He is desperate to get out. Food is brought to him each day and passed through a hole in the wall. Not a day goes by that he abandons his obsession to escape. He attempts to dig his way out beneath the window with his spoon. After a long time, however, he reaches solid rock and gives up. Then he tries using the handle of his spoon to file through the bars of the window, but he makes no headway. He attempts to climb the walls to make a hole in the ceiling, but just falls back again. He even fasts to lose enough weight to squeeze himself through the bars of the window, but to no avail. After twenty years of struggling to escape, he is exhausted. In frustration and resignation, he leans back against the door of his prison cell. To his utter amazement, it swings open! For the first time he realizes that the door was never locked. No one stops him as he walks outdoors into the brilliant sunshine. He had been free from the very beginning! He could have pushed the door open on the very first day, twenty years earlier. He *could* have, but he didn't. No one can say whether or not those twenty years of struggle were a necessary preparation for giving up, leaning against the door, and realizing his freedom.

The Buddha was born in the Sakya Kingdom in what is now Nepal. As a young prince, one who could have all the physical comforts easily provided for, he chose instead to leave his wife and small son, Rahula, and follow an ascetic life in search of liberation. For six years he wandered around, practicing every kind of austerity. He fasted, chanted, and meditated. He stood on one leg, gazed into the sun without blinking, ate one grain of rice per day until his body was reduced to skin and bones. Finally, he took some food, sat down under a tree, and came to the realization that he had always been the Buddha, pure consciousness itself. Later, when he returned to his birthplace, his wife came out of the palace shouting at him, "Where have you been all these years? Couldn't you have had this awakening living in the palace with me and your son?"

"Yes, Yashodara, I *could* have," he replied, "but I wouldn't have. Theoretically, I could have become awake just leading an ordinary life, but somehow it took all this striving and effort to come to a place of effortlessness."

It is hard to say whether the effort and preparation are really necessary. Is it necessary to travel all over the world in order to appreciate your own home? Maybe not, but that is often how it happens. Zen Master Huang Po puts it beautifully, "Suppose that a warrior forgot he was already wearing his pearl on his forehead and sought for it somewhere else: he might search through the whole world without finding it. But if someone simply pointed it out to him, the warrior would immediately realize that the pearl had been there all the time....Eons of striving will turn out to be wasted effort, just as when the warrior found his pearl, he simply found what had been hanging on his forehead all the time, and his discovery had nothing to do with his efforts to find it elsewhere."[22]

To realize the truth of who we are is said to be easier than falling off a log. It simply requires that we look back at the experiencer of this moment without paying attention to thought. It does not require any time for preparation. The Sixth Zen Patriarch was asked what emotion he experienced on realizing enlightenment. "Embarrassment," was his reply. He had missed the obvious for so long.

YET IT IS NOT HABITUAL

The realization of Truth is both easy and difficult. The recognition of the obvious cannot be called difficult, yet the momentum to become identified again is extremely strong. We might say that it is easy to recognize our natural state but difficult to abide in the recognition. We are habituated to believe in separation. As Hakuin puts it in the *Song of Zazen,*

> How near the Truth, yet how far we seek
> Like one in water crying "I thirst!"
> Like the son of a rich man
> Wandering poor on this earth.[23]

It is not waking up, but the permeation of that wakefulness into all the dimensions of ordinary life, that seems to be challenging. Surya Das, an American-born Dzogchen lama, once said, "These days, everyone is becoming enlightened…but no one is staying enlightened!" The tendency towards externalization and dualism is so strong, and the culture in which we live is so deeply steeped in separation, that resting in this state of simplicity is the real challenge. This is the challenge this book aims to address.

A MOMENT OUT OF TIME

Historically, there have been different attitudes toward what is necessary to realize the Self, our original nature. They can roughly be divided into two schools: those who believe in a gradual path with a state of "enlightenment" as its eventual goal; and those who suggest that the Truth can be seen directly in this moment, but that we may need repeated immersion for the seeing to become stable. Those who walk a gradual path spend decades living with a teacher, or become involved in austere spiritual practices, or devote a lifetime to service and renunciation. Those who speak of a sudden flash of lightning in a moment out of time recommend not a gradual awakening, but a constant returning. In this moment out of time, the past disappears, the mind disappears, the idea of separation disappears. Rather than being the fruit of effort, the open secret of our original nature is revealed in the abandonment of all effort.

IT DEFIES INTELLECTUAL UNDERSTANDING

The Self cannot be remembered, forgotten, or somehow held in concept, memory, or belief. How can you remember emptiness? How can you grasp an empty hand? It is that which remains in the abandonment of all belief. Nothing can be said about it except in negative terms. In Vedanta the traditional method of exposition is *neti-neti:* "not this, not that." "The eyes cannot see it, words cannot say it, the mind cannot know it," says the *Kena Upanishad.* "Since we cannot know it or understand it, it cannot be taught. It is beyond all that is known, and also beyond all that is unknown. We know this from every Master who has spoken about this." [24]

When all things have been rejected—not this, not that—the Self is left. Nothing in words can pin down or limit what this is. "However much one may try to explain it," says Ramana Maharshi, "the fact will not become clear 'til one attains Self-realization and wonders how one was blind to the self-evident and only existence so long." [25]

Words are useful only when spoken and heard from direct realization. No word could possibly describe the experience of eating strawberries to someone who has never had one. You could say "sweet," but they might think of sugar. You could say "fibrous," but they might think of a carrot. You could say it has "seeds," but they might think of a melon. But if you both bite into a strawberry, then you can use any word you like. "Mmmm! Delicious!" would be sufficient, because you are speaking from mutual recognition.

In fact, intellectual understanding often obscures the direct realization of Self. For the Self to be embraced, both incorrect *and* correct understanding must be abandoned because even correct understanding will stand in the way. As Sosan says,

The more you talk and think about it,
The further astray you wander from the Truth.
Stop talking and thinking,
And there is nothing you will not be able to know. [26]

There is a delightful story from China about Hui-Neng, the Sixth Zen Patriarch. As a young boy he heard the Diamond Sutra being elucidated and was set on fire with a love of *dharma*. He went to the monastery of the Fifth Patriarch and asked to be taken in, but because he was illiterate, he was put into the kitchen to pound rice. After some years, the Fifth Patriarch, who was now quite old, was ready to name an heir. He asked anyone in the monastery to write a *sutra* expressing his clear understanding of the *dharma*. Whoever wrote the best poem would take the robe and the bowl of the abbot and become the head of the monastery. No one ventured forth, and it was assumed that one of his most learned and well-read students, who presumably had realized enlightenment, would therefore succeed him. Finally his most senior student, Shen Hsiu, felt obliged to write something, so he went to the wall of the monastery in the night and wrote the following four-line stanza:

> *Our body is the bodhi tree,*
> *And our mind the mirror bright.*
> *Carefully we wipe them hour by hour*
> *And let no dust alight.*

He did this in secret because he thought that if the abbot saw the *sutra* and liked it, he would admit to authorship and take over as his successor. If the abbot dismissed it, he would keep quiet.

Hui-Neng, the illiterate kitchen-helper, had a friend read Shen Hsiu's *sutra* to him. Then he composed a stanza of his own and had his friend write it on the wall beside the one already there. This was his sutra:

> *There is no bodhi tree*
> *Nor stand of mirror bright.*
> *Since all is void,*
> *Where can the dust alight?*

When the abbot came out in the morning to look at what had been written on the wall, it was the illiterate Hui-Neng, with no official standing in the monastery, who was recognized as awakened and chosen to be the Sixth Patriarch. His fellow monks were so jealous of his accomplishment that he had to flee for his life and set up his own monastery elsewhere.[27]

Such stories are common to all traditions. Often, it is not the pundits and great scholars who speak from this timeless place of wisdom, but the simplest, most uneducated people, who in the end have the easiest time seeing the utter simplicity of things and becoming free of the dualistic mind. In this seeing, the mind becomes empty and clear like the mind of a child, and yet all religious texts suddenly become accessible as though one had written them oneself.

Realizing the truth of our own essential nature requires the abandonment of all beliefs and concepts. Even concepts that may be correct and reflect the true nature of things have to be rejected, as they stand in the way of direct knowing. Any limiting idea about ourselves or the nature of truth, such as "I am wealthy," "I am poor," "I am intelligent," "I am ignorant," "I am spiritual," "I am unspiritual," even lofty concepts like "All is one" or "God is love," place limits on the ground of being, the original, self-perfected state that cannot be pinned down in concepts. Intellectual understanding is a "booby prize" that can never really satisfy our yearning for Truth.

In San Francisco's Japantown there is a mall full of Japanese restaurants. In the windows of these restaurants, all the dishes available inside are on display. But the food on display is all plastic food. You can see what you want to eat from the display and tell your waitress once you are seated. Although these samples of plastic food look quite tempting, even enough to make your mouth water, if you go into the restaurant and ask for a certain dish and they bring you the plastic food from the window, it will not nourish you. It might look good, and you might feel very proud when the other people in the restaurant see that you have a large lobster before you, but if it is plastic it cannot possibly satisfy your hunger. In the same way, intellectual knowledge may seem impressive—one can quote from religious texts and demonstrate understanding of spiritual scripture—but unless the essential experience of one's original nature is there, no amount of intellectual understanding can replace it.

THERE IS NO TIME OR SPACE

In the recognition that there is no individual identity, what was believed to be so is immediately "seen through" and what actually exists is revealed. It is like pulling back a curtain at night to find that the intruder we had imagined knocking at the window is only the branch of a tree moving in the wind. We feel tremendous relief and a release of the energy that had been held in relationship to an imaginary intruder. In the same way, we find that this "I" thought has been the basis of all that is unreal and that resting in the natural state, an unborn state of consciousness, is the foundation of all that is real.

In the moment of seeing that the person one took oneself to be exists only as a thought, time also disappears. Just as no "I" can be found if it is sought for directly, so it is also not possible to find anything called "past," "future," or even "present." What is left is simply the one eternal "now," unchanging and unmoving. The idea of a past/present/future continuum is revealed to be a concept, an idea that binds us into an imaginary, through-the-looking-glass world of time and separation. When we don't believe thought to be real, there is no time, and what is left, "the Self" or "consciousness," is revealed to be always existing now—and now—and now—always the same indivisible now. In the abandonment of belief in time, all effort to be "here and now" evaporates, for it is the only place where consciousness and life can possibly exist. It is the only choice on the menu. Wu Men puts it in this way:

An instant realization sees endless time
Endless time is as one moment.
When one comprehends the endless moment
One realizes the person who sees it.[28]

Only in a ruthless commitment to this eternal now is one's true nature continuously revealed. That is why it cannot be encapsulated in belief or memory. The memory of Self-realization is not Self-realization—it must be seen eternally in this very moment.

Again, a million universes separate thinking about it, or understanding it intellectually, and actually seeing the simplicity of it face-to-face. Adopting a belief in the fiction of time and personal identity leads to a pretentious state in which one is late for everything because, one insists, there is no time. When asked if one wants a cup of coffee or tea, one replies, "There is no one here to decide." This is a trivialization of real seeing. An actor may forget his real identity and lose himself completely in his part. When he remembers who he actually is, it does not mean that he can no longer act or follow the plot. It simply means that he can participate fully, playing his role, without getting lost in the apparent joys and sufferings of his character.

When we see through the myth of time, awareness rests fully in what is actually real, in its own nature and manifestation as life in this exact moment. In this sense, there is simply a discrimination between what is here, now, and real—and what is only imagination.

THE SELF-PERFECTED STATE

In the dissolution of "I," not only does the idea of past/present/ future simultaneously disappear, but so does the solidity of likes and dislikes, the accoutrements of individuality. Preferences are seen to be arbitrary thoughts arising and falling in consciousness that have no intrinsic meaning or importance in and of themselves. They are only thought-forms. Sosan says:

> When love and hate are both absent,
> Everything becomes clear and undisguised.
> Make the smallest distinction, however,
> And heaven and earth are set infinitely apart.
> If you wish to see the truth,
> Then hold no opinions for or against anything;
> To set what you like against what you dislike
> Is the disease of the mind.[29]

In the transcending of like and dislike, fear and desire, a state of surrender is revealed in which all things are seen and accepted as perfect, just as they are right now. Not perfect because they conform to some idea of how things "should be," but perfect in that they are experienced to be the spontaneous arising of life in this moment, now. In Lao Tzu's words:

> The whole universe is sacred.
> You cannot improve on it.
> If you try to change it, you will ruin it.
> If you try to grasp it, you will lose it.[30]

But to speak of acceptance and surrender is not really enough. For behind the veils of like and dislike, infinite love is waiting to shine. Not the kind of love that is limited to "my" father, "my" mother, "my" boyfriend, "my" girlfriend, but a love that pays no attention to what kind of object is set before it, a love that sees all things in the same light of perfection.

What can be said about this love? When you fall into it, or even towards it, you are overtaken by rapture. This is the state of intoxication with which Rumi's poetry is ablaze. Indeed, it is this love to which all great mystical poetry and testimony pays homage. My teacher was once asked if he still experienced a deepening of this revelation, and he replied, "Yes, even now, even as we speak, there is no end to this love."

This realization expresses itself in heartful, compassionate service to the Earth and all that walk on her, and in the recognition that all is sacred and holy and not other than the Self. This service, devotion, and love is, after all, directed to the Self in all its manifestations and expressions. This is a love affair in which no otherness can be found, a love affair of the Self with itself.

We might fear that, in the release of belief in an individual doer, everything might degenerate into chaos. In fact, quite the opposite is the case. A state of immense Grace is revealed in which each moment unfolds with perfect synchronicity, as though it were carefully orchestrated and taken care of by the unseen hand of an infinitely loving mother. The One who takes care of all these things has never been known, has never been seen face-to-face, and yet His or Her or Its hand is found everywhere in a life lived free from the addiction to separation. We will explore the surrender to this mystery further in Chapter Thirteen.

A beautiful love affair begins to develop between the Self and itself, its manifest form and its unmanifest source, where the relationship is non-dual and undifferentiated, and at the same time more thrilling, rewarding, and meaningful than any dualistic love affair could possibly be. What can we say about it? As soon as we turn our attention to the mysterious beneficence and perfection that is revealed as "doership" is renounced, we are left speechless. No one has ever known the address or seen the face of this formless benefactor, yet there are traces found everywhere in a sacred life.

THIS PERFECTION HAS NO PARTICULAR FORM

Although we speak of a self-perfected state in which all things that arise are seen to be expressions of perfection, it does not mean that our individual lives now conform to some predetermined idea of what perfection should look like, or that our personal problems are externally solved overnight. It simply means that you know who you really are, and who you really are is not separate from life, from God, from consciousness. It is that simple.

Everyone who has walked a spiritual path, studied spiritual teachings, or participated in spiritual retreats has in some way developed a concept about what a glimpse or state of realization should look like. For some it has become associated with no longer having disturbing or negative emotions or conflict with others. For others it means being free from fears and anxieties, particularly regarding money and survival. For still others it is associated with having perfect health. Actually, what is found in the moment of Clear Seeing is that none of these ideas about what Truth should look like has any validity. The way that life shows up is entirely determined by previous actions in the appearance of time that are now playing themselves out. The freedom that comes with the deepening of awakening is freedom from *identification* with that appearance, or from defining oneself as being limited to it. It doesn't necessarily mean that the individual life will appear to be any different from other lives.

It is like a small boy playing on the beach while his mother sits under an umbrella reading a book. He can splash in the waves, make sand castles and watch the surf destroy them. He can play with other children, with toys shared or fought over. He can run and jump and be chased by a dog. But as a substratum to all these activities is the awareness that, "Mother is there for me, she is sitting under her umbrella on this beach, and therefore I am safe and things are essentially okay." In the same way, once the Self is revealed, it is perfectly okay for *anything* to arise, not only good and desirable things, but also what has been resisted and called misfortune, and even the emotions which may accompany them. The unseen magic that has transformed life is the recognition of the context in which all these joys and misfortunes are arising.

After the realization of this ground of being, there can be a return to involvement in duality, a return to activity, even to consciously addressing what may previously have been perceived as issues to be avoided, such as working through conflicts in relationships or business, ill health, money, or coming to terms with the death of a close relative. All of this can be experienced without needing to overshadow the intrinsic wholeness of things. This does not necessarily mean that there will be no more suffering, or at least the outward appearance of it, but it does mean that the true context in which both suffering and joy, gain and loss, ill health and good health, conflict and harmony, all occur does not need to be lost.

THE SELF IS NOT AN EXPERIENCE

Everything that has name and form in life can be known through the five senses and can become an experience with a beginning, a middle, and an end. The Self, however, cannot be experienced. It is the *experiencer* itself. It cannot be seen, tasted, touched, smelled, or heard.

"The big mind in which we must have confidence is not something which you can experience objectively," says Suzuki Roshi. "It is something which is always with you, always on your side. Your eyes are on your side, for you cannot see your eyes, and your eyes cannot see themselves. Eyes only see things outside, objective things. If you reflect on yourself, that self is not your true Self any more. You cannot project yourself as some objective thing to think about. The mind which is always on your side is not just your mind, it is universal mind, always the same, not different from another's mind."[31] You can project any kind of image imaginable onto a white screen, but the screen itself will only be revealed in the temporary absence of images. Self-realization cannot be remembered or grasped or experienced; it can only be fallen into again and again.

Looking for your Self is like looking for a pair of glasses that are perched on your nose. You can look under the sofa or the bed, in the kitchen or the bathroom, on your desk, in the garage or car. But the recognition, "Aha, they are perched on my nose" is a moment of realizing what was already the case, not the result of a diligent search through the house. This is not an external phenomenon, but the recognition of that which has been common to all external experiences. Wittgenstein puts it this way: "The aspects of things that are most important for us are hidden because of their implicity and familiarity."

One of the most common ways that confusion or seeking begins again after this recognition is the fall into making even this another experience in time. For example, one can hold to the idea that, "I used to be an unenlightened person; then, on August 29, I saw the Self, and now I am an enlightened person!" Of course, this is not realization, but the same sense of a separate identity returning, now sprayed over with the glitter paint of "enlightenment." The identification with being a seeker, a finder, and a loser of some experience called enlightenment is mistaken. It is only when attention returns fully to the Self, so that it is revealed only to itself and not to any idea of a person on a path, that it is clearly known to be your original nature.

"There is no goal to be reached," says Ramana Maharshi. "There is nothing to be attained. You are the Self. You exist always. Nothing more can be predicated of the Self than that it exists. Seeing God or the Self is only being the Self or yourself. Seeing is being. You, being the Self, want to know how to attain the Self. It is something like a man being at Ramanasramam asking how many ways there are to reach

Ramanasramam and which is the best way for him. All that is required of you is to give up the thought that you are this body and to give up all thoughts of external things and the not-Self."[32]

THE SELF IS ALWAYS FRESH AND NEW

No memory or previous state of realization can be used as a foundation for wakefulness in this moment. The realization is now—and now—and now—and now. Every moment is an invitation to look back behind the eyes, to listen behind the ears, and to be willing to find out again and again, always as though for the first time, who is really reading these words. This is not a static state, fixed irreversibly in time. It is continuously fresh, rediscovered in every moment.

Justin Golden, Ph.D., also known as Hanuman, a psychologist in San Francisco, fell awake with Poonjaji when they first met in Hardiwar, India in April of 1990. Since then he has devoted his life to sharing this with others. He has noticed that the idea of "getting it" and "losing it," which so commonly clouds the simplicity of things, is often the result of confusing one's true Self with the state of bliss or euphoria which so often accompanies the event of awakening itself. "A state of bliss will eventually pass, as all states must do," he says. "States are time-bound, they have a beginning and an end. When this elation fades away, the mistaken idea often comes that one's true nature has somehow been lost. But where can the eternal go? What has been lost is simply a particular psychological or spiritual state. So the search is picked up again, a search for a new event of awakening with the hope for another state of bliss, one which will last for a longer time, or forever. The identification with the blissful one or the one who has lost the bliss obscures the recognition, here and now, that 'I am the very consciousness in which this bliss arises, displays, and disappears. I am neither the blissful one nor the despairing one. I am that very consciousness, which is unerasable, unlosable, ever present, and always recognized here and now.' Now!!"[33]

Recognition of the timeless is always accessible. The very fact that all of this is being experienced right now bears testimony to the absolute presence of consciousness in this very moment. If consciousness were absent, this moment would not be experienced and, in essence, would not be happening.

HABITUAL ADDICTIONS
OF THE MIND

The recognition of who you really are is relatively easy. The fact that you have taken an interest in this subject, acquired this book, and read to this point means that you have already had some glimpse of this truth. It may have happened when you looked at a beautiful view and lost yourself in the panorama. It may have resulted from sitting quietly in meditation and discovering in the stillness that there was no one to be found. It may even have occurred in a moment of great crisis or emergency, when you spontaneously overcame the sense of separation as you helped others without any conscious concern for your own safety.

Although a glimpse is relatively easy, we find that we are also easily pulled back into a sense of separation by the context of our lives, by the way that we are habituated to having relationships with "other people," and continuously called upon by our society to accumulate things and define ourselves in terms of the acquisition of material possessions.

The rest of this book presents simple exercises that are helpful in deepening the recognition of the unborn nature of awareness and in freeing consciousness from being bound by external stimuli. These processes are not an end in themselves, nor intended to become another addiction. They are simple antidotes to be used when the essential clarity and perfection of things has been overshadowed. Once they have served their purpose, throw them away, as you would throw a stick you have been using to stoke a fire into the fire itself, once it has served its purpose.

The realization of who we really are happens in a moment out of time. It may take the rest of this human life to integrate and dissolve all that arises to obscure that realization. Kabir says, "I saw the mystery of things for fifteen seconds. Now it has made me a servant for life." The processes in this book are designed to be used whenever something arises that "kidnaps" awareness, something that seems to have more importance, relevance, and attraction than the Self itself. They are intended as antidotes to *samsara*, to the addictive quality of phenomenal existence.

CHAPTER 3

RELAXATION

When we become agitated even the simplest things become difficult, so it is very important to learn to relax. When we find a state beyond all our usual tensions, everything relaxes automatically."[1]

NAMKHAI NORBU

As we discussed in the previous chapter, there can be no real preparation for awakening from the dream of separation. At best, we can say that it is more likely to happen in a favorable context, in the right climate. Spiritual inquiry has become associated with relaxation rather than with stress, with solitude rather than with being in a crowd, and with heightened alertness rather than with dullness or intoxication. The Buddha wandered for six years, studying with different masters and trying different kinds of practices and austerities before he sat down under the bodhi tree and relaxed. Many people whose hearts are ablaze with this quest for freedom and wakefulness have practiced meditation, physical exercises, visualizations, and other practices, all of which help bring the body-mind into a state of relaxed alertness and openness. Although meditation itself will not necessarily lead to direct realization, the state of relaxed alertness that repeated practice cultivates may create a fertile soil.

In this book we use induced relaxation, sometimes called hypnosis or trance, to create a favorable context for inquiry. We then use the insights made available through such states to deepen and stabilize the awakening of "the view" which we have discussed in the previous chapter. This is not a substitute for a meditation practice, nor for whatever physical exercises you may use to create relaxation and energetic balance in the body. Nor could anything in this book be a substitute for the presence of a realized teacher. The advantage of inducing relaxation in this way is that it can effectively cut through the old habits of thought and does not require repeated practice as other disciplines may. It also does not create any dependency on membership in a group or the presence of a particular person.

STATES OF CONSCIOUSNESS

The word "hypnosis," from the Greek word *hypnos*, was coined by James Braid in the nineteenth century to mean "gradually induced sleep," or sleep that has been consciously induced by means of intentional direction. Induced relaxation is actually different from sleep, however, because there remains a quality of wakefulness and directed awareness and the possibility of making lucid choices and coming to new understandings. It is also different from waking consciousness because there is a far deeper accessibility to otherwise unconscious material, such as memories, emotions, archetypal patterns, and attitudes. It is also different from dreaming because the subject is simultaneously aware of subconscious material and the immediate environment. A "trance state" is also different from meditation in both its intention and its characteristics. While "meditation" usually refers to a state of stillness, of ceasing to pay attention to mental activity, in a state of induced relaxation we are paying specific attention to the contents of consciousness, particularly its more unconscious aspects, to bring about change.

Recent research into brain wave activity has clarified the distinctions between these states of consciousness and their corresponding brain wave patterns.[2] States of induced relaxation are characterized by greater coherence of the two hemispheres of the brain, as well as brain waves that combine theta (deep relaxation usually associated with dreaming or deep sleep) with alpha (a light state of relaxation and spaciousness) and beta (associated with conscious alertness and focus).

CHARACTERISTICS AND USES OF INDUCED RELAXATION

What is induced relaxation like and how can it be recognized? Such states are generally characterized by deep relaxation of the body and the mental processes. Physiological measurements often associated with stress—like the galvanic skin response, heart rate, muscular tension, and adrenaline accumulation—decrease, while the subjective experience of the speed and intensity of thought is reduced. This kind of relaxation is not unusual. You have probably already experienced it in your ordinary life. When you go to the movies or watch a film on television and become so absorbed in the story that you forget all about the popcorn in your lap and the friend sitting next to you, you are in an alpha state of brain wave activity. You may notice that your limbs feel heavier, your attention becomes fixated, and you forget your usual sense of yourself. You may also go into this state of deep relaxation listening to music, being in nature, or napping, where you are not actually asleep but remain aware of the sounds around you. Hence, induced relaxation has been used therapeutically as a means of reducing stress, since the effects on the body are in themselves beneficial.

In this state of deep relaxation, the "critical faculty" of the mind is bypassed so that there is a direct association between words and their literal meaning. (The books on hypnosis in the bibliography will provide you with many examples of how this works.) As a result, deep relaxation brings us back to a childlike state of innocence, in which suggestions are freely accepted by the subconscious mind. The high suggestibility associated with relaxed states of mind has been used in a variety of ways, from selling soft drinks through subliminal messages to overcoming addictions through therapeutic hypnosis. In a deeply relaxed state, new attitudes and beliefs can be "installed" at a level that bypasses the intellect. This is sometimes known as "direct suggestion" and can be used to help people quit smoking, lose weight, or change other unhealthy patterns.

Because deep relaxation bypasses the critical faculty, it can also be used to access memories, emotions, and hidden core beliefs. Rather as in dreams, or when we are overcome by intense feelings, deeper contents of consciousness are uncovered which were blocked by conscious willpower and concepts. Trance states allow us to access the "subconscious mind" in order to reveal and release the core issues underlying problems. Thus trained practitioners can work with childhood memories, archetypal images, and even past life memories that would not ordinarily be available in the waking state. Because of the direct connection between words and images, visualization is often used in induced relaxation to create new, more desirable blueprints in the subconscious mind.

Here we will be using states of deep relaxation in a significantly different way. Inducing relaxation has been most commonly used to bring about change: to change one set of attitudes to another in order to make life work better, heal the body, or transform emotions so one feels better about oneself. In this work we induce relaxation with quite a different intention. Instead of trying to change anything, we will use the state of induced relaxation to deepen insight into the nature of things as they already are, to see into the mechanics of dualistic consciousness, and hence to bring about its dissolution.

TYPES OF INDUCED RELAXATION

There are many different ways of using states of relaxation. The first and perhaps most traditional way is through "direct suggestions," as we discussed earlier, to cause the unconscious patterns of the mind to operate in new ways. An example might be the suggestion, "Every time you smell cigarette smoke, you will feel how clean your lungs are, and how much you love fresh air." Or, "Every time you go to the refrigerator, you will want to eat fruits and vegetables." Such suggestions are called affirmations when they "affirm" positive thoughts we would rather have about ourselves and our environment: "I am a good and honest person, I deserve love, the world is an abundant place." This approach may be ineffective if the technique used does not take into account the kinds of resistance that may be encountered, and therefore does not really bring about an increase in awareness. But it is certainly the most common use of the suggestibility associated with inducing relaxation.

"Indirect suggestion" was pioneered by the late Milton Erickson and systematized and made popular by Richard Bandler and John Grinder as Neuro Linguistic Programming. Here the subconscious mind is influenced in a more indirect way. Suggestions may be embedded in longer sentences or given in such a way that they are not noticeable, in order to bypass resistance. Although this approach is subtler than direct suggestion, it still does not allow an increased awareness of the mechanics of the mind. It is something done "to" us, of which we may not be aware.

A third approach, sometimes referred to as "secret process," operates in the opposite way, i.e. the facilitator remains unaware of the content, and the participant follows generic instructions. An example might be, "I am going to ask you now to remember a pleasant memory, something that was nourishing to you. When you feel in touch with this, you can allow a movement with one of the fingers of your right hand." The person in a deeply relaxed state might not actually speak out loud at all during the session, and the facilitator might guide them through the steps of a process without ever knowing what content is being addressed.

In this book we use a style that is known as "interactive process." Both the facilitator and the one going into relaxation are involved in determining the direction it takes, and both speak out loud during the process.

Just as there are different styles of working with relaxation, there are different levels of relaxation. Here we will be working in light to medium states in order to maintain awareness throughout the process.

You may have also heard about people going "out" then "coming back" after an experience of deep relaxation as though from another dimension and being unable to remember anything that happened. While that may be helpful in bringing about unconscious behavioral change, we are more interested here in the expansion of awareness and the integration of insights that occur in the session into our day-to-day life. The inductions in this chapter are all intended to bring someone to greater awareness and understanding using a state of deep physical relaxation accompanied by alertness.

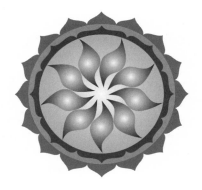

ANATOMY OF A SESSION

Now we will move on to discuss the practical steps needed to guide a friend through a "session" facilitating Clear Seeing. Each session is comprised of a number of parts:

- The **pre-induction talk** allows you to become comfortable together and to explore the focus of your session. During this part of the session you will be practicing the Heart Meditation described in the next chapter.

- The **induction** creates the relaxed state that will be the context for the rest of your work together.

- The **main part of the session** happens interactively and addresses a specific obscuration to the natural state, like an obsessive desire, relationship issue, or confusion of some kind. The outlines for this part of the session are found in later chapters.

- **Suggestions** at the end of the session can dispel and neutralize latent doubts and help bring the habits of thought into alignment with the natural state.

- **Counting back** at the end of the session brings your friend back to normal waking consciousness.

THE PRE-INDUCTION TALK

It is recommended that you spend some time talking together before doing any of the sessions outlined in the later parts of this book. This will allow you to establish greater rapport and trust and to gather information about the kind of obscuration to Clear Seeing that is presenting itself. This information will be useful later on, once your friend is in a state of relaxation, because you will be more familiar with her habitual patterns and you will need to ask fewer questions. Also, those qualities in consciousness that your friend wants to look at can be enlivened and brought to surface awareness by speaking about them before you begin the main part of the session. Ask your friend to tell you everything that she can about this obscuring tendency, about when it is strongest, when it goes away, what kinds of situations evoke it, and how she feels it in her body, emotions, and thoughts when she is caught in it.

The pre-induction talk also allows you to become aware of any counterindications for working in trance or any reasons that you might want to refer your friend to a licensed professional. Unless you are a licensed psychotherapist, you should not try to work with material that carries an intense emotional charge or may elicit memories or feelings that your friend would find it difficult to integrate afterwards. It is also better not to do this work with someone who is under the influence of a mind-altering drug or is chemically dependent.

During a pre-induction talk, the most important thing is to listen from the Heart,[3] from a place of emptiness. The more you can listen from and absorb into spaciousness, the more the content can unfold naturally. In the following chapter we will explore the practice of *Tonglen,* of giving and taking from the Heart, described by the Tibetan Master Atisha in his *Seven Points of Mind Training.* I first began to use this as a daily practice in 1979. It has been both a great gift for me personally and has enhanced my ability to be empty when working with people. If this simple practice of giving and taking on the breath were all the training you had when conducting a pre-induction talk, it would stand you in much better stead than more formal and technical ways for establishing rapport.

This ability to remain present and empty, not only during the pre-induction talk, but also throughout the session, allows unseen magic to work, taking this experience beyond therapeutic intervention into the realms of applied mysticism.

METHODS TO INDUCE RELAXATION

After you have talked together for a while, gathering enough information to be able to be comfortable as a facilitator, you can go on to induce a state of relaxation. There are literally hundreds of ways to do this. Some are simple and easy, others are more rigorous and complicated. The processes of induction given here have been chosen for this book because they can be learned by anyone without formal training.

1. Pacing and Leading.
Pacing and leading honors the way things already are and then uses this to lead deeper into a state of relaxation and expansion. The method is simple: you make three undeniable statements about your friend's experience exactly as it is in this

moment (pacing), then follow them with a statement that takes her deeper into relaxation and letting go (leading).

An example of a pacing statement would be:

You can hear the sound of my voice.

That is not something that anyone could disagree with. If she did not hear what you said, she could not disagree with you! And if she did hear what you said, then it is automatically true. Other pacing statements include:

You can feel the way the breath is coming in and going out.
You can feel the way your body is resting here.
You can feel the way your body is supported by the chair.
You can feel the air on your skin.
You can hear the sounds from outside the room.
You can feel the way your feet are touching each other.
(or touching the floor).
You can feel the way your body is resting.
You can hear the sounds around you.
You can feel the way your clothing is touching your body.
You can notice the way that thoughts arise, persist, and fall back.
You can notice the way that emotions are shifting and changing.

"You can hear the soothing and melodious sound of my voice," on the other hand, would *not* be an example of a pacing statement, as it is not undeniably true. After all, she might find your voice jarring and discomforting!

Each set of three pacing statements is followed by a leading statement. Here are some examples of leading statements:

You are relaxing now.
You are sinking deeper.
Your body knows how to relax.

Now you can combine these into sets of three pacing statements and one leading statement and easily induce relaxation like this:

That's right, you can
Hear the sound of my voice.
You can feel the way
Your body is resting here.
You can notice the way
The breath is coming in and going out on its own.
And in that same, easy, effortless way, you can
Allow yourself to
Sink deeper inside.

The way the pacing statements and the leading statement connect to each other may be directive (sometimes called a paternal style) or permissive (a maternal style). Here is an example of a directive style of connection:

You are resting here.
You can hear the sound of my voice.
You can hear the sounds from outside the window,
And you can
Sink deep inside now.

This kind of directive style is more effective with someone who easily goes into a relaxed state and is not likely to resist the suggestion. Otherwise, a more indirect, invitational, or permissive style would go something like this:

Perhaps in your own way you might
Begin to notice the way that
Your body is resting here.
Yes, that's right.
In your own way, you can
Become aware of the sound of my voice now,
And perhaps you might even
Begin to notice the temperature of the air on your skin.
And who knows,
Perhaps in your own way and
In your own time you might consider
What it might feel like for you to
Sink deeper inside.

For more information about pacing and leading, you can refer to Bandler and Grinder's book *Tranceformations*, which is mentioned in the bibliography.

2. Embedded Suggestions.

Perhaps you noticed that in the sections in italics above, some of the sentences were broken in unusual places, like this:

You can take all the time you need to....
Remember what it feels like to....
Relax deeply now.

As you give such suggestions, you can pause at the end of each line as it is written. "Relax deeply now" and the bigger clause in which it is embedded (beginning "Remember what it feels like to") are called "embedded suggestions." They are easy to use.

Simply take a suggestion like "Sink deeper inside..." or "Relax deeply now..." and put it into a larger sentence. This allows you to deliver the same suggestion to the unconscious mind while bypassing the resistance to the conscious mind. Here is another example:

And I don't know if
You are ready to
Go deeper now.
There is no way for me to tell if
You can remember clearly
How good it feels when
You know that
You can allow yourself at any time to
Sink deeper inside.

It is amazing how well this works. Of course, you should only give the indirect suggestions which your friend has already given you permission to use, either implicitly or explicitly. Since your friend is lying down with the intention of sinking deeper into relaxation, suggestions about relaxation or letting go are implicitly invited by your situation. Other suggestions used in this way should be checked out in the pre-induction talk.

3. Counting Down.
This is one of the easiest and most familiar ways to lead someone gradually into relaxation. Synchronize your voice with your friend's breath so the statements that invite deeper relaxation fall on the out-breath. The script that follows is for someone whose eyes are already closed. Otherwise you can add suggestions that the eyes are becoming heavier and heavier, so that, once you reach the number ten, the eyes will be closed.

In a few moments I am going to count from
One to ten.
With every number that you hear you can
Allow yourself to
Sink even deeper inside,
And return back to a place of
Comfort and ease.
That's right now,
Starting to count,
One,

The body is feeling more relaxed, and heavier.
Two,
There's nothing for you to do now.
You are safe, comfortable and easy.
Three,
That's right.
The body and
The processes of thought can remember how to
Relax deeply now,
All on their own.
Four,
Deeper and deeper.
There's nothing for you to do now,
The body is letting go on its own.
Five,
That's right.
The breath and the processes of thought can
Remember how to
Let go and sink deeper inside.
Six,
Nothing to do.
The body is
Relaxing deeply now
On its own.
Seven,
Deeper inside now.
There is nothing to do but
Relax deeply now.
Eight,
Deeper and softer, with every breath you can
Remember how to
Let go now.
Nine,
That's right, there is nothing for you to do,
And Ten,
The body is soft and relaxed now,
And you can
Allow yourself to
Continue to sink deeper
With every breath that leaves the body.

4. Using the Breath.

The induction described above is not the only time when you can synchronize your voice with the breath. In fact, by slightly raising the pitch of your voice with your friend's in-breath, and lowering it with the out-breath (like a sigh), your voice itself can become a means of induction. Below you can see an example of how the language used can be specific to the in-breath and the out-breath.

> *Just as you're resting here now you can begin to...* (in-breath)
> *...relax deeply and go deep inside yourself....* (with a falling tone on the out-breath)
> *That's right, you can begin to notice the way that the breath...* (in-breath)
> *...goes out and allows you to let go....* (out-breath)
> *And as that breath comes in again...* (in-breath)
> *...you can use it to send you deeper inside....* (out-breath)
> *And who knows? Just as you rest here you might become aware that...* (in-breath)
> *...you are sinking deeper and relaxing....* (out-breath).

Just speaking with the in-breath and the out-breath in this way creates a kind of biofeedback loop, where your friend is able to regulate the speed of your voice through her breath and can feel that she is taking the process deeper. It does not really matter what you say; you could read her the Chicago phone book with this rhythm, and she would relax. Try it and see!

5. Parts of the Body.

Pacing and leading, described earlier, involves paying minute attention to the actuality of what is so. This can also be done through what is occurring in the body. I am sure that at some time when you were unable to sleep at night, someone suggested that you progressively become aware of different parts of the body. Sure enough, if you start at your toes and go slowly enough, you won't make it to your nose before you're fast asleep. Simply noticing the way the body is right now, paying attention to the internal feeling of it, naturally leads it into a more relaxed state. Here is the beginning of a script that you can complete on your own, once you get the hang of how to induce relaxation by simply paying attention to the body:

That's right, you can
Take your own time now
In your own way to
Notice the way
The breath is coming in
And going out.
That's right,
There's nothing for you to do.
In a moment you can begin to
Feel different parts of the body
And as you feel each part,
As you become aware of the sensations in that part of the body,
You can allow a gentle movement
With one of the fingers of the right hand.
Even now you can
Become aware of the right foot.
You can feel the way the right foot feels.

Wait for the finger signal before moving on to the next part of the body. With the foot, you can even go into the feeling in each toe and each part of the foot.

You can feel the right ankle.
Notice the way that the right ankle feels now.
And when you are fully aware of the right ankle,
You can, once again, allow the finger signal.

Wait for the signal each time you bring attention to a new part of the body.

You can become aware of the lower part of the right leg.
That's right, you can feel the muscles and tendons and the bones
In the lower part of the right leg.

(Wait for the signal)

You can feel the right knee.
Notice the feelings inside the right knee.

(Wait for the signal)

You can feel the upper part of the right leg,
That's right, you can
Feel all the muscles, tendons and sensations
In the upper part of the right leg.

(Wait for the signal)

You can feel the way that the right leg connects to the pelvis.
You can become aware of the right hip joint.

Now go through the same process with the left leg, finishing with the left hip. Then you can begin to work up through the main part of the body:

That's right,

You can become aware now of the pelvis,

And all the muscles which attach to the pelvis.

(Wait for the signal)

You can become aware now of the lower part of the back,

You can feel the muscles in the lower part of the back,

(Wait for the signal)

You can feel the middle of the back,

The muscles and sensations in the middle of the back.

(Wait for the signal)

You can feel the upper part of the back,

That's right.

You can continue in this way with the right shoulder, the upper part of the right arm, the right elbow, the lower part of the right arm, and the right hand. Then do the same with the left shoulder and the left arm. Then continue with the belly, all the organs in the belly, the diaphragm, the chest and all the muscles involved in breathing, the neck and throat, and all the parts of the face up through the scalp. Pay particularly close attention to awareness of the eyes, nose, mouth, and ears.

This method of inducing relaxation will work with anyone, no matter how tense they may be before you start. Even if your friend seems to have entered a state of deep relaxation early on, continue with the process. If you are afraid she might have gone to sleep, keep asking for the finger signal.

6. Refractionation.

Refractionation uses anticipation to take your friend deeper in quantum leaps rather than through a gradual deepening process. Decide on an arbitrary signal you will give that will allow her to go three or four times as deep. You might touch her elbow, for example, or say a certain word, like "now." Or you could sound a gong or a chime. This method is most effective after one or two of the other methods described earlier. Here is how you use this induction:

Just because you are

Deeper and more relaxed now, so

In a moment you can
Sink three or four times as deep (on the out-breath).
In a few moments you will
Feel my touch on your elbow.
(or "you'll hear a bell..." or "you'll hear the word 'now'..." etc.)
When you feel that touch,
In some natural, spontaneous way you can
Use that touch to allow yourself to
Sink twice as deep (on the out-breath).
That's right, even now, perhaps,
You might be wondering what
Twice as deep could be like for you.
In the body and in the processes of thought
As they arise and fall,
But there's only one way for you to find out,
Because in a moment when you
Feel my touch on your right elbow, you can
Sink twice as deep inside (on the out-breath).
That's right, I don't know what
Twice as deep (on the out-breath)
Could feel like for you.
I have no idea how your thoughts might move as they
Sink twice as deep inside (on the out-breath).
I don't know how
Your body might relax and let go
As you allow yourself to sink
Twice as deep inside (on the out-breath).
But there's only one way to find out,
Because in a moment when you feel that touch
("hear the bell..." "hear the word 'now'..." etc.)
You can allow yourself to
Sink twice as deep inside,
NOW.

(As you say the word "now," touch the elbow or ring the chime). This process of induction works by creating such a state of boredom and impatience that your friend sinks deeper into relaxation just out of long-awaited anticipation! She will be so eager and impatient for you to finish talking about it and take her twice as deep, that when you finally give your signal, she will actually experience going "twice as deep."

This method is particularly good for someone who is resistant to sinking deeper inside. You are intentionally increasing her resistance, rather like pulling back an arrow in the bow before you release it. When you finally let go, it flies to the target.

7. Flight of Stairs.

This simple visualization is particularly useful if you're doing a session to access memory or visualization. It is best used after two or three of the inductions described earlier.

And just because you are
Feeling more relaxed now,
More comfortable and easy,
So it's easy for you to see yourself,
To feel yourself,
To imagine yourself standing
At the top of a flight of stairs.
Ten steps going down,
Ten steps going deeper inside.
And you can begin now to
Step down the stairs.
That's right,
One, just letting go now.
There is nothing for you to do.
Two, that's right, feeling each step as you touch it with your foot.
There's nothing for you to do now.
Three, that's right.
Gravity is allowing the body to move deeper down the stairs,
Deeper down to a place where you can
(recall a memory, meet someone, or whatever is following)
Four
Sinking deeper, there is nothing for you to do
Letting go, letting go
Five, down the stairs,
There is nothing for you to do.
Deeper and deeper inside,
Six, down the stairs, that's right.
Deeper and deeper inside, and
Seven, that's right, the body is
Becoming softer, easier and more relaxed.
Eight, down the stairs,

Deeper inside now, deeper inside.
Nine, there's nothing for you to do.
Deeper and deeper inside...and
Ten.

Once your friend imagines reaching the bottom of the stairs, it is a good time to move on to some of the other processes described later in this book.

8. Other Guided Imagery.

Guiding your friend through a memory of a time when she felt relaxed and at peace will generally induce the same kind of relaxation again. Some examples include walking in a forest or a meadow; walking along the beach or stepping into a hot tub; or even previous states of induced relaxation. Use the present tense in your induction, and use as many different senses as possible.

9. Tapes and Music.

You can facilitate any of the processes in this book without using formal induction methods. If you want to experiment with a friend, and find the instructions given above to be too much to start with, just take some time together sitting quietly and relaxing. You could play some relaxing, calming music. Alternatively, you can obtain tapes from the Living Essence Foundation with a number of different relaxations already recorded with music for you to use before you move into the interactive parts of the sessions.

THE LANGUAGE OF INDUCED RELAXATION

During the induction process and the session that follows, it is important to use language that takes your friend deeper into relaxation rather than jarring her or bringing her back into normal mental activity. Here are a few indicators of how to talk with someone in a state of induced relaxation.

First, use the present tense as much as possible. Even in the middle of recalling a memory, rather than asking, "What happened next?" it is better to ask, "What is happening now?" or "What can you see now?" or "What is occurring for you in this moment?" In the natural state everything is experienced as occurring in this moment. The idea of past and future only arises in conceptual thought. By maintaining the present tense, you minimize the possibility of becoming lost in concepts.

Use simple language that is not conceptual. When someone enters into a state of deep relaxation, they regain the quality of an innocent child, where the association between image and meaning becomes much more direct. Use words that have an immediate, experiential meaning. In the same way, it is a good idea to use positive words rather than negative ones. It is difficult for someone in an innocent state of mind to be asked to "feel yourself walking on a path, and there are no other people here." When the mind is open and suggestible, just the mention of other people causes us to see them. Instead, you could say, "Feel yourself walking on a path, enjoying how it feels to be alone."

It is also a good idea to repeat certain key phrases like "the body can remember how good it feels to relax and go inside," as the repetitive use of language lends itself to deepening. Although in ordinary communication we try to avoid repeating ourselves to avoid boring others, in a state of induced relaxation this quality of boredom can contribute to the deepening. Although in ordinary communication we try to avoid repeating ourselves to avoid boring others, in a state of relaxation this quality of boredom can contribute to the deepening. Although in ordinary communication we....you get the idea.

Generally you use your voice in a way that induces relaxation, even to the point of stretching out words unnaturally or speaking more slowly than usual. However, if during any of these sessions your friend gets in touch with an emotional charge that she may need help in moving through, make sure you maintain a rapport and empathy by meeting her in that place. Many of the processes described in this book involve moving more deeply into something in order to become liberated from it. For example, if your friend is experiencing anger, you may not want to speak in a calm, slow, gentle voice, as it might actually be more irritating than supportive.

USE OF SUGGESTION

All of the session outlines in this book are designed to return consciousness to a recognition of its original nature and to help stabilize that awakening. When you have finished the interactive part of your time together, you can give your friend space to rest in the natural state, in Self-recognition, before counting her back. You can allow some time of silence, or even play some gentle music. You might also want to use some "direct suggestions" before bringing her back to full waking consciousness.

Because we are not primarily concerned here with symptomatic or behavioral change, we are not using suggestions in the way they are often used in hypnotherapy. But it may be, during this period at the end of the session, that you can use suggestion to dispel doubt that might otherwise arise. Habits of mind are so deeply trained in a dualistic vision of things that they will easily kidnap awareness again and obscure the view.

There is a story about the famous archer Arjuna, who fought in the Kurushetra battle and received the dharma from Krishna in the Bhagavad Gita. It is said that he was such an accomplished archer that he had an extraordinary way of defending himself against attack. When the enemy fired arrows at him, he was so fast with his quiver that he could shoot down each approaching arrow with arrows of his own. Of course, like all good stories, this is partially symbolic. Every Arjuna, ancient or modern, has to learn to shoot down the concepts of illusion with the concepts of truth. The result is an empty sky, no concepts at all.

This is what we are doing with suggestion at the end of the session: suggestions are antidotes. We are not trying to persuade the mind into adopting a new belief system with "enlightened" concepts; rather, we are shooting down old beliefs in order to leave the sky clear.

I find wonderful suggestions to use in this way in ancient (and modern) dharma texts like the ones referred to in the bibliography. Any words spoken from this place of non-dual seeing can become a means of deepening at the end of the session to reinforce the resting in original nature. Here is a suitable piece from the *Ashtavakra Gita*:

> You are free of all limitations;
> Independent, calm, without dimension or form,
> Imperturbable, your nature is unimaginable Intelligence.
> Know yourself to be pure Consciousness.[4]

Or here is a piece from the *Kaivalya Upanishad*:

> From your true nature everything is born,
> In you everything is supported,
> Into you everything is again dissolved.
> You are this Vastness, One-without-a-second.
> Your true nature is of inconceivable power,
> You see all without eyes,
> You hear all without ears.[5]

You can also use your friend's own language from the session to deepen the realization, as in the following examples:

You are this consciousness.
You are unborn and undying.
You are the source of all things.
There is nothing that exists outside you.
You are this Love,
You are this Beauty,
You are this Truth.

You may want to offer suggestions that use the word "I" as well as the word "you" and also those that refer to consciousness in an impersonal way. In addition to the suggestion "You are this formlessness" you can use suggestions in the first person:

And now, resting here,
You can allow the recognition to
Settle more deeply that
"I am this formlessness,"

Or without any personal pronoun at all:

Yes, that's right, this consciousness has no form.

Suggestions cannot create realization, they can only act as antidotes to doubt. By using the first and second person, as well as stating suggestions in an impersonal way, you can shoot down the arrows of all kinds of doubts and beliefs latent within consciousness.

COUNTING BACK OUT OF AN INDUCED STATE

Now you have finished the session. You started with the pre-induction talk; you went on to induce a relaxed state; you worked through obscurations using one of the session outlines later in the book; and you then gave some suggestions to deepen and stabilize the realization of emptiness. Now you are ready to bring your friend back to normal waking consciousness.

When we "count back" out of a relaxed state, we facilitate two things. First, we want to make sure that the body and mental processes are wide awake and alert, aware, and able to deal with whatever arises in day-to-day life. Second, we want to make sure that your friend does not link the realization of the natural state with a particular session or process or think of it as some contingent phenomenon that comes and goes in time. Therefore, when counting back, you can suggest that the

body will return to full waking consciousness and at the same time
that this awareness of the expanded, infinite nature of unborn awareness will continue to deepen.

Here is how to count someone back:

> *In a few moments*
> *We're going to count back*
> *From five to one.*
> *With every breath you take,*
> *This realization can become deeper.*
> *With every situation that arises in life*
> *This realization can become deeper and more profound.*
> *Every movement of thought and emotion*
> *Can take you deeper into the realization of this*
> *Self-perfected ground of Being.*
> *When we've finished counting,*
> *The body and the processes of thought*
> *Will be wide awake, refreshed and alert,*
> *As though after a long, refreshing sleep.*
> *And at the same time,*
> *This recognition of limitlessness,*
> *Of vastness,*
> *Of your natural state,*
> *Can become deeper and deeper.*
> *It may be surprising and delightful to see*
> *In what spontaneous ways*
> *This realization of the emptiness of pure consciousness*
> *Can deepen when the eyes open.*
> *It may be surprising and delightful*
> *To find out how*
> *This deepening can continue*
> *With every breath that comes in and goes out,*
> *And with every new experience that arises and falls in*
> *Day-to-day life.*
> *So, that's right,*
> *Allowing the body now to*
> *Take a breath into the belly....*
> *FIVE... that's right, the fingers and the toes are moving,*
> *And you are resting here,*
> *Infinite, eternal, undisturbed,*
> *The source of all things....*

FOUR... that's right,
The energy is moving more and more in the body,
Becoming more alive and awake as you
Relax even more deeply in
The realization of That which you are....
THREE... the body is becoming more alive,
Stretching, coming back to full waking consciousness
Remembering the room in which you are lying,
As you relax at the same time
Into the realization of being That
In which all bodies move,
In which all time and space is occurring.
You are that infinite emptiness.
TWO... that's right, getting ready for the eyes to open,
The body is fully wide-awake and
Returning to full normal consciousness,
And able to resume its normal activities,
And... ONE.

(As you say the number ONE, snap your fingers).

If you have a sense that your friend is in any way "spaced-out" or disassociated, you can ask her to take some time to reorient herself before she leaves the place where the session took place.

ABOUT GIVING SESSIONS

I have taught the kinds of processes described in this book to thousands of people over the years. Virtually everyone has found them easy to learn, and they do not require special training or expertise. You will be able to use these methods and the session outlines that follow with your friends and dharma brothers and sisters. If you are a psychotherapist, hypnotherapist, or bodyworker, you can easily incorporate them into your practice.

Most of the session outlines, as well as the induction methods described earlier, contain italicized sections that act as scripts for what you could say while your friend is in a state of deep relaxation. These scripts are provided to fall back on when you feel you lack confidence. If you are already trained in hypnotherapy, or if you are a therapist, you may not need the scripts, and you can always use your own language to move through the steps of the session.

You may have noticed that I refer to the friend or client you are working with as "she." I do this for two reasons. First, since the majority of people I have worked with in this way have been women, it seems statistically justified. Second, men have had a monopoly on the generic pronoun used to refer to either sex, and it feels refreshing to reverse that trend.

The sessions in the book are not designed to be used repeatedly, like a practice. They are more like initiations into a new way of seeing. Once the unconscious instinctive patterns of perception have realigned themselves, most of the principles underlying the sessions described will become second nature and will not need to be repeated.

Clear Seeing liberates. Once an obscuring tendency has been seen through, it evaporates completely—no further action is required. Initially we may use these sessions as techniques for providing an insight into the mechanics of how consciousness works. But once something is recognized at more than an intellectual level, it is irreversible— you can't go back any more. For example, when you walk towards a door, you don't walk straight into it. You reach out your hand, turn the handle, and open it. You would not call that a technique or a practice. It is automatic; at some point you saw so clearly into the nature of how to open a door that the seeing became irreversible. Barring severe brain damage, you could not "forget." The processes in this book are like that. Use them as antidotes to the false dualistic notions of the mind, and when they have done their work, throw them away. They are intended to point you back to the unconditioned natural state where life happens spontaneously without any interference.

You do not need any special qualifications to use these processes. They are designed to be done between friends. They work best when two people work together, with one as the facilitator or guide and the other as the participant. The person who is going through the session can lie down or sit in a chair where they can lean back with their head supported. If you do not have a friend to work with, you can dictate the instructions onto a tape, or you can use one of the tapes available from our Foundation which are listed at the back of the book. As we have already mentioned, nothing described here could possibly replace the help of a licensed psychotherapist or health care practitioner. If you feel at all unsure, seek out the help of someone who is professionally trained.

This is the age of the friend. All that is needed is an open heart, and a sincere thirst for freedom and awakening, and it will be easy to use the sessions that follow in subsequent chapters to return to a state of simplicity, innocence, and Clear Seeing.

CHAPTER 4

THE HEART MEDITATION

Whoever wishes quickly to become
A refuge for himself and others,
Should undertake this sacred mystery:
To take the place of others, giving them his own.[1]

SHANTIDEVA

ven more important than a toolkit full of techniques for facilitating others in the journey of Self-awakening is the ability to establish natural rapport or empathy. In the early 1970s, while investigating the work of Milton Erickson, Virginia Satir, Fritz Perls, and Gregory Bateson, Richard Bandler and John Grinder noticed that all four of these great therapists produced extraordinary results. In particular, they had a variety of ways of establishing and deepening rapport. By breaking down their technique into discrete steps and modeling it for others, Bandler and Grinder came up with Neuro Linguistic Programming, or NLP. NLP practitioners are taught to attempt to recreate the same effect that Erickson, Satir, Perls, and Bateson produced spontaneously. Although the approach can be effective, it may also seem mechanical if not practiced with utmost skill—and even then it may not necessarily generate the spaciousness and unconditional love that clients frequently experienced in the presence of Erickson or Satir.

In our training we offer another way to develop deep rapport and to dissolve the feeling of separation between facilitator and client. The meditation technique we teach, which can be practiced throughout the session, is loosely based on an ancient Tibetan practice known as *Tonglen*, which is still used in the *Nyingma* tradition of Tibetan Buddhism to cultivate *bodhichitta* or compassion. Besides being a very effective way to open the Heart and deepen wakefulness, it is the ideal atmosphere in which to practice the sessions outlined in this book.

ATISHA THE THRICE BORN

Although the practice predates him, Tonglen is most clearly elucidated by the Tibetan Heart master Atisha (928-1054). Atisha is known as the "thrice born" because he studied and reached awakening with three different masters: Matriyogin, Dharmarakshita, and Dharmakirti, each of whom demonstrated to him in a different way the capacity we have as human beings to dissolve the feeling of separation between ourselves and others.

Atisha's teachings were condensed into *The Seven Points of Mind Training*. This two-page document is one of the most useful and inspiring manuals on awakening that one can find.[2] The practice of Tonglen is described in the second of Atisha's seven points as "the giving and taking on the breath." Here is how he puts it:

> *Train to give and take alternately.*
> *Mount them both upon your breath.*
> *Three objects, three poisons, and three roots of virtue.*
> *In all your actions train yourself with maxims,*
> *Begin the training sequence with yourself.*[3]

For a deeper understanding of what these short verses mean, I would recommend Dilgo Khyentse's translation and commentary.[4] Sogyal Rimpoche's book *The Tibetan Book of Living and Dying* also explains the practice in some detail, as does Rajneesh's *Book of Wisdom*. The following adaptation of Tonglen is a useful foundation upon which to practice the rest of the sessions presented in this book. Always start the Heart meditation with yourself; once you feel it flowing freely with yourself, you can extend it to someone else.

THE HEART MEDITATION

Step 1: Get Comfortable.

Find a comfortable place to sit with your back fairly straight and your chest area open. Now close your eyes and take a minute or two just to settle and tune in to the environment around you.

Step 2: Fan the Flames of the Heart.

Begin to focus the breath into the middle of the chest in the "Heart center," to the right of the physical heart. As you spend a few minutes focusing the in-breath in this way and allowing a gentle sigh on the out-breath, you will notice the Heart center beginning to radiate or glow. You may find it useful to imagine that you are fanning the flames of the Heart with the in-breath and allowing the warmth of those flames to travel through the shoulders and down the arms into the hands and down the chest into the belly on the out-breath.

Step 3: Mount Form on the Breath.

Once you feel the Heart radiating in this way, you can start to imagine the Heart center as a window into the emptiness or vastness which is your true nature. You might even have the sense of being limitless and looking out through this window into the world of name and form. Now you can imagine breathing in form through the window of the Heart and allowing it to dissolve into formlessness, and then breathing formlessness back out through the window of the Heart into the world of form.

Step 4: Mount Thought on the Breath.

Notice thoughts now as you continue to breathe form through the window of the Heart into formlessness and breathe formlessness out through the window of the Heart into form. You may also begin to notice the way that thoughts arise and fall spontaneously in consciousness. Sometimes we suggest seeing them like little children playing, sometimes squabbling, sometimes running, sometimes slouching. You can begin to use the in-breath as a vehicle to carry thought back through the window of the Heart into silence, into formlessness. Try it now: with the in-breath absorb thought through the window of the

Heart into the silence that is free of thought; with the out-breath allow the same silence to burst forth and permeate the field of thought.

Sometimes people like to visualize this as waves on the shore. A wave breaks on the shore and then falls back into the ocean, drawing with it whatever is on the beach; then another wave breaks and floods the shore again. Continue to absorb thought back into silence with the in-breath and allow silence and formlessness to permeate the field of thought with the out-breath. The feeling is like a mother standing at the door of the house welcoming her children home at the end of the day. With the in-breath you open your arms wide, as if to say, "Come home, thought. It's okay to come home to that which gave you birth." Whether the children have been fighting or playing, lazy or productive, it doesn't matter, for they are all children of emptiness. With the in-breath you can bring them home to rest and dissolve like so many streams and rivers brought back to the ocean from which they originated. You are embracing thought with the in-breath, kissing it, hugging it. With the out-breath you are allowing vastness, silence, and the mystery of formlessness to burst forth once again as Lord into the field of thought: fresh, original, spontaneous.

Step 5: Mount Emotions on the Breath.
Take all the time you need to allow the previous step to become natural, like the waves breaking and disappearing on the shore. Now continue in the same way with emotions. First notice the way the emotions shift and change. Then with the in-breath absorb the emotions back into the stillness of love, and with the out-breath allow the vastness, the security, the warmth of the Heart to permeate the field in which emotions arise. You may find your own images to represent this process.

Step 6: Mount Physical Sensations on the Breath.
Now continue in the same way with physical sensations. With the in-breath absorb all sensation back into the blissfulness of the Heart. With the out-breath, allow that same blissfulness to radiate into the body.

You will need to allow yourself plenty of time with each step to start to feel this becoming real.

Step 7: Mount Everything on the Breath.
Now you can continue to absorb with the in-breath and bless and radiate with the out-breath without making any distinction between thought, emotion, and physical sensation. All form is absorbed and dissolved back into formlessness. All vibration is dissolved back into stillness. With the out-breath the Heart itself is radiating its fullness back into form, permeating form with formlessness. You can continue to practice the Heart meditation with eyes closed, or you can open your eyes and go about your day, continuing this rhythm of absorbing and permeating.

THE RESULTS OF THE HEART MEDITATION

This meditation has been the greatest friend to many teachers and practitioners in many traditions, not only in Tibetan Buddhism. Here Bhagavan Shri Rajneesh (now known simply as Osho) comments on Tonglen in his excellent *Book of Wisdom*. "If you can experience it—this is of tremendous importance—then start absorbing it. Don't throw it away. It is such a valuable energy, don't throw it away. Absorb it, drink it, accept it, welcome it, feel grateful to it. And say to yourself, 'This time I'm not going to avoid it, this time I'm not going to reject it, this time I'm not going to throw it away. This time I will drink it and receive it like a guest. This time I will digest it.' It may take a few days for you to be able to digest it, but the day it happens, you have stumbled upon a door which will take you really far away. A new journey has started in your life, you are moving into a new kind of being—because immediately, the moment you accept the pain with no rejection anywhere, its energy and its quality changes. It is no longer pain."[5]

Rajneesh continues a couple of pages later, "But start with your own self. Make a small experiment with your own pains, sufferings and miseries. And once you have found the key, then you can share it with the whole existence. Then you can take all the suffering of all the world, or all the worlds.

"Ride on the incoming breath and your small heart is bigger than the whole universe, if you know what miracles it can do. And then pour out your blessings. It is the same energy passing through your heart that becomes bliss, that becomes a blessing. Then let blessings go riding on the outgoing breath to all the nooks and corners of existence.

"Atisha says: This is compassion. Compassion is to become a transforming force in existence—transforming the ugly into the beautiful, kissing the frog and transforming it into a prince, transforming darkness into light. To become such a medium of transformation is compassion."[6]

In our training we teach this meditation on the first day, and there is an intensity and wakefulness that fills the air. The beauty of the Heart meditation is that it is essentially natural. Rather than visualizing anything, we are utilizing the quality that the Heart already has to absorb and accept unconditionally and to shine forth and radiate. If you try this on your own for a while, you will notice that it becomes second nature. The meditation simply brings your attention to what is already so.

There is an extraordinary presence and vitality, right from the first time that we do this together. Rather than trying to describe this myself, let me invite you into one of our trainings, just after we have finished practicing the Heart meditation for the first time. Listen to what ordinary people like you and me have been experiencing:

"I notice that all the colors have become brighter, and there is a quality of silence in the air. The silence seems so much more real than the words and the movement."

"Everything feels like it has a sameness to it: the chair and the people and the carpet and the sound of the birds outside. As I absorb all these things as well as my own reactions to them into myself through the Heart, they all become a part of me, and with the out-breath they also become infused with me."

"Feelings of liking and disliking other people become less defined here. When I first came to this class I had subtle likes and dislikes of the different people. Now everyone seems the same! (Laughter). I don't mean that there's no difference, but everyone seems intimate to me in the same way."

"Waves of feeling coming in and going out. It is all me. As I absorb myself back home into myself, in the same way I find that everything and everyone absorbs back home into myself, and is reborn out of myself."

"Even though there are many of us here, I have the feeling that we are like the fingers on my hand—many fingers, but only one hand. In this Heart meditation I feel that all these bodies are just like fingers, but there is only one of us. That one never moves, it was never born, and it never dies."

"There is a peace and vastness deep inside myself. As I rest in that, I find that it has the capacity to embrace everything, and in that way to change everything completely. There is only love, these waves are love, this dissolving is love dissolving into itself, this blessing is love bursting out of itself. I find that I have been looking for love, but actually I am love itself."

I was taught Tonglen in 1979 by a Tibetan lama who came to London, and whom I have never heard of since. It has been my constant companion through years of practicing bodywork, hypnotherapy, and other ways of working with people, and I believe that it has allowed me to be more effective in creating a space in which integrated healing can occur with any of the techniques I have learned.

PRACTICING THE HEART MEDITATION WITH ANOTHER

In his *Seven Points of Mind Training,* Atisha emphasizes that it is important not to practice the Heart meditation with another person until you have first become comfortable using it with yourself. First you must develop the ability to absorb your own thoughts, feelings, and physical sensations back into emptiness and to allow emptiness to radiate back into form. In our training, people generally find that they are ready to extend the practice after trying it on themselves a few times.

Step 1: Absorb and Bless for Yourself.
Repeat the process outlined earlier for practicing the Heart meditation with yourself, but move through the steps more quickly.

Step 2: Face Your Friend.
When practicing this meditation with a friend, sit opposite each other comfortably. Feel the rhythm of the waves of thought and feeling dissolving back into formlessness and bursting forth out of formlessness through the window of the Heart, then let your eyes be open and sit with a gentle gaze across from your friend. You can sit in chairs or cross-legged on the floor. Let your eyes gently rest on one of her eyes in soft focus, without staring. Soft focus means that your gaze is distributed over your entire field of vision and not fixated on one point.

Step 3. Absorb and Bless Your Friend Also.

Once you have established the rhythm for yourself, you can begin to have the feeling of absorbing the thoughts, feelings, and physical sensations of your friend through the window of the Heart into emptiness on the in-breath, breathing out blessings on the out-breath. It is essentially the same process you have already established except that you are now extending your circle of absorbing and blessing beyond what you have labeled as "me." On the in-breath you absorb unconditionally. On the out-breath you breathe out blessings.

Step 4: (Optional). Invite Your Friend to Speak.

Continue to absorb everything on the in-breath, unconditionally, and to bless on the out-breath. You can continue this for as long as feels comfortable to both of you; this might be for twenty minutes, or for as much as an hour. You can also invite your friend to speak out loud about whatever you want to address through this work, as you continue to absorb everything that you hear. As the Heart meditation becomes more natural and familiar (which happens very quickly for most people), you will find that you can also interact verbally with your friend, and acknowledge that you are hearing her, that you are present and open. To add this element of honoring what she is saying verbally is called "reflective listening," but be careful not to give advice, criticism or analysis. The spirit of the Heart meditation is to offer an atmosphere of spaciousness, acceptance and presence.

You can continue to absorb and bless, to dissolve and radiate, in this way together as long as feels comfortable. After you've finished sitting together, you can ask your friend to describe her experience.

Breathing out blessings here means having the feeling of creating or giving birth to the appearance of the other person out of emptiness exactly as they already are. Do not try to change them or improve them in any way. For example, if you experience that your friend is tense, absorb the tension through the window of the heart into emptiness, and with the out-breath, bless them with the sense that "it's okay to be tense. It's okay to be exactly as you are." Or, as Sogyal Rimpoche puts it, "Here I find it inspiring to imagine, as Shantideva suggests, that your *bodhicitta* has transformed your heart, or your whole body and being itself, into a dazzling, wish-fulfilling jewel, a jewel that can grant the desires and wishes of anyone, and provide exactly what he or she longs for and needs. True compassion is the wish-fulfilling jewel because it has the inherent power to give precisely to each being whatever that being most needs, and so alleviate his or her suffering, and bring about his or her true fulfillment."[7]

When practicing the Heart meditation, it is important to absorb form *through* the window of the Heart into formlessness and not to absorb it into your body. This is an important distinction that will become immediately obvious once you experiment. If you absorb another's pain into your chest, for example, rather than through the window of the Heart into formlessness, you may end up drawing energy into your own body that could become draining or uncomfortable. If you feel unsure of your capacity to absorb through the window of the Heart into formlessness, work through the self-inquiry session in the next chapter a few times and then try this one again.

As you continue to practice the Heart meditation, it will become more natural to you, and you won't have to think about it. You will easily recognize the gentle tickle or warmth in the chest and belly. You can even use it with a group of people in a room or on a train or bus, and you may notice that you feel more in tune and more at peace. Other people may notice a shift as well, though they may not know exactly what is the cause of the feeling!

As the Heart meditation becomes second nature, we recommend that you practice it throughout the sessions described in this book. At the beginning of a session, you can practice it during the pre-induction interview and the induction itself, and you can continue to absorb and bless through every step. Students in our training suggest that 90 percent of the effectiveness of these processes is the result of the underlying space that the Heart meditation creates. By absorbing and blessing in this way, you radiate an atmosphere of inspired certainty in which awakening can easily occur.

SELF-PROTECTION

Sometimes people have a resistance to this practice because they have been taught some kind of "psychic self-protection." Many psychic schools teach you how to surround yourself in white light or how to ground cords deep into the earth in order to ward off negative energy from other people. Although that may sometimes be necessary, it is certainly a different way of going about things than we are suggesting in this book. The Tibetan Dzogchen master Namkhai Norbu has said of the need for psychic self-protection, "We have an instinct for self-protection, trying to defend ourselves from imagined harm. But our attempt at self-protection ultimately causes us more suffering because it binds us into the narrow dualistic vision of self and other."[8] The exercises in this book are designed to take awareness beyond the domain in which there is anyone to protect or anyone to be protected from, in which all form dissolves back into formlessness.

CHAPTER 5

WHO AM I?

*I gain nothing from seeing Who I am, yet I gain everything.
This seeing is not to be practiced, yet it requires lifelong
vigilance and dedication. It's no task at all, yet the hardest
of tasks. There's nothing to do, yet all to do. It's the very
end, yet the beginning of the Way.*[1]

DOUGLAS HARDING

For as long as we can remember, we have been obsessed with things that are born and die, that have a beginning and an end. We've been obsessed with relationships with "other people" that arise in time and demand solutions in an apparent future. We've been obsessed with "getting ahead," achieving material success, fulfilling our potential. We've been obsessed with thoughts, beliefs and emotions. Every one of our obsessions has a duration in time: they begin, they last for a while, and then they die. Every experience we have ever had is characterized by change. In fact, change is the only unchanging constant that all experiences share in common. Yet throughout all these experiences that arise and fall, we have overlooked the experiencer. Who is it that experiences thoughts and emotions coming and going? Who is it that experiences situations constantly changing?

Even in this moment right now, as you hold this book in your hands, who is it that registers the meaning of these words? It is possible to respond with an intellectual or verbal answer that has been stored in memory, to say, "Well, I am the one in all things," or "I am me," or even "I am the mind." But this answer is only words and concepts. The question still remains: Who is it that is aware of these words and concepts, which are also events in time? Who is it that understands the meaning of the words? Whatever arises with name or form and limitation as an answer to this question immediately becomes another object of experience itself. The question still remains: Who is the experiencer? What is the medium in which thought is moving?

To know the answer to this question, beyond conceptual understanding, beyond thought, beyond what has been read in books or heard on tapes can be called Self-realization. It is not an experience, and it does not belong to the eternal kaleidoscope of changing phenomena. Rather than being another wave in the ocean, it is the ocean itself. Rather than being yet another image flickering on the movie screen, it is the white canvas on which all movies are projected. It is not an object to grasp, not something that can be held or remembered or forgotten. You can only *be* this, for this is who you are.

In Chapter Two we investigated this realization from a theoretical perspective. Here we will explore ways to come to an experiential realization. The direct recognition of this ground of being has been the preoccupation of almost every mystical school. There have been innumerable ways, practices, and paths tried in different traditions to facilitate this homecoming of attention to itself. In the Dzogchen teachings of Tibet, after preparatory practices the teacher gives "pointing out instructions" to the student. In India, the *darshan*, or look of the teacher, becomes a mirror in which to recognize one's original nature. In *bhakti* traditions, the intense focus on and devotion to an icon of the divine becomes a window to the eternal. Every tradition has prescribed some kind of spiritual practice, whether meditation or contemplation or chanting or prayer, to bring the mind home. And many people have stumbled on this natural state of consciousness while hiking in nature, making love, or facing a moment of great crisis, where the habitual tendencies of thought are transcended.

Here we will use the process of self-inquiry, or *atma vichara*. Ramana Maharshi, who lived in India from 1879 until 1950, prescribed this as the most effective way in this modern age to break through the knot of illusion. "The easy way, the direct way, the shortest cut to salvation is the inquiry method. By such inquiry, you will drive the thought force deeper 'til it reaches its source and merges therein."[2] Many regard him as the pioneer of a new era in the possibility of awakening, and he left behind a number of enlightened spokespersons for truth. As well as my teacher, H.W. L. Poonjaji in Lucknow, Lakshmana Swami is still alive in Tiruvannamalai, in South India, where Ramana himself lived, and Anamalai Swami, Ramana's attendant for many years, died there in 1996. The prolific British author Paul Brunton wrote journals and books that are infused with the teachings of Ramana, with whom he spent time on a number of occasions. And until recently, the American Robert Adams conducted Satsang (gatherings in truth) in Los Angeles and Arizona. Ramana has also been a profound influence on Joe Miller, Carl Jung, Da Free John (Adi Da), and many others.

The essence of Ramana's teachings can be condensed into one very simple question, "Who am I?" He maintained that the recognition of who you really are requires no specific preparation or practice, but simply the willingness to inquire into your own nature. "You have to ask yourself the question, 'Who am I?' This investigation will lead in the end to the discovery of something within you which is behind the mind. Solve that great problem and you will solve all other problems."[3]

The basic session that we will use here embodies the same approach that Ramana Maharshi taught at Mount Arunachala fifty years ago. We will facilitate this inquiry using a relaxed state of body and mind, as we discussed in Chapter Three, so the question can penetrate deeper. Even people who have used self-inquiry for years find that, when it is undertaken in an induced state of relaxation, many of the usual obstacles are removed and the wordless answer is revealed.

Here is the session outline to facilitate self-inquiry as a partner exercise. Work with a friend, or with a client if you are a therapist. You will need at least half an hour to conduct this effectively, and you can repeat it as often as you wish. At every stage proceed slowly and patiently, and remain constantly with the Heart Meditation described in the previous chapter. It is this relaxed pace, as much as the content of your words, that will support your friend in her process. You can use your own words, or use the instructions printed in italics.

Session Outline:
Self Inquiry

Step 1: The Pre-Induction Talk.

Step 2: Induction.

Step 3: Establish finger signals (optional).

Step 4: Noticing Thought.

Step 5: Noticing Emotions.

Step 6: Noticing Physical Sensations.

Step 7: Who Am I?

Step 8: The "I" Thought.

Step 9: Deepening the Realization.

Step 10: Sinking Deeper.

Step 11: Suggestions.

Step 12: Counting Back.

SESSION OUTLINE: SELF INQUIRY

Step 1: The Pre-Induction Talk.
Bring your attention to your friend's present life situations: whatever it is that separates her from the perfection of this present moment. Just speaking about anything that is "up" right now, like emotions, certain thoughts, or physical sensations, will help them to be liberated. In the pre-induction talk, you will be finding out how your friend has become identified with certain habitual ways of thinking, feeling and behaving.

Step 2: Induction.
Induce a state of deep relaxation using the processes described in Chapter Three, or using music or a taped induction. You can also move into the rest of this session without formally inducing a relaxed state; just start asking the questions in Step 3, with your friend sitting with eyes open or closed.

Step 3: Establish Finger Signals (optional).
If your friend is relaxing very deeply, you can ask her to respond to you using finger signals rather than talking:

And just because
You are more deeply relaxed now,
So it is easy for you to
Allow a gentle movement,
With one of the fingers of your right (or left) *hand*
As a way of saying "yes."
You can allow that "yes" signal now.

Wait for the signal.

That's good.
And you can also allow
A gentle signal with another finger of the same hand,
A signal which means "no."
You can allow the "no" signal now.

Wait for the signal.

Now go ahead and ask a few random yes/no questions to get your friend used to communicating with the finger signals. Then you can move on to the next step by asking,

Is it okay to move deeper now?

Step 4: Noticing Thought.

Once your friend is feeling relaxed and comfortable, you can begin to guide attention back to a recognition of the way that thoughts and feelings arise spontaneously in awareness. Begin with the arising of thoughts. Ask your friend,

> *And even now, resting here*
> *Is there any awareness of thoughts*
> *Arising and then falling back again in consciousness?*

Wait for the signal.

> *Do thoughts require any effort or decision before they arise?*

Wait for the signal.

> *Do they just arise spontaneously on their own?*

Wait for the signal.

> *Would it be true to say that*
> *Thought is self-arising and self-creating?*

Wait for the signal.

> *Seeing this about thought, is it okay now to*
> *Let go of control of thoughts, and to*
> *Allow them to arise and fall on their own?*

Wait for the signal.

> *Good. You can relax even more deeply into*
> *Being that which is aware of thoughts arising and falling.*

The above instructions assume that thoughts are arising, that they arise spontaneously, and that it is therefore okay to let go of the need to try to control them. If you get different signals than the ones we have assumed here, you can use your own natural intuition to clarify and reword the questions until your friend can see the self-arising nature of thought in her own way.

Step 5: Noticing Emotions.

Now you can move a little deeper, and come to the same disidentification with feelings and emotions.

> *I'm going to ask you now to find out if*
> *There is awareness of emotional atmospheres*
> *And feelings shifting and changing?*

Wait for the signal.

> *And you can find out now,*
> *Do feelings and emotional atmospheres*
> *Require any effort on your part to shift and change?*

Wait for the signal.

Do they arise spontaneously on their own?
Wait for the signal.
  Would it be true to say that
  Feelings and emotional atmospheres are
  Self-arising and self-creating?
Wait for the signal.
  Seeing this about feelings and emotions,
  Is it okay now to
  Let go of control of feelings and to
  Allow them to arise and fall on their own?
Wait for the signal.
  Good. You can relax now even more deeply into
  Being that which is
  Aware of thoughts and emotions arising and falling.

Step 6: Noticing Physical Sensations.
You can move again a little deeper, to the experience of the physical body.
  Is there awareness now of
  Sensations in the physical body?
Continue in the same way, using finger signals, to establish that sensations require no effort to arise, they come and go on their own, and that it is therefore okay to let go of control of physical sensations and to rest as being that which is aware of thoughts, feelings and sensations.

Step 7: Who Am I?
Now you can begin to introduce your friend to the question that was at the center of Ramana Maharshi's teaching, "Who am I?"
  And now, just because
  The body is feeling
  Softer, more relaxed,
  You can begin to
  Allow this question to
  Penetrate deeper and deeper into consciousness.
  "Who.....am.....I?"
Continue to guide your friend deeper into the question, allowing plenty of silence each time you direct her back to the inquiry. You can ask her to communicate with you through finger signals or in words, saying,

If an answer arises,
Allow yourself to
Speak that answer
Out loud.

Your friend may immediately respond with an answer in words or concepts. For example she might say, "I am me," or "I am the all that is," or "I am endless space without beginning or end, not separate from God, as defined in the Advaita teachings of Swami Banananandaraj." You may get the feeling that this answer has come from concepts, that it is actually a thought generated out of something that has been read or heard. You can then simply ask your friend to notice,

Can you see that
This answer is also a thought,
Which spontaneously arises
In response to the question,
Perpetuates itself, and
Falls back?

As your friend sees this, you can ask,

Who is aware of this thought
Arising and falling?
Keep looking deeper,
Keep falling deeper into being
The one who is able to
Experience all these changes.

We are not using the question "Who am I?" to come up with a correct answer in words, and we need to be aware not to create any pressure to find the "right answer." Use your voice and your language to be supportive, to continue guiding consciousness back into a recognition of itself, back to that place of Clear Seeing that is wordless, descriptionless. Keep encouraging your friend to move back, look deeper, and express out loud in words whatever arises. If what is said is conceptually correct, like "I am limitless space," but seems to be coming from concepts, keep guiding the inquiry back,

Who is aware of
These words arising?
Who is aware of
these concepts?

You can also ask,

If there is anything
With name
Or form
Arising in consciousness,
Who is aware of
That name and form?

Step 8: The "I" Thought.
As you continue this inquiry, your friend will almost certainly keep coming back to the answer "me" or "I am." This is what Ramana calls the "I thought." As attention shifts from other thoughts and emotions to this essential concept of "I," you can ask your friend to directly investigate the nature of this "I" itself.

Turn the attention now to this "I."
Look now,
In this very moment,
And see if there is any thing
To which the word "I" is referring.

This is the essence of Ramana's self-inquiry. "What is the ego?" he asks. "Inquire. The body is insentient and cannot say 'I.' The Self is pure consciousness and non-dual. It cannot say 'I.' No one says 'I' in sleep. What is the ego then? It is something intermediate between the inert body and the Self. It has no *locus standi*. If sought for, it vanishes like a ghost. When one looks for it, it is found to not exist."[4] Through the focusing of attention back to this "I thought" and the direct inquiry into its essential nature, it is found to be only a concept, with no experiential component. In the dissolution of belief in "I," consciousness itself, or "the Self," is revealed.

We find precisely the same thing said by Padmasambhava, twelve hundred years earlier:

When you look and observe, seeking the one who is looking and
  observing,
Since you search for this observer and do not find him,
At that time your view is exhausted and overthrown.
Thus, even though it is the end of your view, this is the
  beginning with respect to yourself.
The view and the one who is viewing are not found to exist
  anywhere.[5]

How will you know whether your friend has relaxed fully into recognition of the natural state of consciousness, or is simply repeating spiritual words and concepts that have been heard from elsewhere? There is no objective way to know another's state of consciousness. Like a headache or any other internal experience, it cannot be measured from the outside but can only be known subjectively. The best way to gauge whether your friend is sinking deeper into her original nature is to notice whether you are sinking deeper into silence yourself. There is a natural synchronicity here, a natural dissolution of boundaries; as consciousness comes into direct contact with its own nature, you will feel it in yourself, and you will start to feel as though you and your friend are merging into one. If your friend says, "I am the Oneness underneath all things!" but you experience rigidity in your mind, it may be a clue to go deeper into the inquiry. On the other hand if you ask, "Who are you now?" and there is just a silent spaciousness, this is a good indication that your friend is experiencing the same thing. Answers that come from Clear Seeing are unmistakable, for they carry the vibrancy, spaciousness, and aliveness of their Source.

Step 9: Deepening the Realization.
Leaving plenty of time for this absorption to deepen, you can begin to ask questions that stabilize the realization of the natural state and bring an experiential dimension to the qualities of wakefulness we discussed in Chapter Two.
You can ask,
> Look now all the way to the left
> As far as you can imagine yourself looking
> Into this which you are,
> And find out if there is
> Any limit to this.

Then ask the same question, directing her attention as far as she can to the right. Ask her to look in the same way all the way in front and all the way behind, all the way up and all the way down, all the time asking her,
> Find out
> If there's any limitation
> To this which you are.

Similarly, you can ask,
> Does this experiencer itself
> Have any content?

Is there any name or form
To this experiencer itself?

Remember to allow plenty of time for these questions to permeate consciousness one at a time. This is a realm where time stands still, and any pressure or hurry may reactivate the habitual tendencies of thought.

You can ask,

Was this ever born?

Could this ever die?

From this Clear Seeing,
Is there any such thing existing
In this moment
Called "mind"?

Wait for a response. If a conceptual answer comes, guide the inquiry deeper by finding out who is aware of the concept arising and falling. You will know by this time, within yourself, if the answer is coming from Clear Seeing without conceptual thought or from memory.

Has there ever been
Any such thing existing
Called "mind"?
Is there any such thing
That exists
Called "ego"?

You can look with this Clear Seeing into any dimension of consciousness, to distinguish between the real and the unreal, between that which exists and that which is only an idea.

Is there any such thing
Which exists in this moment
Called "past"?

Is there any such thing
Which exists in this moment
Called "future"?

Can you find anything

In this moment
Called "time"?

These questions will deepen the realization of Truth. If the answer to any of these questions is yes—if, for example, she says, "Yes, I find something called 'mind'"—ask her to look deeply into that which is found and see if it can be directly experienced or if it is only a concept. Clear Seeing simply means to distinguish between that which is real and that which is unreal. You can also ask questions from the talk which you had in Step One. If, for example, she feels distracted by being in debt, you can ask, "From here, what is 'debt'?" She may have been feeling unworthy, or any other state, and you can ask, "From here, what is 'unworthiness'?"

Step 10: Sinking Deeper.
Progressively throughout the session you can ask your friend,
Find out now if
It is okay to
Go deeper now?
Find out if
It is safe to
Sink deeper into this wakefulness?
Of course, the idea of sinking deeper into infinity does not make sense intellectually. Yet one can continue to experience greater and greater depths of infinity even after the infinite, limitless Self has been realized.

Step 11: Suggestions.
As you bring the session to a conclusion, you may want to allow your friend to rest more deeply in the silence of the natural state and to make certain suggestions that can help cut through doubts and concepts that may interfere with the simplicity of realization. Whenever possible, use your friend's own words and insights when giving suggestions. We have already talked in Chapter Three about the use of suggestion at the end of each session, but here are some specific suggestions useful to this particular session:

You are this formlessness.

You are Silence itself.

You are the source
Of all life.

You are not separate.

You are That
Which moves
In all things.

You are not born.
You cannot die.

In this very moment
You are the One.

You are presence itself.

Whatever sounds arise,
You are the silence
Hearing them.

Whatever feelings arise,
You are that
Which is feeling.

Whatever limits are felt,
You are the limitlessness
In which limits arise.

Step 12: Counting Back.
Now you can get ready to count your friend back from five to one, as we discussed in Chapter Three. Before you do so, you can suggest that this inquiry and realization will continue throughout the day, even in the midst of ordinary waking activity.

In a few moments
I'm going to count back

From five to one.
When I've finished counting,
The body will be wide awake,
Refreshed and alert,
And this inquiry can continue and deepen.
With every thought that arises,
You can inquire
Who is the one
Experiencing this thought.
With every situation
That presents itself,
You can find out
Who it is
That experiences this situation.
It may be interesting
And surprising to
Find out
In what unexpected ways this
Recognition of awareness itself
Can continue and deepen in the days
And weeks to come.

Now count back, as described on page 58. Allow your friend plenty of time to reorient herself to normal activity so the recognition of the ground of Being can be integrated and stabilized in ordinary life.

FEAR AND RESISTANCE

Everyone wants to return home, to know what love is, to be at peace and free of pressure and limitation. Every testimony to the awakened condition calls back words of encouragement, from the mountain peak down into the valley. "This is the easiest thing that can be imagined. There is nothing to lose but the fictitious idea of the person you took yourself to be." Yet despite the suffering that the illusion of separation creates, despite the inspiration and encouragement of every great mystic, there is generally considerable fear and resistance to falling into wakefulness. We are inspired to walk on a path, to follow a teacher, to set up an elusive goal of enlightenment next year or next life, but there is immense resistance to seeing things clearly right now. Why should this be? Why should relaxing into a natural state, in which problems no longer exist, be met with an involuntary contraction within consciousness? It's rather like someone with an excruciating headache being terrified of losing their pain!

The implication of the awakened view is a completely different matter if we see it from the standpoint of the fictitious person we take ourselves to be, rather than from the perspective of Clear Seeing. If we take ourselves to be a limited person who exists in time and space, is born and will die, has certain qualities, likes and dislikes, opinions, material possessions, accomplishments, and friends, the realization of our original nature implies a kind of death. The word *nirvana*, after all, means the "snuffing out" of a candle.

On the other hand, in the clear recognition of that which is real, the person we take ourselves to be is nothing but a bundle of thoughts, emotions, and opinions, a set of memories of a past that no longer exists. The entire edifice is built on a single postulate: the idea of a separate "I." The death of an idea is certainly not frightening. In fact, everyone I have ever met would love to still the onslaught of thoughts and ideas. We are constantly changing our beliefs and opinions. Once we distinguish between the real and the unreal, we see that all that could die is a thought in consciousness, which has less power or reality than a leaf blowing in the autumn wind.

This is the beauty and elegance of self-inquiry. Spirituality has been dominated for millennia by the masculine aspect of the psyche: get rid of the ego; destroy the mind; go to battle with the forces of *samsara*; subjugate and transcend emotions, sexuality, nature, and the body. This approach seems merely to increase resistance and fear. Here we are simply offered an invitation to ask, "What is the nature of this person I take myself to be? What is this 'I'?" This inquiry ultimately reveals that the separate individual is nothing but a concept. There can be no fear in the death of a concept. This is the gift of inquiry as an instantaneous deliverer of freedom. Rather than trying to change or do anything, we are simply looking into the nature of things as they are to find out what is actual and unchanging.

In Clear Seeing, the very concept of enlightenment also disappears. There is only consciousness, which has always and eternally been absolutely awake. It is unenlightenable. This appearance of a person, which is no more than a collection of thoughts, memories, and beliefs, also cannot be enlightened; it is nothing but a figment of imagination.

If fear or resistance arises in this session, you can treat it like any other emotion or thought that arises, persists, and falls away. You can direct attention back to that which is experiencing the fear. Or, if it seems to be too strong, you can use the instructions that follow under the heading "Dealing With Obscuring Emotions."

FILTERS OF ATTACHMENT AND REPULSION

As you pursue self-inquiry, you may notice three basic tendencies of mind arising: attachment, or liking; aversion, or not liking; and indifference, or not caring either way. For example, responses to the question "Who am I?" may have not only a certain emotional flavor, but also an energy of attachment. If your friend says, "Well, I am the One, and I know this already," or "This is fantastic, I am bathed in great joy," you can say,

> Good, and I wonder if you can
> Experience now
> The feeling of holding on to
> This concept (or this emotion).

As she becomes aware of the feeling of holding on to a pleasant experience, you can add,

> Look deeper now, and
> Find out who is aware
> Of this holding
> Within consciousness.

Or your friend may have an aversion to the process of inquiry, saying, "Well, I don't like doing this, and I feel really scared." Rather than dealing with the content, you can ask,

> Can you
> Feel now
> This revulsion
> Within consciousness,
> Can you
> Feel this pushing away?
> Look now and find out
> Who is aware of this disliking;
> Who is aware of this revulsion?

You may also notice a posture of indifference, almost like an internal shrug of the shoulders. In the same way, once your friend becomes aware of this "posture" within consciousness, you can guide attention back to the one who notices this attitude. The tendencies toward attraction, repulsion, and indifference are the basic building blocks of the mind. If there is awareness of this tendency to hold, push away, or feign indifference, consciousness is looking into itself in a much deeper way than it could by looking at the content itself.

As your friend sinks deeper into recognition of her original nature, she will become more and more speechless, and you will need to ask or say less and less. Absorption in this silence and expansiveness is the fulfillment of the Heart's true longing.

DEALING WITH OBSCURING EMOTIONS

Instead of falling back into a recognition of the natural state, your friend may get caught up in obsessive thoughts or emotions. Here we will explore a way to return obscurations to their source. (Other ways will be developed in later chapters.)

The approach we take has its roots in the Tibetan Buddhist Dzogchen practice of "liberating thoughts and emotions back into the primordial state." Patrul Rimpoche, who lived only a hundred years ago, offered this advice:

Don't follow after the object of hatred; look at the angry mind.
Anger liberated by itself as it arises is the clear void.
The clear void is none other than mirror-like wisdom.[6]

If attention is paid to subjective internal experience, rather than to the "story" created by the thoughts, then full immersion in the apparent obscuration will become a doorway back into the natural state. Almost without exception, thoughts, emotions, and physical sensations act to obscure Clear Seeing *only if they are resisted.* In other words, if your friend is trying to stop thought, that is the surest way to perpetuate thought as an obscuration.

Close your eyes right now and try not to think about monkeys, especially monkeys wearing pink pajamas, holding umbrellas over their heads, and riding unicycles on a tightrope. What happens? Pretty soon your mind is inundated with a zoo of primate acrobats. The more you try not to think about something, the more it dominates consciousness. The more you don't want to feel an emotion, the more stubbornly it persists. Whatever is resisted in consciousness, whether it be physical sensation, pain, emotion, or thought, tends to perpetuate itself. In Chapter Twelve, we will find out why consciousness operates like this. Whenever your friend gets caught up in an emotion or a persistent thought, bring attention back to the feeling in the body. From here, consciousness can be directly experienced. You can use these instructions at any point in the session outline above.

> Take a moment now
> To find out where this
> Emotion (or thought)
> Is experienced in the body.
> Look and see if there is a
> Contraction somewhere
> In the body.

Ask your friend now to lay her hand on the place in the body that seems to be the center of the feeling. If she says that there seems to be more than one place, ask her to find the strongest place, the "epicenter." Now you will guide her in letting go of the story attached to this feeling and giving herself completely to the energy or frequency itself.

> That's right.
> And now that
> You have a feeling for this place in the body —
> And now that you can
> Feel this sensation
> Directly —
> So it is easy for you to
> Let go now
> Of the (specific thought, memory, belief, fantasy),
> And drop even deeper into
> The atmosphere of this feeling.

The best way to remove the resistance to feeling something is to consciously attempt to make it stronger. Ironically, it is this very willingness to feel that brings us liberation from what we most resist. Says Ghalib, "Dive deep enough into sorrow, and tears turn to relief. Like this we learn how water evaporates into thin air."[7]

You can ask your friend to make this feeling stronger in a number of ways. You may want to use just one of them, or you can use all of them, if you wish. Use your voice assertively and directively to support your friend in becoming willing to experience what has up to now been avoided.

> That's right now.
> You can allow yourself to
> Dive into this atmosphere
> Like diving into a whirlpool.

Or you can use another metaphor:

> *Let it break over you completely*
> *Like a tidal wave;*
> *Let it swallow you so that*
> *Nothing else remains.*

Continue asking your friend to intensify this frequency until it cannot become any stronger, always using your voice to give authority and strength to the suggestion. Here is another metaphor,

> *Turn the volume up now, like the volume on a stereo.*
> *Turn it up as far as it will go.*

Ask her to give herself so completely to the contraction that nothing else exists in the whole universe. As she dives into it, ask her to allow this sensation, this contraction, to expand infinitely in all directions. Let it pervade and take over every imagined corner of the universe. Encourage her to welcome it and exaggerate it until it cannot be exaggerated any more.

> *Let this become so strong,*
> *So overwhelming, that*
> *Nothing else remains,*
> *So there is only this frequency*
> *In the entire universe.*

She doesn't need to scream or cathart or shed tears, although if she does, just allow it to happen on its own. Like homeopathic medicine, it is the finer energetic levels of phenomena that bring liberation. When your friend is experiencing this frequency as much as she possibly can, have her use a pre-established signal to indicate that it cannot be exaggerated any more.

> *And when this feeling is at its maximum,*
> *When you feel that it cannot*
> *Become stronger,*
> *I am going to ask you to*
> *Make a gentle signal*
> *With one of the fingers*
> *Of your right* (or left) *hand*
> *Or to say the word "now."*

When you get the signal indicating that the contraction cannot become any stronger, and therefore that the resistance has been completely removed, simply say,

> *Let go now.*
> *That's right.*

You can allow yourself to fall back fully
Into relaxation
Into ease and
Find out now
Who is it
That is aware of this sensation?

You will be surprised to find how effortlessly this works. Almost always, you will discover that the obscuration is completely gone, and that there is a natural return to expansion and ease, to the natural state. If it is not completely gone, it means that there was still some resistance to feeling it, so just go through the steps in this section again. If something new or some deeper level has become apparent, repeat the steps with this new sensation.

Once the resistance is removed from anything that arises in consciousness, the self-perfected state of being is immediately revealed. It can only be obscured by that which is resisted. This observation alone makes it easier to rest in the Self, because we start to discover that it is the nature of life itself to be continuously moving and shifting. If you allow yourself to experience an emotion completely, within seconds it has shifted into another emotion. A physical sensation, when fully experienced without any idea that it shouldn't be like this, changes into another one. Thoughts are noticed to be continually shifting and changing. It is only by keeping experiences at bay that we allow them to persist in time.

THE SOURCE OF THOUGHT

As well as the question "Who am I?" there are many other ways that interactive exercises can be used to guide attention back to the natural state. The *Vigyana Bhairava Tantra,* for example, lists 108 methods that were reputedly taught by Shiva to Devi,[8] all of which can be used as the basis for an interactive session. Tibetan Buddhism is overflowing with tasty morsels to tempt attention back to its source. And the brilliant contemporary "scientist of headlessness," Douglas Harding, offers dozens of "experiments" to bring us back to Self-recognition.[9] Two methods in particular are worth mentioning here. Rather than having them spelled out as step-by-step processes, you can experiment with them yourself.

The first involves bringing attention to the movement of the breath. In the *Vigyana Bhairava Tantra,* it is described like this:

Radiant One, this experience may dawn between two breaths.
After breath comes in (down) and just before turning up (out) —
The beneficence.
As breath turns from down to up,
And again as breath curves from up to down —
Through both these turns — realize.[10]

You can use this exercise as part of the self-inquiry session presented in this chapter, or as a separate inquiry. After you have finished the induction, simply guide your friend to pay particular attention to the movement of the breath, to notice the way that energy contracts with the in-breath and expands with the out-breath. As you move more deeply with this, you will become aware of the point where breath is all the way in or all the way out. At that point there is no thought, nothing obscuring the Self. In deep relaxation that point can also become a doorway to the natural state.

The second session uses thought as an invitation home rather than seeing it as an obscuration. We generally regard thought as somehow distinct from the Self and believe that we must stop thought to realize the natural state. We do not investigate thought itself to find out what it is made of, where it comes from, or what it is pointing to. One Dzogchen Master describes the way thought can be seen through in this way: "...you can check back (thought) to find its origin. All things are created by your thought and mind—and if you look back to the source of your thought and mind, you find that it disappears. It dissolves and goes back to its nature. That is the limit; every individual thing is dependent on the mind."[11] "Look back to the origin of thought and inquire where the natural state is, material, visible or invisible. You have to check back. You cannot find where this object is or who is searching for it. When you try, you lose everything. Like the sky—that is the empty mind—you start to realize the empty mind."[12] "When you check back to the source of thoughts, you cannot find anything— you just come back to the nature of mind itself. It is not separate from object and subject, nor from names, nor can any thoughts seize its nature."[13]

Lao Tzu says essentially the same in the *Tao Te Ching*:
To find the source of all things,
Follow any manifestation back to its origin.
When you find the mother, you also know all her children.
Knowing the children, but remaining in touch with the mother,
You are free from the fear of death.[14]

Do this exercise

To facilitate this inquiry in a session, establish finger signals with your friend as we described above. Now ask your friend to begin to pay attention to the movement of thought. Whenever she notices a thought arising or a movement in consciousness, ask her to make the finger signal. Each time she makes this signal, ask her to find out where this thought came from, what it is made of, and where it returns to. When thoughts are observed in this way, they become slower, and the natural state is revealed. As you continue, your friend will come to realize that thought is not separate from the Self, but is a manifestation of it, and a wave within it.

THE BENEFITS OF THIS INQUIRY

As we discussed already, this inquiry has no specific benefits. It does not fit into the usual pigeonhole of psychotherapy or hypno-therapy. In fact people often ask, "What is the good of this way of working? What are the benefits of realizing who you are?"

I remember when I was living with my teacher, Poonjaji, in India, and my father came to visit me from England. A traditionally edu-cated journalist who tends to see things in the conventional wayĺ, he was trying to understand what on earth I was doing in India living with this guru and why I didn't just get on with "ordinary" life. In attempting to explain to him what had brought me there I said, "We've been obsessed with our thoughts and our feelings and our material possessions, and we've never asked the question, 'Who am I?'" Then I asked him, "In this very moment, who are you?" He looked back at me with a shocked expression, as though I had just pulled down my pants in his presence. "Well," he finally replied, "one simply does not ask oneself that sort of question!"

This is the attitude we have been taught from the cradle. Since the time of Aristotle, Western culture has been predominantly ex-centric, and "self-absorption" or "introspection" has generally been regarded as an undesirable state. It is considered well-adjusted to be "outgoing," but a handicap to be introverted. From this standpoint, it is certainly valid to question the value of recognizing the recognizer. Will Self-realization help us make more money or have a better sex life? Will we suddenly have the ability to correctly intuit the winning Lotto numbers or have psychic insight into the contents of Citicorp's mainframe computer? Will we win friends, influence people, and heal the wounds of childhood?

In answering these questions, we need to make a distinction between that which has intrinsic value and that which has learned value. For example, young children don't appear to have any interest in money. They only value it later in imitation of the behavior they see around them. Otherwise, to them it is just pieces of paper and metal. An interest in acquiring money is a learned value, not something intrinsic to consciousness. Similarly, living in a particular location, driving the right car, eating the right kinds of foods, dressing in the right way—these are all learned values, which shift with fashions and trends. We are conditioned and taught what to like and pursue. Consequently, most people lead lives that are not intrinsically fulfilling because they are obediently chasing after all the items they have been told will make them happy.

On the other hand, certain things in life *are* intrinsically fulfilling, like physical pleasure and love. I don't think you need to condition or educate people to enjoy sitting in the sun and feeling the warmth on their bodies. Nor do you need to teach them to enjoy loving and being loved.

In the same way, waking up from the dream of being a separate person, limited in time and space, seems to be intrinsically fulfilling. Those who have fallen into this secret say that to return to the recognition of our original nature brings a deep sense of peace and fulfillment. Indeed, mystics and sages throughout the centuries have considered it to be the culmination of human life, in comparison with which even the most valuable possessions and exalted accomplishments seem paltry and insignificant.

AFTER AWAKENING, AN ORDINARY LIFE

These days, people are finding that falling back into the recognition of who they really are is easy. It is happening to more and more people, and the same Truth beyond the mind is available through more and more traditions and more and more spokespersons. Many people discover that by sitting in Satsang with a teacher or with friends, or by sitting in meditation, they can taste the recognition that there are no boundaries, there is no separation, no otherness. However, most of these same people find that the stabilization of this recognition is extremely demanding.

We still live in a society that is based in separation. Our economic system is based in competition, greed, and an "I-Win-You-Lose" mentality, not in the recognition of Oneness. Our social system is based in hierarchy, in getting ahead of others. The way we have been conditioned to engage in intimate relationships is based in a feeling of lack, of unfulfilled needs. Our political system is based in fragmentation, pitting this country against that country. Our attitude towards the earth is based in separation. We are constantly being exhorted to amass and accrue our own private possessions. Western psychology is steeped in separation and time.

The rest of this book has to do with the stabilization of this realization and its permeation through our lives: in the way we have relationships, in the way we view personal history, in our involvement in the material world and the world of commerce and money, in our feeling of having a body, in our sense of purpose and service. Every assumption about reality and every unconscious mechanism demands to be re-evaluated in the light of what is found, or not found, when we look for this separate "I."

CHAPTER 6

THERE IS NO OTHER

Out beyond ideas of wrongdoing and rightdoing,
There is a field. I'll meet you there.
When the soul lies down in the grass,
The world is too full to talk about.
Ideas, language, even the phrase "each other"
Doesn't make any sense.[1]

JELALUDDIN RUMI

Over the past 19 years, in my own life and in my work with people, I have found that issues of intimate relationship cause us to fall into imbalance and obscure the natural state more than anything else. Particularly when there is some kind of romantic expectation, it is the longing for the other that binds us most strongly. Most of the people who seek therapeutic help do so with relationship issues as their initial presenting problem. Even when you are alone or on a retreat, isn't it the thought of the other that preoccupies you?

We are inundated with cultural expectations about relating. Jung's initially impartial distinction between the introvert and the extrovert has been interpreted culturally as a value judgment. A "well-adjusted" child is outgoing and extroverted, while a child who prefers to be alone or self-contained is more likely to be seen as a problem. From cars to soap to home computers, advertisers present us with images of a harmonious happy family life, while vacations, perfume, alcohol, and chocolates are promoted through the allure of the romantic couple, with glittering eyes and perfect white teeth, lost in each other's magic and the perfection and boundless fun of their life. These stereotypes, reinforced through TV, movies, popular songs, and romantic novels, put a tremendous unconscious pressure on us. We feel that the rest of the world is enjoying a fairy-story scenario, and there is something deeply wrong with us if we are not. As a result, we are always looking for the elusive formula that will create the perfect relationship. Most of the workshops and seminars offered in the name of "personal growth" are oriented to improving relationship, creating more harmony and love, or somehow eliminating the possibility of conflict and misunderstanding.

Yet what is the reality of our experience? Stripped of all expectation, all right and wrong, all guilt and romance, what is the nature of relations between human beings? Look at your own life and the lives of the people you know intimately. Look back through history, even as far back as the *Ramayana* in India or the early stories in the Old Testament, and what do you find? Even examine the lives of undomesticated animals, which have no conditioning about how things should be, and what do you see? Perhaps the ideal of perfect harmony, complete understanding and the elimination of conflict is in itself neurotic and causes us more suffering than the outward circumstances themselves. When we examine the way things actually are, we find that life presents us with a picture of both harmony and conflict, arrivals and departures, understanding and misunderstanding.

Rather than trying to fix things in any way, here we will look into the underlying cause of all suffering in relationship to "another," to the feeling of separation and isolation that arises from identifying with an individual personality in time and space. Wherever there is the idea of two, there must be separation. Krishnamurti puts it like this: "It is separation that brings conflict and ugliness. When there is not this separation, then living itself is the act of love. The deep inward simplicity of austerity makes for a life that has no duality."[2] Or, in the simple language of the Upanishads: "Fear comes when there is the idea of a second."[3] Whenever there is a relationship between two people with different points of view with different sets of conditioning and personal histories, there must inevitably be a degree of misunderstanding and hence conflict. I have met many who claimed to have found the perfect formula to make relationships easy and constantly comfortable. But they always came limping back from the battlefield again some time later. Those who seem to have found peace in relationship have learned to accept the inevitable spectrum of human experience as it already exists. "Opposition brings together, and from discord comes perfect harmony,"[4] says Heraclitus.

What does "relationship" mean? It implies the relating of two separate identities, two distinct points of view on the same situation. If you have already worked through the session in the previous chapter, it must be clear to you now that it is not your original nature, not the Self in its purity, that is in relationship with another. Within silence, peace, infinity, there can be no relationship, because there is no other. It is two temporary identities that enter into relationship. These identities differ in their conditioning, their patterns of thought and emotional responses, and their physiological and psychological habits of seeing the world. Of course, between different identities there must inevitably be places of convergence and difference. "We like the same movies, but we eat different food. We read the same books but have different friends." If there were complete alignment on everything, they would essentially be the same person.

When there is strong identification with the person you take yourself to be, with likes and dislikes and opinions, relating with another eventually brings conflict and suffering because there is a sense of separation. When there is the perception that this relationship is not between "me" and "you," but between arbitrary identities or points of view that are both rooted in the Self, which is what we both are, there is release from suffering. "Behold the One in all things," says Kabir, "It is [the idea of] the second which leads you astray."[5] This is the approach we take here—learning to transcend the sense of "I" and "you," "my point of view" and "your point of view," "my needs" and "your needs." As rigidly held positions dissolve, relationships may become easier and more harmonious, or they may come to a natural and agreeable completion.

We are concerned in this chapter not with trying to change the outward appearance of things, but with the way those things are perceived and the degree of unnecessary suffering involved. As we shift from an isolated, personal point of view to the Clear Seeing of things from the eternal Self, personal "love" blossoms into love without any conditions, which does not discriminate according to the object placed before it.

What we refer to as "falling in love" in this culture usually involves becoming fixated on another person as the source of beauty, wholeness and fulfillment in our lives. When two people do this to each other simultaneously, one of life's greatest joy rides results, which more often than not ends in a crash landing. This is what the Greeks call *eros*. We also speak of "loving" others in a slightly different way, when we have become so deeply familiar with them and in some way attached to them that their absence from our lives would cause us suffering. This the Greeks call *familias*: the love of the familiar, of the family. Of course, these two states are an inevitable part of human experience.

There is another kind of love, however, which is actually not a function of attachment or obsession at all. The Greeks call it *agape*. This is the exquisite recognition of oneness, the realization that the Self is seeing itself and there is no other. It is this love that the German poet Novalis writes of when he says, "We are alone with everything we love."[6] Rumi tells a story of a man who knocks at the door of the Beloved. When asked who is there, he replies, "It is me." He is rejected and sent away to suffer the torment of separation. Finally, after a year he returns and again knocks. This time, when asked who is there he replies, "It is you."

"Come in, my own Self," the Beloved replies. "You know this house is too big for two."

This is the ultimate experience of intimacy—thrilling to the heart and terrifying to the dualistic habits of mind. In this love the lover is consumed in the love for the Beloved, and disappears from the scene. As one Christian mystic puts it, "He who loves with not only a part of himself, but the whole, transforms himself into the thing beloved."[7]

Strangely, this love of the Self for itself seems often to be more readily achieved outside the confines of a personal relationship. We may easily fall into this mystical love with a teacher or a spiritual brother or sister, or even with someone we are meeting for the first time, although we wish we could find it more easily with our spouse or partner. For this love exists out of time. Like a frightened deer it runs from any faint whiff of attachment, need, or definition. In William Blake's words,

> *He who binds to himself a joy*
> *Doth the winged life destroy.*
> *He who kisses a joy as it flies*
> *Lives in Eternity's Sunrise.*[8]

It is this kind of love that Rumi sings of in all his love poems to "The Beloved." Although initially inspired by his teacher, Shams, after Shams' disappearance, Rumi comes to see Shams and his own Self in all things.

This kind of love looks *through* the appearance of the other, rather than at it. It drinks the wine within the cup and does not concern itself with the kind of cup the wine has been served in. It tastes the same wine everywhere. Recognizing That which is undefined and has no fixed identity, yet which is overwhelmingly present, love looks through the window of another human being and sees itself as the sky, looking back at itself. This can be called divine love, unconditional love. It is love as a means of perception, rather than a state of attachment. "Every creature denies it is the other," says Meister Eckhart, "but God is the denier of all denials."[9]

The session outline in this chapter is an invitation to step through the limitations of "I" and "you," into Rumi's field where the words "each other" no longer mean anything. You can use this session outline to dissolve the feeling of separation with anyone, be it a friend, a lover, or a colleague. In Chapter Eight we will look more deeply into the dynamics of romantic love as it is projected outward in desire and fantasy.

SESSION OUTLINE: DISSOLVING SEPARATION

Step 1: The Pre-Induction Talk.
Your friend will need to focus on a particular relationship in her life. Take all the time you need to speak together about this relationship—what has been left unsaid, when there is most separation, when there is most unity. You will probably find best results with a relationship that has some emotional charge, as then there is already an impetus in consciousness to bring it back to simplicity.

Step 2: Induce a State of Relaxation.
Use any of the methods described in Chapter Three or any other induction methods you prefer. It is helpful to finish this induction with the "flight of stairs" described on page 54.

Step 3: Evoking the Presence of the Other Person.
As your friend finishes imagining herself arriving at the bottom of the stairs, ask her to imagine stepping through a door, into a place where she can meet this person with whom there is a feeling of separation.

That's right
And just because you are feeling relaxed now,
Relaxed and easy,
So it is easy for you to feel yourself,
To see yourself
Standing in front of a door.
And in your own time
You can
Open the door.
That's right,
Step through the door
Into the perfect place for you to
Meet (name of the other person) *today.*
And you can take your own time now
To describe this place out loud.

Continue to gently elicit the description of this place. Keep your questions generic rather than specific; for example, if she says "I am in nature," you might ask, "Can you see any trees here?" rather than, "Look and see the giant oaks." Also, keep the description in the present tense, as it will support your friend in experiencing the situation, rather than thinking about it. For instance, if your friend says, "Well, the last time I met Frank it was in a cafe," you would respond by saying, "That's right, you are in this cafe with Frank now, and I wonder if you can even smell what it's like to be here in the cafe."

As she relaxes into being here, ask her to begin to experience the presence of the other person. Start with the feeling in the body.

And I wonder now,
Here in this (forest, cafe, high school gym, office, etc.),
If you can begin to get a feeling
Of (name of the other person) *here with you.*
Perhaps you can even feel
In your body
What it's like to be here with (name of the other person).

When she acknowledges she has this feeling, you can then ask for a description of the other person in the present tense. Ask her what this person's hair is like, what color the eyes are, what the person is wearing, etc. All these details will make the situation more real and evoke the feelings in the body more strongly.

As she imagines being with this other person, point her attention to the feelings.

Step 4: Speak to the Other Person.
Now you can ask her to speak to this other person, giving full expression to how she feels and to everything that has been held back in the past. Because she is in a relaxed state, she will probably be able to speak more honestly and openly than has previously been possible in the physical, face-to-face interactions with the person.

And you can take your time now,
Just being here with (name),
To tell (him/her)
Everything that you need to say.
Tell (name) *how you feel,*
Tell (him/her) *everything that you have avoided saying in the past.*

Here you can add specific details from the talk you had in Step One. This will give her more of a feeling of empathy and rapport and allow you to encourage her expression. For example, you might add, "Tell him how hurt you felt when he did not call you," or "Tell him how sorry you feel about all the things you said to him." Allow your friend at least a minute to speak to the appearance of the other inside herself.

Step 5: Listen to the Response.
After she has spoken to the other person in her imagination, ask her to become passive and listen to how the other person responds. Allow her time to listen to each response and to report to you what the other person says to her.

Step 6: Continue to Speak and Listen, Until There Is a Softening.
She can continue to speak and listen in the same way as the communication begins to unravel. This interchange between the person in relaxation and the imagined other may go backwards and forwards many times. Give her at least a minute of speaking and listening each time, and continue in this way until you notice a shift in the way the other responds. Initially it may follow the old predictable pattern, just as she described it to you in Step One. If there has been conflict or dysfunction, it

will be lived out during the session. However, because she is in a state of relaxation and there is the possibility now of saying and listening to everything freely, rigid boundaries will slowly begin to dissolve. She will generally be able to hear the other's point of view more clearly, the other's position will begin to relax, and the communication will begin to feel more heartful and receptive.

Step 7: Become the Other.
Once the other begins to change in this way, you can ask your friend to shift the focus of identification and *become* the other person. Do not attempt to do this too early, as it will only be comfortable once the surface feeling of conflict has been moved through.

> *In a moment,*
> *I'm going to ask you to*
> *Take a deep breath*
> *Into the belly*
> *And to become* (the other person's name).
> *That's right,*
> *Take a breath now*
> *And allow yourself to fully become* (name).
> *Take your time to feel what it's like to*
> *Feel this body from the inside*
> *To have these emotions*
> *And to have these thoughts and beliefs.*
> *Let yourself fully become* (name),
> *And as* (name) *now,*
> *I'm going to ask you to*
> *Look out through these eyes*
> *And to see* (your friend's name)
> *Here with you.*
> *What do you have to say to* (him / her) *now?*

Give her the time to fully feel in the body what it's like to be this other person, to experience what this person thinks and feels and senses. This is the most powerful moment of the session, in which the gestalt of separation dissolves. You will be amazed to find that your friend lying or sitting there beside you has a remarkable ability to fully embody and speak as this other person, and to fully see things from this other point of view, which had only recently seemed so alien.

Step 8: Move Between Each State of Identification.
Now that she has been able to fully embody each of the two points of view in the relationship, ask her to continue speaking first as herself and then as the other. Allow about a minute for each side of the exchange. As she continues to do this, the feeling of identification with a particular position will gradually diminish. This may lead to a liberation of misunderstanding and conflict as the two points of view come into alignment. A common ground and mutually agreeable solution may begin to reveal itself.

You can continue to move back and forth between these two points of view until she shows no preference for or prejudice against one over the other. This is a state of freedom, in which she fully sees herself to be both of these people and neither one at the same time.

Step 9: Move Beyond Both "I" and "You"; Become Vastness.
When you find that she has developed an ability to move fluidly between these two identities, discovering more common ground between them or perhaps simply clinging less to a particular position, ask her to let go of both.

In a moment
I am going to ask you once again
To take a deep breath into the belly.
And once again to allow yourself to
Slip out of being the person
You have taken yourself to be,
Like taking off a tight glove.
And you can now
Become the space
In which both of the people are existing.
That's right,
You can become the room in which they are meeting,
You can become the space itself.

If she has been able to move fluidly between these identities, she should find it easy now to discard them and see that they are both simply masks she has been trying on. She is neither the person she took herself to be nor the other; or rather she is both, since both are expressions of the mystery she really is. By moving beyond both identities, she can become identified with "identity-lessness" itself, with empty space, with the context rather than the content of the situation. You can support this dissolving of limitation.

> *That's right,*
> *You can allow yourself to be this spaciousness.*
> *And you can now*
> *Allow yourself to expand infinitely in all directions,*
> *And to become the spaciousness*
> *In which all meetings exist.*

Seeing these two forms in relationship, neither one exclusively "me" yet neither one separate from "me," is an invitation to unconditional love. Now your friend has been led up the winding staircase to the viewing gallery on top of the cathedral, and she has a "God's-eye view." "Things are all the same to God," says Meister Eckhart, "They are God himself."[10] She may remain silent and speechless at this point, or she may want to say how the situation looks from the perspective of infinity. Often she will experience deeper insight and deeper acceptance of the way the relationship unfolds, seeing that in fact it is not between two independent people but between two bundles of thoughts, emotions, and conditioning. There is an inevitability, and hence a perfection, to its unfolding, whatever the outward appearance may be. From the perspective of consciousness, the perspective of the aliveness and love *behind* these bundles, she looks through them and realizes that it is in fact the same love behind both pairs of eyes. This leads to a transcendence of the gestalt of "relationship" and an embracing of the *knowing* of oneness, the intimacy that transcends any possibility of separation.

Step 10: Elicit Speaking From Clear Seeing.

Although your friend may in fact be silent and still, it will be helpful after some time to ask her to articulate aloud what she sees when she experiences the relationship in this way. Ask her to look at each of the people in the relationship (the one she has been identified with and the other) as well as to experience the quality of the relationship itself. From this spaciousness, ask her to give voice to whatever she notices, and write it down as closely as possible. Generally, you will hear a clear and detached acceptance of the dynamic as it is, as well as an understanding of the direction in which the relationship is naturally unfolding. This might be towards resolution, dissolution, or just remaining the same. There is often a recognition of the inevitability of these two particular forms interacting in this particular way, as though a hidden destiny is now recognized and deeply accepted.

You can also ask your friend to speak aloud as this spaciousness itself to each of the two identities in the relationship and to share whatever insight arises about where there is stuckness or resistance. For example, as spaciousness, she might turn attention to the person she usually takes herself to be and say, "Cynthia, you really need to let go of this now. It is finished for you. You have been holding on to this situation out of familiarity and fear, but so much more is waiting for you if you can move on."

Step 11: Suggestions.

Now you can ask her to take a breath and with the in-breath to absorb these forms back into the source from which they arose.

That's right,
And as this spaciousness
You can allow a breath now into the body
And feel these two forms
Dissolving back into the formlessness
From which they arose
Like waves falling back
Into the ocean.

In Chapter Three, we talked about suggestion as a means to dispel doubt and to deepen the realizations that come in relaxation. You might want to use some of these now, either from those listed on page 58, or from your own innate wisdom, or from the following list of suggestions that have proved particularly useful with this session:

And it will be interesting to find out
In what new and unexpected ways
This relationship may be seen to
Shift and change in the next days and weeks,
Even as you rest without any activity
In this which you are.
You are this emptiness.

You are this Source beyond identity
From which all identities arise.
And it is easy for you,
Whenever you want to,
Whenever you need to,
To slip out of any state of identification
And to return to this which you are
In this relationship
Or any relationship.
You can easily come to this same
Silence and emptiness
Again and again.

You are Love.
You are Peace.
You are That
Which exists prior to all beings existing.
In the next days and weeks
It is easy for you to
Continue as this vastness,
As this unconditional love,
To see that you are both
The person you took yourself to be
As well as each seeming other,
And you are neither one at the same time.

Step 12: Counting Back.

Now you can count your friend back from five to one, as we described in Chapter Three on pages 58-60. You can suggest, as you start to count, that it is easy to remain as this identity-less source, even as the body returns to normal activity. Your friend will need to take some time to make the transition between the state of relaxation and ordinary life.

Session Outline :
Dissolving Separation

Step 1: Pre-Induction Talk.

Step 2: Induction.

Step 3: Evoking the Presence of the Other Person.

Step 4: Speak to the Other Person.

Step 5: Listen to the Response.

Step 6: Continue to Speak and Listen, till there is a Softening.

Step 7: Become the Other.

Step 8: Move Between Each State of Identification.

Step 9: Move Beyond "I" and "You," become Vastness.

Step 10: Elicit Speaking from Clear Seeing.

Step 11: Suggestions.

Step 12: Counting Back.

THE EFFECTS OF A SESSION

What are the external effects of doing a session in this way? Sometimes it happens that a conflict or misunderstanding disappears. Now that the person who has gone through the session has developed an ability to see the situation from both sides and to surrender attachment to her own fixated outlook, she is able to move more fluidly between different ways of seeing. This doesn't necessarily mean that she will become submissive or easily dominated by the other. It may simply mean that, by letting go of clinging to a rigid way of seeing things, the perspective opens up in which everyone's needs are included. Almost invariably, this shift is also reflected in the other person's attitude.

Or the relationship may continue as before. The ways that human beings relate are generally determined by forces that originate in the past, and stepping back from identification does not necessarily mean that we will arrive at a place of perfect harmony. But the suffering and feeling of bondage in the situation may dissolve, and there may even be a delight in the play of conflict and harmony, as the seventeenth century Christian mystic Peter Sterry celebrates in these words: "O peaceful and pleasant war! Where the supreme love stands on both sides, where, as in a mysterious love-sport, or a divine love-play, it fights with itself."[11]

Often it happens that the process of disidentifying causes the relationship to melt away and disappear because we have pulled the plug on the attachment that held it together. But the beauty of things is that we do not need to be concerned with the outcome. As the vision expands from personal identification to a universal view, we step aside and allow the forces of life itself to determine the outcome.

This process can be especially helpful with grief. By going down into deep relaxation, meeting and communicating with the person who died, and then becoming that person, the one who is grieving can come to a completion and integration that otherwise might have taken a long time. This is especially true with an untimely or sudden death. Many people have told me that after the session something happened in their lives to strengthen the feeling that the relationship with the deceased had been completed. For example, one woman whose husband had died suddenly had been unable to move on with her life and had remained absorbed in a world of memories and regrets. When he was alive, her husband had owned a beautiful crystal with many "phantom" crystals inside it, and she had treasured it constantly, as though it connected her with his soul. We did a session together in which she said goodbye to him, thanked him for all the beauty they had shared, and, most importantly, asked his forgiveness for ways she felt she had disappointed him. He blessed her and encouraged her to move on in life to new relationships and horizons. She slipped out of both identities into spaciousness and saw the relationship moving to completion. When she got home, she told me later, she found that the crystal had been left in the sunlight and had developed a crack in it. But she felt little reaction, seeing it now simply as a beautiful piece of rock.

While the external consequences of working in this way are not necessarily predictable, we are always moving towards freedom from entanglement and attachment, allowing more space for real love, free of old karmic bonds. "When the ten thousand things are viewed in their Oneness, we return to the Origin and remain where we have always been,"[12] says Zen Master Sosan.

The most extraordinary thing about this session is the effect it has on the other person, the one who was not physically present and may not even have known that the session was taking place. Frequently people report that, once they have disidentified from the relationship conflict in this way, the other person begins to behave quite differently, as though it was that other person who had received the session and come to a more open, less identified point of view. Sometimes people tell me, "Well, I didn't feel so differently towards him, but he certainly took a different attitude towards me. Did you call him or something?" Of course, I never do. What causes this to occur?

One explanation is that the external world is in fact a solidification or manifestation of our mind that reflects back to us whatever is now or was previously held in belief and limitation. Only through awareness of the contents of that mind, both in its conscious and unconscious aspects, can we come to understand the external world. In this sense we could say that we live as apparent individuals in parallel universes. "A fool sees not the same tree that the wise man sees," says William Blake.[13] Rather than seeing ourselves as isolated parts of a fragmented universe, we see the world from the inside out. Out of consciousness arises the idea of "I," from this "I" arise personal mental tendencies and beliefs, and from these manifest a body, which projects out of itself its environment and the universe in which it exists. This view, contrary to Western scientific thought, is common to Advaita Vedanta, Dzogchen, and other non-dual teachings. It is now also to be found in quantum physics.

Let's look at several case histories to see what we can expect to happen in a session of this kind.

CASE HISTORY: JANE

Jane was a sensitive, spiritual woman in her late thirties with two teenage children from a previous marriage and a young child with her present husband. Her husband was a successful businessman, active, energetic, outgoing, and not overtly interested in dealing with philosophical, metaphysical, or emotional issues. When confronted with feelings, he became angry and impatient, and she in turn felt unheard and unmet in her essential being. They argued often and he burst into uncontrollable rages whenever she tried to express emotions or analyze things. He felt trapped and dismissed her world as "emotional rubbish." She felt frustrated that the more she tried to engage him in emotional sharing, the more distant he became. This pursuer-distancer pattern is a common one in relationships and can easily lead to divorce.

When Jane came for our session, she was frustrated and angry and felt that the marriage had come to an end. We talked for a while about the dynamics of the relationship, which she felt were entirely his responsibility. As she went into deep relaxation and down the flight of stairs, she imagined meeting him on the beach, which was already a concession since he was a surfer. The first part of the session acted out the familiar patterns of frustration, anger, and eventual cutting off that characterized their day-to-day interactions. She insisted on talking everything through, and he quickly became angry and verbally abusive.

Because she was so deeply relaxed, however, and her usual defenses were down, Jane found herself becoming more honest and vulnerable with this internal husband than she would ordinarily be. For example, she was able to say, "When you're not there for me, it really hurts me, and I'm not able to express the love I really have for you." She told him that she felt confused and at a loss about how to deal with the situation, an admission that had been masked in their day-to-day relationship by her apparent confidence in resolving things through talk and "emotional honesty."

As she loosened up and became more honest, she felt her internal husband become more attentive and present. Then she took a deep breath and allowed herself to become her husband. Suddenly this slight woman's posture changed, her muscles began to ripple, her voice deepened, and her chest puffed up. For the first time in her life she was able to see reality through her husband's eyes and through her husband's energetic structure. She could feel what it was like to be a man who had been conditioned to act tough and deny his vulnerability and softness. She was able to feel and be with his anger.

Because she was deeply relaxed, she was also able to remain awake to her real nature, like an actor playing a part without forgetting who she really was. As her husband, she was able to articulate how difficult it was for him to express emotions and how afraid he felt of emotional entanglement.

Moving back and forth between these two points of view, she could see that both had validity: her own need to talk and be understood, and her husband's integrity and his need to live life dynamically, without getting bogged down in endless cycles of mind and emotion. Neither one was absolutely right, and neither was wrong.

I asked her to take another deep breath, to step out of being both the person she had taken herself to be and the personality of her husband, and to become the space in which they both existed. As this space, she experienced that she had no limits, no boundaries, no past, no fixed point of view, and yet she was still fully conscious and present. Most important of all, there was now immense love and forgiveness for both of the characters in her movie. Empty of content and free of limitation, she was bursting with immanence, mystery, and bliss.

She could now recognize that both points of view were projections of mind. Neither one could contain who she really was, and yet both were children of the same Source, equally loved, protected, listened to, and respected. As she settled into a deeper sense of mystery, expansion, timelessness, and silence, both points of view dissolved back into their origin.

I brought her back from the session as this unidentified, timeless mystery. Although her body and mental faculties were wide awake, she had a strong sense of being the witness to all that occurred, both internally and externally. As she drove her car home, she told me later, she was not the person driving the car, but the consciousness aware of the person driving the car. When she arrived home, she was not the wife meeting the husband, but the awareness of both these forms meeting within herself.

Her relationship with her husband did not change in any overt way. Both maintained their divergent points of view, but they seemed to experience less charge around them. He was more willing to let her talk when she needed to, and she was more willing to let things go. They developed more independent lives, more of a sense of humor about their relationship, and a greater ability to co-exist without having to fit into each other's narrow point of view.

Jane told me later that this had been her deepest experience of what she called "the Self," and that its effect on her marriage was tangential to its deeper significance: a more timeless and impersonal sense of her real identity as Love, as Consciousness, as the Self itself.

CASE HISTORY: CLARK

Clark had been married for almost three years, but he was distant and apathetic in the relationship. As we talked together before the induction, he told me that before his marriage he had lived for almost a year with a woman named Julie. One day he had come home to the apartment they shared and found that with no prior warning she had moved out with all her possessions. She left no indication of any problem in the relationship, and he never heard from her again. "On the rebound," he had met and married his current wife as a way of saying to himself, and to the memory of his ex-girlfriend, that he could carry on nonetheless. But he had never fallen in love with his wife.

In the session he went down the flight of stairs and found Julie in the apartment they once shared. As he expressed his anger and resentment, her response was to distance and tease him. He became more angry, until this remark burst forth from within his chest: "Dammit, Julie, don't you know I loved you more than anyone I have ever loved, and you abandoned me." He began to cry. As the tears poured down his cheeks, he deeply felt the abandonment, pain, and loss he had hidden from himself. As he opened to his feelings, he also noticed that his "imaginary" ex-girlfriend became more compassionate.

When he became Julie, Clark could feel from the inside her deep-rooted sense of adventure. Still in her early twenties, she had felt an urge to explore the world, to meet new people and have new experiences. Living with Clark, she had begun to feel trapped, but had no idea how to escape. He was so attached to her that she saw no alternative but to move out abruptly, without any explanation. As Clark gave full expression to Julie's point of view, he began to recognize how he had imprisoned her in his world and tried to mold her into an extension of his own personality. He felt the core energetic pattern of this need to possess, which we will explore more deeply in Chapter Twelve.

Clark came to see that the situation was a manifestation of his own mind. As he stepped between these points of view, he saw that the way Julie had abruptly left him was an inevitable response to the way he had tried to keep her trapped like a domestic animal. Freed from identification with one perspective, he experienced a release from blame and a seeing of the "suchness" of the situation. He saw that it was not Julie he had been obsessed with, but his own need to possess the other. At last he was able to let her go, say good-bye, and experience the kind of completion and integration inside himself that he had not experienced in real life. He found that he could now see his wife clearly for the first time.

Most important, Clark came to know that the tenderness and honesty uncovered in the session was a revelation of his real nature. He saw that he was the compassion the situation enlivened, rather than a person who felt compassion.

That night Clark called to tell me that when he returned home from work he found a message on his answering machine from Julie, with whom he had not had any contact for more than three years. She had called at about 2:30, just a short time after he had "become" Julie in the session. "I don't know why I'm calling you," the message said. "I found your name in the phone book and felt I *had* to call. You've been constantly in my heart and mind ever since I left that day. I want you to know that I've always felt sorry about what I did, but it was the only way I could deal with the situation. I don't know what's happening in your life right now, but I'd love to get together and catch up on old times." Subsequently, he and his wife met Julie for dinner, he discovered that the charge was completely gone and they became friends. Although this case is unusual in its striking synchronicity, it is representative of what can happen once we see that the roles of "me" and "you," "him" and "her," are just masks that consciousness adopts to play this game of incarnation.

This session is a powerful way to liberate us from the prisons we create in the name of personal identity. Feel free to experiment with your friends. As you get the feeling for working in this way, you will need to rely less on the steps outlined in the book, and you will be able to allow the session to unfold on its own. And don't forget: listen to your inner wisdom about when it is or is not appropriate to work with someone. If you have any doubts, you are better off seeking the services of a licensed professional or contacting the Living Essence Foundation to find someone close by who has trained professionally in this work.

CHAPTER 7

THE PAST IS
NOT NOW

The past and thoughts bring suffering,
You don't need anything to be free.
The boulders of the past rest on your chest
And destroy your life and freedom.
Remove them by finding the origin of the "I" thought.[1]

H.W.L. POONJAJI

Since Sigmund Freud's work became well-known less than a century ago, it has become an accepted assumption in the West that our behavior and personality are shaped by the conditioning of our early years. The fact that much of this conditioning lies outside our conscious awareness has led to the belief in what is called the "subconscious mind" and the view that we may be driven by forces deep within the psyche that we do not fully understand. This view has become so deeply ingrained in our culture as a whole that even the outcome of legal trials can sometimes be altered if it is determined that the defendant was in some way a victim of his or her own past conditioning.

Other cultures have not always seen things this way. Prior to the mid-19th century even our own culture did not hold these same assumptions. In Chaucer's world, for example, the violent, depressed, or deviant tendencies of human beings were attributed to an imbalance of the humors, astrological influences, or even demonic possession. Before Freud, childhood trauma was rarely proposed as a reason for present behavior.

Similarly, in Asian cultures it is difficult for people to understand why anyone would seek Western-style psychotherapy, except perhaps for relaxation and stress reduction. Even among the more affluent and educated classes in India, the practice of psychotherapy is unusual simply because they do not collectively hold the assumptions that we are a product of our past conditioning. I have never heard any Indian, however Westernized, attribute his personality traits or present behavior to childhood trauma.

The same is true in Bali. Balinese culture is finely tuned to spiritual and psychic influences and looks to imbalances in the spirit world as the root of any outward imbalances. Fervently involved in their religion, the Balinese give virtually every activity a deeper mystical significance, and it is hard for them to understand what the work of a psychotherapist would involve. The closest equivalent in their culture is the *dukun*, who is a blend of magician and psychic healer. The *dukun* does some physical healing but more commonly works with the spirit world as it manifests in what we in the West would call mental illness. The *dukuns* I have spoken with in Bali place personal history far down the list of possible explanations of present behavior. More significant by far would be the regularity of offerings made to the gods, the state of physical and energetic balance in the body, and the possibility of possession by a visiting spirit. When I discussed our Western attitudes to conditioning with the *dukuns* I met, they all reiterated that the only important thing about the past is to see that it does not exist. Many cultures do not even have words for past or memory and use a language that does not decline in any tense but the present.

Similarly, the assumptions made in Buddhist cultures challenge our belief in the importance of past conditioning, but in a different way. In the West many people assume that the most significant aspects of our past are the wounds we carry as victims of others' mistreatment—the ways, for example, that we were violated, abused, lied to, or manipulated. In a Buddhist framework, however, it is quite the contrary; it is the things we have done *to other people*, our past karma, that reinforce the core wound of separation and suffering. The hurts we have suffered at other people's hands are a fulfillment of karma and leave us more liberated and clear. Thus Buddha advises us in the *Dhammapada*:

> "He abused me, he struck me, he overcame me, he robbed me,"
> In those who harbor such thoughts hatred will never cease.
> "He abused me, he struck me, he overcame me, he robbed me,"
> In those who do not harbor such thoughts hatred will cease.[2]

Seeing things in this way brings a greater sense of integrity and wholeness. When you blame your pain on your childhood, you are left feeling powerless and choiceless, as if you had lost at some ghastly game of Russian roulette. By contrast, when you interpret your present suffering as the result of your past actions, you are left with the sense that you can change your life by changing your behavior and, even more important, by eliminating the sense of separation that caused your unskillful behavior in the first place. Our shared assumptions in the West, by overemphasizing the impact of what was done to us in the past, risk turning us into hapless victims of circumstances beyond our control.

After all, in this moment what past do you find? As you hold this book and see the black ink on the white pages, can you find anything existing called memory or personal history? It exists only in thought and imagination, and once recreated in this way will appear to be real and perpetuate itself into an imagined future. Seeing the past clearly as merely a thought in this moment causes it to dissolve.

Of course, memory has a place at a certain level. In everyday life we could not function at all without it, and we can learn from the past—for example, when we recall similar circumstances when trying to solve a current problem. But, as Krishnamurti reminds us, "There is a state where memory has very little place. A mind which is not crippled by memory has real freedom."[3] The past has no separate and abiding existence except in the mind.

A TIME OF TRANSITION

We live in unprecedented times in terms of the potential for growth of consciousness and liberation. The generations of Westerners born since World War II have questioned and rejected the status quo and traditional values more than any other generation in history. Deeply aware of the impermanence of human institutions, including marriage, family, governments, and geopolitical boundaries, as well as of the often painful impact of such institutions on our lives, we seem to be far more open than ever before to the possibility of freeing ourselves from *all* conditioning and limitation. Perhaps the closest parallel would be the European Renaissance, when the breakdown of the feudal order and the medieval world-view gave rise to humanism, the exploration of new continents, the birth of a nontheistic political structure, and an unprecedented blossoming of artistic creativity.

We are left with many unanswered questions about the relationship we have formed with our personal conditioning. On the one hand, we see the dangers of repression, where the pain of our own unfulfilled needs is denied. If we treat our psychological wounds and our emotions as though they do not exist, we can become superficial and addicted to New Age platitudes, unable to feel into our own depths. On the other hand, if we overemphasize our past and over-identify with being a victim, we may feel that we are unable to operate in any but a dysfunctional way because of the conditioning into which we were born.

In the past two decades we have seen the emergence of groups whose members are bound by a shared sense of dysfunctional conditioning. There are support groups for adult children of alcoholics, adult survivors of sexual abuse, adult survivors of abandonment, and even adult survivors of Jewish mothers! While this support can be strengthening and reassuring to someone who has lived with their pain in isolation and denial, the fascination with our wounded past can lead us to a more deeply entrenched sense of identity as dysfunctional. While it is important in our search for liberation, truth, and transcendence to acknowledge the "suchness" of the past, it is equally important to find a way that truly and deeply allows us to let go of it and see its potential irrelevance to our present situation.

As we look into the nature of our past, which after all continues to exist only as thought, we see that there is no possibility of liberation from personal conditioning by changing or rearranging its contents. The only way to free ourselves from our individual dream or nightmare is through deep acceptance of its intrinsic nature. George Gurdjieff painted a wonderful parallel in his *Beelzebub's Tales to his Grandson*. He compares our situation to a man in a prison cell. The first and most important step, he says, is to realize that you are in prison and to want to escape. However, he says, most people are content to perpetually rearrange the furniture. This he compares to working on one's personality, trying to change one's conditioning in some way. The way out of the prison is to look beyond the familiar gestalt, to examine the nature of the prison itself and to become truly passionate about emancipation.

Liberation from the past comes not through trying to change, understand, or relive it; that would be like rearranging the furniture in the prison cell. Freedom from the past is available in every moment if we face the dragon directly. In that moment out of time we see that all that exists, at most, is a thought or a feeling in the body *now*. Transcendence of the pitfalls of indulgence and repression can be discovered by questioning what, after all, is the nature of this past right *now*. When attention is not fixed anywhere, when we are just here with whatever is happening, what past do we find? It is by seeing through personal history that we liberate ourselves from it, not by trying to change it.

What possibility could there be of changing it anyway? What happened to you as a child ten, twenty, thirty or more years ago cannot be changed, only abandoned. After all, that is what makes it the past. Traditional psychotherapy and various kinds of hypnosis can help you rewrite the scripts that were shaped by your past, but the facts of what occurred can never be rewritten. Pretending that your past existed differently than it actually did is merely a form of self-delusion.

Although we cannot change the contents of the past, we can change its relative transparency or opacity. It is like a movie that is being projected onto a white wall. Our attention is completely focused on the content of the movie, which seems like reality to us, and the wall may easily be overlooked. But what happens if we project the movie onto an open window looking out onto a garden full of flowers and children playing? The movie may still be running, but the transparency of the medium onto which the content is being projected makes the images seem almost irrelevant. We now have the choice to focus on the images from the past or to look beyond them to the garden and the beauty of this moment.

PSYCHOLOGICAL AND FACTUAL MEMORY

The difference between images projected onto a wall and those projected onto an open window is the difference between psychological and factual memory. The key to switching between the two lies in our willingness to experience memory in the physical body and hence to allow its liberation.

Factual memory means what actually happened, as might be recorded on a videotape or remembered by a disinterested observer. Nothing can be done about it now, because it no longer exists except in collective thought. If your mother left when you were four, or your father died when you were three, or you were sexually or physically abused, nothing can be done to change the factuality of the sequence of events as they occurred. Trying to rewrite the contents of a history book becomes the obsession of a megalomaniac dictator trying to rewrite the history of his country. Such things have occurred.

Psychological memory is stored in the body; it is the way in which we perceive the events of the past as though they are still happening now. This psychological memory can be erased, which means that although the content of the memory may remain perfectly intact, it can become as relevant or irrelevant as we choose to see it. Through the acceptance and absorption of psychological memory into emptiness, spaciousness and love, old memories can become as irrelevant to this moment as a B-movie you once saw. Once we see its inherent emptiness, the past loses its sting. I have seen this occur with hundreds of people over the years. As the kinesthetic charge is removed from memory, it is revealed to be simply a movie, a story we tell ourselves now, which has no substantial reality in this moment, and therefore no relevance for our lives today.

As we let go of psychological memory, we begin to see the transparency of personal identity. After all, when you meet a friend and look into her eyes, what difference exists between the two of you except a different set of circumstances and conditioning in a psychological past? When this psychological past is diffused, discharged, or made irrelevant, what separate identity remains? The Self is the same: it is infinite, eternal, unborn, undying, empty of all content, and yet full of all possibility. As personal history becomes transparent, personal identity dissolves.

Hence it is only by realizing the eternally unchanging Self that we can let go of the past. Otherwise the dissolution of the past is experienced as a kind of death, an abandonment of a part of who we are. This may explain why people are often unwilling to let go of old painful emotions and habits. As long as they are still identified with them, this letting go is considered to be tantamount to suicide. However, it has been said many times that as the Self is realized, karma is burnt up and destroyed. Of course, this does not mean that the body is not still subject to cause and effect, or that it no longer has to experience the consequences of its previous actions. Rather, it means that there is no longer any sense of an individual entity to whom this past karma belongs.

CHARGED AND UNCHARGED MEMORY

We will be discovering how to liberate the psychological memory that has been held in the body, leaving only the factual memory which is free of emotional charge. Of course, not everything that has happened to us is held in the body as an emotionally charged psychological memory. Many events leave no residue and do not inhibit our ability to respond freely to future events. But charged events get imprinted in the body and then determine how we react emotionally to similar stimuli. To illustrate this, consider two simple stories from an anonymous childhood.

In the first story, Tommy, a small boy of four or five, goes to a birthday party and spends his time happily with the other children, eating cake, playing hide and seek, and pinning a tail on the donkey. Finally, at the end of the party, each child is given a packet of candy and a balloon. The mothers arrive at six-thirty, and each child goes home to dinner, happily holding the balloon and the bag of candy. After dinner Tommy brushes his teeth, ties his balloon to the end of the bed, and drifts off into a perfect sleep at the end of a perfect day. This kind of incident would typically carry no charge and may not be remembered. Millions of such events have taken place in your life, but can you remember what you ate for breakfast on the fifth of January twenty-five years ago? Or what you watched on TV just last year? It has been forgotten and has no bearing, positive or negative, on how this moment is perceived.

Charged memory is quite different. Imagine Tommy at the same birthday party, but this time his mother does not arrive when the others do. All the other children leave with their parents, but Tommy is left. The family of the house goes about its business while Tommy waits in the hall. Finally his mother arrives, about an hour late, after an unexplained emergency. She is embarrassed and stressed out, and she whisks him off in the car without taking the time to listen to his feelings. In the process Tommy forgets his balloon and his packet of candy. When he goes to bed that night after brushing his teeth, he spends some time awake, staring silently at the ceiling, feeling sad because his mother did not pay attention to his feelings and because there is no balloon tied to the end of his bed.

If such incidents were to happen to Tommy repeatedly, he might develop the attitude ,"I don't get the things that other people get in life," "Things don't work out for me," or even "I am unlovable." These beliefs about himself and reality would then become the blueprints for more such things to occur in his life. This is an example of charged memory. I imagine you can remember events like this from your own past; you may even feel the accompanying emotion in your body. Although the incident described here was only mildly traumatic, it could easily become lodged in the body as an energetic or physiological holding pattern. More intensely charged incidents include the loss of a parent through divorce or untimely death, various kinds of sexual or physical abuse, and accidents or natural disasters.

Because we feel overwhelmed and out of control, we are unable to fully experience or integrate the emotions aroused by traumatic events. Instead, we numb out or repress them, and the emotions are stored in the muscles and energetic pathways of the body. Untraumatic events, by contrast, are fully experienced and assimilated and leave no energetic residue.

Just as the memory was imprinted because there was not enough space or safety to feel the emotions associated with it, it can also be liberated by creating the space and safety now to experience the feelings that were stored in the body. There is no better way to do this than by absorbing those feelings back into the spaciousness, emptiness, and infinite love of the Self, which we have revealed through Self-inquiry in Chapter Five. In Dzogchen, this way of being with feelings as they arise is known as the "liberation of emotion into primordial emptiness." It is through our increasing absorption into the Self and surrender of the sense of an individual "I," that we have greater capacity to feel and liberate feelings that previously seemed unbearable.

Here is a simple session outline for the absorbing of psychological memory back into the Self and its release into factual memory. You do not need to go through this process for every charged memory. The session is an "initiation." Once the psyche has learned how to liberate feeling through absorption into emptiness, this process will become second nature and can occur throughout the day. Again it should be emphasized that these processes are designed for milder forms of trauma. When dealing with severe trauma, such as physical or sexual abuse, it is best to consult a licensed mental health professional.

Session Outline:
Liberating Charged Memory

Step 1:   Pre Induction Talk.

Step 2:   Inducing Relaxation.

Step 3:   Progressive Regression.

Step 4:   Entering the Memory.

Step 5:   Enlivening the Physical Sensation.

Step 6:   Exaggerate the Energetic Contraction.

Step 7:   Relax back into Self-Inquiry.

Step 8:   (optional) Absorb and Bless on the Breath.

Step 9:   Check the Body.

Step 10: Return to the Memory.

Step 11: Rehearse the Situation in Current Life.

Step 12: Suggestions.

Step 13: Counting Back.

SESSION OUTLINE:
LIBERATING CHARGED MEMORY

Step 1: Pre-Induction Talk.
Prior to inducing the trance, take some time to talk with the person for whom you are facilitating the session. Identify together the recurrent emotional or reactive pattern in your friend's life now, and how that indicates that something has been held from the past as psychological memory. For example, low self-esteem, excessive and irrational anger, or feelings of fear or anxiety.

Step 2: Inducing Relaxation.
Do one or more of the relaxation techniques suggested earlier, or others with which you are familiar. Finish with the flight of stairs, and move into the regression technique that follows.

Step 3: Progressive Regression.
There are many ways to facilitate age regression. If you are already trained in hypnotherapy or psychotherapy, you may be familiar with some of them. The one I prefer is the corridor of memory, which gradually builds confidence in the ability to remember things clearly.

First set up a finger signal with your friend, as you may have already done in previous sessions.

And I'm going to ask you now to
Allow one of the fingers of the (right/left) *hand to*
Make a gentle signal
As a way of saying to yourself
As well as to me
That you are ready to go deeper.

Once you get the signal, you can move into the corridor regression.

And just because you are
Deeply relaxed now
So it's easy for you to
Feel yourself,
To imagine yourself
Standing in a corridor
With doors on the left and doors on the right.

Now ask her to give the signal when she imagines herself in the corridor. When you have the signal, you can begin to move down the corridor to memories from the past. Start with a memory from one year ago.

And I'm going to ask you now to
Move to a door on the right
In this corridor,
To a memory from one year ago.
That's right, you can open the door
And see a memory from one year ago.
Maybe a person,
Maybe a place,
Maybe something which happened.
You can open the door and allow yourself
To experience this memory now.
And when you find that
You are able to remember something clearly
From one year ago,
You can allow the finger to
Make the signal.

She may take some time to get in touch with a memory from a year ago, or she may give the signal immediately. If she doesn't give the signal after a minute or two, simply repeat the instructions until she does. Then you can say:

Good. It's good to know that you can
Remember things from the past
Easily and effortlessly.

Do not spend more than a minute or so on each memory at this point, or you will get sidetracked. Now ask her to move further down the corridor to a door on the left or the right, to a memory from five years ago, and repeat the same instructions. Move back to ten years ago, twenty years ago, and then, depending on how old your friend is, to the age of twenty, fifteen, ten. The point of the regression is to increase her confidence in being able to move back easily through her past and to help her to see that she can remember anything if she chooses to.

Step 4: Entering the Memory.
Now we are going to help her approach the memory that triggers her current pattern of identification. Here are the instructions,

using "unlovable" as an example of the emotion that is arising
as an obscuration in your friend's current life. You would need
to substitute the feeling state that your friend describes to you
in Step One, as well as its opposite (e.g. confident/unconfident,
open/closed, trusting/guarded, etc.).

> *I'm going to ask you now to*
> *Find a door in this corridor*
> *On the left or on the right;*
> *A door which can*
> *Lead to a memory of*
> *A time when you were feeling* (unlovable)
> *But you really wanted to feel* (loved).
> *And when you find that door,*
> *Even though it may be closed right now,*
> *You can allow the finger to make the signal.*

Then wait for the finger signal. You can say:

> *Even though that door may be closed just now,*
> *When you feel ready to open the door*
> *And step into the memory,*
> *You can allow the finger to make the signal.*

When you get the signal, you can ask her to open the door and
move into the memory. When she begins to step into the
memory, you will notice that the eyeballs start moving rapidly
from left to right, even though the eyes are closed.[4] After she
has had time to tune in the memory, you can ask her, "What is
happening now?" "Where are you now?" or "How old do you
feel right now?" Simply ask her to begin to describe the memory
in the present tense. For example, she might say, "I'm in the
classroom. My teacher, Mrs. Skunthorpe, is staring accusingly
over her pince-nez glasses at me, and I'm feeling incredible contractions in my stomach." All you need to do at this point is to
encourage her to continue describing the memory in the present
tense until she gets in touch with the emotion that it is enlivening in the body. Psychological memory is stored in the body,
and it is from the body that it needs to be liberated. As soon as
she starts to feel a sensation, encourage her with statements
like "That's right, you can feel the tension in the body, and of
course it's natural for a little girl like you to feel faint and scared
when Mrs. Skunthorpe is staring at you in that way." Give her
every encouragement that this is a natural way to feel in this

situation. When she is feeling the sensation fully in the body, move on to the next step.

Step 5: Enlivening the Physical Sensation.
Now you can ask your friend to let go of the pictures and the story and simply stay with the feelings in the body. Ask her to lay her hand on the place in the body which is enlivened by the memory. If that is inaccessible to her, you can place one of your own hands there, to help focus her attention at that place.

Step 6: Exaggerate the Energetic Contraction.
Now ask her to drop even deeper than the body, into the energetic contraction or atmosphere associated with this memory.

> *And it is easy for you now to*
> *Feel even more than the physical body,*
> *And to become aware of the energy,*
> *The atmosphere,*
> *The frequency which is causing*
> *The body to feel this way.*

This will usually seem more pervasive than the physical sensation itself. In order to eliminate the repression that has prevented this frequency from being fully experienced, you can ask her to exaggerate it, to make it larger than life. Use the approach we described in Chapter Five, on pages 89 to 92. The point is not necessarily to move into catharsis or emotional release, but simply to feel more completely. Ask her to keep building up this energy so she is consciously creating, welcoming, and absorbing it in this moment. When she has fully welcomed and exaggerated the feeling, so that all resistance has been removed and the feeling has become so vast and overwhelming that it can't be exaggerated any more, have her make a finger signal.

Step 7: Relax Back Into Self Inquiry.
Once she has exaggerated the contraction of energy as much as she possibly can, you can simply ask her to relax back into being that which is aware of energy moving in the body just now in this moment.

> *That's right*
> *You can allow yourself to*
> *Let go,*

And become aware
Of That which is aware of energy
In states of contracting and
Letting go.
You can allow yourself to relax,
Even more deeply,
Once again
Into that same question,
"Who am I?"

Step 8: (Optional) Absorb and Bless on the Breath.
You can also ask your friend to absorb whatever is left back into vastness through the window of the heart. Ask her to begin to absorb the feeling into the Heart on the in-breath and to breathe back the vastness of the Heart on the out-breath. Ask her to allow the feeling to "ride" the in-breath back into the Heart and to allow the vastness of the Heart to permeate, or bless, this place in the body. You will find more complete instructions in Chapter Four on the Heart Meditation.

That's right.
And just because you can
Feel this sensation in the body now,
So it's easy for you to
Absorb this feeling
With the in-breath
Into the emptiness of the Heart,
Like a mother
Welcoming a child home,
Like you would greet
A long-lost friend.
Use the in-breath
To bring this feeling home,
To drop this feeling into the Heart
Like into an infinitely deep well.

You can take a deep, audible in-breath now yourself to encourage her to use the breath to absorb the feeling back into the vastness of the heart.

That's right.
And with the out-breath

You can allow the quality of the Heart
To permeate this place in the body,
To breathe out the vastness of the Heart
And fill this place in the body with blessing.

Continue in this way for as long as it takes this feeling to be completely absorbed or liberated back into its source.

Step 9: Check the Body.

Once your friend has returned completely to relaxing in her own natural presence, through Self Inquiry and the Heart Meditation, check to see what is left in the body.

What do you experience now,
In the body,
Under where your (left / right) *hand is resting?*

When the feeling has been completely dissolved, she may be surprised and reply, "Nothing" or, "It's just warm," or she may just say, "Space." But take your time. Once you have "unvelcroed the story," feelings in the body are usually liberated in a couple of minutes, but there is no reason why you should not take ten or twenty minutes to breathe together in this way.

If the sensation in the body does not seem to dissolve at all, it is probably because it was not fully exaggerated in the previous steps. You cannot absorb what is still being resisted. Go back and repeat Steps Five to Seven, until it cannot be exaggerated any more and all resistance has been removed.

Step 10: Return to the Memory.

Like rewinding a videotape, go back to the beginning of the factual memory and replay it again, to see if there is any charge remaining. Almost always, if you have brought your friend to an experience of emptiness in the body, she will be able to run through the memory without any reaction. People sometimes report that it seems like a movie or a TV show they once saw. It has become irrelevant, perhaps even funny. If any charge remains, simply go through Steps Four to Nine again: feeling the sensation in the body, letting go of the memory and the story, consciously exaggerating the feeling in the body until it is at its maximum, then relaxing back into being awareness itself, and checking the body again.

Step 11: Rehearse the Situation in Current Life.

Continue this process until the memory has lost all psychological charge. Although this may seem like a mammoth task,
you will actually be surprised by how easily mountains are
reduced to molehills in our willingness to feel, particularly
when it occurs in a state of induced relaxation. Now you can
return to a current situation in your friend's life in which these
feelings arose, or could possibly arise, and run through the
situation again, in imagination. The charge should be gone
completely. If it is still there, run back to another earlier or
different memory.

Step 12: Suggestions.

Once the charge has left the memory, as well as the triggering
situation in your friend's current life, you can ask her to dissolve
both fantasies and rest as spaciousness. It is through dissolving or liberating overshadowing emotions that the natural state
is revealed. This is a time to allow her to enjoy her own silence,
her own absorption in the Self. You might also want to use
some suggestions before bringing her back. You can use the
suggestions from Chapter Three or create your own out of the
content of the session. You might like to try the following suggestions, which work particularly well in changing how we
see the past.

> *That's right.*
> *It is safe for you to feel*
> *Everything that arises.*
> *Every emotion,*
> *Every sensation in the body,*
> *Every memory moving in consciousness*
> *Is safe for you to feel.*
> *You are limitless.*
> *You are the source and destination*
> *Of all that arises and falls back again.*
> *And it is good to know now,*
> *Isn't it,*
> *That all memory is just*
> *A thought moving in this moment,*
> *And it is safe for you to*
> *Feel and experience that completely.*

Step 13: Counting Back.

Now count your friend back from five to one, as described in Chapter Three. As you count back, you can suggest that it will be easy to liberate all emotions as they arise in this way.

WHAT YOU RESIST PERSISTS

We free ourselves from what is held in the body by our willingness to feel it fully. Of course, we need to be careful that we are not trying to feel it fully in order to "make it go away." We need to be willing to have it remain forever, fully enlivened, as a part of our universe. Only by fully embracing, accepting, and absorbing feelings will we find ourselves able to integrate and liberate them.

Psychological charge can be held almost anywhere in the body. The most common place is the abdomen, which contains many of our most vital organs and is the only part of the body not protected by bone. Most other animals walk with this part of the body facing down, but man and certain primates expose their bellies to the world, thereby creating greater vulnerability. Emotions can also be stored in the chest, the arms, the legs, the back of the neck, and the facial muscles. There have been fascinating studies by bodyworkers and other healers that explore this kind of emotional anatomy.[5]

THE RESCUE MISSION

For childhood memories where there was an ongoing atmosphere of unfulfilled needs, rather than specific trauma, there is another kind of process called the "Childhood Rescue Mission," which was developed by David Quigley as part of the approach he teaches called Alchemical Hypnotherapy.[6]

Although you will not be able to master this process with the few pages of instruction provided here, we can say briefly that the regression used is more or less the same as the one described earlier in Step Three. You move back to a specific memory in which your friend, who is now regressed to feeling like a child again, is able to describe what is happening in the present tense and to feel the emotions in the body. Instead of focusing on the sensations, however, you now bring your friend back to being the adult, lying in relaxation with you in this moment. You then ask her how she feels seeing this little child, who usually seems lost, unloved, and uncared for. Generally the adult self will be overcome with compassion and tenderness. You ask her if she would be able to rescue that child and take care of her in a way that she has never been taken care of before. The adult personality returns to the memory to bond with the child personality, to listen to its needs, and to give it love and nurturing. Eventually, having said good-bye to the original family and the atmosphere of trauma, the adult brings the child back to become a part of the adult's current life.

This rescue mission may initiate what is often referred to as "inner child work." As such, it can be useful for those who have had so little emotional nurturing that a general atmosphere of sadness and hopelessness, rather than a specific response to a specific stimulus, has come to permeate their lives. By talking with and holding this imaginary child, they can create a feeling of being worthy of love. Of course, this kind of approach has its pitfalls. We can become so hypnotized by the symbol that we have created that we develop an addiction to our own imagination and become even less available to the mystery of this pristine moment, in which there is neither a child nor an adult personality to be found. I talked every day with my own little Nicholas for more than ten years, and I am immensely grateful to David Quigley and Jehru Kabbal for the liberation from the past that both their approaches allowed me. Over many years I have also shared this process with hundreds of people in individual sessions and trainings. While working with the inner child can be a wonderful way to acknowledge and be with our feelings, there also comes a time when it is necessary to give it less significance and to move on. In the rediscovery of the Self, feelings and memories can be absorbed back into our original nature, where the appearance of a personal history and identity dissolves.

PRESSING THE PAUSE CONTROL

There is a third way of working with the past that is worth mentioning, called "pressing the pause control." While the child rescue mission is helpful where feelings have been completely repressed, this session is helpful for the opposite kind of situation, where there is a strong identification with emotional states and a tendency towards indulgence.

Once again, you induce a relaxed state and do a regression, as described in Steps One to Three on page 126. Once you enter into the memory and the emotions are enlivened, you ask your friend to pause the memory, just as you would press the pause control on a VCR. You can even ask her to see the memory as though it were displayed on a TV screen. Once the memory is on pause, ask her, "Where is this memory now?" or, "What existence does this memory have in this moment?" The strong feeling of identification is broken, and a realization occurs that this is only a thought now, in this moment. It is not real.

Rather than absorbing and integrating the feelings, this is a simple way to see that in this moment there is no past; in this very moment the memory is nothing but a thought or an energy arising in consciousness. For someone who has had a lot of therapy and is overly concerned with the effects of the past, this is an antidote—to see that the past is as transparent or opaque as one wants it to be. If she has been identified with being a victim of the past, your friend may have some resistance to seeing through memory in this way and bringing it to transparency. She may want to cling to the story. If you continue to ask her, "Yes, but in this moment, with these feelings in the body, what existence does that have?" she will eventually come to see that this is merely a picture in consciousness now, and as a picture it cannot hurt her. One of my teachers many years ago likened this to a photograph of a tiger. While a real tiger can eat you alive, a photograph of a tiger is harmless and need not concern you at all.[7]

I remember when I returned from India in 1992 after living with Poonjaji. I had previously loved movies, and of course I was at least two years behind with the current releases. I was giving Satsang on Orcas Island in the beautiful, remote house of my friend Judy McClenaghan. I went to the movie rental store to look for something soft and gentle to watch, as a gradual reintroduction to the world of films. Finally I found a title that sounded just right, like it might even be for children; it was called *Silence of the Lambs*. Without bothering to look at the back of the box, I took it home. After Satsang, everyone left and Judy went to bed. I decided to stay up a bit late to watch my soft and gentle film. Well, if you know the movie, you can imagine my predicament in that remote country house, with the wind blowing the trees outside and making the house creak! This was an invitation to press the pause control every now and then and ask myself, "What is real in this moment? Is this real or is it just images on a screen?" I silently paid homage to my teacher from years before who pointed out the difference between a real tiger and a photographic image!

You will need to be sensitive to discover which approach to the past will work best with your friend. With a simple recurring emotional state

associated with a charged memory, we can create enough spaciousness and emptiness to absorb the feelings into consciousness, back into
the original nature of mind. If there has been a general tendency to
discount all feelings, and thus to feel unworthy, the childhood rescue
mission can be helpful as a transition toward dissolving feelings once
they have been felt. If there has been a tendency to overindulge in the
past, we can re-educate consciousness to be able to freeze memories in
mid-frame and to see that this is only a picture or an energy that is
being created now in this moment. It can be switched on or switched
off as we choose. And once again, in the case of any severe trauma or
otherwise overwhelming material, you are advised to refer to a licensed
health care professional.

CASE HISTORY: GAIL

Gail was brought up in Australia in a large family with an authoritarian father. He took to physically punishing his children for misde-
meanors ranging from not finishing their food to answering adults back
at the table. As a consequence, Gail grew up with a fear of asserting
herself or putting herself out in any way. When I met her, she had already meditated daily for more than twenty years. As a result, she had
developed quite a cushion of silence and emptiness, but she remained
unconfident in all her social interactions. She worked in a newspaper
office, and although she had excellent relations with her co-workers,
she was thrown into panic by even the faintest suggestion of criticism.

We decided to do a regression to a time when she wanted to be
spontaneous and natural, but felt criticized and shut down. She
returned to a memory of sitting at the family table with her eight brothers and sisters. Her father was criticizing her for speaking out of turn
to one of her siblings. With the enlivening of that memory, she felt the
contraction in her chest, the feeling of needing to hold back any spontaneous expression and natural arising of childlike exuberance. As she
experienced the feelings in her body, she was able to let go of the story
and the picture of her father and stay with the feeling in the chest,
contracted in denial of her spontaneity and exuberance. As she
dropped deeper than the body, she exaggerated the frequency, allowing it to overwhelm her to the point that she felt completely numb
and dead. Because of her long background in meditation and her
absorption in silence, it was easy for her, once she had exaggerated
the frequency to the maximum, to relax back into being spacious.

When she returned to the memory, she found herself feeling much stronger than her father. This was not a strength that needed to confront him, but a feeling of vastness, emotional stability, and deep love and compassion. Now she found that her father's rantings and ravings became irrelevant. They only reflected his own insecurities and his need to maintain control. The charge was gone from the memory. The tiger was reduced to a stuffed animal. We returned to the situation in her office in her imagination, where she could now experience criticism, or what actually now seemed like constructive suggestion, without the same reaction. She later told me that this equanimity also spread into the real life situation in her office, and although there was still the same instinct towards contraction in the face of potential criticism, there was also now a much greater cushion to fall back into. The session had been an initiation into a different way of seeing.

Of course, this is quite different from changing the contents of memories in an attempt to rewrite one's past or working with affirmations without dealing with the underlying feelings. If Gail had tried to replace her feelings of fear with the opposite by trying to affirm her spontaneity or exuberance, she would have found herself unknowingly reaffirming her old sense of identity. By dissolving the holding patterns that create a fixed sense of personality, we are left with a greater depth of silence, vastness, relaxation and love.

CASE HISTORY: JANET

Janet was born in the north of England and also grew up in a large family. She describes her childhood as basically happy and peaceful. Because her father was busy earning a living and her mother was looking after seven children, Janet came to regard her own emotional needs as unimportant. Feeling invisible as a person, she constantly needed to define herself through others. Throughout her adult life she sought a sense of definition and personal identity through her husband, her children, and any activity that involved putting other people's needs before her own. Rather than seeing through the ego in a transcendent way, Janet was attempting to subjugate or suppress the ego. She was a perfect candidate for learning how to establish a relationship between the adult, capable personality and the inner child whose needs had never been addressed.

When Janet regressed, she found that as a child, rather than feeling any strong emotions, she just felt numb and blank. This little girl had elder siblings who ignored her and younger siblings who were being cared for by her mother. Somehow Janet had slipped through the cracks and was never recognized to be of any intrinsic worth in her own right. We found her wearing hand-me-down clothes and playing with weeds and dirt in the garden. At this regressed age, she was unable to say much; she was so deeply habituated to being ignored. After some talking, we established that she would in fact like to have someone to take care of her, but she considered this to be an almost impossible fantasy, something she could not believe she deserved.

We then came back to the adult Janet lying in relaxation and asked her how she felt to see this lonely waif playing in a cold garden in northern England. The adult Janet was overwhelmed with compassion. After all, she had spent her entire life taking care of others, and it was easy for her to feel compassion for a child. Janet's adult then returned to the memory also, but it took some time for the child to trust and bond with this adult. She simply did not feel that she deserved any quality attention. Janet was able to bring this little child back into her adult life, to talk with her on a daily basis, and to keep reassuring her that her needs and her feelings were important.

During this period Janet kept up her daily meditation practice, which created space for her feelings to be experienced fully and then absorbed into silence. She maintained a relationship with this child over a period of several months, during which she regularly did a gestalt exercise in which she became first the adult and then the child. Soon she was able to recognize when she was having emotions, rather than following her previous pattern of being completely numb to them. As this capacity to feel was restored, she was able to absorb these emotions back into their source.

CHAPTER 8

THE BELOVED

*The minute I heard my first love story
I started looking for you, not knowing
How blind that was.*

*Lovers don't finally meet somewhere
They're in each other all along.*[1]

JELALUDDIN RUMI

In Chapter Five we examined our interpersonal relationships and saw how the fixation onto another in some way creates obstacles to resting in the natural state. In this chapter we will explore the fantasies and idealism of romantic love and how they lead us from a state of balance into an obsession with the idea of the other as the source of beauty, truth, and wholeness.

For the most part we will focus on the dynamics between men and women in romantic love, simply because heterosexual affairs are statistically more common, and because we are concerned here mainly with the interaction of male and female energies within the psyche. Those who are oriented towards same-sex relationships should translate the material to fit their own orientation.

It is not only the negative, unhappy, problematic aspects of life that obscure the natural state. It is equally our idealism and our hopes, our tendency to chase after the pot of gold at the end of the rainbow, that causes the innate perfection of things to be obscured. We tend to focus more on negative states because they are uncomfortable and cause pain. Naturally we would like to be rid of them and hang onto the positive. But this is actually a short-sighted approach to becoming free. There is a saying in Tibet, "What tastes sweet in the beginning is often bitter in the end; and what tastes bitter in the beginning is often sweet in the end." It is rather like a Chinese pill that has sugar coating on the outside. When you put it in your mouth and begin to suck, it tastes sweet, but it doesn't take long to reach the bitter herbs on the inside. Similarly, people often say that when they start to eat simpler food, such as a macrobiotic diet, they find it repulsive at first. Then slowly they develop a taste for it, and what was once repugnant becomes delicious. In fact, those things that appear most appealing and seductive often cause us the greatest unhappiness and plunge us most deeply into hidden foolishness. Whereas the willingness to endure painful and difficult states often leads us to our greatest internal source of strength and sweetness.

Rather than trying to get rid of what makes us unhappy and acquire more of what makes us happy, we will be learning here to see through the tendency of consciousness to chase after external phenomena and look for happiness outside our own nature. Many New Age therapies assume that it's better to be more successful and more powerful, to have more money, more things, and better relationships with more powerful and impressive people. In this way such therapies tend to support the underlying assumptions of the mind. The dharmic perspective, on the other hand, while not trying to destroy these aspects of life, leads us to question whether fulfilling desires in the external world is not in fact deepening our entanglement in craving and thought. Desires that until now have been externally directed can be seen through, made transparent, and internally fulfilled.

THE DREAM WE HAVE BEEN SOLD

In Chapter Five we discussed how the media persuade us that it is through relationships that we can fulfill our needs. Almost everyone in the West is somehow preoccupied with romantic love. We are inundated with television, motion picture, and advertising images of idealized heterosexual lovers in fond embrace. We have already discussed how many products are sold to us on the strength of these images, which promise a kind of security, caring, union, and aliveness that we all dream of finding. We are also presented with pictures of the perfect nuclear family, riding in their new convertible or brushing their teeth together with the latest smile-enhancing toothpaste or sitting down to breakfast with the latest cereal. The mother and father look relaxed and comfortable, in total harmony with each other. The children look up adoringly to their parents as perfect role models of wisdom and maturity. Healthcare products, children's toys, stylish clothing, and vacation packages are all purveyed to us with images like this.

Yet how often do we actually see this ideal lived out in our own lives or the lives of the people we know? Of course, life brings moments or even periods of this kind of happiness. But if we are really honest and step back for a moment from the mass hypnosis to which we have been subjected, we may find ourselves wondering how many romantic liaisons we know of where this kind of harmony and nourishment is ongoing and truly fulfilling. How many nuclear families with a mother and a father and two-and-a-half children living together in a little box somewhere do we find that reflect what we see in the shampoo ad, the cereal commercial, or the TV sitcom?

If we open our eyes from the American dream, we discover that in the United States more than 50 percent of all marriages end in divorce, whether or not children are involved. And this figure may be misleading because the 50 percent of marriages which survive includes people who live in such obedience to a social or religious framework that divorce is out of the question. Many parts of American society are so dominated by religious beliefs or the expectations of the extended family that it would be impossible to dissolve a marriage even if one wanted to. Thus, among people who are relatively free to divorce without being ostracized or condemned, the statistic is much higher than 50 percent. What percentage of the couples you know remain together until their children are grown, let alone spend their entire lives together? Indeed, how many couples stay together for more than a few years?

A SHIFT IN CONSCIOUSNESS

Why should an institution so appealing that it can be used to sell almost anything be so doomed to failure? A plethora of books and workshops have emerged in recent years to address the failure of romantic love to live up to its promise. The fundamentalist right blames it all on moral decline and prescribes a return to discipline and "family values." Both women's and men's liberation groups have their own interpretations. In his best-selling book, *Men Are from Mars, Women Are from Venus*, John Gray suggests that the primary reason relationships don't work is that men and women don't know how to communicate with each other. One popular workshop leader even suggests that in 1952 a giant explosion threw the sun 15 percent off its normal magnetic alignment. As a result, the sun (masculine energy) and the earth (feminine energy) are now 15 percent out of balance, and communication between men and women will continue to deteriorate until the earth also makes the accompanying shift. He predicts that this will happen in the next few years, solving many marital problems, but also melting the polar ice caps in the process![2]

We can also view the crisis of the sexes in terms of the evolution of consciousness throughout human history. The stages of this evolution correspond to the seven energy centers, or *chakras*, in the body.[3] From the base level, corresponding to the *Muladhara*, or first chakra, relationships between men and women are dominated by food, shelter, procreation, and physical survival, much like the relationships between dogs, monkeys, and other animals. Very little emotional bonding occurs at this level.

The second level, which corresponds to the *Svadhisthana*, or second chakra, located above the genitals, emphasizes emotional bonding and security. At this level the external family is created. Interpersonal conflicts are seen to be of secondary importance to the internal security of the family. This form of bonding still dominates many Asian cultures, particularly in India, Indonesia, and most Muslim countries. In this view, marriages are more likely to survive because the survival of the family is invariably seen as more sacred than individual needs. This level of consciousness also dominated Europe until the mid-20th century. Indeed, prior to 1945, the divorce rate in the West was far lower than it is now, and the extended family was much stronger.

The third level of consciousness, which corresponds with the *Manipura*, or third chakra at the solar plexus, is concerned with willpower and individuality. At this stage the ego, the individualized self, becomes fully crystallized. The United States, particularly since 1945, represents the culmination of this level of consciousness. We can see how America moved from the second level to the third during this century and how Europe followed suit. Now the same kind of shift is beginning to occur among the younger generation in Asia. This level of consciousness is least conducive to stability in marriage, since the individual tends to feel trapped and inhibited from expressing himself.

The dawning of widespread "awakening," which we have referred to in earlier chapters, represents another level in the evolution of consciousness. Like the shifts that preceded it, this awakening begins with a few individuals, then becomes the norm in certain communities or areas of the country, and finally grows into the dominant state of consciousness of humanity. This level corresponds with the *Anahata*, or fourth chakra at the Heart, where the crystallized ego is seen through and duality dissolves into non-duality. In this level there is the birth of the ability to see the other as Self in another form. It is the dawning of *agape*, unconditional love. Here the power struggle gives way to synchronicity as the external lover becomes an icon of the eternal Beloved. In the fourth level there is meeting without attachment. The family expands to become all sentient beings.

The three higher levels represent the unfolding of this non-dual vision and its permeation into every aspect of our lives. The movement from the third level to the fourth happens when the individual ego is seen through, and attention shifts away from external phenomena to the Self. Whereas in the lower three stages of consciousness, completion is sought through bonding with or overpowering another, in the fourth stage wholeness is found through the discovery of our original nature.

Nowhere is the effect of this evolution of consciousness more apparent than in the relationship between men and women. When attention goes out in search of the other as a source of wholeness, the result is greater and greater entanglement. When it goes inward to find wholeness, there is increased simplicity and completion.

THE SEARCH FOR WHOLENESS

Even with the recognition that possessing another cannot bring lasting happiness and that living from the Heart does, why is it that we become so obsessed with seeking our fulfillment in external circumstances? What leads us to believe that if we could only find our ideal mate, we would experience perfect happiness?

This tendency is to some extent instinctive and biological; it is hard-wired into the DNA. The built-in attraction of the male and female assures the survival of the species. But there does seem to be something deeper also at work here. The tendency to romanticize and idealize the other appears to transcend body and biology. For a more satisfying explanation, we need to look into the nature of consciousness itself, and how individual identity has arisen out of it.

In an earlier chapter we looked at the mechanics whereby undefined, limitless, eternal consciousness—call it God, Tao, Self, or Source—is concentrated into a postulate, an idea of "I," and then seeks to further define itself. As soon as consciousness seeks a definition for this "I" idea, it has to restrict itself to "this" or "that," and it begins to create polarities. One of the first of these polarities is male and female: "I am a man" or "I am a woman." Subsequent definitions become progressively more complex: "I am intelligent/I am unintelligent," "I am worthy/I am unworthy," "I am rich/I am poor," "I am from a developed/undeveloped country," "I am conservative/liberal," "I am a spiritual/materialistic person"—as more and more detailed distinctions are made to define the false sense of a separate identity. The more we define ourselves in this way, the more incompleteness we experience, and the further we stray from our original nature as undefined, whole, and containing all possibilities.

Once postulated, the "I" thought begins to attach more and more definitions to itself; in fact, its greatest fear is of being undefined. It does this in the same way that a piece of tar paper attaches to itself anything that blows by: leaves, dirt, twigs, bugs, sawdust, and so forth. Just as the individualized identity craves more and more definition, so there is a corresponding force within consciousness to return itself to wholeness. The first is the incessant appetite of the mind to categorize and define what does not really exist; the second is the longing of the Heart to return to what is real. In this sense, the force of romantic love can be seen as the urge to become whole again. Man, having identified himself as being male, has disidentified himself from being female. In fact, each gender inadvertently cuts off half of its original wholeness when the man adopts his identity along masculine lines and the woman adopts her identity along feminine lines. This very act of fragmentation, of no longer identifying with the whole but becoming a "part" of God, initiates the search for this integration once again. As soon as we say, "I am a man," we cut off the feminine energy within us. As soon as we say, "I am a woman," the male becomes something external to us. The return to wholeness is a journey to being that consciousness which is neither male nor female, but the source of both. You may have noticed that mystics or others who have truly transcended the forces of duality have both masculine and feminine qualities. Poonjaji, my teacher in India, could exhibit qualities that were ferocious and warriorlike, but could just as easily become as soft and gentle as the most feminine woman.

We have been deeply conditioned to look outside ourselves for what is missing rather than to look within. There is a wonderful story from Persia of Rabia, a Sufi mystic. One evening at dusk she was found outside her hut on her hands and knees looking through the grass.

A friend stopped and asked, "Rabia, what are you doing?"

"I've lost my only needle," she replied. "I use it for embroidery, so I have to find it." Rabia's friend also got down on her hands and knees and started to look in the grass. Soon other friends also came and asked what was happening, and they, too, joined in the search. After a while there were more than a dozen people on their hands and knees helping Rabia search for her lost needle in the moonlight.

After twenty minutes or so someone stood up with frustration and said, "Tell me, Rabia, where exactly did you lose your needle?"

"Oh, I lost it inside my hut," she replied matter-of-factly. Everyone stopped in disbelief while the one who first stood up asked, "If you lost it in your hut, why have we just spent the last twenty minutes on our hands and knees outside looking in the grass?"

"Well," Rabia sighed, "it was too dark in the hut. At least outside we have moonlight and it is easier to look."[4]

The story comes straight to the point. We prefer to look outside because somehow it is easier to look there, even though what we have lost may be within our own Heart. We are hypnotized into believing in the independent reality of the external world, as opposed to seeing the world as a projection of the mind, which is the more prevalent view in Eastern psychology. Thus we seek our lost wholeness in external things. Identifying ourselves as one gender or another, we long for a feeling of completion which we feel will only result when our perfect "other half" is found again. Rather than looking back to our own nature to find this wholeness, we look to the external world to find what we have lost in name and form. Of course, the more we look to external form to complete ourselves, the more we are frustrated, because our inner experience is one of incompleteness and fragmentation. Feeling that our original wholeness, which is a blessed state of completeness and happiness, has been lost, our fantasy is that by finding our lost half "out there somewhere," we will experience that completeness again.

THE ROMANCE CYCLE

Looking outside the hut gives rise to the cycle of romance. At the beginning of the cycle, we start with a sense of incompleteness—a vague feeling that something important has been lost and that we must find it again in the quest for the Beloved. It is this feeling of incompleteness that gives rise to the myth of the soulmate—the myth that somewhere out there in the confusing minestrone soup of humanity is our perfect other half, the one who can complete us and make us whole.

I had a friend who was strong on this topic of soulmates. He believed that by eliciting the energy of the soulmate within himself, he would draw the perfect external soulmate who was already out there somewhere waiting to meet him. In his opinion, the first woman he married was this perfect soulmate. A year or two after we met, however, he decided he had been mistaken. Now, he told me in glowing terms, he had found his real soulmate, who was even more perfectly attuned to him in every way. His faith in the process of locating his soulmate had been reinforced. Well, to make a short story even shorter, the second soulmate only lasted a couple of years, and that relationship also ended in disappointment and frustration. Not for long, however, for he then found a third perfect soulmate (the two previous perfect soulmates having been gross errors of judgment), who was in fact the ideal woman and the other half of his soul. As I write this book, my friend is going through his third divorce. This kind of mythology arises out of the belief that "I am an individual person; I am incomplete; and somewhere out there in time and space is the other half of me, who will complete me and make me feel whole again." Many films and popular novels reinforce this myth.

In the second phase of the romance cycle, we meet an external person and project these expectations and fantasies onto them. If the other is willing to play this game, unbridled euphoria may result as both people have the illusory experience of having found their other half after so many lonely eons of searching. Of course, this euphoria is reinforced by various biological urges. This "honeymoon" period is accompanied by a euphoric high not significantly different from the bliss of mystical experiences. Although the house seems well-built, the foundation is laid on shifting sand.

The third stage of the romantic cycle is one of disillusionment. We start to find that the other, whom we had taken to be our perfect other half, the solution to all our loneliness and longing, is not in fact living up to the fantasy we have projected onto them. Simultaneously, the ways in which we have subtly compromised our own life to fit in with the other's needs and expectations become an unbearable strait-jacket. In the third phase of the romance cycle the feeling of incompleteness and fragmentation is actually amplified, and we end up feeling more incomplete, dysfunctional, and neurotic than we did before. Rather than a completion, the other becomes a mirror in which we see reflected our own experience of fragmentation. Soon we find that the one we have taken to be our missing half also feels fragmented and incomplete, and we are left with two fragments who increasingly mirror each other's frustration and unhappiness. This is the dilemma and pain of romantic love.

The fourth stage of the romance cycle is one of dissolution. It is characterized by anger, disappointment, a feeling of entrapment, and a desperate need to return to the now-idealized state of aloneness and self-sufficiency. It usually involves a sense of waking up from a dream. We ask ourselves how we could have been so stupid. We look at the other with fresh eyes and see them as another human being just as incomplete and neurotic as we ourselves feel inside. At this stage we become disillusioned and cynical about the idea of romance. It is this phase that brings the formerly starry-eyed couple to divorce court and returns them to a feeling of abandonment and isolation.

In the fifth stage of the romance cycle, we return to being alone. It is often a phase of healing, in which we experience our greatest growth in maturity and come closest to perceiving the true reality of the situation from a greater perspective. Slowly, as learning is integrated, we come to forgive the other with the realization that it was not their "fault" that the relationship unfolded the way it did. This is often a time of introspection and spiritual inquiry, and it may even be the springboard that catapults us out of the romance cycle altogether and leads us to search for the Beloved within. Unfortunately, however, this phase often gives rise to loneliness and despair, causing us to miss the opportunity to grow as a result of the pain we have endured. It is at this stage that we rats are most tempted to go back down the maze in search of that imaginary chunk of cheese. In giving in to this familiar urge, we start the process all over again, and we "fall" back into a state of infatuation.

MEETING FROM WHOLENESS

How are we to break out of the cycle permanently and find wholeness? It is clear that most of us are not inclined to don the robes of a monk or a nun and live apart from ordinary society. We feel that our place is in the world, yet we recognize the emptiness of the fantasies we continuously live out in our externalized search for wholeness. What models do we have in our lives of mature and balanced relationship? What characterizes the co-existence of male and female incarnations where real love, *agape*, flourishes? Like many of us, I have looked long and hard to find the answer to this question. Clearly, relating is nourishing when it is a meeting from wholeness rather than a search for wholeness. We have all encountered those rare couples who come to mutually discover a place of self-sufficiency, a recognition of their own innate wholeness and therefore their own internal masculinity and femininity. Now, rather than looking to the other to feel good, we look through the other, like a window, and see looking back at us the same Beloved that is our own eternal nature. This meeting arises not out of need, but out of an overflow of wholeness rejoicing in meeting itself.

The most beautiful and inspiring examples of this kind of meeting from wholeness are two people who join together out of a shared commitment to freedom and awakening. There is the sense of walking together hand-in-hand, rather than walking towards each other hoping that the meeting will fulfill some need. In the same vein, it is like looking out towards a gorgeous view and enjoying it together, rather than looking to the one sitting beside you to see the view reflected in their eyes. Joe and Guin Miller, who lived in San Francisco sharing crazy wisdom with others, shared this kind of love between them. And Stephen and Ondrea Levine have made it their life's work to share with others their discovery of this secret.

We find this kind of mature meeting also occurring when two people have dedicated their lives to something greater than their own individual needs. Couples who join together in an environmental, social, or political cause may find the same kind of wholeness if their attention is thoroughly given to something greater than themselves. Similarly, it may occur where there is a shared devotion to children, though in my experience this is more rare than when there is a spiritual or dharmic basis to the meeting.

Occasionally with older people who have been married for a long time we find a sweet friendship that transcends the romance cycle because they have simply outlived or exhausted it. They may have gone through the cycle enough times to recognize the futility of looking to the other for fulfillment. But even this kind of friendship, which develops over time with older couples, may entail a large measure of compromise and restriction.

THE BLUEPRINT

In this chapter we are concerned with dissolving the romance cycle in the recognition that what is being sought outside is in fact inside, that the needle was dropped inside the hut. The very fact that we look outside for completion shows that we carry a blueprint inside of what we are looking for. It is like looking for a lost book. To carry out the search, you must have an internal image of what the book looks like. It is only this internal picture that allows you to determine whether the book you have found is the one you have been searching for.

The same is true for anything we seek. In many ways the internal image that fuels the search for romantic love is shaped by our conditioning. We tend to fall in love with an approximation of what we lack within ourselves. Most men and women fall in love with the same type of person physically, emotionally, and mentally time after time. For example, a driven, "type A" person may subconsciously be drawn again and again to a soft, affectionate, easy-going lover. Similarly, a shy, withdrawn person may subconsciously be drawn to an extraverted, outgoing mate. Someone who is feeling bored or unfulfilled in their life may carry a romantic image of a lover who would bring them adventure. In one sense, our external romantic quest is an attempt to find the qualities we have been missing in ourselves that we believe would restore us to a sense of wholeness. Or it may be that our subconscious image is based on the qualities we loved, or found missing, in one of our parents.

Some of these internal images are based on the collective stereotypes we share as a culture. These days the desirable woman is fun-loving, slim, athletic, and outgoing; the ideal man is muscular, cool, and affluent. In the forties and fifties, the ideal woman was a homemaker who took care of her children, while the ideal man was responsible, hard-working, and dependable. In the nineteenth century, the ideal woman was plump, a desirable sign of the times. These cultural forces all take a part in shaping the subconscious images we project onto others.

Everything in the romantic search for opposite-gender love can be equally true with same-gender love. In a homosexual love relationship a woman might feel that she is missing within herself certain aspects of the feminine or masculine psyche, which she looks to another woman to complete. Likewise, a man may look for a composite of male and female qualities in another man for his own completion. Generally it is only when we have explored this tendency to externalize and have been disappointed enough times that we are willing to look beyond the myth of the external lover to find the true Beloved within our Self. (For a detailed discussion of the quest for romantic love from an archetypal perspective, see the work of Jungian analyst Robert A. Johnson, particularly his three popular books *He*, *She*, and *We*.)

Through the repeated frustration and disappointment of searching externally, we are led to an internal search. We could call this spiritual maturity, when we come to see that all the outgoing tendencies of the mind are leading us away from real happiness. The way to return to this innate wholeness and happiness is to directly recognize and experience the images we project onto the external world.

The wholeness we are looking for is androgynous; it is neither male nor female, and at the same time both male and female. Initially, it may be difficult for most people to experience this in a completely disembodied form; instead, we can allow this energetic blueprint to manifest itself as an image in consciousness. Once it has been directly experienced and brought out of the shadows, we can merge with it completely and come to a place of integration that includes both the qualities we are familiar with and those we have projected outward. We see this same merging in the sacred art of Tibet and India, where Vajrasattva and other deities have their consort sitting astride them, locked in sexual embrace, depicting the wholeness of the male and female aspects of consciousness together as they continuously replenish each other.

In the session outline that follows, we use the energy of the external search for romantic love to return us to a recognition of our own innate wholeness.

Session Outline :
The Beloved

Step 1: Pre-Induction Talk.
Step 2: Relaxation Induction.
Step 3: Setting the Scene.
Step 4: Enlivening the Heart.
Step 5: Emanating the Beloved
         from the Heart.
Step 6: Speak to the Beloved.
Step 7: Listen to the Beloved.
Step 8: Move Fluidly from
         Speaking to Listening.
Step 9: Become the Beloved.
Step 10: Speak as the Habitual Identity.
Step 11: Merging and Harmony.
Step 12: Merge both Forms
         Back into Emptiness.
Step 13: Suggestion.
Step 14: Counting Back.

SESSION OUTLINE:
THE BELOVED

Step 1: The Pre-Induction Talk.

Speak with your friend about her experience of falling in love and going through the romance cycle, particularly about any relationship in which she is currently involved. From this information you will be able to find out where she is in the cycle. You also might want to ask about her previous experience of romantic relationships and see to what degree she has seen through the myth of trying to fulfill needs externally. Generally you would not do this session with someone who is madly in love, i.e., in the throes of stage two. They would have no incentive to let go of the outer image and find the internal blueprint. This session works well when some state of disillusionment has set in.

Step 2: Relaxation Induction.

Induce a state of relaxation in one or more of the ways described in Chapter Three.

Step 3: Setting the Scene.

Guide your friend to find an appropriate place where she can meet this internal blueprint. Here is how you could say this.

> *And just because you are deeply relaxed now,*
> *So it's easy for you to imagine yourself*
> *To feel yourself*
> *Walking in a natural place.*

Using the present tense, you can ask your friend to notice flowers, the sunlight, and other sensory details, using as many of the senses as possible. Ask her to imagine a place where she can sit quietly and alone.

Step 4: Enlivening the Heart.

Now, as your friend is sitting quietly and alone in this place in nature, ask her to begin to bring the breath into the Heart, like this:

> *And now that you are*
> *Sitting comfortably and alone*

Here in this place in nature,
I'm going to ask you to begin to bring the in-breath
And to center it into the middle of the chest.
So with every in-breath you enliven the quality
Of the Heart.
That's right, and with the out-breath
You can allow this place in the Heart
To expand,
And to permeate more of the body.
With the in-breath, focusing the attention into the Heart,
And with the out-breath allowing this place of the Heart
To expand and to permeate the body.
You can begin to do that now.

Give your friend enough time to continue to use the breath in this way to enliven the quality of the Heart with the in-breath, and with the out-breath encourage her to feel the quality of the Heart permeating the body.

If you are trained in any kind of energy work, like Reiki or pranic healing, you can use your hands to increase the focus of energy in the center of the chest, in the Heart.

Step 5: Emanating the Beloved From the Heart.

When the energy feels more intensely centered in the Heart and there is more of the longing that gives rise to the romantic quest, ask your friend to allow this energy to project itself out from the body and to become externalized as an image in front of her, the image of the Beloved, which until now has been projected onto other people.

And now, as this energy in the Heart
Becomes stronger and stronger,
You can allow it to
Burst forth like a flame,
To burst forth and to become a form in front of you,
This form of the lover,
This form of the Beloved
Which you have always been seeking in the outside world.

Give your friend plenty of time to notice as many sensory details about this Beloved as possible: the hair, the color of the eyes, the way the Beloved is dressed, and so forth.

Step 6: Speak to the Beloved.
Ask your friend to tell this projected image of the Beloved about all her needs, all her fears, and everything she has sought in the external world.

Step 7: Listen to the Beloved.
Ask your friend to become soft and quiet and to listen as the Beloved speaks back to her.

Step 8: Move Fluidly From Speaking to Listening.
Move freely between talking and listening as this dialogue ensues. Encourage your friend to be as vulnerable and open as possible, expressing everything she has held back.

Step 9: Become the Beloved.
Once the dialogue has become more intimate, and an honesty and openness has developed, you can ask her to become the Beloved. Just as you did in Chapter Six, allow plenty of time here for your friend to feel what it is like to be this apparent other, to feel how it is to embody the Beloved from the inside. If your friend is a man, ask him to feel what it is like to be soft and feminine and to have breasts. If your friend is a woman, ask her to feel what it is like to be in a male body and to have male genitals.

As the Beloved, ask her to look through these eyes and see the person she has taken herself to be and to speak from here. In particular, ask your friend, as the Beloved, to tell this habitual identity how much love he (the Beloved) feels for her, how he will always be there for her, and how he is actually a part of her true identity.

Step 10: Speak as the Habitual Identity.
Ask your friend to come back to being herself again and to speak once more from this place. Keep encouraging the expression of feeling. In this way the pathways of the Heart are opened. If the emotional aspect of the meeting seems suppressed, use the breath to enliven it.

Step 11: Merging and Harmony.
Continue to shift between embodying the Beloved and embodying the habitual identity, speaking back and forth. Encourage your friend in both roles to express the unconditional giving and fulfillment of internal needs. In this way the kind of harmony and merging that has always been dreamed of in the external world occurs internally. Pay as much attention as you can to physical sensations, to the way it feels in the body to be here in this place.

Step 12: Merge Both Forms Back Into Emptiness.
Now ask your friend to come closer and closer to the Beloved until they embrace. Some people like to play music during this part of the session. During this embrace, you can suggest that the two identities are merging together into one wholeness that includes all the male and female qualities. Finally you can suggest that even this integration merges back into the formlessness from which it arose, leaving neither one nor the other. Now, as this unmanifest spaciousness, she can feel both the male and the female emanations latent within her own nature.

Step 13: Suggestion.
Now you can use the kinds of suggestions mentioned in Chapter Three, but here you can particularly use suggestion that transcends the limiting sense of gender. The best thing is to use language that your friend has already used herself during the session, but here are some other examples for you to experiment with.
You are both male and female.
You are whole.
You are undivided.
You can fully allow this male energy
And this female energy
To express in every aspect of life.

Step 14: Counting Back.
Bring your friend back by counting from five to one, as we described in Chapter Three. Encourage her to fully embody this feeling of integration and wholeness.

THE EFFECTS ON OUTER LIFE

What effect does this session have on an individual life? I have done it with many different kinds of people in different life circumstances. In every case there was a return to feeling more whole and integrated and a transcending of the obsessive needs that are generally projected outward. Nevertheless, the way the session affected each person's outer circumstances was quite different. Letting go of a need-based way of relating doesn't necessarily lead to celibacy. But it does generally lead people to approach relationships in a more whole and self-sufficient way, with a feeling of an overabundance of love, rather than from a need to be loved.

When someone is not in a relationship, this way of working tends to break down the neediness that can lead to isolation or unhealthy relationships in future. When we are alone in life for a period of time, the feelings of incompleteness, neediness, and loneliness that arise can make it more difficult than before to meet someone new. All the world loves a lover, but "nobody wants to know you when you're down and out." When we move through life from this feeling of wholeness and integration, there is more of a chance of experiencing healthy love and connection outwardly without its being based in obsessiveness or fear.

With people who are already in relationship, this session has the effect of taking their partner "off the hook." Now the external lover is no longer seen as the source of all nourishment and wholeness, but rather as a friend—someone who is essentially whole, but who also may experience feelings of incompleteness. The sense of walking together side-by-side is restored, and there is no need to rush towards each other in desperation. Most commonly, this kind of session leads towards what we call a "dharmic relationship," a meeting to support wholeness and integration. Stephen and Ondrea Levine speak about this eloquently in their book *Embracing The Beloved*,[5] and anything I say about such relationships merely reflects what they have already said so well. Their book is highly recommended.

Of course, some external relationships do break up once this sense of integrated wholeness is restored within. This is especially common when one member of the couple finds a greater source of internal wholeness and the other is unwilling to let go of the addiction to otherness. For many who are sincere about waking up from the dream of separation, the greatest challenge is to let go of the attachments that were formed in the past out of a sense of need and to be willing to move forward alone, if necessary. This was Gautama's dilemma when he returned from the trip outside the palace with his charioteer. Legend has it that he stood in the doorway for an agonizing moment, poised between his attachment and responsibility to his wife and young baby and his allegiance to the longing in his Heart to live a life dedicated to the Truth of the Self. I have also stood on the same razor-sharp threshold, although perhaps I did not have the courage to jump one way or the other as decisively as Gautama did. This can be an excruciating place to be, especially when children are involved, as it carries with it feelings of guilt, the stigma of society, and the pain of residual emotional attachment. Once this mystery of the whole Heart reveals itself, however, nothing that is out of tune with it can remain for long in one's life.

The following case histories reveal what happened to two very different people in two very different situations after disengaging the tendency to obsess over the external. These vignettes illustrate the possibilities inherent in this kind of session.

CASE HISTORY: ELIZABETH

Elizabeth had devoted her life to awakening and freedom and had spent much of it living in spiritual community or on retreat. When she came to see me, she was in her mid-forties. Despite the many retreats she had attended, the diligence of her practice, and the depth of her insight and realization, she was still haunted by a lingering feeling of sadness and deflation. When we first talked, she was unaware of the source of this feeling, attributing it to some forgotten "past karma." As we talked further, however, it became clear that she deeply regretted that she had never been involved in a romantic love relationship for any extended period of time. The more we spoke, the more it became apparent that she secretly feared that the rest of humanity was enjoying some forbidden fruit called "romantic love," from which she was sadly excluded.

In this particular case, the session required a much longer pre-induction talk to help her feel comfortable with exploring what she felt she had been missing. As our examination deepened, so did her feelings of sadness and failure; at the same time, the image of romantic love and a romantic lover crystallized in her awareness. After we did the induction, she was able to get in touch with the longing in her heart. As we intensified this feeling through the breath, Elizabeth was able to visualize and sense the blueprint that had been locked until now in the hidden recesses of her imagination. One of the reasons she felt justified in her loneliness was that she was uncommonly tall. As the emanation of her lover became more embodied, Elizabeth found herself meeting face-to-face with a giant, an impossibly tall man to whom her height was of no concern. The session then unfolded in a deeply touching way.

Elizabeth found that she was able to fall into a spirit of trust and vulnerability with this image, which was indeed a projection of her own mind. As a result, she was able to release and express all the pent-up feelings of longing, awkwardness, and disappointment that had characterized her adult life. What unfolded between this masculine and feminine dimension of her own Heart was a gentle, sweet friendship characterized not by passion or attachment, but by honesty and tenderness.

Because Elizabeth had adopted many typically male characteristics over the years, so her inner man similarily embodied many feminine qualities. Just as she had become somewhat tough, disciplined, and self-critical, he was loose, soft and forgiving. We actually went back and developed this nurturing internal relationship over three consecutive sessions. Each time her pent-up feelings of undeservedness melted as she was able to find the fulfillment of her romantic dreams within herself, with this internal lover.

By the end of the third session, she told me that she felt free of the need to look outside herself. She was no longer eyeing each new man who arrived at the retreat center to see if this might finally be "Mr. Right," and she felt resigned to live out the rest of her life devoted to the inner marriage only.

Less than three weeks after our last session, Elizabeth made a new friend. Significantly, it never crossed her mind in the initial meeting that this was anything more than a friendship between a dharma brother and a dharma sister. She told me that her new friend had a similar background to her own and had used the spiritual life as a way to deal with his deep feelings of isolation and unworthiness. He was, incidentally, almost seven feet tall!

As their evening walks and talks became longer over the days of his visit to the center, a deep empathy developed between them, not out of any sense of romantic expectation, but out of a profound understanding of the condition in which they both found themselves. As of this writing, Elizabeth and her new friend are living together. And, interestingly enough, their relationship seems more stable and less subject to the usual tensions than romantic liaisons entered into with higher expectations.

CASE HISTORY: ANNA

When I met Anna, she was in her late fifties and had already been married with children for more than twenty years, although she could hardly bear to be in the same room with her husband. A "social drinker," he treated his wife more like a cook and laundry service than a marriage partner. Over the decades, she had found ways to anesthetize her feelings and her expectations of any emotional nourishment in life.

Our first session focused on her relationship with her husband, using the framework we have discussed in Chapter Five. For the first time she experienced herself setting boundaries in the relationship. By becoming herself and then fully embodying her husband's point of view, she came to realize that she had withheld communicating the many frustrations in her marriage. The more the communication with her husband deepened, the more clear it became that it was time to separate and move on. Her children were now grown, and she realized that the only thing that still kept her in the marriage was a feeling of lethargy and hopelessness.

After our second session, Anna told her husband that she wanted a divorce. In our third meeting we explored her romantic longing, which had been stifled by a marriage that had lost its nourishing quality. As she was able to allow the emanation of her internal masculine qualities to present themselves and to find the flow of nourishment between her habitual identity and the part of her that had been suppressed, quite the opposite happened than in the previous case history. She felt less and less of a need to look outside, and as she merged this internal lover back into her own Heart, she sank more deeply into a place of silence, integration, and wholeness.

She and her husband did separate a few months after her last session, and for the first time in her life she began to enjoy her solitude. She realized that she had always looked outside herself for what she wanted, but that what she was looking for all along was her own Self, which was always readily available. Anna now lives by herself and carefully balances her time so that she is able to spend as much as she needs alone, tuning in to her own Heart, her own feelings, her own being.

CHAPTER 9

THE GURU IS IN

The question of whether there is God, truth or reality can never be answered in books, by priests, philosophers or saviours. Nobody and nothing can answer the question but you yourself and that is why you must know yourself. To understand yourself is the beginning of wisdom.[1]

JIDDU KRISHNAMURTI

We have explored how both negative, problematic states and positive, desirable states can act as obscurations to resting in our original nature. In this chapter we will see how even our attachment to the teacher or guru can become an impediment to freedom.

Throughout recorded history, awakening has occurred through direct connection with a living teacher. In the *Guru Gita*, one of the oldest scriptures in India to talk about the guru-disciple relationship, it is said that one moment of the guru's grace is equivalent to unimaginable amounts of practice. Many teachers maintain that it is impossible to be liberated from the grip of *samsara*, from the endless cycle of birth and death, except through the grace of a realized Master.

Traditionally an aspirant who has glimpsed the possibility of liberation approaches a teacher and then undergoes a series of tests before being accepted as a disciple. This often begins a long and arduous relationship in which the disciple's surrender and complete obedience is tested and molded in rigorous ways. Detailed accounts of this kind of guru-disciple relationship can be found in Irina Tweedie's book *Chasm of Fire*; Reshad Feild's *The Last Barrier*; Paramahamsa Yogananda's *Autobiography of a Yogi,* and in all of Ouspensky's descriptions of his relationship with Gurdjieff.[2] The traditional guru performs many functions for the disciple, all of which contribute to the journey home. Initially the guru provides the disciple with a living testament to the fact that it is indeed possible in this lifetime to wake up from the dream of separation and to embody the beauty and radiance of the Self. A master also dispels the student's intellectual doubts by explaining the true nature of reality in words and concepts, thus sharpening the desire for direct experience. The Sage Vashishta brings Rama to awakening in this way in the *Yoga Vashishta.*

In addition, the guru's presence emanates a transmission of energy, or *shakti*, an aura of blissfulness, an expansion and heightened alertness that is transferred to the disciple who is open to receive it, awakening the dormant energy in the disciple and provoking a direct realization of the Self. Lastly the guru provides a focus for the feelings of devotion which arise in the opening Heart, a means whereby the limited, selfish desires and motivations of the student can be channeled towards a higher teacher and teaching.

We often forget that this kind of master-disciple relationship took place historically in rather isolated, intimate contexts. Traditionally, in Tibet or India, the guru had a handful of close disciples with whom he or she worked intensively in isolation from the rest of the world. Hence the relationship was not subject to many of the pitfalls that occur in the world at large, outside such a protected environment. In this chapter we will examine these pitfalls and see how they can be circumvented by a direct approach to the Self. We will present session outlines that can remove the feeling of separation and hierarchy with a teacher and can deprogram an old relationship with a teacher that is now acting as an impediment to awakening.

A MEETING OF CULTURES

The guru-disciple relationship is not indigenous to our culture; it has been transplanted, sometimes awkwardly, in the past few decades.

In the generation born here in the West beginning shortly after the Second World War, the thirst for liberation has been extraordinarily intense. When this generation began coming of age in the late sixties, it called forth many teachers from Eastern traditions. The most famous of these included Maharishi Mahesh Yogi, Swami Muktananda, Yogi Bhajan, A.C. Bhaktivedanta, Bhagwan Shree Rajneesh, and Guru Maharaji. There were also countless other less conspicuous Buddhist, Taoist, and Hindu teachers who established followings in the West. The sixties and early seventies were a time when the promise of awakening and the scent of the Divine (not to speak of marijuana and patchouli oil!) wafted in the air.

By the mid-seventies, what had begun as a wild and spontaneous infusion of mysticism into Western culture became more institutionalized. Around many of these teachers there developed an inner circle, a hierarchy, accompanied by a massive acquisition of real estate and the solicitation of large donations of money from devotees. This phenomenon involved scores of spiritual groups, millions of seekers, and billions of dollars in assets. Each organization claimed to be *the* catalyst for a transition to a new age of spirituality. In the name of their own particular mission to save humanity, followers sometimes found themselves behaving in ways that on later reflection appeared to be in violation of their personal integrity.[3]

During the 1980s, a number of these organizations began to experience serious internal political conflicts and media exposés. Of course, the Western press added an unnecessary dose of cynicism and had difficulty understanding the original motive and purpose of such groups. Nevertheless, the downfall of these organizations as the result of alleged corruption, sexual misconduct, and misuse of funds was widespread.

By the early 1990s, a shift had taken place among the children of the sixties in their relationship to gurus, spiritual organizations, and "Truth." Many who had been most ardent in their devotion became disillusioned and bitter. Others, while grateful for the doorways that had been opened and the gifts that had been received, left their interest in organized spirituality and returned to the world of business or established society. Many became confused about how the sweet nectar of divinity could have been sipped from a cup that later turned out to be chipped and cracked. *Yoga Journal* covered these issues in depth, as did *Common Boundary* magazine, which published interviews with a number of ex-devotees from different groups who had undergone a process of recovery.[4]

Today we are faced with a new challenge. Among many, the passion for awakening to truth, love, and the dissolution of the old is stronger than ever. At the same time, those who have passed through the maturation of the past few decades have developed a resistance to hierarchical spiritual organizations. Now we are called upon to find the same Grace, silence, and mystery we felt at the feet of charismatic teachers in our own presence and in the meeting of friends.

Joe Miller was an ex-Vaudeville performer who fell awake (as he put it) here in the West, catalyzed by the teachings of Ramana Maharshi. Joe's teaching is completely Western in its language, its earthiness, and its insistence on democracy; no translation is required. Until his death in 1991, he conducted weekly walks in San Francisco's Golden Gate Park, followed by an evening of music with his wife, Guinn, on the piano. "I don't consider myself a teacher," said Joe. "I consider myself a friend, and that's the way I have always dealt with people. I look at it this way: one on one, that's where something happens. Sometimes it happens with a group, but that's not because you have communication. It is because you have communion."[5]

Joe Miller was a torchbearer. We need to have a more mature understanding of the nature and purpose of gurus, and we need to examine the ways in which an external teacher can be both a help and a hindrance, depending on our phase of development. Some movement is afoot in our collective consciousness in which the Heart itself is demanding that we embrace truth without the confines of a tradition, a label, or rules set down by an organization. Through the disintegration of spiritual hierarchies and organizations, we are being forced back into reliance upon our own nature, to meet in the Truth itself, without any implication of higher or lower.

THE PITFALLS OF THE MODERN GURU

When one enters into a guru-disciple relationship, especially when the guru is Eastern and the disciple is Western, there may be a tremendous amount of projection and fantasy, as well as differences in cultural expectations, of which the student is quite unaware. The traditional guru in Vedic or Tibetan cultures, or the traditional Zen master in Japan or China, had dozens or at most several hundred disciples. Hence he or she could maintain a personal relationship with each of them in which the specific needs and circumstances of the disciple could be addressed directly. Many of the spiritually oriented groups that have arisen in the West in the past few decades have gathered not dozens or even hundreds of disciples, but thousands or, in some instances, millions. Hence the original nature of the master-disciple relationship has undergone a metamorphosis in its translation from East to West.

We have treated the charismatic teachers who have come to the West like rock stars, idealizing them and imagining them to be beyond the pale of our ordinary sphere of human experience. We have created a mythology that distorts the facts of their past and fantasizes that their lives are different in every respect from our own. We have become fascinated by their habits and attempted to imitate them by eating the same foods, wearing the same kinds of clothes, and using the same language and mannerisms. Thus our emphasis has been more on a personality than on liberation, more on a phenomenon in name and form than on the namelessness and formlessness of our own Divine nature.

Competition and political manipulation inevitably develop in these groups through people's attempts to get closer to the teacher or to achieve what appears to be a position of greater importance in the organization. This also distracts them from their original motivation, the original call of the Heart that drew them to the teacher in the first place. Because the dynamics of the situation invite fantasy and projection, the perception of the teacher is often clouded by leftover disappointments with parents and other figures of authority, and by the unprocessed emotions and behaviors of childhood.

To perpetuate the movie of adulation, of course, we must leave only one part available for the Awakened One on the throne and thousands of parts available for the "extras" who must, because of their role in the drama, remain identified with seeking. The more we project the source of Truth, enlightenment, and love up there onto the teacher's podium, the more we remove the essence of guruness from the sphere of our own life. The less accessible the teacher is to direct interaction, the more invitation there is to project and fantasize, thus solidifying our identification as a seeker, one who does not know and is not identical with the same source of Truth and light. The higher the guru is placed in our projection, the lower we create our own identity.

In Monty Python's *The Life of Brian*, an essentially ordinary and innocent "bloke" named Brian is mistaken by the mass New Age culture of the time to be the Messiah. At one point in the film, Brian wakes up in the morning and throws open the shutters to find thousands of screaming would-be disciples waiting in the courtyard below.

"Please, Master, give us some guidance," they call out to him.

"I don't have any guidance," he replies. "Go away; leave me alone; piss off!" he shouts.

There is a shocked silence in the crowd. They look at one another in confusion. Then, out of the silence one meek voice calls out, "But Master, we do not know *how* to piss off. Please Master, teach us, that we may be able to piss off as you have instructed!"

Jack Kornfield, an eminent Western Buddhist teacher, has spoken and written about the complexities of the relationship between Eastern teachers and Western students. Not only are gullible Westerners the casualties of this phenomenon, he suggests, but so are the teachers from the East who are worshipped as spiritual super-heroes. Just as nothing corrupts like power, no corrupting power is so subtle and difficult to catch as spiritual power, with its seeming immunity to outside inspection. In their excellent book *The Guru Papers*, Joel Kramer and Diana Altstadt look deeply into the ways in which we miss the boat through our projections and fantasies.

Even when the teacher may be attempting to point the students' attention back to their own nature, the context in which this teaching is happening and the appearance of hierarchy and assigned roles can be counterproductive to the teaching itself. "The medium is the message," Marshall Macluhan pointed out more than thirty years ago. As long as one individual is placed on an elevated platform and made the special focus of attention, the meta-message is not, "We are all the same Self," but, "The one up front is the Self, and we who are on the floor listening are somehow lesser beings."

Meeting Poonjaji broke this habit in me. I had spent more than twenty years, more or less full-time, with teachers who were physically inaccessible, and hence very easy to project fantasies onto. I had benefited immensely from them in many ways, and I have tremendous gratitude for the lessons I learned. But the realization that "I am also the Self," that this Consciousness, Beauty, Truth, and Divinity is also my own nature, could never really be embraced because of the dynamics of the relationship. Poonjaji welcomed me in sameness from the very beginning. Not only his words, but his behavior in every moment dispelled any idea of hierarchy. He openly complained about the pains in his body. He admitted mistakes he had made in his life. He made no attempt to hide his ordinariness as a human being. Yet through this appearance of a human life, the mystery of the disembodied Divine essence, which is every being's true nature, shone through.

There was one particular afternoon, soon after our initial meeting, that really exposed my childish tendency to adulate and project outwards. I had gone to his house to return some work he had asked me to do. When I arrived he was dressed to go out to the market, and he invited me along. Believe me, this sort of outing had not been available before with other teachers I had deified. Now I was going shopping with God!

When we arrived at the covered market close to Poonjaji's house, he went to the stall where raw dhal and rice are sold. The shopkeeper wanted 14 rupees (about 50¢ in American currency) for a kilo of mung dhal. Poonjaji inspected it carefully and decided he only wanted to pay 13 rupees for this particular quality. So they began to dispute the price together. In that moment, I stepped back from the situation and saw what was happening. Everyone was behaving normally. The shopkeeper was being an ordinary shopkeeper, Poonjaji was being a typical Indian customer, and the other people in the market were all behaving quite sanely. Except me. I was staring in nervous adulation at my teacher, much as a teenager might behave on a shopping trip with Sting. In that moment, I saw the game I had been playing for so many years, which had actually kept realization at bay and had prevented me from hearing the essence of any teaching.

Poonjaji's ordinariness and accessibility, which deflate fantasies and addiction to idol worship, have made him a powerful catalyst for awakening in others. I saw the same thing in Krishnamurti when, after a talk in 1981, he joined the lunch line with everyone else, paper plate and plastic spoon in hand. Ramana Maharshi constantly refused special treatment, insisting that everyone visiting his ashram be served food before him, as a sign of respect to his guests. It is vitally important that we learn to distinguish between this genuine embodiment of our true Self, reflected back to us, and the "show biz" variety of personality worship, of which we have seen so many examples in the West in recent decades.

In Douglas Harding's futuristic novel, *The Trial of the Man Who Said He Was God*, the protagonist is forced to defend himself in court for acknowledging the awakened view that we discussed in Chapter Two. At one point in his defense before the jury, he says this about gurudom: "You'll gather that I'm not one of those spiritual teachers who gives his pupils the option, 'Either see who you are, or else surrender to me. If you aren't ready to find the true guru in yourself, at least find Him provisionally in me, as a first step. The second step, from me as your authority to yourself as your real Authority, may then follow.' Those aforementioned teachers include some great souls, and I'm not saying they are wrong. It's not that this roundabout road to enlightenment via devotion to a guru is closed, but that it's a long and difficult diversion, and few they are that emerge from it onto the main highway. I still have to meet a devotee who has come through and will tell you so. Accordingly, my message, day in and day out, to anyone who has half an ear, is, 'What, for heaven's sake, is wrong with the direct road to Yourself? It couldn't be better paved and easier going and safer—and shorter. In fact, all you have to do is face the right direction, and—like a shot—you've arrived at the Place you never left!' That 180° turnabout of attention is enough to see you right Home, instantly. But you are responsible for making it. Your attention isn't something I can get hold of like a wrong-pointing signpost, and twist around to point the right way. It's you who have to do that."[6]

Obviously, the tendency in human consciousness to create hierarchies has to be transcended if awakening is to become more commonplace. In a pyramid, there is room for only one at the top and multitudes at the base. In a circle, by contrast, every point is equidistant from the center. Thus the guru can be everywhere and nowhere at the same time. By discovering and enlivening guru as our own essential nature, the external teacher becomes a mirror to remind us of who we are, an externalized image of our own Self. Therefore, all of life becomes the teacher. When Poonjaji asked me to teach a few years ago, he told me, "Share this with your friends. Travel door to door." He told me that from his awakening with Ramana in 1943 until his health forced him to stop traveling in 1992, he never allowed more than 15 people to gather around him. "Once a big crowd develops," he said, "you can be sure that something is no longer pure."

Tung-shan had this to say more than a thousand years ago. He could have written it today, as it sums up this theme so well.

If you look for the truth outside yourself,
It gets farther and farther away.
Today, walking alone,
I meet him everywhere I step.
He is the same as me,
Yet I am not him.
Only if you understand it in this way
Will you merge with the way things are.[7]

THE ROLE OF THE TRUE GURU

When the sense of separation between external guru and one's own Self has been dissolved, the teacher is revealed to be an externalization of that which is otherwise invisible behind one's own eyes. "The Master is within," says Ramana Maharshi. "Meditation is meant to remove the ignorant idea that he is only outside. If he is a stranger whom you await, he is bound to disappear also. What is the use of a transient being like that? But so long as you think you are separate or that you are the body, an external master is also necessary and he will appear to have a body. When the wrong identification of oneself with the body ceases, the Master will be found to be none other than the Self."[8]

We find that all the roles the outer teacher performs—inspiration, provider of teachings, giver of understanding, transmitter of energy or shakti, object of devotion—can be fulfilled internally when we deepen our understanding of what the word *guru* really means.

The word *guru* in Sanskrit can be literally translated as "that which causes uproar, fear, and alarm to go away."[9] The meaning has slowly shifted in colloquial usage to refer to a person giving a teaching. But what actually causes the turmoil of the fearful mind to disappear? Surely it is only the Peace and Silence of the Self. This Peace and Silence and Truth is who you are. Its reflection may be found by fixating onto an outer form, or it may be found by turning the attention back to your own nature.

There is a deep resistance, especially in the Western psyche, to fully acknowledge that what we are seeking is our own inherent nature. Perhaps because we are so aware of the insanity of the posturing ego, we are afraid to bring the search home to our own subjectivity. Carl Jung talked about this antipathy in the Western mind to owning Truth: "The identification of the Self with God will strike the European as shocking. It is a specifically oriental realization as expressed in Sri

Ramana's utterances. Psychology cannot contribute anything further to it, except the remark that it lies far beyond its scope to propose such a thing."[10] And yet we do find this view expressed occasionally by Christian mystics like St. Athanasius, who said, "God became man in order that man might become God."[11]

Here in the West, we have sought out teachers from other cultures partly out of a need for practical guidance. The values we inherited from our parents no longer satisfy us, and we see our culture in decay. As a result we look for someone to provide a structure, a set of do's and don'ts to ease our discomfort. We want formulas about what to eat, how to deal with our sexual energy, what kind and color of clothes to wear, where and with whom we should live. While the external teacher may initially fulfill this need and provide prescriptions and rules for a spiritual life, this help can easily become a hindrance. To use the words of an external teacher in this way leads to dogmatism and ultimately the dog house.

As soon as we try to use a teaching to make a generalized set of rules that apply to all people at all times, we become followers of a fundamentalist cult, rather than responsible, awake expressions of consciousness responding purely to the demands of each moment. You might assume, for example, that vegetarianism is an unquestionable basis for a spiritual life and liberation. Yet Buddha, for many the quintessential example of enlightened consciousness in world history, was not vegetarian. Rama, the avatar of Hinduism, hunted deer for sport, and Jesus also ate meat. You might assume that smoking cigarettes could never be compatible with awakening, yet Nisargadatta Maharaj, revered by many as one of the greatest exponents of advaita in this century, not only chain-smoked during his discourses, but was even a beedie salesman by profession![12] Some would assume that celibacy would be an absolute requirement for a spiritual life. After all, Buddhist and Christian monks and nuns and Indian sadhus all take vows of celibacy. Still, we find that many of the greatest exponents of liberation, like Krishna, Rama, Ramakrishna, and Padmasambhava, were married, and many had children. Perhaps beyond question would be the assumption that the awakened state could not include violence or killing, yet Krishna's advice to Arjuna in the battlefield five thousand years ago was to fight and vanquish his enemies.

Every time we try to follow a set of rules as the basis of a spiritual life, we only trip over ourselves in guilt and hypocrisy. There is a wonderful story from the Tendai school in Japan that illustrates this. Four monks agreed to observe seven days of silent meditation together. For the first day, no one said a word and their meditation retreat began uneventfully. When the first night came and the oil lamps were growing dim, one of the monks could not help exclaiming to a servant, "Fix those lamps."

The second monk was surprised to hear the first one talk. "We are not supposed to say a word," he remarked.

"You two are stupid. Why did you talk?" asked the third.

"I am the only one who has not talked," concluded the fourth monk![13]

Rather than have us look to an external code of behavior, the real teacher encourages us to rely on our own nature for guidance. As a result, we discover that the Self is not different behind our own eyes than it is behind those of the teacher. Joe Miller puts it like this: "Each one of us is a microcosmic reflection of the macrocosm. In other words, within each one is a replica of everything that is contained in the solar system. All of the answers are within you. You have to find them by looking and inquiring into yourself."[14]

Initially, we may turn to a teacher for practical guidance only. As the thirst for the divine becomes stronger, however, we will seek instruction in how to quiet the mind and realize the Self. In the same way, when we look outward for spiritual instruction, we become fixated on the spoken words of the teacher or on books, audiotapes, videos, or discussion groups. We may accumulate an impressive spiritual library without necessarily comprehending the meaning.

One Zen Master exhorted his students, "Don't look at my finger, look at where it is pointing!" The true external teacher is pointing us back to the internal teacher, our own Self nature. "The guru is both external and internal," says Ramana Maharshi. "From the exterior, he gives a push to the mind to turn it inwards. From the interior, he pulls the mind towards the Self and helps in quieting the mind. That is guru's grace. There is no difference between God, Guru, and the Self."[15] The contemporary Dzogchen master Namkhai Norbu puts it this way: "The master will not say, 'Follow my rules and obey my precepts!,' but will say, 'Open your inner eye and observe yourself. Stop seeking an external lamp to enlighten you from outside, but light your own inner lamp. Thus the teachings will come to live in you, and you in the teachings.'"[16]

Divine guidance does not need to come through an external source; rather, it is available when we pay careful attention to the silence, to the source of our own consciousness prior to all conditioning. It is fully present now, even as I write and as you read these words. The place from which the words arise and into which they are received is the same. Pay attention to that place now and the purpose of all words and teachings is fulfilled. In this knowingness, when we discover gurudom as our own intrinsic Self, the need for an external source of guidance is transcended. Then we can take the same attitude as Yun Men, who suggests, "When you hear that some great Master has appeared in the world to liberate all beings, you'll immediately clap your hands over your ears. As long as you aren't your own Master, you may think you have gained something from what you hear, but it is secondhand merchandise, and not yours."[17] We are tuning in to a part of the mind which Patanjali refers to as *ritam bhara pragya* or "consciousness which knows only Truth."

Of course, we do not only look to the external teacher for words and instructions. There is a profundity of silence and a *shakti* that emanate from an awakened being. We may get divinely drunk on Grace and be transported beyond the confines of the mind. Some people experience profound awakenings of energy, movements of *kundalini*, or showering lights. However, the belief that these experiences are transmitted from the outside becomes an addiction that draws attention away from our own true nature. As Joe Miller puts it, "The meaning of transmission isn't that the teacher gives you anything. All he does is act as a reflector, so that the light that he has, or the mirror which he is, bounces back into you and you'll put out a little more."[18]

For several years after Poonjaji asked me to "share this secret with my friends," I did so in the traditional manner, by sitting at the front of a room and answering questions. An extraordinary grace and magic would infuse those meetings, which the people in the room often attributed to something I was doing or emitting. I knew full well that this was not the case, since I felt like I was basking in the same magic myself. Over the years, we have made a shift of gestalt. In our trainings and other gatherings we sit together in a circle of about 20 or 30 people. When anyone in the circle is willing to share their own immaculate Being with others, Grace is there, just as it is when one person sits at the front. I look around the circle and see the same depth and mystery looking back from every pair of eyes. In this way the guru is everyone and no-one at the same time. The guru frequency is fully present, but no one is excluded from it.

Try this with your friends. Invite them to come together once a week and sit silently for 30 to 40 minutes, turning their attention to their own nature, prior to concepts, emotions, thoughts, and changing phenomena. Then, when you have finished the silent sitting, invite them to speak in a way that fully acknowledges the experience. You can use a talking rock, just as some American Indian tribes have for many generations. Whoever has the rock has the right to speak, and everyone else in the circle listens. It is interesting—when you listen to someone with the respect you would pay to a teacher, they become infused with the wisdom and authority of the teacher. It may take a period of adjustment, but I suspect that the same Grace that comes over us in our gatherings will come over you, too.

"Grace is the beginning, middle, and end," says Ramana Maharshi. "Grace is the Self. Because of the false identification of the Self with the body, the guru is considered to be a body. But from the guru's outlook, the guru is only the Self. The Self is one only, and the guru tells you that the Self alone is. Is not then the Self your guru? Where else will Grace come from? It is from the Self alone. Manifestation of the Self is a manifestation of Grace and vice versa. All these doubts arise because of the wrong outlook and consequent expectation of things external to oneself. Nothing is external to the Self."[19]

Finally, we find in the external guru an object of devotion, a focus for the feelings of the opening Heart. As we discussed earlier, when this adoration is fixated on a specific name and form, on that which is born and will die, it only becomes the basis of fanaticism and isolation. How many wars have been fought in the name of undying love for and loyalty to a religious teacher? As we discover that Guru is the spontaneous arising of the Self which we are, then this devotion can burst forth freely without any feeling of separation arising. All of life is taken to be an embodiment of the Self, of guru. Nothing occurs which is not in some way a teaching. Ramana Maharshi referred often to Dattatreya, a figure famous in Indian mythology, who had 24 teachers that brought him to liberation, including the earth, the air, the sky, water, fire, the sun, the moon, a wild pigeon, a python, the ocean, a prostitute, and a child. "Who is a Master?" Ramana asks. "He is the Self after all. According to the stages of development of the mind the Self manifests as the Master externally. The famous ancient saint [Dattatreya] said that he had more than twenty-four Masters. The Master is one from whom one learns anything. The guru may be sometimes inanimate also, as in the case of [Dattatreya]. God, guru and the Self are identical."[20] Ramana Maharshi's guru, the founder of the lineage that includes Poonjaji, Robert Adams, Paul Brunton, Lakshmana Swami, and many more, was a mountain!

As we discover that guru is our own nature, so we also discover that it is constantly manifesting itself through every form in our life. "If you set the compass of your being right," says Joe Miller, "there isn't anything or anyone you encounter that you don't learn from."[21] The Native American traditions also cultivate the keen awareness that all of life is a teacher.

We are not suggesting here that there is never any benefit to associating with someone who has awakened to the Truth of things. That would be like throwing the baby out with the bathwater—and yes, there is a baby to be found in the bathwater. The processes that follow, which we teach in greater detail in our training, are designed to remove the feeling of separation from, and obsession with, the personality of the teacher, allowing the real role of guru to be fulfilled. We will cover three kinds of sessions. The first is designed to deepen the connection with an existing teacher and to remove the quality of externalization. The second is intended to be used with someone who carries feelings of fear and disappointment associated with a teacher who is no longer in his or her life, which may in some way inhibit the realization of Truth now. The third session is a way of accessing the qualities we may have shelved for later use, deferring them "until I am enlightened."

We are also not suggesting that you replace the dependency on an external guru with a dependency on a process or a technique. The processes suggested in this book are in and of themselves completely worthless if you see them as ends in themselves. It is only the state to which they can lead that is important. We are just as capable of worshipping a process as we are of worshipping an individual, and the practice of a technique can become as much of an addiction as spending time with a particular teacher in order to achieve a certain status in his or her spiritual hierarchy. The processes that follow are all playful ways to direct our attention back to inner guruness, to that which truly dispels ignorance and darkness.

These processes may deepen and enrich the connection with an external guru by revealing it as a meeting of the Self with the Self. This is the end to which every real teacher is anyway pushing us. We come to see that these roles are arbitrary identities within consciousness, and what we really are is both guru and seeker and, at the same time, neither guru nor seeker. The relationship between seeker and finder, between student and teacher, between *chela* and guru, is actually all happening within the consciousness that we are.

Session Outline :
The Internal Guru

Step 1: Pre-Induction Talk.

Step 2: Induction.

Step 3: Set the Scene.

Step 4: Invoke the Presence
of the Teacher.

Step 5: Speak to the Teacher.

Step 6: Listen as the Teacher Speaks.

Step 7: Alternate Between Speaking
and Listening.

Step 8: Become the Teacher.

Step 9: Speak as the Teacher-Self.

Step 10: The Touch and the Gift.

Step 11: Absorb the Form of the Teacher
back into the Formlessness.

Step 12: Suggestions.

Step 13: Count Back.

SESSION OUTLINE:
THE INTERNAL GURU

This session will allow you to help someone deepen the connection with a living or ascended guru and to dissolve any feeling of separation.

Step 1: The Pre-Induction Talk.

Talk about your friend's history with spiritual teachers and disciplines, and ask if there is someone she regards as a teacher now or any figure she turns to in this way without necessarily having a personal relationship. You could do this session with Jesus or Buddha just as well as with a living teacher. Finally, you might ask if she has had any negative experiences with teachers in the past who may have caused her pain. Although we will deal with this more directly in the second session outline, it is useful to obtain the information here, as such experiences might color her feelings toward the guru-frequency in general.

Step 2: Relaxation Induction.

For this session, you might want to use inductions that promote an increased awareness along with relaxation. One way to help facilitate awareness is to ask your friend to sit in a chair rather than lying down. You can also ask her, on the in-breath, to focus the breath between the eyebrows and, on the out-breath, to allow this focus to diffuse into the rest of the body. As she remains focused on the space between the eyebrows, you can count from one to ten, suggesting that the body will become more and more relaxed as she does so, and that awareness will simultaneously increase.

Step 3: Set the Scene.

Once you have finished the relaxation induction, you can ask your friend to create a suitable environment within herself in which to invoke the presence of the teacher.

And just because you are
More relaxed and comfortable now,
More inside and spacious,
So it is easy for you
To find yourself,
To imagine yourself,

To see yourself
In a place where you can
Feel comfortable to find (teacher's name)
Today.

She may find this place in nature or in an inner sanctuary or meditation room. Some people even find themselves meeting with the inner guru suspended in infinite empty space. Whatever place feels most suitable to your friend, ask her for as many sensory details as possible, all in the present tense. Now you can ask her to feel herself becoming relaxed and comfortable, sitting in a posture where she can invoke the presence of the teacher. This time of preparation and waiting becomes a second induction, within the one that you have already conducted.

And I'm going to ask you now,
Just because you are relaxed and comfortable,
Waiting here,
To begin to bring the breath up into the space
Between the eyebrows.
That's right,
To bring the in-breath into the space between the eyebrows,
And with the out-breath to allow this place
To radiate down into the rest of the body.

You can continue this kind of breathing for several minutes. Continue to guide her verbally throughout this time to keep her from daydreaming. After a few minutes, she will be very relaxed and, at the same time, more alert and conscious.

Step 4: Invoke the Presence of the Teacher.

Now you can ask her to begin to feel the presence of the teacher in this space. You can do this in a number of ways, depending on what she has told you in the pre-induction talk. If she already has a sense that the true teacher is within, you can ask her to allow this space between the eyebrows to project out an image or presence into the empty space before her. If she has a teacher in her life now to whom she looks for guidance and support, you can ask her to begin to feel the teacher's presence here in this space. You can facilitate this process by asking her to remember how she experiences her body, her emotions, and her thought processes when she is in the presence of the teacher. You can help to invoke this presence through music, chanting, or incense that reminds her of the teacher's presence, or even through a tape of the teacher's voice. Or she may have a connection with a teacher who is no longer in the body or whom she has never met in form. It doesn't matter which approach you choose; the main point is to invoke the spirit of guruness that speaks through all teachers. The more slowly this invocation unfolds, the deeper it will be.

Step 5: Speak to the Guru.

Now ask your friend to say whatever needs to be said to this teacher. She might want to ask specific questions, to burst forth in gratitude and devotion, or to express the longing to sink deeper into the mystery of the Self.

Step 6: Listen as the Guru Speaks.

Ask her to become quiet and to hear the response of the teacher. The more receptive she can be, the deeper will be the response. Sometimes there will be a long silence before any words come, and sometimes the silence itself may be the response.

Step 7: Alternate Between Speaking and Listening.

Now you can facilitate a dialogue between your friend and her teacher, asking for guidance and receiving answers. Of course, both the question and the answer are arising in the field of unlimited consciousness which is our true identity. This session allows the dance of seeking and receiving guidance to take place internally.

Step 8: Become the Teacher.

After your friend has asked and listened a number of times, she will exhaust her questions, and a silence and a spaciousness will fill the room. You will feel as though you are in the presence of awakened consciousness. Now you can ask her to take a deep breath and slowly to become the teacher.

This is the most powerful moment of the session. There is often a dramatic and palpable shift of energy as your friend shifts her identification from seeking to knowing. She may experience herself bathed in light, expanded and silent. Her speaking may feel like it arises from the depths of awakened consciousness itself. Allowing her to rest in this expanded silence will be more powerful than any words.

Step 9: Speak as the Teacher-Self.

Now you can see if she has anything to say, as the teacher, to this sense of self which has been habitual to her. You can encourage her to shift freely between identifying with the seeker who asks questions and becoming the Teacher-Self, which is the source of all answers. As she moves between these two, consciousness is learning that it can assume any point of view it chooses within the spectrum of seeking and awakening. It can place itself anywhere in an imagined journey from sinner to seeker to saint. All of these points of view are available to a consciousness that is liberated from the fixated addiction to a particular identity.

Step 10: The Touch and the Gift.

You can also ask your friend to experience the teacher reaching out and touching her somewhere on her body, sending a transmission of energy. She may also receive a gift from the teacher, an object or a sound or word, which she can put somewhere in her body. These are both ways of anchoring this meeting so it can be accessed again at any time.

Step 11: Absorb the Form of the Teacher into Formlessness.

Now you can ask her, with the in-breath, to absorb the form of the guru back into the place between the eyebrows and to find herself alone again. You can also ask her to absorb her own form back into formlessness in the same way, so she rests as the space in which both of these forms arise.

Step 12: Suggestions.

As your friend rests silently as this spaciousness, you can use suggestions to integrate the session into the rest of her life. You will be able to use suggestions that utilize her own language from the session or the pre-induction talk, but here are some others to fall back on.

You are this spaciousness.
You are the infinite source
Out of which all questions
And all answers arise.
You are this silence.
This silence is teacher itself.

There are some beautiful passages in *I am That* by Nisargadatta Maharaj and in David Godman's anthology of Ramana Maharshi's teachings, *Be As You Are* , that speak of teacher as a manifestation of the Self. You might like to read these passages aloud at this point in the session.

Step 13: Count Back.
Count your friend back from five to one, as explained in Chapter Three.

FANTASY OR INNER REALITY ?

There are a number of effects that come from accessing the spirit of teacher internally. First, we may receive answers to many of the practical questions we have sought to have answered externally: "Should I eat meat or not? How should I make money? What should I do about this particular health problem?" Although we may have teachers who are still alive, it may not be possible to turn to them for answers to every concern with which we need guidance. By accessing the teacher within consciousness, a channel opens that is permanently accessible. Second, even if we do have sufficient access to an external teacher, we may have questions we do not feel comfortable or confident enough to raise. For example, I know many Westerners who experience difficulty in discussing sexuality, money, or childhood conditioning with teachers from a very different cultural background.

Most important by far, awakening the internal teacher allows us to fulfill the true role of the outer teacher: to point us back to our own nature as the source of guidance. We tune in to a deeper, more silent level of the mind, from which all scripture has been written and from which all transmission of Truth has been spoken. This is Patanjali's *ritam bhara pragya*, consciousness that knows only Truth, which we referred to earlier. We are also cultivating devotion, surrender, and a sense of listening to something far more profound and reliable than the conditioned, conscious mind.

Zuigan was a Zen master who practiced this kind of internal dialogue. He used to call out every day, "Master!"
He answered himself, "Yes, sir."
Then he said, "Wake up!"
Again he answered, "Yes, sir."
After that he continued, "Do not be deceived by others."

"Yes, sir; yes, sir," he answered.[22]

We might question the validity of this kind of session. Are we really accessing the teacher within, or are we just using the limited mind to fantasize? Particularly if we meet Jesus or Paramahansa Yogananda, we might wonder whether it isn't just our own imagination telling us what we want to hear. We might believe that the enlightened state is far beyond the capacity of the limited mind to imagine or comprehend. Of course, this internal teacher is the product of imagination, a projection of the mind. But so is the external teacher in name and form. When unable to listen to the silence of its own nature, the Self creates an external image as the teacher to mirror its own essence back to itself.

Every teacher speaking *dharma* has told us that the awakened state is already your nature right now. The belief that it will only happen after so many decades or lifetimes of spiritual practice is the barrier that prevents us from experiencing illumination in this moment. Many of us have had the experience, whether in the presence of an awakened one or through the serendipity of life circumstances, of being thrown into a state of illumination, awakening, transcendence. We know that these states are possible now. By asking our friend to experience the presence of the teacher and then to become the teacher, we trick the mind out of its habit of identification with being bound.

As a facilitator, you will be able to distinguish between answers arising from the conscious mind and those that arise from silence by the extent to which they return your friend to a sense of her own inner knowing. When you hear an answer coming from a particular teaching or set of spiritual principles, such as, "You should be celibate because it says so in the Upanishads!" or "You should never eat meat because it violates the principles of Kashmiri Shaivites," you can tell that it is based on mental conditioning. You will be able to address this with the instructions we give later on dissolving points of view. However, when the answer that arises reflects a deeper knowing or sense of compassion, you will feel the silence reflected in your own nervous system.

We might also wonder whether the answer that arises is coming from the teacher as another being or from the inner space of "teacherness." Is this actually a form of channeling? It is this ambiguity toward which we are pointing attention. Is there any real separation between the Self and the external teacher? By working in this way, we are breaking down the imagined boundaries between our own consciousness and the teacher's. We can begin to see that the question and the answer both arise from silence. This session takes us deeper into the place from which divinity and Truth arise. How can we ever know what is the product of the creative capacity of thought and what is in some way independent of that? When awareness awakens from the appearance of separation and sees into the nature of things, it sees that no thing exists, internally or externally, that is other than the product of mind. "Guru is not the physical form," says Ramana Maharshi, "so the contact will remain even after the physical form of the guru vanishes. One can go to another guru after one's guru passes away, but all gurus are one, and none of them is the form you see. Always, mental contact is the best."[23]

ASCENDED MASTERS AND DEITIES

You can also use this session to meet and talk with masters who have been out of the body for a long time, like Padmasambhava or the Buddha, or even with angels or deities. Not only can it provide answers to questions, but it can enliven the particular aspect of the Self that the deity represents. For example, in the Hindu pantheon, Durga is an emanation of the Divine Mother who is both powerful and beautiful. Invoking and then becoming Her would enliven that aspect of consciousness in the person receiving the session.

Every culture and tradition has its own stories and icons to represent the ways in which the various aspects of the Self manifest and interact with each other. For example, the soft and beautiful aspect of the feminine principle appears as Tara in Tibet, Uma in Hinduism, and Aphrodite in the Greek myths. Ares, the Greek god of war, who embodies the fierce and warriorlike masculine qualities of the Self, is found as Subramanya in Hinduism and as Mars in the Roman Pantheon. Every culture on Earth has personified the various emanations of consciousness in this way, and it does not really matter which tradition you draw on to do this kind of session. None of these icons is external to you; they are all aspects of your own nature as it arises and gives birth to creation. For example, Anu Yoga, a Tibetan Buddhist practice, uses visualization through sudden manifestation and embodiment. Namkai Norbu describes it like this, "Anu Yoga uses a method of visualization only found in that school. The visualization is manifested in an instant, rather than built up gradually, detail by detail. One visualizes oneself as being the deity, and the sensation is more important than the details."[24]

Hameed Ali (who writes as A.H. Almaas) is the creator of the Diamond Approach, an integration of Western psychotherapy and mysticism. He feels that for the Self or Essence to become fully realized, each of its aspects, such as compassion, discernment, and strength must be awakened and embodied. By invoking and then embodying the deities who represent these qualities, you can facilitate this process.

DEPROGRAMMING EXISTING TEACHERS

There is another session that addresses teacher in a different way. Rather than deepening or strengthening the connection with a teacher, you can also clear the psychic presence of a teacher whose influence no longer seems to be healthy. While we will not go through this way of guiding the session step by step here, we do explore this way of working in our training.

Once you have finished the interview and induced relaxation, you continue to invoke the presence of the teacher. But now, instead of asking questions, you encourage your friend to go through a process of completing the relationship. She may want to express her gratitude for everything she has received, but you need to also explain why she needs to move on and to say good-bye. Sometimes people even need to express feelings of hurt, disappointment, or anger in the completion of the relationship. Because this session goes through a number of stages, it may take considerable time.

Robert, for example, had spent almost twenty years with a well-known and controversial Western teacher we will call the Master. Over the years he had risen to a position of importance in the Master's organization. He had known intense devotion and great intimacy. He had been singled out as the best disciple, while simultaneously being subjected to humiliation and sometimes totally ignored for months at a time. Finally he moved out of the center and for the first time in his adult life was no longer living in the Master's direct physical presence. Several months later, he had a powerful awakening to his own true nature. When I met him, he was immensely grateful to the Master for the preparation he had received during those grueling two decades. At the same time, he felt that the full flowering of his own realization was hampered by the extent to which his relationship with the Master remained unresolved. The Master appeared to Robert in dreams and left him with a feeling of residual dependency.

When we did a session together, Robert saw himself in a favorite place in nature. He had a feeling of being on his own ground. Then he invited the Master to join him there. He expressed his immense gratitude and love and then told the Master that he was unable to meet him in the same hierarchical way any more. He said that he would love to be friends and to meet as the Self meeting the Self, but that he was unwilling to set the Master above him and continue a subservient relationship.

When Robert became the Master, his voice and mannerisms completely changed as he fully embodied his former teacher's energy. The Master admitted that he had no one in his life he could really call a friend and that he would secretly love to meet someone in this way. All his relationships were from a podium looking down. Still, however, the Master, speaking through Robert's body, expressed his unwillingness to accept Robert's offer of friendship, because he remained convinced that his condition was somehow different from Robert's. Finally, Robert asked the Master to leave this sacred place in nature and not to return until he was willing to meet in true mutuality. He then invited all his current friends who were ready to meet him in a spirit of wakeful mutuality to come join him. The serious and stern atmosphere of the meeting with the Master was replaced by friendship and celebration.

Jean-Luc had been a Hare Krishna monk in the sixties and had taken a lifelong vow of celibacy. During his twenties he had traveled around the world for years in orange robes with no personal money or possessions. During this period he enjoyed a close personal relationship with the movement's founder, A.C. Bhaktivedanta Swami Prabhupada, and saw him as a savior who was beyond reproach.

In his late twenties, Jean-Luc met a woman through his travels as a missionary and discovered that his attraction to her felt much more important than his vow of celibacy. He disrobed as a monk and married her. They went on to have four children together and remained married until she died recently. Overnight, he found that he had become a demon in the eyes of the movement where he had previously been an apostle. He suffered ostracism, humiliation, and the threat of eternal hell.

When we did a session on this, Jean-Luc had already been out of the Hare Krishna movement for more than twenty years, and his teacher had died years before. But he still carried a deep wound which left him cynical and defensive about his own deep longing for awakening.

In the session, he met Bhaktivedanta on a beach. While his old teacher approached him in the traditional orange robes, shaved head, and staff, Jean-Luc was wearing fluorescent colored surfing shorts and sun glasses. Initially, it felt important to him to express his anger and hurt, not only about his own confusion, but also about his friends from that time, some of whom had committed suicide under the pressure of vows they felt unable to keep. As the session wore on, Jean-Luc began to feel divided between the deep gratitude and love he still felt towards Bhaktivedanta and the resentment he needed to release. Eventually he was able to experience two Bhaktivedantas. One was the head of a modern religious order and obliged by his beliefs to maintain a strict code of discipline and obedience. This one of the two identical twins on the beach spoke in a deep, monotonous voice and resembled a robot from a science fiction film. Next to him was an identical figure who was human, feeling, and heartful. When Jean-Luc saw this more human version, he could express his gratitude but also tell his old teacher that he did not have a deep enough understanding of the Western psyche. By forcing vows of celibacy and life-long austerity onto Westerners in their teens and early twenties, Jean-Luc explained, his teacher had hurt many people, albeit without malicious intention.

This human Bhaktivedanta simply looked down at the ground without saying anything. The gesture, which let Jean-Luc know that he had been heard, released him from the grip of fear and guilt that had haunted him since his abdication two decades before. He looked up into the sky, into the vastness that contained both Bhaktivedanta and Jean-Luc, and merged with it, with the real Krishna, who is after all an icon for the Self at the Heart of all beings. As a result of this session, Jean-Luc's passion for awakening to Truth was rekindled.

I have done this kind of session with many people who were involved with large hierarchical organizations where there was some degree of intimidation and fear. Often the teacher was seen with confusion as both the initiator of freedom and its inhibitor. Leaving the teacher— or, more accurately, asking the personality of the teacher to leave the inner world—carries with it the threat of damnation or of postponing liberation for millions of lives. However, once these two identities, seeker and teacher, are seen as manifestations of the mind, they can be dissolved back into the Self, into the real source of all teacher manifestation.

THE FUTURE SELF

There is a third session that can help people become one with what they project as the enlightened state. Instead of meeting with a currently embodied teacher or even an ascended master, they meet with the fantasy of the person they take themselves to be in some imagined future, where the spiritual journey has been completed.

Like a builder who carries a blueprint in his mind of the finished house, those who consider themselves to be on a progressive spiritual path carry an image of what the enlightened state will eventually be like. This image, which exists in consciousness now and is experienced energetically, emotionally and physically, is labeled "future." If the spiritual seekers are optimistic, the future label reads "after the next retreat." If they are less optimistic, it reads "later in this lifetime." If they do not hold out much hope, it reads "after many eons of reincarnation." Or, if they believe in the Buddhist bodhisattva vow, it reads "after all sentient beings have been liberated." Whatever the future label reads, they carry an image based on their reading, their fantasies, and the role models they have encountered. We can shortcut the idea in the mind of a future resolved state by meeting and then embodying this future self now.

In the future self session, you can conduct the pre-induction talk and the induction as in the session described earlier. Then, once your friend is in a deeply relaxed state, you can guide her through a future progression. There are a number of ways to do this. You could ask her to experience herself drifting up in a hot air balloon or on the back of a bird, or she could sprout wings and float above her present condition. Ask her to see herself flying above a river, which at its present location shows her life as it is right now. As she flies above this river, she follows its journey downstream towards the sea. With each new stage in the river, she is moving forwards in time, perhaps ten or twenty years. Move forward to the time when she imagines she will be finished with seeking. You could also induce the relaxation in a chair and then help her to actually stand up and walk forward, with each step representing a year into the future.

Once you have progressed your friend into the imagined future, you can guide her to the house where her future self lives. This might be her "enlightened" self, or simply a future self who has learned and integrated lessons she is still learning today. Ask her to notice the environment, the context. Is she living alone, with a family, or communally? Is it in the country or the city? All of these external factors could, of course, become the context of her life right now. She can ring the doorbell and meet her future self, who is now quite old, or perhaps aged only a few years. She can find a place where they can sit down and speak together. Now you can proceed as in the session outlined earlier:

she can ask questions, listen to answers, become the future self, and then come back either with a gift or merged energetically with the future self.

You can remind your friend of the issues she is facing now and help her progress to the imagined future where those issues have been resolved. This can be a helpful way to deal with any apparent obstacles to liberation. If anyone has the authoritative solution to a problem, it is your *own self* in a future state where the problem has been overcome. You can become that future self, look back, and say, "This is how I overcame that obstacle."

For example, she might say, "I cannot be liberated now because I am still concerned about money." As her future self she might observe, "There is no need to have your issues around money completely handled in order to be aware of who you are," or, "This is how I handle my money issues." Whatever advice is given can be utilized by your friend now.

The assumption behind this "game" (and I do suggest that you take these exercises playfully) is that any problem we postulate as existing in our lives also carries within itself its own solution. We have a thought that says, "This is the problem now, I am in the process of solving it, and at some imagined future time I will have solved it." We also carry an image of a future in which we will have solved it, if not in this life, then in some imagined heaven or future life. By becoming the image that holds the solution, we take perfection out of an imaginary future and embrace it in this moment.

Of course, this session is tricking the mind that wants to postpone until the future what is already the case in this moment. By working in this way, you can support the mind's assumptions while bypassing the imaginary time interval between the future state and now. Richard Bach's book, *A Bridge Across Forever,* allows its protagonist to meet his future self, who guides him through difficult circumstances. Later he travels back in time to meet and guide an earlier version of himself. The book brings us to the awareness that all these stops along the timeline exist now, some with the label "present" written below them, some with the label "past," and others with the label "future."

I encourage you to take the sessions in this book lightly and playfully. Remember that true fulfillment comes from silence, infinity, the mystery of the Self. These sessions are merely antidotes to the fixed idea that we are limited and imperfect and hence the only possibility of freedom and perfection lies out there in someone else or in some faraway future. Of course, we can also become fixated on another idea: "Now I am a great enlightened guru." You may know people who have fallen into this equally deluded state. These sessions offer the opportunity to remove the concept that I am suffering and bound in time—and therefore the opportunity to leave ourselves *undefined*. After any of these sessions, you may prefer to help your friend return from the session, not as her habitual identity, her future self, or the teacher, but as the ground of being out of which each of these forms has arisen.

CHAPTER 10

FROM GREED TO GRATITUDE

Fame or your True Self, which is more important?
The Self or wealth, which is worth more to you?
Gain or loss, which hurts you more?
Holding on to things only brings you pain,
Amassing wealth leads in the end to losses.
Be content with what is and you will not know
disappointment.[1]

Lao Tzu

Second only to the relationship issues we have discussed in earlier chapters, the challenges of making money and dealing with the materialism of Western society cause us the most difficulty in resting in our original nature. Once there has been an awakening to the Self, there is often a sense of disorientation that follows, as life begins to spontaneously reorient itself. There is a natural purification of everything that does not fully support the freedom of the Heart. We find old relationships and friendships dropping away, routines changing, the balance of the body shifting, and, more than anything else, the relationship to career and money being turned upside down. Work that was primarily motivated by greed, power, or fear becomes impossible to continue.

We spoke about this together at a Satsang I facilitated in Seattle a few years ago. Out of about seventy people present, all but two felt that their outer life was in transition. Many reported that the work they had done up to this point no longer seemed fulfilling and that the outcome of their lives no longer seemed to be so clearly within their own control. Some spoke of stepping into something unknown and unstructured.

As the realization of the Self deepens, it becomes our greatest priority, eclipsing anything else that had previously captivated our attention. This expresses itself in many ways. First, we see a dismantling of the complicated edifices we have created in our lives and a return to simplicity. Pursuits that had previously seemed essential to fulfillment lose their meaning, and our lives undergo an alchemical process of distillation. Second, with the erosion of belief in a separate identity, we move from isolation and an emphasis on individualism to co-operation and a focus on community. Many people, after awakening to the mysteries beyond the appearance of separation, move into communal housing or a rural community. Third, the life that had been devoted to serving the needs of the separate "I" is frequently given over to service, whether to the planet, to spiritual teaching, or to social change. In this chapter we will examine these three qualities and offer ways in which each can be cultivated and midwifed into manifestation.

These three consequences to the awakening beyond the dream of "me" emerge naturally on their own. As the boundaries between the individual and his environment evaporate, so do the structures that have been built on separation. When the relaxation into simplification, co-operation, and service is resisted, however, great suffering may result, sometimes far greater than had been present before. You may have already noticed this in your own life. When we can relax and allow the death and resurrection to occur on its own, the changes in our outer life can bring a deepening and stabilizing of realization and a further dissolution of the sense of "I."

People often complain that the glimpse of the awakened state is unstable. Sitting in meditation or in Satsang with a teacher, they may experience silence and clarity, but in their everyday lives they find it difficult to maintain. When we examine this issue together, we find that the difficulty results from an unwillingness to let life change and reorganize itself around this new sense of limitlessness.

For example, I knew a man in his early thirties who had met several awakened teachers. Many times he had glimpsed his own nature as vast, empty, and silent. His life had oscillated between phases of accumulating money (he had a knack for business) and phases of devoting himself fully to the mysteries of the Heart. Although he was pulled towards simplicity, he believed that he must first accumulate a certain amount of money through his business activities. He had worked out a five-year plan that would allow him to eventually retire and lead the life to which he was really drawn. No matter how much effort he put into his schemes, one thing after another went wrong, his life became more and more complicated, and he was miserable. When he came to Satsang with us in Seattle, where he lived, the misery would abate for a few hours, but it was immediately recreated by a life out of tune with his Heart. Finally the business went bankrupt, and he could no longer resist the direction his life was taking. Only then was he willing to relax into the simplification that was already trying to occur, and he no longer felt split between his Heart and his life.

SIMPLIFICATION

We live in a society that has gone mad with materialism and greed, and is structured around and supports separation, isolation, and a spirit of individualism. Particularly in the United States, but also increasingly in other countries, the primary measures that people use to evaluate the quality of their lives are their income and their ability to accumulate possessions. The American dream offers each family the promise of owning its own home, its own land, several cars, and every kind of modern appliance. Technology that was once a novelty few would embrace quickly becomes a necessity. Witness the meteoric rise of the answering machine, the fax, the home computer, the cell phone, the beeper, the high-speed modem for Internet access—the list of indispensable devices seems to grow from month to month. When I was a child in the 1950s, you could consider yourself lucky if you had a typewriter and a TV!

The American Dream turns into a global nightmare as we become enslaved by this need to possess. Besides the impact on the planet of constant manufacturing and the depletion of natural resources to create energy and goods, our devotion to this dream of comfort and convenience enslaves us. We devote all our energy and time to being able to own more and more. Joe Dominguez and Vicki Robin, in their book

Your Money or Your Life,[2] make the important distinction between our standard of living and the quality of our life. The standard of living is measured in purely material terms; it is determined by how much you earn, what kind of car you drive, how much your assets are worth, and how often you travel to exotic places to recover from the stresses of paying for all of the above. The quality of life, maintains Dominguez, is a more accurate measure of fulfillment. It takes into account whether you have time with your family, how relaxed you feel, whether you laugh a lot and have time to do the things you really enjoy. While our standard of living has undoubtedly improved over the last century, Dominguez maintains that our quality of life has been in steady decline. Beyond this understanding of the quality of life, we might even postulate another measure: the quality of consciousness, which is determined neither by material measures nor by one's degree of leisure, but by the degree of freedom of consciousness one experiences.

We are the only species on the planet that accumulates in this way. Neither cows, horses, lions, nor monkeys require transportation or clothing or homes made from other than immediately available materials. Even dolphins, which have a proportionally larger brain than humans, and quite possibly a more developed intelligence, do not seek to possess or accumulate. And it's only quite recently that this tendency has become so obsessive. Less than two hundred years ago this valley in Northern California where I sit to write was inhabited by a culture that lived in harmony with, and had deep respect for, Mother Earth.

Fortunately, I have had ample opportunity to see beyond the myth of accumulation as a means to fulfillment. In Marin County, California, my clients park their BMWs and Mercedes in my driveway when coming for individual sessions. I have also travelled in rural India, Thailand, and Indonesia, where I met people living on a few hundred dollars a year. Despite the material poverty, a greater prevalence of illness and infant mortality, and the pollution that has resulted from Westernization, I saw people laugh more in poorer countries and sensed more contentment and acceptance of life. I did not observe the anxiety and desperation that my California clients bring to our meetings.

Recently I attended a workshop where two of the participants were Western Theravadan Buddhist monks. During the meal breaks, they sat in a corner with their food bowls, which, along with their robes, were the only possessions they owned. At the end of the workshop some curious participants asked them why they had decided to give up so much. The reply was touching. "I don't really feel that I have given up anything of value," one of them replied. "On the contrary, I feel that I now have what is most valuable to me—my freedom."

Only by waking up from the dream of separation can we dismantle the structures held together by greed. Once the real source of happiness is revealed, the desire for more and more stuff will naturally fall away.

Of course, Western culture also has its advantages and its gifts. Diseases that once wiped out millions of people and made infant mortality commonplace have become extinct in the West. We are able to travel to different parts of the planet with relative ease, and we can learn from every culture through developments in technology and media. At this point no one could seriously suggest that we should return to the tribal life lived in the jungles of Africa or South America. As we awaken, however, from the collective trance of greed and separation, we do have the possibility of enjoying the developments we have made without being enslaved by them.

IMAGINE THIS

When I was in England recently, I had an interesting insight into our intuitive sense of the natural life. A group of us were watching a TV show about alien abductions. After the program ended, we began to discuss what a more intelligent life-form visiting earth would be like, and we considered how science fiction has generally painted this picture.

You might like to try this experiment yourself, as an indication of the assumptions you carry about life's potential. Imagine that an alien spacecraft visits this planet and that it is inhabited by beings of higher intelligence who have benevolent, or at least neutral, intentions.

- How would their social structure be organized?
- Would there be a leader, or would there be a sense of equality and co-operation?
- How would they communicate? Would it be through language or through the psychic transfer of thought-forms?
- Would they experience any kind of internal conflict, or would there be perfect harmony?
- Would they have individual possessions and individual living quarters, or would the material objects on the spaceship be shared and used as needed?
- Would they be motivated in their actions by individual self-interest, or would there be mutual intention behind their actions?

Now take a moment to reflect on your assumptions.

Of course, this is just a game. We could just as well ask the same questions about a more evolved human society in the future. Later I asked these questions in workshops I offered, and it was fascinating to see that almost everyone made the same assumptions. I wonder if they are the assumptions you made as well.

Everyone thought that this society of visitors would be leaderless and that its members would spontaneously act in perfect harmony, in the same way that a flock of birds creates a perfect formation without needing to be organized or trained. Hence there would be no need for language; thought-forms would spontaneously flow between them. There would also be no internal conflict. They would work together as part of one greater organism, continuously aware that the members of the spaceship are all expressions of the same source. Finally there was an almost unanimous assumption that they would have no individual possessions, but that the instruments and objects on the spaceship would belong to no-one in particular and would be used by whoever needed them at the time.

The assumptions we make in fantasy about life in the future and alien cultures reflect our assumptions about how things could or should be for human beings, were they to operate in a more intelligent and conscious manner. As the sense of separation and the need to define an identity dissolves, so does the need to possess things and define oneself through material objects. As we awaken, we find ourselves less willing to function in the stressful, technologically complex, time-pressured corporate world; we develop a preference for simplicity. The following session can evoke this natural tendency for life to simplify itself.

SESSION OUTLINE: THE GREAT PLAIN OF ACCUMULATION

This session, which is adapted from a Tibetan Vajrayana visualization, creates an internal spirit of renouncing clutter of all kinds: physical, emotional, social, and mental. It allows your friend to recreate a life that supports freedom. Since you have already become familiar with how to conduct these sessions from previous chapters, we will use fewer italicized scripts, allowing you to improvise in your own language.

Session Outline :
The Great Plain of Accumulation

Step 1: The Pre-Induction Talk.

Step 2: Induce Relaxation.

Step 3: The Great Plain.

Step 4: Seeing the Content of the Plain.

Step 5: Absorbing Back into Emptiness.

Step 6: Absorb the Body Back into Emptiness.

Step 7: Absorb the Plain Back into Emptiness.

Step 8: Recreate Life Out of Emptiness.

Step 9: Suggestions.

Step 10: Count Back from Five to One.

Step 1: The Pre-Induction Talk.
Talk with your friend about the current state of her life. Which areas feel like a burden or an unnecessary attachment and which feel like the natural expression of flow and service? Sometimes the areas that feel the most burdensome or cluttered are also those that are the hardest to let go of.

Step 2: Induce Relaxation.
Use any of the methods in Chapter Three, or others with which you feel comfortable.

Step 3: The Great Plain.
Ask your friend to imagine herself standing in the middle of a vast plain extending infinitely in all directions. This plain is filled with all of the components that constitute her life as it is now.

Step 4: Seeing the Content of the Plain.
Now, based on the conversation you had together in Step One, help your friend to see, hear, and feel the specific contents of this plain. Include everything to which she is attached: people, objects, places, memories. Leave out nothing that is important.

> *And now,*
> *Just because you are*
> *Relaxed and present*
> *Here in this plain,*
> *So it is easy for you*
> *To begin to notice*
> *All the objects and people*
> *Which are here in this great plain*
> *Of your life.*
> *That's right,*
> *You can see* (your mother)
> *Here with you in this plain.*
> *You can hear her voice,*
> *And notice what she is wearing now.*

Continue with father, spouse or lover, children, past lovers, friends, teachers, business associates. Include people she likes as well as people she does not like. Include people from the present, as well as everyone from the past who shows up. Be thorough.

The idea of this session is to overwhelm her with how stuffed this closet of her life is.

Now continue in the same way with objects: houses, cars, possessions, everything that shows up from the past or the present.

That's right,
And now you can
Begin to notice that
The house where you live
Is also here on the plain.
Notice the color of the front door,
The space in front of the house.
And now step inside the house.
And as you walk around it
You can describe
Out loud
Whatever you see here.

It is important to move slowly and experience each person and object, not just to list them like a catalog. Your friend will realize how long it has been since she spring-cleaned her life. This session is an inner form of renunciation.

Continue in your own way to include books, music, pictures, favorite places, and specific memories. Include not only people and things that are personal to your friend, but also those that have become familiar through the media and the collective culture. For example, President Kennedy, Jesus, Mother Theresa, Donald Duck, the Apollo space shuttle, and characters from various soap operas have all shown up in this session at various times.

It does not matter in what order you populate the plain. You can start with people, switch to objects, then to childhood, then back to current people. But be thorough. Continue until she has the sense that it has become extremely crowded and cluttered. Usually this step takes about thirty minutes.

Step 5: Absorbing Back into Emptiness.
This is the step of renunciation, the dissolution of form back into formlessness. There will only be the energy and the willingness to do this if you have reached a state of overwhelm and exhaustion in Step Four. To absorb the contents of the plain back into emptiness, use the breath as a medium. Start with the people and things your friend feels most ready to let go of.

That's right,
And I'm going to ask you now
To choose any person
Or any object here in the plain
Which you feel ready to let go of now.
(Wait for response)
And as you see this (person or object)
In front of you now,
It is easy for you to take a breath
Into the heart —
That's right —
And to absorb this (person or object)
Back into the formlessness from which it arose.
Yes,
Take your time now
To use the breath like a vehicle
To absorb this (person or object)
Back into the Source of all things.
And with the out-breath, you can
Allow the emptiness of the Heart
To fill this place again
In your plain
Leaving it empty and free.

It will be easiest to start with things that are old and to which there is no longer any attachment. You can absorb the contents of the garden shed, or old relationships. Some parts of the session will go quickly, and some will take longer to absorb and dissolve. She can absorb some people and objects in groups all at once. (For example, *with the in-breath now you can absorb your high school and all the students you knew there.*) Some people and objects will need to be absorbed individually.

Then ask her to absorb even more, to absorb and dissolve the objects and concerns that give her some pleasure but belong to the past and therefore create a sense of clutter. She can start to clear out whole rooms in her house, giving up activities for which she at one time felt a desire but that have now become habitual. Continue this process of dissolving and renouncing until she works through all her possessions and relationships, from those she is most ready to give up to those she cherishes most.

Ask her to dissolve and discard all her beliefs, starting with those that have become outmoded and those that have been inherited from her family or culture, and ending with her current spiritual beliefs, including the belief in giving up itself. She can do this by absorbing the books or people from whom these beliefs were taken. Of course, she may have some resistance to dissolving those aspects of her life to which she has been most attached.

Ask her to dissolve all roles and identities, to experience herself resigning from boards, clubs, and other activities, even those she considers worthwhile. Ask her to dissolve the home in which she lives. Continue absorbing until the plain is empty, and your friend is standing alone. Ask her to absorb the clothes the body is wearing.

Step 6: Absorb the Body Back into Emptiness.
Now ask her to use the in-breath to absorb the body back into the emptiness of the Heart. This may sound a little paradoxical, but it happens quite naturally at this point, carried by the momentum you have already created. The body feels like it is imploding in on itself, leaving only spaciousness.

Step 7: Absorb the Plain Back into Emptiness.
Now use the breath to absorb the plain itself, the time-space continuum, back into the Heart. This is the most powerful moment in the session. Many people say it gives them their most potent realization of the true meaning of emptiness, because of the gradual process of absorption and dissolution that preceded it.

Let her rest for some time in this spaciousness, giving adequate time for the silence to deepen, until everything has been renounced and dissolved back into its source.

Step 8: Recreate Life Out of Emptiness.
After she has rested for some time as the unmanifest source of all things, you can tell her to begin to fill the plain again with what feels useful and supportive for a simple life. Begin by recreating the body out of emptiness and then clothing it. Although I never suggest restrictions, people typically recreate a small selection of clothes where there had been a huge wardrobe, a

few good dharma friends in place of a crowd, a few special possessions in place of a clutter. You might ask her to use the breath to recreate first that which feels most essential: clothing, a place to live, work. Then invite her to populate the plain with whatever feels attractive. When she has taken back as much as she wants, you can suggest that she repeat this process, with you or alone, as often as she feels she needs to.

Step 9: Suggestions.
Make whatever suggestions you feel are appropriate about her ability to dissolve and recreate form in her life.

Step 10: Count Back from Five to One.
Use the instructions in Chapter Three.

In this session we never put pressure on people to permanently dissolve anything to which they feel attached. If during the first part of the session they feel a resistance to dissolving something, remind them that they can always take it back afterwards. Also, in the second part of the session, they are free to take back everything if they choose to. However, most people find that they recreate far less than they have dissolved, generally only that which is important, nourishing, or supportive of a truly meaningful life. For everyone with whom I have done this session, the recreation has led to far greater simplicity.

CASE HISTORY: JEFF

Jeff had spent more than twenty years with spiritual teachers and practices. In his mid-thirties he met his present wife, and they started a small business together in the garage, making meditation cushions. She sewed and cut and designed, and he got on the phone and made deals with local shops. Still deeply connected with their teacher and community, their business allowed them a modest income doing something they loved. Then Jeff's wife Karen became pregnant. Not only did they need to get help with the business, but for the first time in his life Jeff had to start planning for the future. So Jeff started a small catalog to sell the cushions by mail order, and gradually added incense, soap, and then books, T-shirts and music tapes.

After a few years Jeff had a beautiful small boy, and a thriving business. By the time we did our session he had 10 employees, a catalog with a circulation of 200,000, a large office, and chronic backache. He felt overwhelmed, and longed for the simplicity of his old life with his teacher and community.

We stepped down the flight of stairs into the plain, and, needless to say, found it crammed in every direction. From one corner his wife was needing him, from nearby his son wanted to go and play, and from another his employees were lined up with lists of questions. He found friends from every phase of his life, business associates and people from his spiritual community, and found them all battling for spaces in his appointment book, like pawns on a chess board. He found his parents, his family, and all their friends. As we turned to his material possessions, we found his office in the plain, every shelf crammed with New Age gizmos. We found his house, overflowing with children's toys, and not only the three cars that his family currently owned, but also every car that he still felt identified with from the past.

As we continued in this way, he became more and more overwhelmed, and visibly anxious. He felt that the conditions of the plain, a representation of the conditions of his life, were suffocating him. At this point we were ready to dissolve the plain back into emptiness. With delight he absorbed the office, the clutter, his large house and all its contents, and all his friends and associates. He also absorbed the possessions he felt more attached to, like the vintage Mercedes he once bought for a song. Then he absorbed his parents, his child and his wife back through the Heart into emptiness. The plain became very quiet, and consequently the atmosphere in the room became very still. He was left with his teacher and a few spiritual friends, just as he had been before his marriage. I encouraged him to also absorb these people, and hence this identity, back into emptiness through the Heart, and so he was left alone. Finally he absorbed his clothing, then the body, then the plain itself back into himself, so only silence remained: emptiness, peace. He rested like this for many minutes—the room was suspended in a pindrop silence, as though time had stopped completely.

When we recreated the plain he kept things very simple. Although he did recreate his family once again, he also created more space and more time to enjoy being with them. Although he did recreate his work as a way to support himself, now he also created a competent manager to whom he could delegate most of the day-to-day pressure. And now space and relaxation became the main themes of his life. After the session was complete, Jeff reported to me not only that this had given him an opportunity to step back from the priorities which were running his life, but that it had also given him the deepest immersion in his own natural Peace he had ever known.

COMMUNITY

The second tendency we mentioned as a result of awakening is a movement towards community and co-operation. As the boundaries between our sense of identity and our environment erode, so the motivation to go it alone, to succeed, and to dominate gives way to a spirit of interdependence. Many of the people I know who have embraced "the view" later move into shared housing or even rural communities.

Often, when I meet with people individually, at some point in our sessions we do an exercise called "Time Line." They start by sitting in a chair situated in present time. Then they stand up and slowly begin moving step by step along a line on the floor into the future. The first line we create is a continuation of their present life circumstances, in which nothing really changes. Most people are not satisfied with seeing their future in this way. In fact, a few have said that if they thought their external life would be the same in ten years, they would rather kill themselves.

A second line, for which they choose the direction themselves, leads into a future in which there are no regrets, a future in perfect harmony with the Heart. As they step along this line, they come to a place, perhaps five or ten years in the future, from which they can look back and not wish to change anything. Many of the people I have helped to do this exercise see themselves living in the country with a group of friends. Without exception their lives are much simpler than the ones they are living now. Generally they see themselves owning fewer things privately and sharing more with others.

Admittedly, I keep company with a rather small segment of the population, hence the same experiment might yield different results in other parts of the country, or the world. It has been interesting to note, however, how many people share more or less the same vision of the natural life, and how few have found a way to actualize it. The time line session motivates people to bring outward circumstances into alignment with their internal vision. Because it is so unusual to live this way in our society, it takes a certain amount of midwifery to birth this vision into being.

Living in community provides one with a group of friends who share the same world-view and can support each other. The pressures of the media and society to accumulate and compete are reversed, as the emphasis is no longer on individual possessions but on communal ownership. The community creates a culture favorable to the awakening of consciousness.

As a result of the breakdown of the extended family since the Second World War, we live in a society fragmented into isolated individuals or small nuclear families. Outside the self-sufficiency of the modern American home we often don't even know the names of the neighbors who share the same block or apartment building with us. In India, Indonesia, and Thailand, by contrast, children, parents, grandparents, and even great-grandparents still tend to live together in the same building or family compound. In many cultures that are commercially less developed than our own, the boundaries between individuals and biological families within tribes barely exist; hence there is much less of a sense of "me" or "mine."

As we awaken from the nightmare of isolation, we find that we are less able or willing to participate in a social and economic system that supports separation and competition. Despite the popular myth that the communities movement came and went in the flower power days of the sixties, there has in fact been an enormous resurgence of intentional community in the past few years in the United States. *The Directory of Intentional Community*[3] lists more than twelve hundred such communities, with membership ranging from a handful of people to seven thousand. Geoff Schwaltz, who was one of the compilers of the directory, has personally visited and documented more than five hundred communities over the last few years. He estimates that there may be three times more communities in existence than are listed in the directory, the remaining two-thirds preferring the cloak of anonymity. Today there are far more people living in communities than at any point in the sixties.

Jack Lessinger, a retired professor of sociology at the University of Washington, has traced five distinct population movements since the pilgrim fathers arrived in the seventeenth century.[4] The fourth such movement came after the Second World War with the development of the suburbs. The fifth movement, which he sees as happening now in the nineties, is away from larger metropolitan areas altogether, towards small towns or villages, like Pagosa Springs in Colorado, or Sandpoint in Idaho, both of which have dramatically increased their population over the last decade. This movement is fueled by a greater need for community and a slower pace of life. The next such movement, which he predicts will take place on a large scale in the mid-twenty-first century will be towards intentionally created community.[5]

Some intentional communities are based on an environmental or political vision or on a belief in communal life itself as the common unifying factor. But many have a spiritual basis, ranging from those that are organized around a particular teacher or teaching, often involving a hierarchy of some kind, to more loosely knit communities like Lama Foundation in New Mexico, where there are shared dharmic values and spiritual practice but no individual leader. Lama was founded in the sixties by Ram Dass and others, and is still going strong thirty years later despite a recent fire that destroyed many of the buildings. There was enough community enthusiasm to begin rebuilding almost immediately. At Lama they have no leader; decisions are made entirely by consensus. There is no fixed teacher or teaching, and yet there is a sense of reverence and sacredness brought to every activity in the community. They meet together for daily silent meditation practice, although almost every member of the community embraces a different teacher and tradition as their inspiration.

This kind of community supports the simplicity which we discussed above. Once the land has been paid off and the infrastructure has been built, as it has been at Lama, the cost of living can easily be reduced to a few hundred dollars a month per adult. Expensive appliances and luxuries, once they are shared by twenty or more adults, become more affordable. The habit of individual accumulation and hoarding is broken down, while the benefit of material possessions can still be enjoyed. Most of the communities in the directory have communally owned tools, washers and dryers, communal meditation halls, food preparation and eating areas. Although each individual might own their own dwelling and possessions, they can be much simpler than in a conventional life.

As our artificial sense of separation from others dissolves, so does our separation from the Earth on which these bodies walk and out of which they were formed. We come to recognize this planet not as a commodity to be used, but as a sacred manifestation of the same divine Self that now perceives it. Many communities foster such a relationship with the Earth, whether through the rediscovery of Native American rituals, the cultivation of the land through permaculture, or the production of organic foods.

Of course, there may be an enormous rift between the utopian dream and its actualization. Many communities fold within the first few years, primarily because their vision has remained a material one and has not provided a way to transform the consciousness of the participants. As long as the sense of "I" and "you" remains intact, rather than a Zen temple to contemplate the sound of one hand clapping, we create an arena in which to witness many egos clashing. There has been considerable research on what makes communities work and what causes them to fail, and best-selling author F. Scott Peck has even established a foundation to explore these variables.

The following session provides a basis in consciousness for this dream of community to become actualized.

SESSION OUTLINE:
THE GOLDEN CITY

As we have already discovered with our space alien fantasy, we all carry an image, however indirect or hidden, of the potential for human society. In Chapter Nine we discussed how we carry a blueprint of our future self. In the same way we carry an image of a society free from the belief in a separate "I," free from the need to accumulate and hoard things individually, free from interpersonal conflict and competition. Although we have mentioned the resurgence of interest in community life, the number of people living in this way is still quite small compared with the number of those who see it as their long-term goal. Of the people I have worked with over the years, most see a simple life in rural community as their ideal. This session can help bring the circumstances of life closer to this ideal.

Step 1: Pre-Induction Talk.
Speak with your friend about her vision of how she would really like to live. Inevitably, this will involve speaking together about the ways in which her current life is not satisfying to her. Most people see stress, lack of time to meditate and connect with others, and city dwelling as the limiting aspects of their life; consequently they see relaxation, communion with other people, and living in a rural environment as their utopian ideal. Although these values are almost universal, few people feel that their life will ever come close to matching them. This session addresses this schism.

Step 2: Induce Relaxation.
Use any of the methods described in Chapter Three, or others that are familiar to you.

Step 3: Begin the Journey to the Golden City.
Ask your friend to imagine or visualize herself walking in nature along a path. As she walks, she can see a Golden City somewhere in the distance, which deep in herself she knows is her real home. Ask her to describe the sounds, the smells, and the feeling of the path under her feet.

As an optional step, you might encourage her to see if there is any obstacle preventing her from approaching this city. When I have conducted this session, people have met a stern parent, symbols of parts of themselves, or symbolic objects that stand in the way of their living a life in harmony with the call of the Heart. As they overcome or dissolve such obstacles, the vision of the Golden City becomes clearer and more realizable.

Step 4: Enter the Golden City.
As she enters the gates, you can suggest to her that this is where she lives; this is her natural home. Ask her to notice how people are moving and interacting with each other. She might also notice how the community is organized. Do they use money? Do they have any rules or leaders, or is there a spontaneous synchronicity between the inhabitants?

Now you can ask her to find the house where she lives in the Golden City. Most people describe a simple room with just a bed and a few possessions. You can ask her to feel herself going through the activities of her day, which often comes as a great surprise. A corporate attorney who worked every day in San Francisco in his current life found himself working as a carpenter in the Golden City. A woman who worked as a secretary found herself doing healing work.

Step 5: Integrate the Feelings Into the Body.
Now make sure that she fully feels in her body what it is like to be involved in this kind of activity. This will accelerate the process of bringing day-to-day activity into alignment with what has been experienced internally. Feeling fully in the body can also bring up and stabilize past-life capacities, such as

Session Outline:
The Golden City

Step 1: Pre-Induction Talk.
Step 2: Induce Relaxation.
Step 3: Begin the Journey to the
         Golden City.

Step 4: Enter the Golden City.
Step 5: Integrate the Feelings
         into the Body.

Step 6: Dissolve the Vision Back
         into the Heart.

Step 7: Suggestion.
Step 8: Count Back from Five to One.

forgotten healing gifts or the ability to play a musical instrument.

Step 6: Dissolve the Vision Back Into the Heart.
As you did in the previous session, you can now ask your friend to absorb the vision of the Golden City back into the Heart on the in-breath.

Step 7: Suggestion.
Using your friend's language, you can suggest that this vision will become increasingly real in her day-to-day life now.

Step 8: Count Back From Five to One.

In one sense, of course, this session is merely a fantasy, a guided visualization. However, because we are not imposing any content, but are simply creating a context in which the Heart's vision can unfold, we are uncovering the blueprint of a meaningful life that has been repressed. We not only repress dark and negative emotions, we also repress our higher potentials, labeling them as unattainable. I almost always do this session with my clients because it reveals how much or how little their current life reflects their Heart's vision. Everyone finds that their work in the vision is simpler, less cerebral, and more service-oriented than the work they are actually doing.

SERVICE

The third consequence of awakening to the Self is a shift from a self-serving life to a life of service. The automatic dictates of "my needs" are eclipsed by the command of the Heart to serve and to give to others. When the sense of "I" with all its needs begins to evaporate, then the needs of all sentient beings and all existence becomes the responsibility and concern of this body. It is taken up and used by the creative force underlying all life. This may happen in obvious and overt ways, like teaching the dharma or healing, but it can also happen through social or even political service. We will discuss this natural surrender to life and the flowering of compassion in subsequent chapters.

As the sense of an individual doer disappears, one's *"dharma"* or duty or appropriate service in the world becomes clear. It does not require any figuring out or thinking. It quite simply reveals itself in the absence of an apparent "I" interfering with existence. Often people find that what brings them the most peace, love, and connectedness is the channel through which service can flow. For example, in my own case I have always found meditation and speaking of *dharma* to be my greatest joys, and life has continued to offer me opportunities to let those activities be my service in one way or another. A friend of mine loves to play the didjeridoo, but for a long time she thought that her didjeridoo playing and her way of being of service in the world could never coincide. Then she met other people who were working with the didjeridoo, she put an ad in the paper offering didjeridoo "healings" by donation, and now she's busy using her didjeridoo as a tool for serving others. Again and again we find that when the mind quiets down, life itself reveals the way in which service can happen. The following session helps to clarify this process.

THE FINANCIAL QUESTION

In India and most other Asian countries where *dharma* is taught, there is a long tradition that teachers will never ask for money for what they offer people. When money is charged, it is said, the teaching loses its benefit. Even an Ayurvedic doctor who requests money for healing people will purportedly lose his power to heal. Nothing could be more different from the way we practice medicine in the West! Many who have brought *dharma* to the West have tried to maintain this tradition of never charging fees.

Just as a true teacher will never ask money of his students, so it is a well-established practice in the East to approach the teacher with fruit, cloth, flowers, and food, which symbolically represent all of the teacher's needs. In the *Guru Gita*, the book of etiquette in these matters, Shiva advises his consort, Parvati, that one truly interested in liberation should present to a teacher "furniture, bedding, transportation, ornaments, and all things conducive to his happiness."[6] In Buddhist cultures this giving back to the teacher is known as *dana*, or generosity, and has been practiced for more than 2,500 years.

Over the past few decades there has been an attempt to translate these traditions into Western culture, with mixed results. On the one hand, there have been well-publicized cases of Indian teachers coming to the West and living in luxury quite out of keeping with the circumstances of their students: i.e., driving in expensive cars and living in lavishly decorated, air-conditioned surroundings. This image has become the epitome of the Eastern teacher in the media. On the other hand, there are many lesser-known teachers who have come to the West to teach *dharma* in the traditional way, by offering it freely, and have found great difficulty in supporting themselves because the tradition of *dana* is not established in the West. Some have tried to overcome this difficulty by asking for donations, which can easily become such a preoccupation that it eclipses the essence of the teaching. Some have simply abandoned the tradition of making teachings freely available and have resorted to charging fees, which can put a price tag of anything from a few hundred to a few thousand dollars on meditation practices that have traditionally been available without cost. Similarly, with the introduction of Chinese and Ayurvedic medicine in this culture, some practitioners have attempted to maintain the tradition of freely giving away their services, while others charge fees comparable to or even higher than their allopathic counterparts.

One approach that has worked well for many is the creation of a non-profit corporation or trust through which service-oriented activity can function. A non-profit corporation with well-designed bylaws allows service to be offered while at the same time safeguarding both the practitioner and those being served from the possibilities of greed. Practitioners can receive a modest salary to support their day-to-day expenses, and any profit can then be donated to other kinds of dharma work. The formation of a non-profit corporation can provide a useful safeguard on your integrity. You can ask sympathetic friends who support your work to be board members or trustees. This protects you and your clients from cultural pressure to accumulate more and more and to measure your self-worth by your salary.

SESSION OUTLINE: RIGHT LIVELIHOOD

Step 1: Pre-Induction Talk.
In the pre-induction talk find out what your friend understands to be a spirit of service and heart-oriented action. Ask her to give examples from her own life of times when she has felt herself to be of real service. Bear in mind that service may be quite a different phenomenon for different people in different ways. For some, service might involve direct political action; for some it might involve giving massage; for some it might involve spiritual teaching. For my wife, her highest service is in her parenting.

For some, taking the responsibility to meditate and be at peace with oneself is an act of service toward the rest of humanity. In talking about service (and you can do this for some time while practicing the Heart meditation described in Chapter Four), you will be cultivating the spirit of service and loving kindness to which the rest of the session is devoted.

Step 2: Inducing Relaxation.
Do any of the inductions described in Chapter Three, or any others with which you are familiar.

Step 3: Enliven a Memory of Service.
Go back now to a memory of being of service or an act of lov-ing kindness that your friend has already described to you in your pre-induction talk. Guide her into this memory, and ask her to describe to you, in the present tense, all the details: where she is, the sounds she can hear, what she can see, any tastes or smells. Let her move slowly through the memory, particularly emphasizing the feelings she has in her body. Ask her to speak out loud to whoever else is there, in the present tense, embody-ing this feeling of being of service.

Step 4: Build Up the Energetic Frequency.
As the feeling of service becomes stronger in the body, ask her to fall back completely into this feeling and to consciously exaggerate this frequency, this atmosphere of selfless service. Because you are starting with a memory of when this felt good, you are cultivating the feeling of service rather than a moral injunction that she should be of service in some way. Now ask her to let the images of the memory fade away, leaving her with the energy and the sensations of being of service.

Next ask her to take a deep breath into the place in the body where this feeling is strongest (often the middle of the chest) and with the in-breath to "fan" this place, like giving oxygen to a flame, making it burn more brightly. Ask her with the out-breath to feel the spirit of service, loving kindness, and giving infusing the rest of her body. She will use the in-breath to expand and exaggerate these feelings and the out-breath to allow them to permeate the body and her environment.

Step 5: Anchor the Feeling.
When she feels that this spirit of service and loving kindness has become as strong as it can, ask her to invoke a situation from her present life where there is an opportunity to be of service in some way. She might even become aware of how the longing to be of service and embody loving kindness is drawing that situation into her life and her awareness.

She may find herself with someone who needs her help or in a situation where she can be of service to a number of people. Ask her to allow the image to arise as a receptacle into which this overwhelming loving kindness can pour itself. Ask her to move fully through this situation in her present life. You can also ask her to hear the response of the person or persons she is helping and to receive their gratitude into her heart.

Step 6: Receiving Exchange (Optional).
You do not need to do this step with everyone; for most people the preceding steps are enough. However, some people have no problem in being of service to others, but they have great difficulty receiving money or exchange for their services. Hence they are unable to do what feels natural to them, and instead work at another occupation to pay their bills. If this is the case, you can ask your friend to become the person she has just helped and to feel the gratitude and generosity in her heart. Then you can ask her to become herself again and to feel what it is like to receive in exchange. When the ability to receive is blocked, it can take some back-and-forth movement between being the habitual self and being the other before a natural give and take becomes comfortable.

Step 7: Future Pacing.
There is an optional further step that you might like to add. You can ask your friend to experience how this spirit of service and loving kindness, which is pouring forth as a spontaneous act, could become a way of life for her. For example, if her act of loving kindness was to rub someone's feet, she might imagine becoming a massage therapist. This use of future fantasy is called "future pacing." If her act of loving kindness was to help homeless people get back on their feet, she could imagine turning her energy towards alleviating the problems of poverty in her area.

Session Outline:
Right Livelihood

Step 1: Pre-Induction Talk.

Step 2: Inducing Relaxation.

Step 3: Enliven a Memory of Service.

Step 4: Build Up the Energetic Frequency.

Step 5: Anchor the Feeling.

Step 6: Receiving Exchange (Optional).

Step 7: Future Pacing.

Step 8: Dissolve the Images back into the Heart.

Step 9: Suggestions.

Step 10: Count back from Five to One.

Step 8: Dissolve the Images Back Into the Heart.
Just as we have already done many times, now you can dissolve all the external images by asking her to dissolve them back into awareness through the window of the Heart. Allow her to rest as the Heart itself, vast, at peace, as the very source of all giving and generosity.

Step 9: Suggestions.
As she rests in her own sense of natural presence, you can offer suggestions to deepen her experience that all of life can become an opportunity to be of service and to share freely from the fullness of the Heart.

Step 10: Count Back From Five to One.

CASE HISTORY: ALAN

Alan had a very high-powered job in the city when he came to see me for bodywork, complaining of chronic backaches. As I took notes on his symptoms, I asked him when it was worse and when it got better. He told me that the thing that irritated his condition most acutely was driving or sitting still for long periods. Hence the symptoms came on in the morning while driving over the Golden Gate Bridge and gradually worsened during the day in his office. He had the least problem when walking his dog or hiking.

I first noticed a potential flaw in this explanation for his condition when he told me about the cross-country camping trip he and his wife had taken in their VW camper left over from student days. For two weeks behind the wheel there had been no backache; and he also told me that he enjoyed reading (generally also a sedentary activity, unless you read on the treadmill at the gym).

As we moved into the bodywork session, we simultaneously induced a relaxed state, and I guided him through the steps of the session above. His memory of being of service was of making a new gate for an elderly neighbor. We dissolved that image and went on to another: he was making a tree house for his nephew. Each new image we got involved working outdoors with his hands and with wood. As we anchored this in the body in Step Five, Alan's face lit up: hammers and nails were obviously his path to liberation. But this feeling of being of service in an earthy way was still divorced from his practical life, particularly from his way of making money. So we did some future pacing in which he found ways to offer his services with his tools to neighbors and friends. Alan became an independent consultant with his company, and reduced his work in the city to three days a week. The rest of his time is now devoted to making garden furniture, which is in high demand at the local garden store. Alan's back condition dramatically improved as a result of his less sedentary life style and the bodywork he went on to experience.

The sessions in this chapter have more of a quality of creative visualization to them than we have explored in other parts of the book. However, we are not primarily interested in changing the circumstances of external life, but instead in using visualization to enliven the Heart's true longing to express itself. In this way we can initiate the process of bringing our outward life in tune with our vision.

"Trust in Allah, but first tether your camel," they say in Sufi circles. These sessions alone may not lead to a new source of livelihood or dramatic changes in life circumstance, but they can help clarify and free the natural flow of the Heart in your friend's life.

CHAPTER 11

DESIRE AND FEAR

When love and hate are both absent,
Everything becomes clear and undisguised....
To set up what you like against what you dislike
Is the disease of the mind.[1]

SOSAN, THE THIRD ZEN PATRIARCH

Whenever attention is distracted from the purity of this moment, we lose the simple perfection of things. Whenever attention returns to what is real in this moment, the natural state is restored. In this chapter we will see how we are distracted from "the view" by the constant play of desire for and fear of that which is not real in this moment. In the following chapter we will deepen this inquiry into an examination of systems of belief. And in Chapter Thirteen we will taste what life is like when experienced without the distractions of desire, fear, or belief.

When consciousness is neither moving towards something in desire, nor trying to avoid something out of fear, nor in a fixed posture of indifference, it rests in its own original nature, which is infinite, eternal, and filled with love. Although desire and fear have

two names, we will discover that they are simply two ways of looking at the same phenomenon. Any movement in consciousness is
simultaneously towards something and away from something else.
When you drive from San Francisco to Los Angeles, you are simultaneously moving away from one place and towards the other.

For example, the desire to acquire wealth and possessions is
another way of expressing the fear of poverty, of not having enough.
Similarly, the desire to be in relationship is another expression of the
fear of loneliness. Desire and fear arise simultaneously; they only
appear to be different from within the story they each create. The movement away from and the movement towards are simultaneous.

In working with desire and fear we will be working with two
expressions of the same phenomenon; it is the same movement in
consciousness, the same "disease of the mind," as Sosan puts it, to "set
up what you like against what you dislike" and to then try to eliminate one and sustain the other.

ANATOMY OF DESIRE AND FEAR

We have been so driven by desires and fears, yet we seldom step
back long enough to find out what they are made of, or what exactly
is occurring when attention is fixated in this way. Take a moment now
to watch the movements of consciousness in its waves of attraction
and repulsion. What is actually happening? Later we will make the
distinction between mental desire and the longing for freedom, and
also between desires and biological instincts. But just now, when you
observe desires in the mind, what is actually happening?

We could say that desire is the tendency in consciousness to set
up a model of reality as somehow preferable to our immediate,
sensory-based experience and then to move toward the model, rather
than accepting things as they are. Let's say you are driving down the
freeway in your used car and you find that in the next lane is a brand
new Mercedes. A desire arises to have a car like that too. A fantasy is
created in which you see yourself as the owner of a different car
from the one you are driving. Interwoven with this fantasy is the
assumption that owning the other car will bring you more happiness and fulfillment and will free you from any suffering you have
associated with owning your present car. Such a fantasy is created
in consciousness and labeled "future." We do this with desires for

all kinds of objects, for sexual experience, for power and fame and money.

Perhaps the ultimate and most deceptive desire is the desire for enlightenment, in which we use the fantasy of some exalted state to distract us from what is real now. In fact, it is this desire to be an "enlightened person" that most clearly demonstrates to us the futility of all desire and the way that desire works against what it most deeply longs for. I have been involved in spiritual groups of one kind or another for more than twenty-five years, and I have seen and experienced how we collectively project a "state" onto a teacher or master and call it "enlightenment." We fantasize that this state, far removed from our own, involves never having any thoughts or emotions, or sleeping only two hours a night, or living only on juice, or never having any desires! Some people fantasize perfect omniscience and omnipotence in which there is never discomfort, shyness, or vulnerability. The fantasized projected state is set up as preferable to the state in which we find ourselves right now.

Of course, the true teacher shows us that it is this desire for "enlightenment" that keeps us from fully sinking into the experience of who and what we are now. Whenever we do relax into the perfection of this moment, into what we call "Clear Seeing," it is revealed to be simply the abandoning of all ambition, including spiritual ambition, and the sinking more deeply into the actuality of this moment, including its emotions, thoughts, vulnerability, and discomfort. The incomparable Zen poet Basho puts it like this:

> Though I'm in Kyoto
> When the cuckoo sings
> I long for Kyoto.[2]

Although already totally present in this very moment of perfection, when the cuckoo mind sings its song of desire, we start to long for what already is the case.

Of course, the same is true of fear, which is no more than an image, established in consciousness, of an undesirable state that we then make every effort to avoid. Almost without exception, the object of our fear is not currently being experienced; rather, it is something that could or might happen later. For example, someone who is afraid of losing all their money is usually not bankrupt *right now*. Once you have run out of money, you're not afraid of being bankrupt; you simply do whatever is required to move on to the next step. Similarly, the tension and anxiety associated with the fear of abandonment comes before the moment of actually being abandoned. One finds much less psycho-logical fear in India than in the U.S., although the difference in average income is huge. We only fear our fantasies, not what we are actually experiencing. Just as with the desire for enlightenment, there is noth-ing that can be done to alleviate the fear of separation but to awaken from the dream of separation.

DESIRE AND LONGING

We can make the distinction between hankering after external experiences, which we will call desire, and the Heart's yearning to re-turn home, which we will call longing. Longing is the desire for God, for Self-realization, for Peace, Love, and Beauty. There is an enormous difference between desire and longing. We desire what is not here right now. When you desire a new car, you are experiencing dissatisfaction with the car you own, and you are creating a desire for something you don't already have. When you experience the desire to be with some-one, you are craving what is not the case in this moment. Desires cause suffering both because we are generally unable to fulfill them and because, deep down, we know that even if we do, it will only lead eventually to frustration and the creation of new desires. Longing, by contrast, is for a deeper relaxation into that which is already the case.

Suppose that an American has the desire to become a German citi-zen. If he currently holds only an American passport, it would take a major effort to become German. He would have to find a German wife or perform a service that is urgently required in Germany and that no German national can perform, or he would have to be so wealthy that he could settle in Germany on the basis of passive income. In one way or another, the process of going through the application process and changing citizenship would take enormous time and work. Or what if the same American had the desire to become an Indonesian citizen? It would be virtually impossible. At this time the Indonesian govern-ment does not grant Indonesian nationality to any foreigners except under the most unusual circumstances—for example, someone who had succeeded in befriending the Indonesian president or performing some heroic deed for the Indonesian people. Since this desire would be almost impossible to fulfill, a fixation on fulfilling it, or equally a fear of its not being fulfilled, would cause immense suffering.

By contrast, what about an American citizen who develops the desire to become an American citizen—or the fear of not being an

American citizen? How much effort or time is required to satisfy that? None. He only needs to look at his passport to realize, "Aha! I am an American already! My desire to become American was creating a false sense of not being what I already am."

Longing is like wanting to be an American when you already have an American passport. Desire is like wanting to be German when you have an American passport. Desire, because it is for that which is not the case, can only lead to effort and frustration. There is a separation in time between the inception of desire and its fulfillment. Desire ultimately creates more desires.

Longing, by contrast, leads to realization, peace, and contentment, because it is for that which is already the case but was overlooked. Longing leads to the cessation of effort because it is for that which is already real; longing is enough, it requires no further action. The stronger the longing, the deeper the realization will be.

There is a wonderful Zen story that illustrates how longing is all that is needed to be free. A Zen student who came to live with the Master Suiwo was given the koan, "Hear the sound of one hand clapping." The pupil remained with the master for three years but could not pass this test. One night he came in tears to Suiwo. "I must return south in shame and embarrassment," he said, "for I cannot solve my koan."

"Wait one week more and meditate constantly," advised Suiwo. Still no enlightenment came to the pupil. "Try for another week," said Suiwo. The pupil obeyed, but in vain.

"Still another week." Yet this was of no avail. In despair the student begged to be released, but Suiwo requested another meditation of five days. It was without result. Then he said, "Meditate for three days longer, then if you fail to attain enlightenment, you had better kill yourself." On the second day the pupil was enlightened.[3]

When the longing is so intense that there is nothing else left, no back door, no escape route, the simplicity of things is revealed. When you are consumed by the longing for Peace, it brings you to Peace; the longing for Love brings you to Love; the longing for God brings you to God. When longing is total, there is no separation in time between the longing and its fulfillment. The more intensely we long for God, for the Beloved, for Freedom, the more we realize that we are already free. The more we desire money, sex, and power, the more frustrated and entangled we become because those things never deliver. No external desire has ever delivered what it promised. Joe Miller put it like this in one of his talks: "You overcome attachment by a change of focus, a change of viewpoint. If you must be attached, be attached to the very essence itself. And if you point at the very essence itself, whatever comes down is no longer an attachment to you."[4]

No effort is required to be present here, where you already are. It may require vigilance, awareness, mindfulness, but no action. You are already fully Here Now, whether you like it or not. Where else could you possibly be but here? Which moment could possibly be available to you but this one? You are permanently nailed to the Here and Now; there is no escape from it. The only choice on the menu is this moment and this place; the rest is fantasy. To desire what is already so, to long to "Be Here Now" with your whole Being, as Ram Dass advised us 30 years ago, brings its own immediate fulfillment. To turn the energy we call "fear" towards separation and duality brings the realization that there is nothing to be afraid of.

When Zen monks come to this realization, or *satori*, often after many years of practicing koans, the most common response is to burst out laughing.[5] Why? Because they realize they are already free. They realize that the state they were seeking is already and has always been their true nature. It was only the fantasy of separation, the fantasy of desiring to become that which they already are, that created the appearance of a journey in time.

A DHARMIC APPROACH TO FEAR AND DESIRE

Conventional hypnotherapy and much of Western psychotherapy tries to help you fulfill desires and avoid what you most fear, usually through some kind of external change. If you desire to be in a relationship, most therapeutic approaches will help you find the right mate and learn all the necessary skills to have a successful relationship. Similarly, if you have the desire to be affluent, most conventional hypnotherapy will help you to create the right mind-set to accumulate more money—to "think and grow rich," in the words of Napoleon Hill. But does this lead to freedom? By making the dream more comfortable we may be dampening the longing to return Home.

Some desires are part of the built-in survival mechanism of the body; we could call them natural instincts. The desire for food when you have not eaten is a good example, or the desire for sleep when you are tired, or the desire for sex, to the extent that it's a purely physiological rather than a mental urge. These natural, instinctual bodily functions do not disappear when desire returns to longing. On the contrary, when attention relaxes into this moment without the distraction of mental desires and fears, natural instincts can be fulfilled without interference. When you are tired you sleep; when you are hungry you eat.

To realize the fulfillment of all desire means to enjoy the perfection of things just as they are. It is a state not of passive resignation, but of passionately and fervently embracing the fullness of each moment. It means shifting the object of desire from that which is not so to that which is already the case, which ultimately means moving the focus of desire from an external object to one's own intrinsic nature. Rather than craving possessions and accumulations, it means realizing that you are the Source out of which all possessions and accumulations arise. Rather than craving relationship with another person, it means awakening to the reality that there is no other to find, that what you are is all that moves, all that is conscious. Rather than running from fearful stimuli, it means resting as that which cannot be destroyed. This is when we are spontaneously in a place where all desire is fulfilled at its inception, and all fears are dissolved as they arise.

There is an understanding in New Age circles that we create our own reality, which is another way of saying that thought and desire have consequences, that our personal reality, our relationships and the universe we see around us are a product of thought and belief. Obviously this is true. Before the stirring of thought there is only consciousness; out of that consciousness arises thought and belief; and out of those thoughts and beliefs arises the context of our life. Therefore, the New Agers argue, we should try to think the right kinds of thoughts to ensure that we have as much stuff as possible: think abundant thoughts so we can be abundant; think loving thoughts so we can be surrounded by love; think successful thoughts so we can be successful. This has given rise to a popular West Coast sport called "manifesting." The testimonies on the back of every metaphysical pamphlet demonstrate that it works. "Through applying the simple tools in this workshop I was able to double my income, meet the woman of my dreams, and cure myself of a lifelong disease."

But there is a piece missing from this equation. In the discovery that thought creates reality, we overlook that this ability to manifest can be a limitation rather than a blessing! There is nothing wrong with creating reality consciously, but for some people it simply ceases to be interesting. How many times can you put your coin into the slot machine and pull the handle before you run out of interest? Eventually the Heart calls out for something beyond our limited ideas of "I want this" and "I want that."

Poonjaji tells a wonderful story about a king who had no heir. The king was getting old, so he asked his ministers to send out a proclamation throughout the land that on a certain day he would be conducting interviews with anyone who would like to apply to become the next king.

On the appointed day the palace gates were opened, and hundreds of applicants poured in. They had all come to see the king. Before they were allowed to have an interview, the king had arranged all kinds of luxurious experiences for them. First they were directed to the royal bathhouse where they could enjoy saunas, showers, hot tubs, and massage. Then they could use all kinds of beautiful and costly perfumes, and they were dressed in the finest silks and beautiful robes.

Once attired, each applicant was treated to a sumptuous feast, a buffet with more than a hundred dishes and beautiful wines to choose from. Then there was music, dancing, and all kinds of entertainment. Finally, the end of the day came and it was time to leave. As each applicant left the palace, he tried to carry with him as much as he could—bottles of perfume in his pocket, a leg of mutton under his arm, a bundle of beautiful clothes on his head. But the guards were under orders to ask each person to leave everything behind.

After everyone had left, the king called his chief minister. "Where are the applicants to inherit the kingdom?" he asked. "Was it not today that I called them all here to be interviewed?"

"Yes, your majesty," came the reply. "But they have all left already. They became so interested in the luxuries and entertainments you provided that they forgot why they had come to see you!"[6]

Similarly, when we become fascinated with manifesting our own reality using the creative powers of the mind, we forget why we came here. We become so interested in wanting this and wanting that, and so clever at "creating it" that we forget to claim our inheritance to the kingdom. "This" and "that" will be taken away, but the kingdom is forever. We inherit the kingdom when we give up our addiction to creating our own personal reality and are willing to rest in and live from a thoughtless, conceptless space where we can experience real blessing. We can allow the magnificence of life to happen on its own, without the interference of individual doing.

That thou mayest have pleasure in everything,
Seek pleasure in nothing.

That thou mayest know everything,
Seek to know nothing.
That thou mayest possess all things,
Seek to possess nothing,

said St. John of the Cross.[7]

This is not the exclusive domain of reclusive mystics. We have all experienced moments of "letting go" in which we have given up our addiction to manipulating reality through either action or metaphysics. In these moments the unseen hand of the divine takes over and blesses us in countless ways. Of course, the divine is not separate from who we really are, but it is vaster and more intelligent than the individual we have taken ourselves to be.

BRINGING DESIRE BACK TO LONGING

How can we bring outwardly oriented desire back to pure longing, which is the initial impulse in consciousness from which it arose? Once desire has become rooted in the body, it can take us over completely, dominating our dreams at night and our fantasies during the day. In the session described later we will experience how all desire is the distorted cry of consciousness to come home to itself. Once desire has been distilled down to pure longing, there is no longer any gap, no separation in time, between the longing and its fulfillment.

The immediate object of desire may differ from moment to moment and from person to person, but the impulse is the same. Whenever we understand this, not just with the intellect but in our very core, we bypass the endless tossings and turnings in *samsara*[8] that have dominated our lives.

Imagine a group of cars that set off from Seattle bound for Miami. One driver might decide to drive via Portland, Oregon. Another might choose to drive across the state of Washington to Coeur d'Alene, Idaho. Another might drive diagonally across Washington through Boise, Idaho. Although each driver may take a different route, all have the same intention of reaching Miami. At any moment each car may be in a different place, traveling on different terrain at a different speed with different obstacles to overcome, but each shares the same intention.

When you look at a map of the United States, you see countless rivers and streams. They may seem to be moving in different directions. They may merge with each other. Up close you might see all kinds of currents, eddies, and whirlpools. But all of these rivers and streams are heading towards the ocean. Once they arrive and discharge themselves, there is no longer any separation between them.

One person might say, "I want a new car." Another might say, "I want a better relationship." A third might say, "I want more money, financial security, a house in the country." But to what are all these desires finally pointing? As we strip away the layers of complexity, we find that all desire is an expression of the longing for Peace, Love, and Beauty. The individual expression may seem distorted. For example, the desire to dominate another with bloodshed or oppression may be an extremely distorted form of the desire for Peace. The desire to abuse and pollute the earth may be a distorted form of the desire for Beauty. Underneath this desire may be the desire for money, underneath the desire for money may be the desire to feel secure, and underneath this desire is the longing for a relaxation and peace that cannot be taken away. Whenever we distill desire down in this way, we discover the longing of the Self to know itself. Similarly, each fear may initially seem different from other fears. But when we look underneath, we find the same movement away from powerlessness, isolation, contraction, and separation.

Because we cannot see, hear, touch, taste, or smell our natural state directly, the mind has become addicted to seeking it in transitory experiences. But when we examine our experience carefully, we realize that our natural state cannot emanate from an object.

You can look at a painting and be moved to tears by its beauty. But the person standing next to you may not find it beautiful at all. Or you can look at someone special to you and be moved by a feeling of overwhelming love. Yet someone else who knows your beloved may not feel that way in the slightest. Beauty is not intrinsic to the object, nor is Love or Peace or Truth. Rather, it is the experiencer who projects these qualities onto the object. Why is nature and the wild outdoors so universally effective at bringing us home to ourselves? Being natural, not being a distorted expression of source but a direct, natural expression, does the wind in the trees somehow remind us, act as a pure mirror of our original nature, and bring us back into resonance with who we really are? It is unusual to see something in nature which we consider to be ugly; ugliness is usually a product of the mind's distorted expression of Source.

You are the Source of all the Love, Beauty, Peace, and power that you desire and perceive as existing in an object. But you can only *be* this; you cannot know or experience or touch it through the senses. "It's closer than your hands and feet, closer than your jugular vein," says Joe Miller. "It's your heart. It's the love within. And anything that goes in another direction sooner or later destroys itself."[9] It is perhaps this quality of consciousness that gives rise to manifestation. As undifferentiated, contentless, timeless infinity, consciousness cannot perceive itself. It has to polarize itself into self and other, man and woman, parent and child, giving the appearance of otherness in order to love itself.

When we sit in a tub without moving, we do not experience the bath as warm. We have to move the water a little to experience its warmth. In the same way, a movement within consciousness is required for consciousness to experience its own nature and love itself. Once identity and duality have been created, we define ourselves more and more and forget who we really are. Consciousness cannot see itself; it can only see its creations in name and form. Soon it starts to define itself according to these names and forms. The true Heart wants to know itself, wants to taste its own beauty and fall in love, and it can only experience love by creating a feeling of otherness. To experience manifestation in the unbroken realization of your essential nature requires remaining aware at all times that the beauty and peace you see everywhere is an expression of who you really are.

In *Waiting for God*, Simone Weil puts it this way: "It is not for man to seek or even to believe in God. He only has to refuse his ultimate love to everything that is not God. This refusal does not presuppose any belief. It is enough to recognize what is obvious to any mind: that all the goods of this world, past, present, and future, real or imaginary, are finite and limited and radically incapable of satisfying the desire that perpetually burns within us for an infinite and perfect good."[10]

And here is the Tibetan Buddhist master Padmasambhava, eleven centuries before:

> *To desire something other than this*
> *Is just like having an elephant (at home),*
> *But searching for its tracks elsewhere.*
> *Even though you may try to measure the universe with a tape*
>   *measure,*
> *It will not be possible to encompass all of it.*
> *(Similarly) if you do not understand that everything derives*
>   *from the Mind,*

It will not be possible for you to attain Buddhahood.
By not recognizing this (intrinsic awareness for what it is),
You will then search for your mind somewhere outside of
*   yourself.*[11]

To miss this is to be driven by instinct, biology, and greed. To recognize the way in which desires repeat again and again is to free yourself from this pattern. After understanding, no further action is needed.

Once the mechanics of desire have been seen through, not just intellectually but with the whole being, a state of desirelessness naturally arises. Everybody has had this experience in certain areas of their life. When you were a child, for example, you may have had the desire to eat enormous quantities of ice cream. If you did that often enough, you began to understand that the bellyache you had on Thursday morning had something to do with the ice cream you ate on Wednesday. Eventually your desire for ice cream naturally diminished. Similarly, many people these days are seeing that the endless tendency to fall in love with another and invest all our attention and energy in the way another feels for us and the way we feel for another just brings frustration. In this seeing, the desire also drops away. I have met people who were addicted to the desire for power and money and who at a certain point saw through it because it was not providing them with what they really wanted. In that seeing through they were liberated from the addiction.

In this session you will help your friend or client to see that all outwardly directed desire only leads us into another cycle of frustration; looking for the sun in a rain puddle just leaves you with agitated water. The puddle is reflecting the sun to you, but it is not emanating light on its own.

SESSION OUTLINE: DESIRE TO LONGING

Step 1: Pre-Induction Talk.
Identify together a particular desire that stands in the way of resting in the natural state. This might be an obsessive desire for money or power or love—some habitual tendency for the mind to be directed outward.

Session Outline:
Desire to Longing

Step 1: Pre-Induction Talk

Step 2: Induction

Step 3: Imagine Fulfilling the Desire

Step 4: See What Is Left

Step 5: Move to a Deeper Desire,
until no more desire remains.

Step 6: Dissolve the Outer Image

Step 7: Return to the Original Desire

Step 8: Suggestions

Step 9: Count Back from Five to One

Step 2: Induce Relaxation.
Once you have identified such a desire together, induce a relaxed state as described in Chapter Three.

Step 3: Imagine Fulfilling the Desire.
Now tell your friend:
> *Imagine yourself, see yourself, feel yourself in a situation where you are able to fulfill this desire.*

For example, if the desire is for a new or better car, she can experience herself moving through a situation where she gets the car she wants; if it is for romance, she can imagine going out with the man of her fantasies.

Ask her to move into an imaginary scenario or fantasy where she can completely fulfill her desire. Make sure that she uses all her senses in fulfilling this desire while speaking in the present tense. Ask her to experience the situation directly, through all the emotions and senses, rather than speaking about it as an outside observer. Ask her to move through the cycle of the desire so that it is completely fulfilled or burned out.

Step 4: Ask What Is Left.
From here you can ask her,
> *Now, what is it you want or need?* or
> *What is missing?*

There are now two possibilities. Either she will drop to a deeper, more fundamental desire, or she will say, "There is nothing that I want now." If there is still desire, move to the next step. If she is resting in a desireless state, move on to Step Six.

Step 5: Move to a Deeper Desire, Until No More Desire Remains.
Having fulfilled the desire in Step Three, help your friend see if there is another, deeper desire underneath. For example, if she desired a car, there might be a deeper desire for the perfect companion to sit in the passenger seat, or for a home where she can park the car. Keep looking for what is still missing. As you move to deeper desires, keep repeating Step Four, allowing the desire to be fulfilled in fantasy through all the senses, and keep asking about what feeling states accompany the fulfillment of the desire.

As you continue to do this, the desires will become more expanded, more generic, and more inwardly directed. As each layer of desire is fulfilled and transcended, she will move towards longing, i.e., "I want to be at peace; I want to experience love; I want beauty; I want expansion." Now ask her to find a way to fulfill this desire completely and remain resting as that. As she moves deeper into her own essence, you can spend more time asking her to rest in the feeling of fulfilled desire. Through your session together, she will come to the feeling of desirelessness and fullness.

Step 6: Dissolve the Outer Image.
Once your friend has come back to rest in the feeling of wholeness through the distillation of desire, ask her to let go of the fantasies and images that led to this state and to relax fully into the feeling itself. Allow several minutes for this. If you like, you can play soft music or give suggestions of the kind we discussed in Chapter Three.

Step 7: Return to the Original Desire.
Now ask her to return in imagination to the desire with which you started the session together and see if any clinging remains. If it does, you can repeat the steps, encouraging her to move more fully into the feeling of fulfilling desire at each step. Keep going until she has burned out all outwardly directed desire.

Step 8: Suggestions.
You can use any of the suggestions from Chapter Four, and you might also like to include these:

> And it is good to know,
> Isn't it,
> That desires do arise and fall
> Spontaneously and
> Effortlessly.
> And whenever desires come
> For new sensations and experiences
> It is easy for you to
> Discover
> In new and interesting ways
> The place where all desire is fulfilled
> And to which all desire is pointing.

Step 9: Count Back from Five to One.
Count back as described in Chapter Three.

CASE HISTORIES

Bob was a real estate developer addicted to the perfect deal. Although he had more than enough money to live off his interest for the rest of his life, he found himself incapable of turning his back on a new opportunity. He came to see me for stress reduction, complaining that he was always overwhelmed with unexpected complications and never had any sense of relaxation or peace.

We started out by returning in fantasy to a situation in which he was being offered a share in a new resort complex. He recreated the feeling in his body, the rush of excitement and power. As we moved through the fantasy to its fulfillment, he experienced himself signing the papers, completing the deal in the way he wanted it, and shaking hands with his new partners.

I asked him what was still missing, what desire remained. He said he wanted to find the right people to manage the project so that he could relax and know that everything was properly taken care of. We moved through this fantasy until it too was completely fulfilled.

Now his desires became more generic and non-specific. He wanted to relax more and to enjoy what he already had. He wanted to experience being loved and taken care of. As he was able to feel these qualities, he became quieter and more internal, and a glow of peace came over his face. Finally, as he moved through each new layer of the mind's craving, he came to a place where he whispered: "I don't need anything more, I am complete. I feel at home and at rest." I invited Bob to relax and enjoy this homecoming to himself. Incidentally, he was a good example of how this kind of dharmic approach can work with anyone. Although he had no overtly "spiritual" background, he had an innate human longing to know himself more deeply.

When we returned to the original memory, he perceived the new resort deal from this place of peace and integration. The compulsion was now gone, and he saw that he would be equally happy entering into the project or passing on it. He also saw that his peace and expansiveness was more important than any deal could be, and he found himself setting limits on what he was willing to sacrifice in his personal life.

Moving through this session does not lead one to become completely passive, like a tiny boat tossed on the waves of a turbulent ocean. By removing the obsessive charge of externally oriented desire, you are free to exercise preferences in a relaxed way. When desire is understood for what it is, there is immediate liberation from its addictive effects. Many people, like Bob, still experience preferences when they return to the initial situation in Step Seven. If one can have the money or the girl or the goodies, so much the better. But it makes no difference to the essential sense of well-being.

This session may seem similar to "creative visualizations" aimed at obtaining the object of your desire. However, our purpose in experiencing desires internally is to transcend them and return to the Self. From here, if you still want a car, it may come more easily, but it is no longer crucial to your experience of fulfillment. Fulfillment now comes from the realization of who you are.

WORKING WITH ADDICTION

In our training we present a different session specifically designed to address addictions. We will not cover the details here but will briefly discuss how addiction would require a different approach.

There are many ways to deal with addiction, whether to cigarettes, alcohol, drugs, food, work, sex, or even shopping. Conventional hypnotherapy is often associated with addiction control, and more serious addictions require the services of licensed therapists who have been trained to specialize in this area. In a sense we are all addicts of one kind or another; the outward-directed tendency of the mind is itself an addictive tendency. It can manifest itself in all kinds of ways, but the basic craving remains the same. I have worked with people hooked on tobacco, food, sex, and just about everything else in between. When we take the time and attention to sink to the energy beneath each addiction, we find the same constant craving to fill an inner void.[12]

Addiction is a fixation onto some experience that has the capacity to overwhelm the sensory nervous system and temporarily give us pleasure, dissipate the feeling of craving, and return us to peace. All addiction is a way to avoid pain and experience the cessation of craving. We become addicted to the habit or experience that seems to do that for us most effectively.

Over many years as a hypnotherapist, I did countless sessions with people focusing on simple addictions like cigarette smoking, overeating, and workaholism. It became clear to me that the only long-term resolution of every addictive tendency is to introduce consciousness to its own nature. Otherwise, the addiction will reappear in another form because the basic tendency has not been addressed.

Although the object of addiction may vary from one person to another, the underlying feeling in the body is always the same. If you have ever smoked cigarettes or used alcohol regularly, you know this feeling of craving in the solar plexus that can completely cloud your reality. We ask the person receiving the session to dive into this feeling completely and allow it to take over consciousness to the exclusion of everything else; even the object of addiction (the substance or activity) is forgotten. She continues to do this until it cannot be amplified any further and is no longer being resisted in any way. Once the resistance and externalizing tendency have been removed, the craving itself is allowed to flow in its natural direction, which is usually experienced as expansion, peace, love, relaxation. You can ask the person to continue doing this until all of the craving has been internalized. When you ask her to return attention to the original object of addiction, it is almost invariably experienced without any charge and is no longer connected with physiological craving. Once a cigarette or drink or sweet can be experienced in this way, the feeling of craving has been "reframed" and is now associated with the longing to return home.

WORKING WITH FEAR

At the beginning of this chapter we discussed how fear and desire are two facets of the same movement in consciousness. We have already explored how all externally oriented desires can be brought back to the essential longing for wholeness and peace. Similarly, although each fear may initially appear to be different from other fears, underneath we find the same movement away from powerlessness, isolation, contraction, and separation.

We have explored how we can distill desire into longing. Now we will see how fears of potential external events can be distilled down in the same way to the essential fear of disappearing or being annihilated. When desire was distilled into longing, it led spontaneously to the realization that the true longing is for the Self. In the same way, we will now experience that all fear is essentially the fear of what cannot occur: the extinction of the eternal.

REAL AND PSYCHOLOGICAL FEAR

We made the distinction earlier between desires that arise in the mind, like the desire for more money or power or prestige, and basic instincts like the desire to sleep when you are tired or to eat when you are hungry. The first will dissolve when it is traced back to its essence; the second will increase and become more urgent once concepts and limitations are removed.

The same is true of fear; we can distinguish between real and psychological fear. Real fears have some authentic basis; they are instincts that protect us from actual dangers. We instinctively move out of the way when we see a truck coming down the street or back away in the face of overwhelming aggression. Real fear is an intelligent response to the circumstances of our environment.

Psychological fear, on the other hand, is created through projecting imaginary states into the future, much as we do with desire, except that the desire projection is fueled by what consciousness is moving *towards*, and the fear projection is motivated by what consciousness is moving *away from*. Psychological fears are the cause of most of our anguish and stress, particularly in Western society. They are created in thought and entirely fueled by false assumptions about our true nature.

There is a story told in India that illustrates the illusory nature of psychological fear. A man is strolling along a cliff at night, overlooking the sea. Walking a little too close to the edge, he loses his foothold and falls. In terror he reaches out and catches hold of a branch growing from the side of the cliff, and he holds onto it for dear life. Finding a foothold for his feet just a few inches wide, he stays in that position the whole night—his hands holding onto the branch above his head, his toes resting on the rock beneath him. Further below he can hear the thundering sound of the waves breaking on the rocks. He knows that if he relaxes his grip, even for a moment, he will be doomed. It is pitch dark, and he spends the night in abject terror of his fate were he to lose his foothold or let go of the branch. When dawn finally comes, he looks down and sees that just twelve inches below the rock on which he is perched is a large ledge that would have provided him comfortable rest for the night. He actually had nothing to fear except the assumptions and fantasies in his mind.

"Most of the things that we worry about never come to pass anyway," says Joe Miller, "...unless we do something to encourage the worrying and add a little jab on the off-beat and then sometimes it comes true. Then you're as lousy as you think you are or whatever it might be. You've got to understand that it's all a Oneness."[13] All our psychological fears are like this. We can spend hours, even weeks or months, hanging onto our assumptions about the sheer drop down to the ocean, only to find in retrospect that there was a ledge just a few inches below our feet.

In Western society there is a tendency toward chronic mental and emotional anguish; we are constantly afraid for our security. I have lived both in Asia and in the West, and the contrast is striking. In India, for example, it is quite common to meet a man bicycling a rickshaw who might hope to earn a hundred rupees a day, about three dollars, on which to feed his wife and perhaps four or five children. At night many of these drivers sleep on the backs of their rickshaws. Most of the people in countries like India, Indonesia, and Nepal live without even the faintest hope of finding financial security, yet, despite the illness and material poverty, they laugh far more often than we do here in the West. It is our psychological fear that causes us the most suffering. I'm sure you have experienced physical pain or real misfortune at one time or another in your life; everyone has had an accident or lost somebody close to them. Once we actually experience what we fear, however, we find that nothing is as bad in actuality as it was in anticipation.

I have had the privilege of working with people who were dying. They can be our greatest gurus because they have the opportunity to step into the dark caves that we have huddled in front of for so long, afraid to enter. Once fear is abandoned and death is accepted, dying is a delightful state of letting go, of giving back to the material world that which has been borrowed. To accept the pain and suffering that is inherent in the human condition is true freedom. To refuse to accept it is to live in anguish.

Session Outline:
Facing Fear

Step 1: Pre-Induction Talk.

Step 2: Trance Induction.

Step 3: Enliven the Fear.

Step 4: Move Through to the
Worst Possible Outcome.

Step 5: What Could be Worse Than This?

Step 6: Move Through to Worst Outcome.

Step 7: Move into the Experience
of Annihilation.

Step 8: Who Is Aware of This?

Step 9: Dissolve the Images Back
into the Heart.

Step 10: Return to the Original Fear.

Step 11: Suggestions.

Step 12: Count Back from Five to One.

SESSION OUTLINE:
FACING FEAR

Here is the session outline we teach in our training to transform psychological fear into the realization of the eternal nature of the Self. Do not use this session with someone who is so overwhelmed by fear that she is unable to remain present and conscious. Like all the sessions in this book, it is intended for those in a "normal" state of mind who want to dissolve deeper into the Self. Anyone experiencing more extreme states should be referred to a licensed psychotherapist.

Step 1: Pre-Induction Talk.
Talk to your friend about any habitual fears that may tend to obscure the original nature of consciousness. Find out which experiences in the past have fueled that fear and which experiences have dissipated it. For example, if your friend has a fear of speaking in public, find out which experiences have made speaking in public more terrifying and which have actually been satisfactory.

Step 2: Induce Relaxation.
Do any of the trance inductions described in Chapter Three.

Step 3: Enliven the Fear.
Use the flight of stairs or any other transition to help your friend imagine a situation in which this fear is enlivened. For example, if she is afraid of being exposed, your friend could experience herself performing on a stage or being interviewed on TV. Ask her to describe the situation out loud, in the present tense, being specific about sensory details—colors, sounds, smells, and tastes. Keep asking her what she feels in the body. Continue this fantasy until the fear has been fully realized. If she enters states of contraction or resistance, invite her to fully experience that in the body, before moving on.

Step 4: Move Through to the Worst Possible Outcome.
Ask her to continue the fantasy, letting it unfold to its worst possible outcome. If she is experiencing herself on stage or TV, she might stutter or go completely blank and have nothing to say. Continue until it cannot get any worse.

Step 5: What Could be Worse Than This?
Once this point is reached, asking her to remain in touch with the feelings in her body, ask her:
> What are you afraid of now?

or
> Is there anything worse than this?

Step 6: Move Through to Worst Outcome.
Now move through another layer of fantasy, again remaining in the present tense and staying focused on sensory details. Keep moving through layers of fearful worst-case scenarios until you can go no further.

Step 7: Move Into the Experience of Annihilation.
If you keep moving through worst possible scenarios and dropping to deeper levels, you will finally come to some form of conscious dying experience. This may involve the death of the physical body, or it may be the death of individuality in some other way. You will know when you have reached this point because when you ask "What could be worse than this?" your friend will not find any further levels to move to.

Step 8: Who Is Aware of This?
Once you have facilitated the realization of your friend's worst fear, ask her to sink back into being the One who is aware of the experience itself, and into the recognition that even in the death of the physical body, the annihilation of the identity, or madness, the experiencer itself is left untouched.
> And now,
> Even as you are aware of
> This experience of (death, bankruptcy, illness etc.)
> Happening to you,
> You can
> Allow yourself to
> Relax even more deeply,
> And find out now
> Who is aware of this event unfolding
> You can allow this question
> Who...am...I?

Since this session may have required some courage and determination, allow your friend plenty of time to rest back into the natural state and to allow the feelings to dissolve in the body.

Step 9: Dissolve the Images Back Into the Heart.
Ask your friend to use the in-breath to dissolve the images, the story, and the bodily feelings associated with them back into the Heart, and then to breathe the quality of the Heart back into the body on the out-breath. Allow her to continue with this until all fear and contraction has completely dissolved.

Step 10: Return to the Original Fear.
Ask your friend to return to the original fearful situation from Step Three, to see if any charge remains. Generally, once the deepest underlying fear of death or annihilation has been exposed and moved through, the superficial presenting fear will seem to be an acceptable and relatively insignificant part of normal life.

Step 11: Suggestions.
Use suggestions that encourage your friend to extrapolate her experience into the broader context of her life, allowing the realization that, no matter how intense the fear, whether of bankruptcy, death, or loss, her essential nature and source of fulfillment remains untouched.

Step 12: Count Back From Five to One.

A FATE WORSE THAN DEATH

Between my individual clients and the students in our training courses, I have witnessed this session many times. One might imagine that all fear would condense down to the fear of physical death, just as all desire distilled down to the longing for freedom. Actually, however, we have discovered that most people carry fears that they consider to be "worse than death" and that they would gladly use death as a means to avoid experiencing. The particular flavor of this "ultimate fear" seems to be influenced by the individual's personality style.[14] For example, one man's fear of confronting his housemates about a messy kitchen distilled down to a fear of becoming a victim of persecution with nowhere to escape. The threat of exposure and persecution instilled more fear in him than physical death. Another man's fear distilled down to becoming a living vegetable who had lost the use of his physical body. For him, life without creative expression and constant activity was worse than death. For one woman the loss of the spouse to whom she had devoted her life was a fate over which she would unhesitatingly choose her own death. For her, life without service to another was not worth living.

To the deeper levels of the mind, physical death is not such a threatening outcome. Since we carry within us cellular memories of previous incarnations, we know at some deep level that birth and death are experiences we have already passed through and survived many times. But the loss of a fortune to a man deeply identified with financial power, the loss of the capacity to work to a workaholic, or the loss of a relative to a co-dependent represents a much deeper kind of identity annihilation. It seems to be this loss of a sense of separate self that we most instinctively avoid, and that this session can help us to face and accept.

FREEDOM FROM FEAR

Some students in our trainings have raised objections to this session because they fear that it might be a form of "creative visualization" that could cause our worst fears to come true by actualizing them in consciousness. Of course, the human mind is a creative instrument that is capable of influencing the outcome of events through its creative power. But I would suggest that working with fear in this way has exactly the opposite effect. It liberates us from our worst fears rather than binding us to them. When an image is locked into the subconscious levels of the mind and resisted, this very resistance causes the image to persist and to grow in potency. Our willingness to face fear in this way, however, takes the charge off and allows us to realize that even when our worst nightmares come true, we remain essentially untouched and whole.

CASE HISTORY: THERESA

Theresa was a student in one of our training programs who tended to keep herself protected and private with people. She noticed that it was much harder for her to share details of her life than it was for the other people in the training. We did this session as a demonstration, which incidentally was already an act of courage and a breaking of habits for her. We talked about her fear of being overwhelmed, and the need which governed her life for privacy and self protection. Theresa had a slight and frail body type, and jumped easily in reaction to sudden loud noises.

We went down the flight of stairs together in imagination, and found ourself in a typical anxiety-provoking situation: a large number of people were visiting her home, and giving her the feeling of being invaded. We exaggerated the image to include kids running wild and spilling food on her rugs, loud and aggressive people she did not know watching TV, and piles of dishes and a mess in the kitchen. Allowing her to exaggerate her fear in this way made it into a creative and playful exercise: now instead of resisting these events she was having fun seeing just how awful she could make it. When the house was completely invaded, I moved on and asked her what could be worse than this. Initially she had trouble coming up with anything, but we did continue with another fantasy, this time experiencing her unwanted visitors and their children moving into her house for an indefinite period, moving into her room, leaving chewing gum in the bathroom, and endless unwashed dishes. On and on her fantasy continued, each time with her own sense of space and privacy eroded even further.

This experience reached a point of complete saturation: we could not make it any worse. Theresa was left an outcast in her own home, with all her normal coping mechanisms and security dissolved. It was at this point that we moved into the Self inquiry, and found out who or what was experiencing this invasive nightmare. She found out that although within the story she was experiencing contraction and irritation, the Self watching this was perfectly expansive and at peace.

When we went back to the initial provocation in Step Three, she was able to face the situation without any internal reaction. Not only did this mean that she could allow her boundaries to be eroded without experiencing fear, but that she now was able to take action cleanly without being crippled by that fear. Cheerfully she told everyone that it was time to go home now!

If you choose to try this session, be careful not to take the fantasy too far. We are helping people face fear and so discover courage and the molehills within our mountains; we are not trying to torture or traumatize anyone. If at any time your friend moves into a contracted state, use the Heart meditation from Chapter Four to absorb with the in-breath, and to create more spaciousness with the out-breath.

CHAPTER 12

BEYOND BELIEF

There is no longer any need to believe,
When one sees the Truth.[1]

AL ALAWI

Do not search for the Truth
Only cease to cherish opinions.[2]

SOSAN

We tend to refer to the person we have taken ourselves to be as an entity, a "thing" subject to birth and death. We call this thing "ego," "personality," or even "soul." When we examine the nature of this person more closely, however, we find that it is not really a linear, coherent individual at all, but a *collection* of masks, or roles, that only appear as a person when referred to collectively.

We are constantly shifting and adapting to the situations life presents. If you have children, for example, compare the way you behave as a parent with the way you behave with your employer or clients. If you have employees, compare your interactions with them with the way you interact with your spouse or lover. Look at the way you behave with your parents compared to your behavior with the cashier in a supermarket. The roles we play reveal to us that the personality is not coherent or linear. In fact, we have many personalities, differing with the situations in which we find ourselves. Even within a single context—a romantic relationship, for example—we may find ourselves shifting between the hurt child that needs to be nurtured, the strong parent who cares for the other, the mystic who wants to meet in tantric union, and the friend who is ready to curl up by the fire and read books together.

The only real difference between you and me, or between any "you" and any "me," is a different set of habitual responses based on specific points of view about reality. Without these "postures" in consciousness, there is no individuality; there is only the purity of consciousness itself. When you take a flashlight and move it around quickly in the dark, there appears to be a circle of light. But the circle is only a by-product of the movement of the bulb. Likewise, the picture on a TV screen is the by-product of the rapid movement of charged electrons. In the same way, individuality is nothing but a by-product of rapidly moving desires, fears, and beliefs about reality. When consciousness moves rapidly enough between these conflicting points of view to create a pattern, we can speak about a person or a mind, as though the movement were a thing. As we dissolve these points of view, we simultaneously dissolve the sense of an apparent separate identity. What is left is simply consciousness itself.

SUBPERSONALITY THEORY

The understanding of the fragmented "parts" between which awareness alternates has been explored extensively in Western psychology and is referred to as "subpersonality theory." A subpersonality is a point of view, a crystallized belief about ourselves, the environment in which we live, and reality in general. Each subpersonality carries with it a mental attitude, an emotional posture, even a way of holding the body. Most subpersonalities are unconscious, which means that when one is dominant we are unaware that we are adopting a posture; we simply see life through a particular tinted pair of glasses. For example, we may see life in terms of the belief "Life is dangerous and I am afraid," and overlook our projected fear. Or we may believe, "There's not enough money to go around," and overlook the filter that is causing us to see things in this way.

This understanding was first brought to the West by the Russian mystic George Gurdjieff and his Western disciple P.D. Ouspensky.

Gurdjieff spoke about the different "I's," which are protected from each other by "buffer zones." When we feel strong, capable, and free of self-doubt, the part of us that feels afraid, contracted, and unable to cope with the world seems ridiculous; we have no way to relate to it. When we feel small, contracted, and afraid, the part of us that feels confident and competent seems like an unrealistic aggrandizement of our abilities. Because of the buffer zones, Gurdjieff believed, subpersonalities are often unable to connect with their counterparts. Gurdjieff liked to put people into such intense situations that hidden subpersonalities revealed themselves. He also worked with the nine fixations of the Enneagram, an ancient Sufi system with which we work extensively in our training.

Roberto Assagioli, an Italian disciple of Freud, developed the approach known as psychosynthesis. Rather than psychoanalyzing, Assagioli recognized that we are already fragmented and are crying out to rediscover our essential wholeness. Psychosynthesis is primarily concerned with recognizing and accepting the parts of ourselves we have rejected. Assagioli encouraged giving each part a name, like "the lost child" or "the seducer," and visualizing its age, voice, and appearance. Fritz Perls, the creator of Gestalt therapy, also worked with these fragmented parts, giving them names like "top dog" (the boss) and "underdog" (the victim). He helped his students create dialogue between these parts and between each part and the witness, or observer.

Perhaps the most sophisticated approach to working with subpersonalities is Voice Dialogue, developed by Hal Stone and Sidra Fieldman. Their first book, *Embracing Ourselves*, gives the best explanation I have read of how opposing subpersonalities develop and become fragmented out of the original integrated sense of Self.[3]

David Quigley, in his Alchemical Hypnotherapy, also works with dialogue between subpersonalities, this time in a hypnotic state. In the Conference Room technique he developed, the client sees as many as ten or twenty parts gathered in a circle, each with their own unique point of view on the issue being discussed. In Quigley's approach, the emphasis is on creating alignments between opposing parts, so the personality can become more unified, integrated, and capable of taking action in the world.

We will be taking yet another approach here. Rather than trying to align and integrate fragmented parts, we will see how easily they can be dissolved into a state of Clear Seeing free of any perceptual bias.

Rather than becoming an integrated personality, we will return to being the Self that cannot be fragmented. Our interest here is to reveal and embrace hidden points of view, or subpersonalities, and to recognize them as perceptual filters rather than our true nature. Rather than giving these parts of ourselves a name, an appearance, and a separate identity, as described earlier, we will feel into the essential frequency, or energetic contraction, and dissolve it back into its source. In the rest of this chapter we will refer to our fragmented voices as "points of view," which can be experienced as mental, emotional, kinesthetic, or archetypal dimensions.

We will discover here that the process of dissolving belief has a practical dimension. Once perceptual bias has been eliminated, we can see the situations of our lives clearly and allow the solutions to so-called problem states to reveal themselves from within the situations themselves. This is what the Taoists call *wei wu wei*, or action through non-action, accomplishment by allowing life to move rather than making something happen.

FACETS OF A DIAMOND

Every point of view has multiple dimensions. It can be experienced mentally as beliefs, emotionally as feelings, and kinesthetically as bodily sensations, tensions, and muscular contractions. These are just different ways of experiencing the same phenomenon which exists as an energetic frequency deeper than all of them. If we are not willing to experience points of view as parts of ourselves, they can be personified as mythical forces, experienced in dreams and fantasies, or experienced externally as the inhabitants of our world who become the objects of envy, judgment or pity.

Let's look at a few examples. When a point of view is primarily experienced mentally, we cling to our opinions about the way things are and rigidly defend them as objectively verifiable. We might talk for hours about how unfair and difficult life is and how we have to fight to get anything done. We might believe that all men are sexist pigs who would like nothing better than to rape every woman and beat their kids. Or we might be convinced that the planet is being over-run by aliens who control the federal government and might see every new law as evidence for this view.

Once we latch onto a system of belief, there is no exit through the mind because the belief becomes a self-fulfilling prophecy. Many points of view seem perfectly logical and well thought-out; one cannot deny, for example, the validity of environmental concerns, the women's liberation movement, or various forms of political activism. The danger of a point of view is not that it is *wrong*, but that it is a limited expression of the truth, leading us to forget that its opposite is also true. When we cling to a belief that life is dangerous and scary, we seek out and attract (albeit unconsciously) situations that prove our point. When we believe that relationships are inevitably disempowering, we see the other as wrong, as the cause of the problem: "You always criticize me and make me feel bad." In this sense, beliefs give rise to personal reality.

Once beliefs have been projected outwards, it is almost impossible to release them through the mind because reality just seems to reinforce them. We also exaggerate our identification with subpersonalities by attracting others who hold a similar point of view. People with strong "victim" subpersonalities, who feel crippled by their past and unable to cope with life because of strong childhood conditioning, may join support groups made up of others who see life in the same way. The lifestyle we choose, and those we choose to "people" it, intensify our identification with certain points of view.

The same point of view that was experienced mentally can also be felt as an emotion. This is not to say that beliefs *cause* emotions or that emotions cause beliefs; they are just two ways of experiencing the same contraction within consciousness. A conspiracy theorist, for example, if he shifted attention from a mental window to an emotional one, might experience suspicion, fear, or even anger. Much psychotherapy is concerned with shifting attention from a mental way of experiencing a point of view to an emotional one, helping us to "get in touch with our feelings." It is easier to release fixated views of reality from an emotional perspective than from a mental one, because our attention shifts to a more subjective dimension. We no longer see the cause of our views to be "out there," but experience it as arising within us.

We may also experience points of view symbolically as archetypes, mythical forces in consciousness that are common to every human psyche. For example, the heroic warrior is an archetype found in every mythology, as well as within our own mind. The damsel in distress, the wise woman or wise man, the king, the inner child, the joker or fool are all archetypes. We experience these archetypes most commonly today through characters in films. Many Hollywood movies present "two-dimensional" characters who display no internal conflict, but an entirely coherent and consistent view of the world.

Watching such two-dimensional characters working out their drama together allows us to experience the unfolding of our own internal fragmentation. Superman, Batman and Robin, James Bond, and Indiana Jones and their respective villains are obvious examples of archetypal, good-versus-evil polarities. When a "bad guy" falls to his death, we feel no sorrow or concern for his family because the character was more an archetypal force than a real person.

In many cultures, both religious and secular mythologies have enacted the full spectrum of potential points of view through a pantheon of deities or archetypes. For example, the Greeks had a cast of gods representing many of the diverse ways in which consciousness can express itself. Ares shows us our warrior-like anger, Aphrodite reflects our feminine beauty, Zeus reflects our power and our magnanimity, and Hades shows us our shadow, our internal underworld. The Tibetan pantheon of gods and demons creates a somewhat different palette of potentials within a field of all possibilities. The same is true of the Hindu pantheon, pagan pre-Christian myths, and William Blake's mythological world. Through familiarity with these stories we come to a greater understanding and acceptance of the infinite ways in which unmanifest Being can manifest itself.

Finally, points of view can be experienced as contractions in the physical body. In the example given earlier, the conspiracy theorist might discover tight muscles in the upper body associated with feelings of fear and anger. Points of view can even become associated with specific organs in the body. For instance, the belief "You *always* make a mess, and you *never* clean up after yourself" may be a mental reflection of irritability and self-pity, which in turn may be an expression of a liver imbalance. Similarly, paranoid beliefs about reality and emotions of fear may be associated with the kidneys, and optimistic or pessimistic beliefs about the future and emotions of enthusiasm and depression may be associated with the spleen.

The mental, emotional, and kinesthetic dimensions of any experience are inextricably entwined, and we can choose which frequency we wish to give our attention. Because physical feelings are the most immediate and can be experienced directly, apart from any accompanying story or rationalization, they are the most direct route to releasing attachment to limited views. The session later in this chapter will allow us to recognize points of view simply as energetic contractions, without worrying about their content. In this way we will see how easily we can dissolve them. The body is like the "hard drive" in which points of view get stored and through which they can also be erased. Without the story or justification behind the point of view, people often come to realize that "it can be any way I see it to be" and that there is nothing in the universe that has any intrinsic meaning other than what you give it.

THE DEVELOPMENT OF PERSONAL REALITY

How does our original, natural state of wholeness fragment itself into these different parts and their beliefs about reality? Both the newborn infant and the enlightened mystic are free of a sense of separate identity and hence have no fixed beliefs about the way things are. In his work on child development, Piaget discovered that, prior to about two years of age, the child has almost no barrier between self and environment.[4] In a newborn, there is even no perceptual separation between the one seeing and that which is seen. How then do we learn to define ourselves in these fragmented ways and lose our way in a maze of our own creation?

In the introduction to his first book, Hal Stone gives a brilliant account of the process of ego fragmentation.[5] In summary, he claims that newborns and young children have no subpersonalities and hence no beliefs; there is just an integrated wholeness and acceptance. In our subsequent conditioning, however, we learn that certain qualities are more conducive to our survival and well-being and certain other qualities cause us pain. We differ, of course, in the lessons we learn and the ways in which we learn them.

In a confusing and seemingly threatening environment, children may simply imitate the behaviors they see around them. By mimicking their parents and siblings, they assimilate the subpersonalities that are predominant in their family. For example, an intellectual couple in Manhattan are likely to teach their offspring that a quick mind keeps you ahead of the pack. In the neighboring Bronx, by contrast, a young child may learn by imitation that the world is a tough and scary place and you need to fight back in order to survive.

The child may also stumble upon behaviors that are rewarded every time they are exhibited. For example, a first or only child of doting parents who is rewarded whenever he behaves in a "cute" or "lovable" way will learn to replicate these behaviors in order to gain reward. Eventually he may develop a "pleaser" or "conformist" subpersonality, accompanied by the belief that "I must be nice in order to get by."

Or certain behaviors may repeatedly lead to some kind of pain or punishment, which causes that aspect of the Self to be repressed and separated from an integrated sense of presence. For example, if every time a child acts rambunctious or wild, she gets physically punished or banished to her room, she may develop a "rebel" subpersonality that is suppressed in favor of its "quiet, well-behaved" counterpart. Later in life she may find herself vacillating between the two extremes.

As certain qualities are cultivated, their opposites are inevitably repressed into what soon becomes the "shadow-self." We develop polarized points of view, where "I am strong" may co-exist with the repressed "I am weak," or "everything is fine and we are having a great time" keeps at bay the repressed possibility that "we are about to fall apart at any moment."

Points of view also develop through social conditioning or peer pressure, which can create perceptual biases that are shared across the culture or subculture. For example, people born in Switzerland tend to share certain highly developed points of view associated with cleanliness, order, and time. People born in India, by contrast, tend to share quite different cultural conditioning on these matters. Today we see parts and points of view shared through the role modeling of television characters. My sons, for example, are willing to clean up their playroom because a jolly maroon dinosaur named Barney makes it seem like a really cool thing to do.

WAVES FALLING INTO THE OCEAN

Once parts have been formed in the ways described earlier, they become rigidified, and constitute the person we take ourselves to be, with its habitual perceptions, emotions, and patterns of tension. When we dissolve a point of view by directly experiencing and accepting the energy contraction out of which it is made, we do not lose that quality of being, but reintegrate it into an undifferentiated wholeness, just as the water in a wave does not disappear when the wave falls back into the ocean.

For example, through early conditioning we may have fragmented within ourselves an internal judge or critic. This subpersonality may be experienced as an inner voice that keeps telling us we're not good enough or we didn't work hard enough. When split off in this way, the judge creates a feeling of internal pressure, a sense that we've never done quite enough to be able to relax. You can no doubt experience this frequency in consciousness; perhaps you can even imagine the kinds of clothing this part of you might wear, or the tone of its voice. As we release resistance to this fragmented part, experienced as "other than me," it is allowed to melt back into the wholeness of consciousness out of which it took birth and to become a quality of "that which I am." We discover that, once the resistance to it has been dissolved, every point of view has a positive, loving, creative intention at its core. Essentially, there is no such thing as negative energy; there is only misunderstood and resisted energy. The judge eventually relaxes into the part of us that has standards, keeps us motivated, and maintains order in our life.

Similarly, we may discover an energy within us that is cowering, disempowered, and afraid. You might call it the "inner victim." It has a point of view that says, "I can't cope with life. I'm not good enough. I can't make it. I need help." In the same way, you can experience this as a disowned part of yourself and imagine an age, clothing, and a voice. You may also judge this energy when you perceive it as "other than me." Woody Allen generally plays this kind of character in his films.

The key to integrating parts and points of view is to understand and embrace their underlying positive intention. When judged or kept at bay, the victim becomes a saboteur, the part of us that can't cope with life. But it is also the part of us that can ask for help, be vulnerable, and keep a lifeline to the world.

You can explore other disowned aspects of yourself in this way. When you remove all trace of resistance and judgment, you can discover the hidden treasures they may be concealing. You might like to experiment with the "prince/princess," the part of us that loves to dress in fine clothing and act charming, or the "inner rebel" or the "monk" or "nun."

ALL POINTS OF VIEW ARE EQUAL

We are accustomed to seeing points of view through evaluative filters; we speak of "positive thinking" and the need to be free of "negative emotions." Most hypnotherapy is based on encouraging what are considered socially desirable contents of consciousness; for example, anger is bad, love is good; harmony is good, conflict is bad. We talk about how we must rid ourselves of negative thinking in order to become better and more powerful people. Although this approach has its value, it is not what we are presenting here.

We are concerned not with trying to change content but with dissolving the filters of perception without replacing them with "better" beliefs. We are exploring what is revealed when we can view ourselves and our environment without any point of view at all. From Clear Seeing, which is the perspective of consciousness itself rather than of the judging mind, there is no good or bad—things are just occurring as they are.

When we return home to Clear Seeing, we discover that all points of view, whether they seem to be positive or negative, are contractions within the limitlessness of our true nature. To hold either that "I am a worthless sinner" or that "I am a superior person" equally limits the underlying and indefinable Truth of our true nature. To hold either that "Life is abundant and I always have everything I need," or that "Life is a bitch and I never have enough to get by," equally limits an underlying reality that contains both and transcends both at the same time. The Tibetan *Six Vajra Verses* put it like this:

> *Staying free from the trap of any attempt*
> *To say "it's like this," or "like that,"*
> *It becomes clear that all manifested forms are*
> *Aspects of the infinite formless,*
> *And, indivisible from it,*
> *Are self-perfected.*[6]

The points of view that can be most difficult to recognize are those that masquerade as spiritual expressions of no point of view. "I have no opinion about this, I just flow with everything. I don't mind what I do, I just go along with whatever happens." Although this may appear to be an expression of Clear Seeing, it may actually be reinforcing a subtle sense of identity and belief. Whatever quality we claim as a definition of who we are ("This is what *I'm* like") is generally compensating for its opposite held in the shadow. Why else would there be a need to hold the belief in the first place? Thus, the more we assert that we have no point of view, the more we may discover an underlying rigidity.

Poonjaji once threw me one of his enigmatic statements: "The real freedom is from the need to be free." As long as we hold on to a belief in enlightened/unenlightened, free/still in bondage, we are caught within the web of our own concepts. I remember meeting another of Poonjaji's students here in the West, who proudly announced, "I have not had a thought in six months." Another friend, who was listening quietly asked him, "Well, what was that then?"

As we dissolve points of view, concepts, and limitations, we also dissolve our precious spiritual beliefs, which we have used to define the very context of freedom and bondage. All understanding, including this sentence, is misunderstanding, because it limits the experience of the inexpressible. As we discussed in Chapter Two, we can start to use language together in the same way that we might talk about the taste of strawberries or great sex. It cannot convey the flavor, but it can be used to refer to a shared experience that is non-conceptual.

THE OPPOSITE IS ALSO TRUE

In Clear Seeing there is no point of view about anything. There is seeing beyond belief, and things are just as they are. As soon as consciousness polarizes and says, "Things are like this," the opposite is simultaneously postulated and given reality. You cannot split wholeness into a fragment without creating another fragment. If you cut a melon in half, you will inevitably get two halves. Points of view always exist on a spectrum ranging from one extreme to another. A belief cannot exist in isolation. If we attach to the belief "I am strong and capable," we automatically create, either consciously or unconsciously, another that says, "I am weak and cannot cope with life." If we create a point of view that says, "I am affluent and prosperous," we automatically create a hidden subpersonality that is afraid of and resistant to poverty. "Every soul which flees away from poverty and non-existence is misfortune fleeing away from prosperity and good fortune,"[7] says Rumi.

To the degree that one part of the polarity is being outwardly asserted, its opposite is being repressed with equal force in the shadow. The greater the repression, the stronger the opposite becomes, until it begins to sabotage the natural flow of life. This is why affirmations don't really work. The more we affirm the positive, the more energy we give to its negative counterpart.

We may either find ourselves slipping into the opposite end of the spectrum from time to time, or we may project it onto other people. For example, we may believe that we don't have what it takes to succeed, but we may idolize or envy those we perceive as successful. Or, because we have disowned this position in consciousness, we may even feel scornful and judgmental of successful people, whom we call "pushy" or "arrogant."

When we experience points of view through the mind only, we may be unable to sense the intimate connection between polar opposites. For example, people who identify themselves with power or strength are generally unwilling to accept that they have an equally strong relationship with weakness. As feelings, however, power and weakness are actually quite similar, as you may experience when you have a fight with someone. The same is true of confidence and insecurity. When we drop even deeper and experience points of view as contractions in the body, we find that the opposite ends of each spectrum are generated from the same physical location. In the chest, for example, we find both love and hate; in the legs we find both indecision and the ability to act. Even deeper is the *frequency* of the point of view, the *contraction within consciousness itself*, which gives rise to the continuous spectrum of opposing beliefs.

Over the full spectrum of belief, we tend to swing from one extreme to another like a pendulum. The swing may take hours, days, weeks, months, years, or even lifetimes. For example, we may spend one lifetime begging as a monk and the next pursuing material success. What would it be like if we could dissolve the entire spectrum and perceive reality from a place that transcends both extremes? What would it be like to be free of both greed and renunciation? Perhaps that could be called gratitude, accepting whatever is given and enjoying it fully. I have known people who live in this way, who expect nothing from life and live very simply, yet feel great abundance.

Or what might it be like to transcend the spectrum of victim and victimizer? Instead of intimidating some of the people in our life and feeling intimidated by others, we might experience empathy without needing to locate ourselves on some hierarchy of power and domination.

When we dissolve belief it is important to dissolve the whole spectrum. Otherwise, we simply swing to the other extreme, leaving the plane of belief in which the opposites coexists still in place. There is always the danger that you may think you have dissolved a point of view, whereas in fact you have merely reinforced its opposite. Anyone who grew up in an alcoholic household is familiar with the seesaw reality of repression–expression–guilt–repression.

In our attempt to define who we are, we have created innumerable spectrums of belief. You can experiment with the chart opposite by writing some of your dominant points of view on one side and their opposites on the other. For each pair, consider what reality might look like if you released the whole spectrum from your perception.

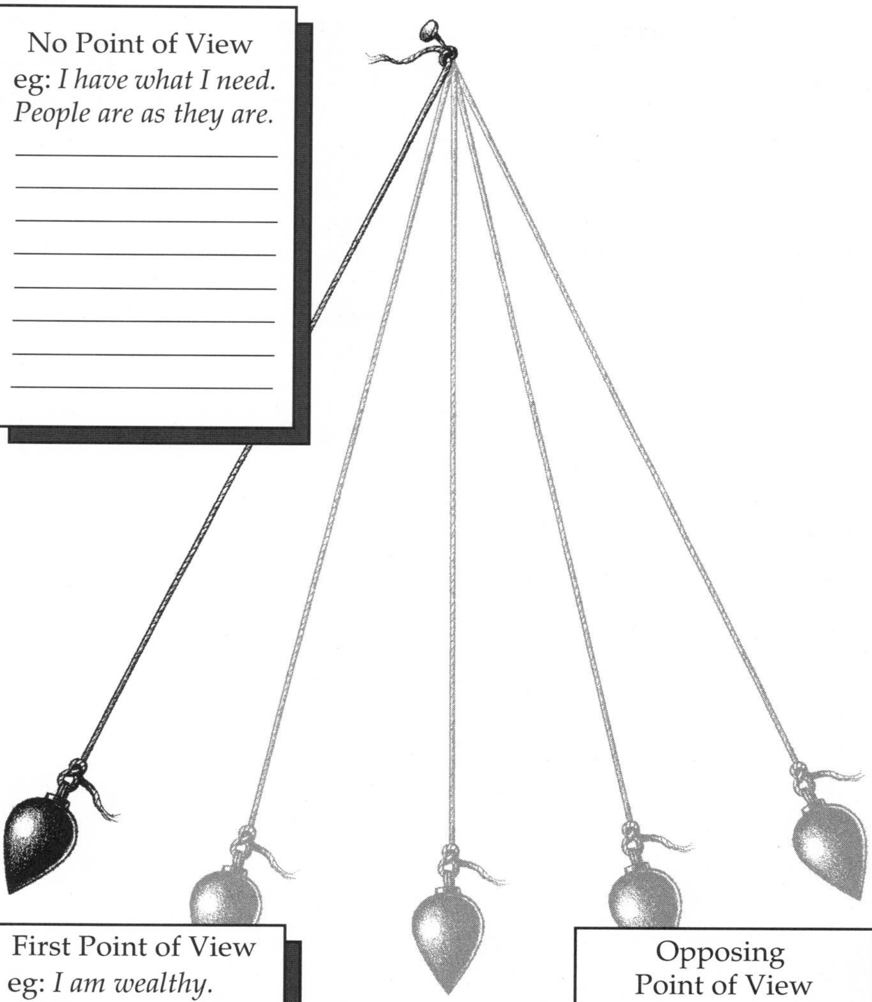

No Point of View
eg: *I have what I need.*
People are as they are.

_____
_____
_____
_____
_____
_____

First Point of View
eg: *I am wealthy.*
People are honest.

_____
_____
_____
_____
_____
_____
_____

Opposing
Point of View
eg: *I am poor.*
People are dishonest.

_____
_____
_____
_____
_____
_____
_____

In the brilliant essay from the 1950s in which he coined the phrase "double bind theory,"[8] Gregory Bateson suggests that we grow and evolve toward wholeness by being repeatedly presented with impossible choices, either of which seems to be a form of death. In these experiences of extreme stress, either we become schizophrenic and dissociate from our environment, or we make a quantum leap to a broader view of reality by finding a solution to the problem that is not to be found within the original parameters. By transcending these "double binds," Bateson maintains, we transcend the duality of the mind and are returned to a state of Beingness.

Hamlet represents a classic double bind:

> Whether 'tis nobler in the mind to suffer
> The slings and arrows of outrageous fortune,
> Or to take arms against a sea of troubles
> And by opposing end them.[9]

And Arjuna, a few millennia before, is faced with the double-bind choice of killing his kinsmen or disgracing himself as a coward. Both Hamlet and Arjuna solve their koans by transcending the very context in which the problem occurs. Hamlet returns from his brush with death on the ship to England able to resolve the polarity and to take action. And Arjuna, once he receives the eternal dharma from Krishna and realizes his true nature to be eternal, is able to face death, both his own and his kinsmen's, as an inevitable dimension of life.

In our session outline later we will find a way to transcend the double-bind choices that define our lives through the willingness to experience points of view energetically, outside of the stories they create.

TRANSPARENT POINTS OF VIEW

The points of view that most affect our lives and most obscure the natural state of consciousness are those of which we have no awareness. Like a pair of glasses, we see *through* the filter rather than experiencing the filter directly. Once we become enmeshed in such a transparent point of view, our personal reality shifts to provide evidence that our point of view is not a belief, but an accurate perception of reality. We forget that there are alternative ways of thinking and feeling. Here are some hints that we may be functioning on the basis of a transparent point of view:

- We easily become emotional over an issue that does not directly affect us.
- We become overly attached to a particular outcome or overly fearful of its opposite.
- We experience the same kind of problem repeatedly, but attribute it to "bad luck" or hold someone else responsible.
- We rigidly defend a position as being exclusively right and refuse to accept any alternate view as viable.

When situations recur in your life, ask yourself, "What would someone have to believe, consciously or unconsciously, in order to experience this repeatedly?" By discovering what you are proving to yourself by repeating this experience, you can uncover the hidden point of view.

For example, one of my clients told me he had repeatedly been the victim of financial swindlers. Altogether, he had lost money to unscrupulous characters four times over the two years prior to our first meeting. When we looked into the points of view he was secretly holding that were contributing to his experiencing life in this way, he initially protested his innocence. "I have absolutely no motivation at all to meet these kinds of people," he remonstrated, "Life is simply like that. The world is full of dishonest people." I stopped him in his tracks and pointed out what he had just said. Until then it had been unconscious; in fact, he consciously held the opposite belief, that everyone is essentially good and trustworthy. We released the whole spectrum, and he was able to see that people are neither essentially trustworthy nor untrustworthy, and that they can be both at the same time. Since that session two years ago he has stopped attracting spurious deals into his life.

As we bring our awareness to the points of view that obscure our original openness, those points of view tend to intensify before they are released. You may already have noticed that everything in life seems to conspire simultaneously to teach you the same lesson and provoke the same letting go. When we are releasing a hidden belief in our own insecurity, for example, every apparently secure structure in our life may suddenly become shaky and unreliable. As we begin to recognize the thought-form that is creating the external pattern, however, it loses its power to control our lives. The session outline we will practice together later in this chapter can accelerate and smooth out this process.

Transparent points of view actually exist in multiple layers, with one core belief giving birth to a variety of related beliefs. "A man has many skins in himself covering the depths of his heart," says Meister Eckhart. "Why, thirty or forty skins or hides, just like an ox's or a bear's, so thick and hard, cover the soul. Go into your own ground and learn to know yourself there."[10] For example, "I have to save and be careful with my money," "it is risky to lend people money," and "waste not, want not" may all be offspring of the core belief that "there is not enough to go around."

Our perceptual bias has been that our beliefs are objective conclusions, founded in our experience, about a fixed reality. With that body of scientific data securely tucked under our arm, we defend our beliefs as having objective truth. But just the opposite reveals itself to be the case: as we expose transparent beliefs, we discover that our points of view are the blueprints upon which our personal experience is based and that the blueprints always exist prior to our experience. In many cases this may be a bitter pill to swallow, but a constant willingness to explore the internal landscape has revealed this to be the case time and time again.

For example, I have spent quite a bit of time in India and other parts of Asia. Having grown up with a mother who saw germs everywhere, I went to India the first time with a certain trepidation and half a suitcase of little bottles. I got miserably sick with every kind of parasite and germ the continent had to offer. Needless to say, it was not hard to discover countless other Western travelers in the same predicament, all swapping advice about the best treatment—allopathic, ayurvedic, or herbal. For years, each trip to Asia was accompanied by the latest cure for the diseases I had already unconsciously decided to contract.

When I met Poonjaji, I was still in the midst of my love affair with Asian maladies. His response to my predicament was shocking to me. "There are no parasites," he said. Initially, I thought he was misinformed. Later, I saw a Western doctor present him with a book about parasites and how to cure them, as a support to his ailing students. Poonjaji promptly threw the book away. As time went on, I saw him repeat the same tactic with many visitors, and I realized that he was fully aware of the medical information but refused to invest it with any objective truth. Often when he succeeded in persuading visitors that they did not have the problem they thought they had, it disappeared, sometimes for good. Later, I traveled to other parts of India and met many different kinds of Western visitors. Slowly I began to notice that there were plenty of people who ate at the food stalls on the street, drank the tap water, and some who even ate raw vegetables. What they had in common was an assumption that "if the Indian people don't get sick, why should I?" I realized that it was, in part, the belief about how clean or dirty India was that would determine its effect on one's body. As I have dissolved the layers of Dettol-inspired points of view inherent in my British DNA, I have been increasingly able to visit Asia without sickness or an apothecary of little bottles.

Our beliefs affect our relationship with money as well. I have friends who always seem to have plenty of everything without making much effort. Abundance just seems to fall out of the sky without being asked for. Then I have other friends, particularly those of us born on the eastern shores of the Atlantic Ocean, for whom financial survival is always a struggle. In the same set of circumstances, one person might find greater ease and comfort, and another would find more struggle. We carry beliefs about money and the ease of its availability, and we constantly make those beliefs manifest as apparent realities in our lives.

We know people who never lock their houses or cars and never have anything stolen, and others who perceive their environment as untrustworthy and threatening and have amassed data that substantiates the need to own a gun and a guard dog.

To accept the universe as a solidification of our beliefs, we must be willing to take a stand against the history of Western thought as far back as Aristotle. Plato, his predecessor, saw the body and its environment as a manifestation of thought-forms. But Aristotle initiated the belief in an independent, objective reality, laying the foundation for the Western scientific world view. In seventeenth-century Europe, Newton and Locke further solidified the understanding that the objective is "real" and exists independently of the observer. Ironically, the Western scientific tradition has returned full circle to recognize the supremacy of consciousness through the work of Werner Heisenberg and others. Yet the belief in an objective reality, out there, independent of awareness, remains the predominant paradigm in the West.

Heisenberg discovered that the participation of the observer actually determines whether subatomic phenomena exist as particles or as waves. In a similar vein, when Captain Cook, who discovered Australia in the eighteenth century, sailed his enormous ocean-going vessel into a bay in the south of Tasmania, the aborigines on the shore appeared to be unable to see it. Because it did not conform to their pre-existing beliefs about reality, it was essentially invisible to them. Only when Cook's men lowered their rowboats into the water did the natives jump up in alarm and begin preparing for conflict. This story always makes me wonder what kinds of enormous spacecraft might be circling overhead, only made invisible by my transparent beliefs!

Our points of view about reality—about what makes us sick or healthy, what is easy or difficult, what is possible or impossible—are self-fulfilling prophecies that obscure the mystery of what is actually so, independent of the machinations of the mind.

Although we may be willing to acknowledge that our limiting points of view are responsible for our present life circumstances, for most people the buck stops dead when it comes to the circumstances of our early life and particularly our birth. After all, as babies we were innocent and helpless, and we are aware of no previous link in the chain of cause and effect for which we can take responsibility.

Jane, for example, experienced repeated rejections, not only in her love life, but in her work and among her friends. We were able to identify the core belief, "The world is an unloving place; you can't trust people because they'll abandon you," and she could recognize that this belief had a formative effect over the circumstances of her life. But she also realized that she felt justified in holding this belief because she was abandoned by her father in childhood. As Westerners, we find it difficult to disidentify from the circumstances of our childhood for a number of reasons. We perceive ourselves to have been powerless over that period of our lives and therefore out of creative control. Also, we share the cultural viewpoint, popular for only about the past 50 years, that our current behavior and unconscious beliefs are the product of our childhood circumstances.

But what if the opposite were true? What if our childhood was the solidification of a pre-existing point of view that existed in consciousness, prior even to our birth? Just the willingness to consider this possibility, without coming to any conclusion, allows us to experience core points of view without needing cause and effect. Jane's willingness to dive into the "abandonment" frequency and release her resistance to it began her liberation from the tendency to be rejected; she did not need to know if the point of view created her childhood or was caused by it.

As we release the unconscious layers of limiting belief, we may be left with many beliefs and perceptual biases about reality over which we have choice and awareness. They no longer prevent us, however, from resting in the natural state because they are not being resisted in any way and therefore do not take any psychic energy.

EXERCISE: ELICITING POINTS OF VIEW

You can do this exercise with a friend, sitting together on chairs. You do not need to do a formal induction; the Heart meditation described in Chapter Four is enough. The point of this exercise is not to change or dissolve anything, but to notice how many layers of belief we hold around any one aspect of our life.

Talk with your friend or client about an issue or relationship that is prominent in her life right now. Ask her to talk to you about it innocently and spontaneously. You may ask questions from time to time or acknowledge that you are listening, but do not add to or try to change the points of view as they arise. Every time you hear a point of view, write it down, and notice how many you find.

In particular, note the ways in which she alternates between opposing points of view; you may even wish to bring this to her attention. For example, regarding a need to earn more money, you may find the point of view, "I don't want to participate in the imprisonment of the corporate world." This might be contradicted by the statement, "I'm tired of all this messing around with spiritual values! I need to get on and earn a living!" Two other opposing points of view might be, "I'm a talented person. I can do whatever I choose to do in life," and, "Whatever I try to do just fails. I can't cope!"

Since not all of your friend's points of view are conscious, you may notice some that are implicit but not articulated. For example, she might give you a list of inconsiderate things her husband has done to her. Implicit in this list may be the point of view, "No one ever pays any attention to me." Or your friend may describe the many ways her boss has been unfair to her, in which you may hear the implied belief, "Life is unfair. I never get an even break."

Notice that for each point of view that is directly expressed, your friend will also have a relationship with its opposite. For example, you might note a statement like, "It's so hard to make enough money." If you ask, "Well, do you believe it should be easy to make money?" you may find that your friend also buys lottery tickets, believing, "Money should be easy to come by!" Similarly, if your friend says, "No one ever notices me; I feel so unattractive," you can assume that she has a relationship with the opposite point of view, which holds, "I am beautiful; I'm the center of the universe." You might elicit this spectral opposite by asking, "How would you like this to be?" or, "Who do you know who least has this situation in her life?"

If your friend begins to blame another person or the environment, you can also turn this into the recognition of a hidden point of view by asking questions like, "Do you believe that you always get a raw deal?" or, "Do you feel that you aren't safe?"

Make it safe to express negative points of view that may be socially unacceptable. Somebody might hold a point of view about getting revenge, for example, but they might not feel safe expressing it. You can elicit this by inquiring in a way that makes it clear that you do not have any judgment about the desire for revenge. Or you might use parallel stories from your own life or the lives of other people you have known to make it safe to have feelings and points of view that might otherwise be judged or repressed. Acknowledge the fear and resistance we all naturally feel to accepting certain points of view, such as anger, terror, lethargy, or resentment. Help your friend to see that these are merely thought forms and not essentially personal at all.

Throughout this exercise, elicit core feelings and beliefs. If your friend gets lost talking around the issue, use your questions to go deeper to the core point of view. Continue with this exercise for about twenty minutes, then note how many points of view you have recorded. In our training most students will discover between eight and thirty points of view connected to any particular issue.

RELEASING POINTS OF VIEW

Once you have recognized the multiple points of view that exist for your friend in a specific area of her life, it is relatively easy to dissolve these postures within consciousness back into the undifferentiated field from which they arose, simply through relaxing the resistance that has held the point of view locked in place.

Let us review what we have discussed about fixed points of view:

- Points of view exist simultaneously as mental belief, emotional states, physical contraction, and pure energy.
- When experienced mentally or emotionally, points of view always exist in polarities; every belief co-exists with its opposite.
- Once experienced in the body or as pure energy, this duality is dissolved, and the suchness of the energy in this moment is revealed.
- Points of view are generally transparent; we see reality through them, but we do not necessarily experience them directly.

- Points of view have no absolute, objective validity. They cause reality to appear a certain way but have no verifiable cause. They just are.

By returning attention to the body and then to the invisible field of consciousness itself, we can dissolve fixed points of view with relative ease. Energy is always moving within consciousness; that is its nature. You can verify this for yourself at any time. Close your eyes for a moment, and notice first how the energy manifests itself in the body and then notice the energetic atmosphere beneath that. Don't even try to label it, just allow it to be as it is. Take a breath, welcome it, embrace it, invite it. Now look again, as though for the first time. What happens? When we invite this kind of inquiry in our training, people invariably report that things are constantly changing. Sadness, if welcomed and celebrated, may shift to softness, which changes to excitement, which becomes sexuality, which turns into raw aliveness, and so on. It is all changing for no external reason at all, except that its nature is to be constantly fluid and constantly restoring itself to a new state of balance.

The art of facilitating the release of points of view is to guide attention to the field of consciousness deeper than thought, emotion, or sensation. People are generally not familiar with this dimension. It is the ocean in which waves of thoughts, emotions, and sensations are arising, and at the same time it is the One who is perceiving the arising itself. At this level of ourselves we experience points of view as contractions within consciousness itself, like a thickening within an infinite membrane. Einstein came to the same conclusion about matter, seeing it as a ridge in an otherwise unified field.

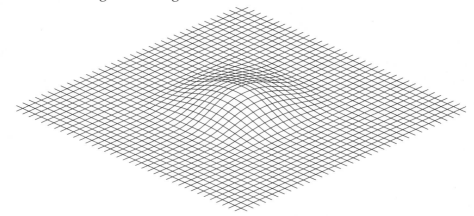

a ridge in an otherwise unified field

The waves of energy that move through consciousness are natural; in fact, this movement is the very essence of life. In small children, the waves shift and change all the time. They only become persistent and solid because they are resisted. These waves can be amplified or subdued. They are generally subdued because our attention is focused on accomplishing external tasks.

Although thought and emotion are always moving naturally within consciousness, they have had evaluative filters superimposed upon them in the form of beliefs. We cling to some waves, push others away, and remain indifferent to others. Systems of belief cause us to regard every aspect of our experience as positive or negative, which means that each wave in consciousness is met with a wave of resistance. It may be resistance to its arising (dislike), resistance to its departing (clinging), or resistance to its being fully experienced (indifference). The meeting of the original wave with the resisting wave creates a seemingly solid ridge within consciousness, which becomes persistent over time and becomes a state of identification. These ridges, created through the interaction of natural energy with resistance or control, become the personality and are stored in the body as habitual patterns of holding.

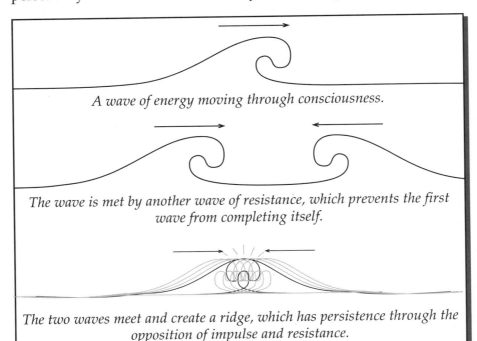

A wave of energy moving through consciousness.

The wave is met by another wave of resistance, which prevents the first wave from completing itself.

The two waves meet and create a ridge, which has persistence through the opposition of impulse and resistance.

As it resists and controls the energy, the mind puts labels on the waves that arise. We say, "I am depressed" or, "I am angry," and inhibit the wave's natural tendency to keep shifting and changing. States can shift in a fraction of a second. You have probably noticed, for example, how depressed feelings can turn into sweetness, openness, or gratitude. As soon as we label or define them, however, we inhibit their ability to change. The ultimate expression of this process of labeling is the pathologizing of experience by modern psychotherapy and the solidification of feelings into diagnostic states.

The key to releasing solidified points of view is to remove the resistance so the original wave can complete its movement and fall back into the ocean of awareness from which it arose. For most of us, however, the habit of resisting and controlling is so strong that the suggestion to "allow" energy to be there can easily be interpreted as complacency or indifference. Particularly among Westerners who have practiced Eastern meditation techniques like vipassana or zazen, I have noticed that "witnessing" or "allowing" energy often leads not to a relaxed awareness, but to a detached form of repression. This leaves both the repressed and repressing energies locked in place, but now with an overlay of "spiritual" calm.

We have found that resistance generally needs to be transformed into amplification. Fueled by the energy of what was once resistance, the original resisted energy can now break like a wave and return awareness to the natural state.

We will take this approach in our session, allowing what had been an obstruction to presence to become an invitation, a wave we can surf deeper into the natural state. In the Dzogchen teachings, this approach is called the liberation of thought and emotion into the primordial state. Patrul Rimpoche, the great Tibetan Dzogchen teacher, puts it this way:

Don't follow after the object of hatred; look at the angry mind.
Anger, liberated by itself as it arises, is the clear void;
The clear void is none other than mirrorlike wisdom.
In the self-liberation of hatred, recite the six-syllable mantra.[11]

He goes on to show how pride, desire, jealousy, and conceptual thought obscure clarity only when they are resisted. When experienced as pure energy devoid of any story, they are seen to be emanations of the vastness—and invitations to return to it.

When we feel upset, reactive, or frustrated, blaming the object of our emotions only leads deeper into identification. As an alternative, we can recognize that this experience is a meeting of a neutral external phenomenon and a fixed point of view. When the phenomenon is discarded, the feeling is left, as frustration for example. In the willingness to experience frustration as it is, without attributing it to some outside source, the frustration can be fully allowed and even enjoyed, and so it is clearly seen as an emanation of the natural state. No matter what its content, any emotion, thought, or sensation, when experienced without relation to an external cause, can return us to wakefulness. In this way, everything we encounter becomes guru, because every experience has the potential to provoke liberation.

The energy which has been resisting and creating the ridge…

can be used instead as fuel to increase the original wave…

…thus transforming resistance into amplification…

…and causing the original resisted energy to break and return awareness to the natural state

SESSION OUTLINE:
DISSOLVING POINTS OF VIEW

Step 1: Pre-Induction Talk.

As described earlier, talk together about an aspect of your friend's life and identify the related points of view that obscure Clear Seeing. It is not unusual to spend an hour on this talk.

Step 2: The Induction.

You can do this session sitting or lying down. Use any of the inductions you learned in Chapter Three, or any other methods you know.

Step 3: Elicit the Situation.

Ask your friend to feel or experience herself in a situation where these points of view are enlivened. If it is about money, she may be in a situation where all her fears and anxieties are brought to the surface, such as getting a bill in the mail or staring at the deductions on her paycheck. If it is a relationship issue, ask her to imagine herself with that person.

Step 4: Elicit Points of View.

Ask her to fully experience the situation in the present tense. Ask, "What can you see? What can you hear? What can you feel? What can you taste? What can you smell?" Make it fully experiential. Keep going until one of the points of view becomes enlivened, which means that she starts to speak about the situation from that point of view. Help her to identify fully with the point of view in a simple statement like "No one cares about me," or "I hate having to go to work." Ask her to repeat this key statement a few times until it has an energetic charge behind it.

Step 5: Bring the Attention to the Body.

Ask her where this statement resonates in the body, and ask her to put her hand there. Have her continue making the statement a few times, to feel the way it resonates from that place. Once she feels the physical contraction, ask her to let go of the outer situation or person and just feel the contraction in the body.

Step 6: Drop Into the Energetic Contraction.
This is the only part of the session your friend might find challenging, as we are not used to feeling energy in its purity, without reference to some manifest form. Ask her to feel the energetic contraction deeper than the physical sensation. You can say,

Feel the atmosphere of it, or
Feel the frequency of it within consciousness.

You will find your own language. Ask her to keep her hand or hands on this place while she drops the attention deeper.

Step 7: Find a Number for the Intensity.
Ask her to find a number from one to ten to represent the intensity of the contraction, where zero means it cannot be felt at all and ten means it cannot become any stronger.

Step 8: Consciously Exaggerate the Energetic Contraction.
Once she is feeling the energetic contraction within consciousness itself, ask her to consciously make it more intense. This means that the energy that was being used to resist the movement is now amplifying it, but without reference to any story. Ask her to use everything available to bring about this amplification: breath, sound, movement. Here are some statements you might use to facilitate this process.

Dive into it like a whirlpool.
Let it take over every corner of the universe.
Turn up the volume completely.
Let it take you, overwhelm you.
Let yourself become this energy.
Let this energy break over you like a huge wave.
Let the feeling become so strong that
Nothing else exists but this.

After she has started to exaggerate it, ask her again for a number from one to ten. Simply stay with the direct experience of the energy of the point of view, without thinking about what it means or attaching emotional significance to it. Turn the volume up on it as far as it will go, until it cannot be intensified any more. Ask her to continue building up the energetic contraction until it is a ten and cannot be exaggerated any further. This means that the resistance has been completely taken off, and there is now only the original energy. This step may take anywhere from two to ten minutes.

Step 9: Relax Back.
Now ask her to relax back into being that which is aware of the energy itself. You can do this by asking her to simply cease amplifying the energy, to switch it off, or just to let go. Or you may simply say:

Now, you can simply relax back into
Being That which is
Aware of all energy moving, expanding and contracting.

This is similar to the way we can make a clenched fist tighter, tighter, tighter—and then, all at once, relax it. If all the resistance has been turned into amplification, the energetic contraction will actually disappear when she stops intensifying it. Allow her time to let go and rest in the natural state.

Step 10: Check the Body.
Now ask her:

What is underneath your (left / right) *hand right now?*

If you have completely removed the resistance to the original energy, it will have dissolved back into the natural state of awareness and there will no longer be any charge in the body. Usually when we ask what is underneath the hand people respond with, "It's empty," or "nothing," or "space," or maybe "warmth." If she still experiences any charge or sensation in this area of the body, it means that there was some resistance to intensifying the energy completely. Repeat Steps Five to Nine until she reports that nothing remains when she feels the body under her hand.

Step 11: Return to the Point of View.
Now you can check to see if the full spectrum of point of view, from the one you worked with to its opposite, still holds any meaning. You will repeat the key phrase you found in Step Four and ask her what it means. For example, you might ask:

What happens when you hear the statement
"I never have enough money"? or
What does it mean when you hear the statement
"No one cares about me"?

Almost invariably, your friend will laugh or even be unable to understand the meaning of the statement. The entire universe in which that statement had reality has been erased, not only for this moment but also when she tries to recall it in memory.

Step 12: Check the Opposite Point of View.
It is important to check the opposite point of view in the same spectrum, to ensure that the whole range has dissolved. So ask the same question about the opposite point of view:

What does it mean when you hear the statement,
"I always have enough money"? or
What does it mean when you hear the statement
"Everyone cares about me"?

You will know that it has cleared when both points of view become meaningless thought-forms, devoid of substance.

Someone once said in one of these sessions, "I hate my boss." We built the energy up to its maximum and then dissolved it. Then we checked it by asking, "How do you feel about your boss now?" "He is just a man," she said. "He is as he is." She laughed. So I asked, "Do you like your boss?" She laughed again. She didn't hate him or love him, but was completely neutral. Neutrality does not imply apathy, however; it just means that things are seen as they are.

If any attachment remains to the point of view, you will need to be patient and repeat Steps Four through Nine until it becomes completely clear.

Step 13: Continue With Every Point of View That Arises.
You can repeat these steps for every point of view that arises. You may notice that many points of view seem to be similar. By "popping" one core point of view, you can pop many subsidiaries at the same time.

Continue in this way until she simply cannot find anything more to say. People usually become quiet and deeply accepting of the way things are. There is a depth, a willingness to experience things completely without resisting in any way. You will know she has come to a place of Clear Seeing because her view will be permeated with a lightness and humor that is completely devoid of cynicism and filled with gratitude, trust, and internal strength.

Step 14: Speak From Clear Seeing.

This is the most important step in the session. Although your friend may not want to say much, continue to ask her questions, both to ferret out any additional hidden points of view and also to give expression to a state of seeing beyond belief. Write down or record everything she says, and let her take it with her after the session. She will articulate right action and solutions from a vision uncluttered by conceptual thought. Thus far, everything said in the session has been an expression of the insanity of the mind. This step allows your friend to articulate from a place of true sanity.

We will discuss the qualities of Clear Seeing in the next chapter. Let it suffice for now to say that this state is extremely dynamic, proactive, solution oriented, and defies linear thought. Solutions arise that completely transcend the original problem state.

Step 15: Give Suggestions.

In this step, you can lead your friend into a deeper state of relaxation and continue to support and amplify the vision she came to in Step Twelve. Also, you can suggest that she can return to Clear Seeing easily with other situations or issues in her life.

> And it is good to know now
> That whenever you want to,
> Whenever you need to,
> You can recognize that
> Any opinion or belief held in awareness,
> Has a beginning and an ending in time, and
> You do have the possibility to
> Return that back into its source and to
> Allow it to dissolve.
> It is good to know that
> Every moment
> Just now
> Between the dissolving of one thought
> And the arising of another is
> An invitation to
> See things clearly,
> Just as they are.

Step 16: Count Back From Five to One.

Session Outline :
Dissolving Points of View

Step 1: Pre-Induction Talk.

Step 2: Induction.

Step 3: Elicit the Situation.

Step 4: Elicit a Point of View.

Step 5: Bring the Attention to the Body.

Step 6: Drop into the Energetic Contraction.

Step 7: Find a Number for the Intensity.

Step 8: Consciously Exaggerate the Energetic Contraction, until it is at a maximum.

Step 9: Relax Back in Self Inquiry.

Step 10: Check the Body.

Step 11: Check if the Point of View still has meaning.

Step 12: Check the Opposite Point of View.

Step 13: Continue with Every Point of View that Arises (steps 4-12).

Step 14: Speak from Clear Seeing.

Step 15: Give Suggestions.

Step 16: Count Back from Five to One.

CASE HISTORY: MAGGIE

Maggie had been diabetic for most of her life and was constantly having to monitor her insulin levels, test her blood sugar, and watch her diet. She had multiple layers of beliefs, emotions, and energetic charge around her condition. We did a long pre-induction interview, and we discovered layer upon layer of both resentment and also attachment to her condition. It was surprising to Maggie to find out that she had hidden motivation (sometimes called secondary gain) for her physical condition. Some of the points of view we discovered were:

- This is not fair: I have it harder than most people.
- I will never heal my body from its condition.
- This is a punishment from God for something I did wrong.
- I should be able to learn from this experience.
- It is the fault of the doctors; I was not treated properly.
- I have to learn to accept this without complaining.

Once we moved into the session itself we shifted quite quickly through many layers of transparent belief. For each point of view that we dissolved, its opposite was also rendered transparent: for example as we dissolved the belief that "I have it worse than other people," we also discovered and dissolved the belief that "I am blessed and lucky" (which Maggie held to, and used as a way to keep herself separate).

As we moved through more layers, they dissolved more quickly. This is highly typical with this session: after a few layers of belief have been surrendered, the rest just drop away in handfuls. Maggie began to laugh even as we started to dissolve each new layer, so the process of "popping" we described earlier took less than two minutes for each new point of view we discovered.

We finally arrived at the core contraction around which her diabetic condition was centered: "I cannot participate fully." She had always seen this belief as the result of her condition, but for the first time she saw that it was an arbitrary belief held about herself which *caused* her condition as much as was caused by it. She recognized that she had, in a sense, "hired" the imbalance in her pancreas to validate and justify a subtle sense of separation that she had always maintained from her universe. As we moved into this sense of sitting on the side of the playing field while other kids played, sitting aside with her sandwiches while the other kids ate cake at a party, and later sitting out the dance to protect her energy, she discovered that this relationship to life was universal, and she had the intuitive sense that this stance had a history far longer than her memories of this lifetime. She came to a place in the session where she could no longer attribute meaning to the idea of fully participating, or of not participating. Life simply is happening as it is, and the level of engagement is inextricably inter-twined with the very essence of life itself.

The results of this session were not overtly dramatic. Maggie cer-tainly experienced no overnight cure to her condition. She did not throw her insulin needles into my trash bin, and rush to the local bakery with cries of "Miracle!! I am healed!" The effect of her relaxing into clarity was more subtle. She no longer instinctively held a physical condition as a reason to define herself as a person, or to define her relationship to life. When I last spoke to her she told me that she still experiences fatigue from time to time in the same way, and she still has to monitor and maintain her insulin level; but none of that needs to interfere with a full experience of her life and her true nature.

Through this session, solutions reveal themselves from within the problem state like diamonds hidden in the mud. Generally, these natu-rally occurring solutions have been obscured by layers of concepts. "Say you are in a tight bind mentally," says Joe Miller, "and you don't know what to do about it. I've had any number of people come to me with difficulty they were going through in their consciousness, and nine times out of ten they only saw a couple of sides of it, the positive and the negative. By just being still and looking at it as if it isn't you—my, my, my—you find out multitudinous ways that you can come back to the same thing and take care of it."[12]

In our next chapter we will examine more closely what the state of Clear Seeing reveals, and how it can be distinguished from a state of apathy or gullibility. Before you read further to learn what other people have discovered through this process, try it for yourself with a friend.

CHAPTER 13

SWEET SURRENDER

*It is enough that one surrenders oneself. Surrender is
to give oneself up to the original cause of one's being.
Your source is within yourself. Give yourself up to it.
Seek the source and merge in it.*[1]

RAMANA MAHARSHI

ead this chapter and consider the questions raised here only
after you have explored Chapter Twelve, so your exploration
of this material is coming from your own experience of the
state of Clear Seeing, not from any concept or fantasy. Once you have
done the partner exercise in Chapter Twelve, take a sheet of paper and
write down five to ten answers to the following questions:
- What is revealed to me in a state of Clear Seeing when I have
  dissolved all points of view?
- What is revealed about any part of my life when I no longer
  hold on to beliefs?"

Take your time in answering these questions now, and then turn the
page to find out what others have reported from this state of awareness.

In the previous chapter, we recognized that we see life habitually through points of view that are for the most part unconscious. When we explored what those points of view contain, we discovered that they have a mental, an emotional, and a physiological component. We recognized that every point of view is registered in the body, and we dropped even deeper into their energetic frequency, where points of view can be "popped" or evaporated by removing the resistance to experiencing them fully. We allowed points of view to dissolve back into the ocean of awareness from which they all arose, and we came to perceive reality nakedly, without any filters of belief. In this chapter we will consider what it might mean to face a relationship or situation with no point of view at all, from a place of Clear Seeing.

Here are some statements that were made, both in training programs and in individual sessions, after all points of view had been dissolved.

- I can't remember what the problem was!
- Things are just as they are; it is all happening perfectly.
- It is all being taken care of; there is no need to worry.
- The only thing is to relax; everything is happening on its own.
- Things are always finding their own balance.
- Now it is so obvious what needs to be done.
- Problem? What problem?
- I am awareness itself. I am not these thoughts and feelings.
- It is all always changing. It always has. No one is doing it.
- There is deep longing to co-operate with the will of the vastness.
- There is such certainty that things work out beautifully.
- The flow is already occurring within itself.
- I feel happy for no reason at all.
- There is only God; there is only love; there is only this.
- This "I" is a creation of the spaciousness.
- The right thing will happen at the right time. It always has.
- Each new step happens on its own.
- There is only love—I feel so much love.
- It is all peace; it is all silence; it is all beauty.
- All my effort has been counterproductive.
- I feel so much gratitude, for everything in my life.

Through the relaxing of belief, an unwavering recognition develops, an inspired certainty in the innate perfection of things. Whether we call it Tao, God, Spirit, or Existence, a natural trust of and surrender to the Great Order emerges spontaneously.

THE QUALITIES OF CLEAR SEEING

When people speak from this dimension of themselves beyond the mind, they do so in certain specific ways. First, they tend to speak of perceiving things directly, free from duality. "Things are as they are" has no opposite point of view; it is a perception and expression of "suchness" rather than of opinion or belief. Simultaneously, such dualities as "past" and "future" are distilled into "now," and value judgments like "good" and "bad" are condensed into "what is."

Second, the capacity to view life from Clear Seeing reveals a vision that is overwhelmingly optimistic and trusting of the "bigger picture." Painful experiences are seen to be temporary and potentially beneficial, while happiness and love are understood as the natural state to which we inevitably return. There is a tendency to relax the pressure of blaming oneself or others and to see things as occurring just as they are, without the need to single out a particular individual as being uniquely responsible. Negative experiences are viewed as isolated cases of misfortune, while the general state of life is recognized as benevolent. There is a difference, however, between an optimistic *point of view*, which contains and hides its opposite, and a state of Clear Seeing, which recognizes the vastness of experience containing both negative and positive experiences and, at the same time, the context in which both occur. I have noticed this natural optimism revealing itself equally in those who started the session with a pessimistic attitude and those who started with an optimistic one.

When we relax into an acceptance of things as they are, a natural humor simultaneously arises, an ability to laugh at oneself and one's seeming misfortunes from a larger perspective. This quality is completely different from the "gallows" humor we so readily use to deny pain and disguise vulnerability. There is nothing cynical or cruel in the humor that arises in Clear Seeing; it is the benevolent chuckle of the sage rather than the cruel wit of the cynic.

Lois, for example, was referred to me by her doctor; she had fairly advanced breast cancer. The negative attitude with which she viewed her medical condition and the circumstances of her life was masked by a dark sarcasm and pessimistic dry wit. She focused her attention on everything she lacked—the unlikelihood of being able to have children even if she made a full recovery, the cruelty and coldness of her husband, and the ways she had been mistreated in her job. At the start of our work she doubted whether she really wanted to recover her health, and she even doubted whether she had the choice. We did many sessions together before we were able to begin the challenging task of dissolving points of view and returning to Clear Seeing around the cancer. When she began to realize the ways in which her illness had enabled her to free herself of many constraints in her life, she began to laugh. The recognition that her illness had been somehow helpful to her allowed her to see her recovery as a choice she could make. She reduced the pessimistic and hopeless voices that had dominated her experience to cartoon characters in her imagination, and she laughed at the absurdity of their obstinacy.

Above all, in the Clear Seeing that is revealed in the dissolution of point of view, there is the recognition of a great perfection in life underlying all our personal desires, fears, and attempts to manipulate reality. This sense of wholeness and perfection, in which distinctions of good and bad have no meaning, is felt as a whole-body knowingness, rather than thought out as a belief system.

I love the story of the awakening of the Zen monk Banzan. When he was walking through a market, he overheard a conversation between a butcher and his customer:

"Give me the best piece of meat you have," said the customer.

"Everything in my shop is the best," replied the butcher. "You cannot find any piece of meat here that is not the best."

At these words Banzan became enlightened.[2]

Robert had been a highly successful real estate developer in southern California. He specialized in buying undeveloped land zoned for commercial use, taking out multi-million–dollar bank loans to develop it, and then turning a big profit at the completion. In the late eighties he had eight or ten such projects in progress, with loans out on each one. When real estate in southern California took a huge dive within a few months, however, he was left owing more on each property than its total worth. Robert went from being a multimillionaire to facing bankruptcy, and he lost any interest in or appetite for the usual pursuits in his life.

This seeming misfortune, however, prompted a deep restructuring of the filters through which he saw reality. As he slowly stripped away points of view, which were mostly pessimistic, he came to view the situation free of evaluative filters. In our work, he dropped easily into Clear Seeing and began to see the hidden blessings in his so-called misfortune. He saw that he had been driven by financial ambition for decades, and that this act of "divine intervention," as he came to call it, had slowed him down enough to find his heart again. He began to practice meditation and Tai Chi and spend more time with his family. He told me that this shift would never have occurred if he had continued his old style of life. As he continued to rest in and speak from Clear Seeing, his view changed from pessimism and disappointment to a feeling of gratitude.

Robert's experience is typical of a return to Clear Seeing. Although one still has the capacity to recognize pleasure and pain, gain and loss, both are seen to be reflections of a higher benevolence. In Clear Seeing comes the recognition that although, "You can't always get what you want," in the words of Mick Jagger, "if you try sometime, you just might find you get what you need."[3] In fact, you always have, and you always will.

This recognition of a higher purpose or bigger picture is not an ethereal concept. It is expressed most fervently by those who have been sobered and grounded by the most challenging life circumstances. The recognition of perfection that our students and clients experience is the same state that the Dzogchen teacher Namkhai Norbu describes: "Seeing that everything is self-perfected from the very beginning, the disease of striving for any achievement is surrendered and, just remaining in the natural state as it is, the presence of non-dual contemplation continuously, spontaneously arises."[4]

With this recognition of life's perfection, it becomes clear that *my* beliefs, desires, fears, and plans were never what caused life to flow, but that things have always been taken care of by the unseen hand of some benevolent, loving, and intelligent force. For most of us this is a staggering realization: that everything just naturally works better when we give up trying to control things according to our idea of how they should be. In John Lennon's words, "Life is what happens when you're busy making other plans."[5]

Once we relinquish all conceptual knowledge, the fingerprints of this hand of Benevolence are discovered on every aspect of our life, although the name, address, and phone number of the Benefactor have never been known. In this mystery is born the awe and devotion that inevitably arises out of all we have explored together in this book, like a perfume from a rose once it opens. For in the absence of an individual doer, what is left is not void at all, but an omnipresent fullness of immense love. In this recognition, trust is born.

Trust can be a cultivated quality, or it can be the natural, spontaneous result of direct seeing. When trust is artificially cultivated, it hides within itself its opposite, distrust. You have probably experienced this at one time or another. The more you try to trust, the more distrust you feel, because anything cultivated or imitated contains its opposite. You may have also tasted the nectar of real trust, which is simply the recognition of something far greater than individuality at work. I saw this in both my sons when they learned to walk. At first, they would need mother's or father's hands holding theirs above their head to be able to take tiny steps. First one hand would be released, then the other, but they had to feel us there as resources. Our presence gave them the confidence and trust to know that, if they fell, there would be someone there to catch them. At such a young age, this attitude is not based on any indoctrinated system of belief; it simply arises out of the direct experience that mummy and daddy will be there when you need them. This is trust: the realization or recognition that something is there to take care even when the idea of "me" is abandoned.

Poonjaji tells a wonderful story to point our attention to this unseen Benevolence. Although we may never have experienced such extreme intervention, each of us could no doubt find a parallel in our own experience that elicits the same question that Poonjaji ultimately asks. The story, which comes from his days in the mining industry in India, is reprinted here in its entirety, in his own words, and with his permission.

"In 1953, I was delivering a load of manganese ore to a ship in Mangalore. I spent the whole day on the ship, and once the ship had been fully loaded and the hatches were closed, I got a bank draft from the captain and a certificate stating that the ship had been loaded with 10,000 tons of manganese ore bound for Rotterdam. I wanted to cash the draft at the bank in Bangalore by the following morning, which was about 500 miles away. It was already about nine o'clock at night, and I was exhausted, having worked the whole day from morning to evening. This was offshore loading, not near the wharf where I could easily have got off of the ship, and it was very warm.

"I knew I was very tired and that I needed to rest, so I should set off early in the morning. But then I thought it would be too late, the banks would be closed by the time I arrived, and it would be better to cross the mountain road right away, which climbed from sea level up to 5,000 feet. The road went through eleven hairpin bends before reaching the summit of the hill and descending down the other side. I decided to cross to the other side of the hill, have a coffee and a short nap, and then continue on to the bank in Bangalore.

"I do not know what happened. I had simply decided that I could not stop on the mountain because there were wild elephants that had already lifted cars and thrown them down into the valley, which was one mile deep. I knew that it was better to go on to the other side and take a rest. When I arrived on the other side of the mountain, however, my head was resting on the steering wheel, and I felt totally fresh. I had awakened from a deep sleep. I no longer even wanted to take a cup of coffee, I felt so fresh. I continued the journey to Bangalore, with the feeling that I had already had a complete, sound, deep sleep. Who was the driver? I had slept; my head was on the steering wheel. I no longer needed rest or coffee, I was so fresh, as if I had slept a complete eight hours. Now, 'Who drove the car?' is still a problem that I cannot solve. Even drivers who are wide awake sometimes have accidents, as you often see on the freeways. But I was fast asleep. There was no accident, the road was very narrow, no more than 15 feet wide. On one side [was] a high mountain, and on the other side a very deep valley; and I cut every one of those eleven hairpin bends. So who did it, who drove the car? I still cannot find an answer to this question!"[6]

At some point everyone has felt the touch of this ever-forgiving, unstintingly patient mystery in their lives. Some people seem to experience it most perceptibly when traveling in another country, when they have set aside their usual agendas and judgments. Some call this force "God," some call it "Spirit" or "Tao." By whatever name it is called, its power and intervention reveal themselves more as we relax into Clear Seeing and leave personal point of view behind.

This Benevolence does not start with its recognition, however. Rather, we come to the realization that things have always been taken care of by this same Benevolence, and action from a personal point of view has only been an interference in the great perfection of things. Suzanne Segal fell into the recognition of her true nature with relatively little external support. In a recent account of the metamorphosis of her view of reality in the ten years following her awakening, she writes: "It also became apparent that there never was a personal reference point, and that everything is being done and has always been done by an unseen doer. This doer does not start doing only when it is seen to be the doer. It has always been the doer; the personal self has never been the doer. Thus, life as usual continues to unfold, everything gets done, just as it did before the realization of vastness occurred.

Since there has never been a personal doer in any case, the realization of its truth does nothing to change how functioning occurs."[7]

In Clear Seeing, the recognition of the Great Perfection brings the capacity to respond to life and flow with each situation without any fixed agenda. In the session we explored in Chapter Twelve, clients speak about the "obvious next step," the now unmistakable ways in which life is calling for a specific action to be taken, and the knowing that each moment will always call forth the appropriate response. "Become one with the Tao," says Lao Tzu, "then relax and be natural, and everything happens on its own."[8] Twenty-five centuries later Patrul Rimpoche, from another tradition, repeats the same message: "Leave everything as it is in fundamental simplicity, and clarity will arise by itself. Only by doing nothing will you do all there is to be done."[9]

The trust that arises in the recognition of this Benevolence leads to a way of responding to life that has been called "spontaneous right action," where thought, action, and speech are no longer dictated by limiting points of view, but arise spontaneously when we step aside and allow the force of Benevolence to move through this apparent individuality. Joe Miller puts it in his usual fresh and original way: "Your surrender is signing off from personality and ego standpoint, then living from the One. The inspiration is always there. Mind is a wonderful tool and must be developed, but it's a lousy boss. You've got to go up to headquarters and let it come from there. Then, whatever happens, you can speak with spontaneity."[10]

In Taoism, this has been called *wei wu wei*, action through non-action, where speech occurs without the sense of speaking, walking occurs without the sense of walking. In the Dzogchen teachings, it is described like this: "This term means no action, but, from the practitioner's point of view, this is not a choice—one just does what comes next in the natural state. Whether it is to look or not to look, to act or not to act, everything is self-liberated; therefore there is no missed view or right view—one simply does not care."[11]

Culturally, we have tended to associate virtue with following an objective moral code. For example, Buddha laid down Four Noble Truths, the fourth of which is known as the Eightfold Path. These eight tenets of spiritual life are usually taken to be eight sequential steps in a gradual path towards liberation: first learn right thought, then master right speech, then move on to right action, and so forth. This view has kept practitioners busy for centuries. But one may also see these eight "steps" as the natural qualities of a life of Clear Seeing, which simultaneously and spontaneously arise in the absence of conceptual thought. Levi Dowling makes the same suggestion about the Ten Commandments in the *Aquarian Gospel*, a Christian mystical text written earlier this century. Ramana Maharshi says the same thing, quoting Patanjali, in these words: "Friendship, kindness, happiness and such other qualities become natural [to one who is awake]....Affection towards the helpless, happiness in doing good deeds, forgiveness towards the wicked, all such things are natural characteristics."[12] All morality is fulfilled when points of view are dissolved and action is surrendered to that which guides life in the absence of our interference.

It is this cognizance of the Great Perfection that opens the heart to a Love that is not object-specific, a love that shines equally onto all that it perceives. Nisargadatta Maharaj, the great teacher of non-dualism who lived and taught in Bombay, spoke of it this way: "Having realized that I am one with and yet beyond the world, I became free from all desire and fear....Spontaneity became a way of life, the real became natural and the natural became real. And, above all, infinite affection, love, dark and quiet, radiating in all directions, embracing all, making all interesting and beautiful, significant and auspicious."[13]

Spontaneous right action is simply the result of dissolving limiting points of view around a specific aspect of our lives and allowing a response to arise on its own from Clear Seeing, without the interference of thought. I am sure you can remember a time when there was no thought of past or future, of individual "I" or belief, and yet action still occurred. Some people have experienced this state in a time of emergency. Last time I was in England, I read in the newspaper about a big fire in an apartment building. An older man who had never been known for courage or bravery rushed suddenly into the burning building, with no concern for his own safety, to save the lives of three children he had never met. When he was interviewed later, he said, "I don't know what came over me! I acted in spite of myself." This is the feeling one gets. It can happen in an accident or a crisis; what is needed spontaneously bursts forth, no longer held back by the limiting ideas of who we are or what we are capable of.

In his passionate book on the Persian poet Rumi, Andrew Harvey presents us with a vision of how this surrender can become a channel of planetary transformation. "How will we save the planet? Only by awakening to who we are. And how will we act when we awaken to who we are? We shall act with Divine love, with Divine passion, with

Divine power, with Divine truth, and that Action, because it will have upon it the seal of the Beloved, because it will be springing out of the will of the Beloved, will give us the solutions that cannot be obtained in ordinary consciousness, that cannot be even understood, glimpsed, aimed at, or even sketched while we remain in the prison house of the ego."[14]

Some people experience spontaneous right speech and action when life thrusts them into a teaching or healing role and something greater takes over and uses the body as a channel. When I first returned from India and began to give Satsang at Poonjaji's request, I would frequently find that my responses to people's questions would appear mysteriously and would be as much of a surprise and a teaching to "me" as they were to "them." In those moments, some greater intelligence than this limited personality would speak through this body, and spontaneous right speech would occur on its own.

With the recognition of the Great Perfection that comes in Clear Seeing, a deep longing spontaneously develops to hand all of life back to that unseen hand of perfection. As the poet Kabir says of himself in the third person, "Kabir saw that for fifteen seconds, and it made him a servant for life."[15] Where life has previously been motivated by desire and ambition, now there is a constant craving to allow the great Benevolence to act through this body and these thoughts. This very craving has been the driving force of the greatest mystical poetry and literature for thousands of years, and it can even be heard in contemporary secular music. Mary Fahl of October Project sings:

Come take my body
Come take my soul
Come take me over
I want to be whole.[16]

The lyrics of k.d. lang are overflowing with the language of surrender.

Wash,
Wash me clean.
Mend my wounded seams,
Cleanse my tarnished dreams.[17]

And George Harrison's music, from *Within Without You* in 1967 and *My Sweet Lord* in 1970 to *Extra Texture* in 1994, are a constant testimony to the sweetness of surrender.

No one expresses this craving more poetically than Swami Vivekananda, Ramakrishna's ambassador to the West early in this century. "Behind my work was ambition, behind my love was personality, behind my purity was fear, behind my guidance the thirst for power. Now they are vanishing and I drift. I come...floating wheresoever Thou takest me—in the voiceless, in the strange, in the wonderland."[18]

Ramana Maharshi, although primarily an advocate of self-inquiry, saw surrender to the hand of Benevolence as an equally valid path home to the Self. "If one surrenders oneself there will be no one to ask questions or to be thought of. Either the thoughts are eliminated by holding on to the root-thought 'I,' or one surrenders oneself unconditionally to the higher power. These are the only two ways for realization."[19]

Surrender is sometimes spoken of as if it were a choice, a decision, or an activity. Some spiritual organizations that prescribe surrender as a path home require that you follow the guidance of, and hence surrender to, a specific leader or hierarchy. This kind of "cultivated" surrender is actually closer to obedience, with the hope of enlightenment as a "payoff" in the future if one is a good enough disciple or follower now. The spirit we are recognizing here in a state of Clear Seeing is a natural surrender, not based on blind faith or obedience, but on the innocent recognition that life always flows more smoothly in the absence of an individual's interference. "Trying to intefere with the Great Plan is like trying to do the work of a Master carpenter. The chances are you will cut your hands," says Lao Tzu.[20]

In this same recognition lies the key to being of service to others. We can learn all kinds of techniques and tools to assist other people in healing and awakening; but as long as these learned skills are used with the sense that we are an individual doing something it is like a boat with a magnificent and expensive sail, but no wind to pick it up. There is also a way of being with people in natural presence, in which we hand the process of healing back to the mystery itself and allow it to speak and move through this body. When the wind is strong enough, the boat will move smoothly across the water with even a tiny sail.

I have learned so many skills over the past twenty years as a bodyworker, hypnotherapist, and breath therapist. But the most important capacity by far has been the willingness to step out of the way altogether and rest in the awareness that I don't know anything at all. From the feeling of complete incompetence comes the force that can truly allow magic to happen on its own. As years have gone by, this exquisite inadequacy has grown and grown, to the point that I throw my hands into the air and give up before even starting. "Die while you're alive," says Bunan, "and be absolutely dead. Then do whatever you want: it's all good."

DESTINY AND FREE WILL

This leads us to a question that has haunted us eternally as human beings. Do we actually have any choice in what occurs in our lives, or is every event and every action from birth to death predetermined by an endless chain of cause and effect? "You must believe in free will," said Isaac Bashevis Singer. "You have no choice about it!"

In Clear Seeing comes the recognition that both are simultaneously true, in a delightful and provocative way that defies the dualistic mind. In Clear Seeing, there is the recognition that the events of our lives are the inevitable by-product of thoughts and emotions that have become locked into persistent points of view. Thoughts arise spontaneously in response to events that were in turn caused by thoughts and emotions. There is no person to be found, only an endless chain of events, responses, and subsequent events. Simultaneously, there is the recognition of the constant freedom to resist this natural flow of life or to relax into it, and in that relaxing to surrender to life itself. Surrender is the first and the last freedom; it is both the death and the rebirth. In the moment of surrender, there is at once the apparent death of an egoic self, which was after all only a mass of predetermined thoughts, and the birth of consciousness incarnate within matter, completely free and unconditioned.

It is this dual awareness of the predetermined nature of events and the absolute freedom of consciousness at any moment to identify fully with form or formlessness that infuses such grace and richness into the surrendered Heart. For surrender does not allow us either to abandon personal responsibility or to turn our backs on the effects of past actions. The Christian mystic Fenelon puts it this way: "One who has surrendered to God is not blinded to their own faults or indifferent to their own errors, but is more conscious of them than ever, and increased light shows them in plainer form, but this Self-knowledge comes from God, and therefore it is not restless or uneasy."[21]

FEAR AND RESISTANCE

In most people, there is both a longing to let go and dissolve and a deep fear and resistance that sets in. For this reason, the session outline that follows can be helpful, because it supports and deepens the power of surrender and at the same time reveals the illusory nature of our fears.

Most of us have a deeply held belief, substantiated by experience, that unless we are assertive—unless we push for what we want—we are going to be victimized or manipulated. Even after we have glimpsed the power of the Benevolence, the fear arises that in surrendering life back to itself we may become weak or docile. Quite the opposite is the case; in fact, the tendency to be manipulated or controlled, or to relinquish control to another, is in itself a rigid point of view, which has underneath it a sense that "I'm not good enough," "I can't cope," or "Someone else knows better than I do." Once this layer has also been dissolved into Clear Seeing, the unseen hand of Benevolence, which is the ultimate authority and power, can now speak *through* and embody this physical form. We hand over power to the real source of power; then, when strength and clarity are called for, they burst forth with far more totality than if they had arisen from an individual point of view. When the money changers have taken over the temple, we don't rely on our personal strength; instead, Divine power impels us to rush in, turn the tables, and kick butt.

People also fear that they would lose any sense of reliability without a fixed set of beliefs, that their position would be continuously shifting and changing—married today, but single tomorrow; fully engaged in work one day, goofing off the next. The indecision we fear is actually the result of alternating between opposing points of view, both of which are unrecognized. When we abandon all points of view and rest in Clear Seeing, that which is actually right, good, and correct can arise spontaneously out of itself, and we can begin to allow problems to present from within themselves their own solution.

The fears and concerns we pass through in our process of surrender are not entirely unfounded. As we let go of fixed positions, we give up our life the way we (or at least our conditioned beliefs) would have it and relax into acceptance of what comes to us. Although this seems to lead inevitably to more happiness, love, awareness, and expansion, the gateways of initiation through which we pass may test the old habits of the mind. We are reminded of the Biblical character

Job, whose faith in God was challenged as he moved into deeper layers of trust: his family got the plague, he lost all his money, on and on his troubles mounted, yet he continued to trust in God. "God instructs the heart, not through ideas but through suffering and adversity,"[22] says one Christian mystic. It seems that the more we rest in our true nature, the more rigorous and challenging the testing becomes, as though life rises to match our capacity to experience difficulty. Any remnants of clinging to "I," to separation, any subtle holding to points of view or limited identities, can and will be deeply challenged by the unseen force of the divine.

With his permission, I would like to tell you the story of one of my best friends, Isaac Shapiro, who has also been asked by Poonjaji to teach on his behalf in the West. When we first met, Isaac appeared to have everything going for him. He had a beautiful wife and two gorgeous children, and, because his wife had inherited a fortune from her family, they were able to travel throughout the world teaching together without any concern for income. They were everybody's idea of the ultimate couple.

Looking back on that period of his life, Isaac realizes now that he carried a subtle layer of complacency and aloofness, a subtle point of view. "There are no flies on me. I've got it all together!" Quite abruptly, while they were traveling together in Europe facilitating *Satsang*, his wife fell in love with another man, took the two children, and left him. She filed for divorce, which would cut him off from the inherited fortune to which he had become accustomed and make it difficult for him to see his children. His external life went through what many would describe as a kind of hell, in which everything to which he had become accustomed or attached was taken away from him. From the outside, it certainly seemed like a negative situation. But Isaac reports that, unbearably difficult and painful as it may have been, the experience took him far deeper into his heart, intensified his compassion, and burned out whatever subtle arrogance and complacency he had been carrying. Recently he described the situation in retrospect without regret, in fact even with gratitude. He is remarried now and has another child. But he recognizes that this sequence of events was necessary to drop him into an even deeper state of surrender.

Isaac's story is not an isolated one. Of the people I know who have stepped into the fire of surrender in recent years, many have experienced challenges and the death of attachments far more difficult than anything that came before. Long marriages and relationships have dissolved, and there have been physical illnesses and dramatic changes in financial circumstances to pass through. Such stories merely illustrate that the process of life itself is constantly deepening our surrender, whether we overtly desire it or not. The more resistance we have to seeing our hidden identities, it seems, the more painful these lessons become.

Maybe not everyone in the process of awakening goes through such extreme circumstances, but we are all tested to whatever degree is necessary to teach us unconditional surrender to the source of life. "When all the world is filled with evils, place all setbacks on the path of liberation,"[23] Atisha advised us a thousand years ago. These situations arise, it seems, to help us recognize hidden points of view and let them go, so that there may be a more complete relaxing into wakefulness and surrender. "Into any man who is brought low, God pours His whole Self in all His might, so utterly that neither of His life, His being, nor His nature, nay, nor of His perfect Godhead, does He keep ought back," says Meister Eckhart. "He empties out the whole thereof as fruits into that man who in abandonment to God assumes the lowest place."[24]

There are so many reports in every tradition of the experience of being tested in this way; what is today integrated and accepted with balance might have been unbearable five years ago. Madame Guyon refers to the shift like this: "It does not involve the cessation of suffering, but of the sorrow, the anxiety, the bitterness of suffering."[25] Awakening to the Self inevitably involves surrendering life back to itself. If the surrender is resisted from within, external circumstances will keep hammering at the door until we finally give in and let go. The session in this chapter facilitates surrender and allows the inevitable to take its natural course.

BOTH WAVE AND OCEAN

The surrender that arises out of Clear Seeing presents within itself another paradox to the old habits of the dualistic mind: Who is the one surrendering, and who is the one being surrendered to? Who is the devotee and who is the object of devotion? These words—"devotion," "surrender," and "trust"—have almost always been used in a dualistic context. In other words, "I" surrender to "you," or "I" surrender to "God," with the idea that God is separate from who "I" really am. The surrender that occurs in Clear Seeing is a surrender of the illusion of separation to the reality of Oneness. It is a surrender of a false sense of self to the realization of the True Self. It is the handing over of that which is born and dies in time to the unborn and undying. Consequently, surrender is not separate from or different from awakening. Surrender is the handing over of the illusory to the real.

In the surrendered state, you are revealed to be both the one surrendering and the one surrendered to. This session will allow you to help people to pass life's issues and challenges from the individuated identity back to the True Self, which is not separate from Life itself. "It is enough that one surrenders oneself," says Ramana. "Surrender is to give oneself up to the original cause of one's being. Do not delude yourself by imagining such a source to be some God outside you. Your source is within yourself. Give yourself up to it. That means that you should seek the source and merge in it."[26]

In most of us there is a deep resistance to dropping this dualistic relationship with God. We carry vestiges of Christian conditioning in which we fear the wrath of the Almighty if we rise up for a moment out of our gutter of sinners. Carl Jung acknowledges this in his foreword to the teachings of Ramana Maharshi. "The identification of the Self with God will strike the European as shocking. It is a specifically oriental realization, as expressed in Sri Ramana's utterances. Psychology cannot contribute anything further to it, except the remark that it lies far beyond its scope to propose such a thing."[27]

We can also see that the postulation of "me" and "God" in relationship is the real arrogance, for it presumes that there is something other than God that can choose whether to surrender to the divine or not. "'I am God' is an expression of great humility," says Rumi. "The man who says 'I am the slave of God' affirms two existences, his own and God's, but he that says 'I am God' has made himself non-existent and has given himself up....He says 'I am naught, He is all; there is no being but God's.' This is extreme humility and abasement."[28]

In Clear Seeing, we realize that an unseen Benevolence takes care of things perfectly and that, at the same time, this Benevolence is not separate from That which we really are. "All talk of surrender is like pinching brown sugar from a brown sugar image of Lord Ganesha and offering it as *naivedya* [food offering] to the same Lord Ganesha," says Ramana. "You say you offer your body, soul, and all possessions to God. Were they yours that you could offer them? At best, you can only say, 'I falsely imagined till now that all these which are yours were mine. Now I realize they are yours.'"[29]

This is the great mystery, that I am both wave and ocean simultaneously. I am the Son of God as form, and I am God itself as formlessness. I am both devotee and the object of devotion. A mysterious, constant craving arises to surrender more and more fully to That which I really am, and so a dialogue begins between individuality and universality. This is the song of the wave to the ocean, neither separate nor fully dissolved, which we call prayer.

Many of us, brought up with a dualistic notion of prayer, have rejected it as the infantile mumbling of the mind to an object of its own creation, the projection of a parental figure in the sky, occasionally benevolent, but also capable of fury and revenge. This kind of projection causes supplicants to believe that they can beg for favors (or boons, as they are called in Indian literature) like money, a spouse, prestige, and the alleviation of suffering. That is not the kind of prayer that unfolds out of Clear Seeing. Here we have instead the cry of form to dissolve back into formlessness, which is a dialogue between dimensions of the Self. The great Christian saint Julian of Norwich said, "Prayer makes the soul one with God."[30] We will facilitate this kind of nondual prayer, which imagines no God outside of one's true nature.

In our trainings we do an exercise together, which is a wonderful way to learn about the nature of prayer. Students work in pairs. While person B takes notes, person A just prays spontaneously, without censoring what comes out. It might be "God give me a new truck" or "Let my enemies be boiled in hot oil." It might be "May Aunt Gladys be healed of her cancer," or "Divine Mother, please may I merge with you more and more every day, and let your will be done through me." Then the participants switch roles. After both partners have spoken their spontaneous prayers for about 20 minutes each, partner B induces a deeply relaxed state in partner A and moves through dissolving points of view, as described in the previous chapter. Once A is resting in a spacious state free from perceptual filters, B reads the list of prayers back to A, now in this open and empty state. A listens to her own prayers and notices how they sound from the natural state. On average, about 80% of the prayers on the original list no longer seem important when heard from a state of Clear Seeing.

All prayer distills down to the same place when it arises from and is heard by a silent mind. Once all points of view have been left by the wayside, the only prayer left is "Thy will be done." Exhausted by a lifetime of struggling to impose our separate will and realizing that it only increases our suffering, we fall at the threshold of the divine and whisper in supplication, "Have your way with me, I am through; take this body and mind and this life and use it for your Divine Will."

Prayer works. I do not know why or how, but once we have abandoned our attachment to outcome, prayer brings resolution and causes problems to disappear. Prayer may be answered by a disembodied voice out of the sky, by a strong felt sense, or by the events that unfold naturally in the process of life itself. It might take the form of something a friend says to us, a chance meeting, or lines in a book that suddenly jump out at us. When the prayer comes from a place of connection rather than from the cravings of the conditioned mind, it always brings a response.

In a recent book that documents his dialogue with the unseen hand of Benevolence, Neale Donald Walsh writes that God has this to say about the way he answers prayer: "I do not communicate by words alone. In fact, rarely do I do so. My most common form of communication is through feeling. Feeling is the language of the soul.... Hidden in your deepest feeling is your highest truth.... I also communicate with thought.... In communicating with thought, I often use images and pictures.... In addition to feelings and thoughts I also use the vehicle of experience as a grand communicator. And finally, when feelings and thoughts and experience all fail, I use words. Words are really the least effective communicator."[31]

SESSION OUTLINE: SURRENDER

This session is intended to be done with someone who has already experienced moments of surrender to Divine Will and trust in the Benevolence, and hence feels a longing to hand life back to itself more fully, but at the same time recognizes the power of old habits of grasping and control. The session facilitates returning the steering wheel to the one who negotiates all the hairpin bends, and always has.

Step 1: Pre-Induction Talk.
Together you can recognize an issue that seems to be unresolved and to demand some kind of action, but where the specific action is not yet clear.

Step 2: Relaxation Induction.
Use the techniques described in Chapter Three, or any others with which you are familiar.

Session Outline :
Surrender

Step 1: Pre-Induction Talk.

Step 2: Relaxation Induction.

Step 3: Come to Clear Seeing.

Step 4: Bow to Benevolence.

Step 5: Surrender the Situation to Divine Will.

Step 6: Listen to the Voice of Divinity.

Step 7: Become the Force of Benevolence (Optional).

Step 8: Merge the Individuality. Back into Formlessness.

Step 9: Rest as Formlessness.

Step 10: Suggestions.

Step 11: Count Back from Five to One.

Step 3: Come to Clear Seeing.
You may want to go through the process of dissolving points of view described in Chapter Twelve. Or, if your friend is already in a state of Clear Seeing, proceed to the next step.

Step 4: Bow to Benevolence.
Ask your friend to get a feeling in her body of the presence of Divine energy. It is important to start with the body in order to prevent this session from becoming just a mental exercise. First sense the Divine presence in the Heart, then let it grow and expand.

Some people want to give formlessness an icon, depending on the spiritual tradition with which they are familiar. If they come from a Hindu background, it might be the form of Ram or Krishna; if they come from a Tibetan Buddhist background, it might be the form of Shakyamuni Buddha or one of the Buddhist deities or teachers. For Christians it might be Jesus or one of the saints. It does not really matter what form appears, or even if there is a form at all. The form is a mirror of formlessness, through which love can prostrate to itself. Some people are comfortable approaching formlessness directly and prostrating to emptiness itself.

Without losing sight of the recognition that this form has arisen as a manifestation of her own formless Heart, let your friend speak to it, prostrate to it, sing love songs to it. She may be moved to singing, to tears, or to dancing. To give space to this feeling of devotion is to deepen the realization of the Self, which is both emptiness or formlessness and Divine Love. Find a way to help your friend prostrate to the unseen hand of Divine Will, whether through an internal visualization or through an actual physical posture of prostration. The feeling is one of handing over control of life from our limited point of view to that which is really taking care.

Step 5: Surrender the Situation to Divine Will.
Now help your friend to speak out loud to the Benevolence. Encourage her to hand the issue you discussed in Step One over to the Divine, to acknowledge out loud, "I know nothing, I am just a wisp on the wind. Please take me over, I surrender everything to you." The language people use in this step will

vary from person to person, depending on their background, culture, and personality. Some may become deeply devotional and use words like "My Sweet Lord, I lay my life willingly at your feet, and throw all I have in your service." Some may be more detached and scientific. Your role as a facilitator is simply to support and witness whatever occurs.

Here the false sense of identity is handing back mastery of life to that which is absolutely real. The changing, prejudiced mind is handing back authority to the unchanging, Clear-Seeing mind.

Step 6: Listen to the Voice of Divinity.
In this step it is very important to allow your friend the space to be still, listen, and wait. The whole session is infused with a silence and a waiting in relaxed alertness. Nothing may come for many minutes, and nothing may come in words at all. What is most important about this session is the attitude of handing things back, which develops in Step Five. As long as the process has momentum, continue to help your friend to surrender and listen.

Step 7: Become the Force of Benevolence (Optional).
You might now ask your friend to become this nameless, formless force of Divinity. If she is using an icon, ask her to become the representation of her icon (Buddha, Krishna, Jesus). If there is no icon, you can say,
> *Let yourself expand infinitely*
> *In all directions and*
> *Become the space in which*
> *All this is occurring....*
> *The space in which*
> *The person you took yourself to be is occurring,*
> *And from this,*
> *Now look at the situation, and*
> *Allow its resolution to*
> *Arise from within itself.*

This is an optional step that allows your friend to look at the situation without the prejudice of a personal point of view and to give testimony to its resolution. Or it may simply be enough in the handing over to allow the resolution to arise spontaneously in the course of life itself.

Step 8: Merge the Individuality Back Into Formlessness.
You can ask your friend to become the spaciousness in which this is occurring (if you have not already done so in the previous step) and to absorb the form of individuality back into the formlessness of universality.

Step 9: Rest as Formlessness.

Step 10: Suggestions.
Here you can use whatever suggestions feel appropriate to anchor the feeling that all of life can easily be handed back to Divine Will.

Step 11: Count Back From Five to One.

CASE HISTORIES

Both in our trainings and in private practice, these have been the deepest and the most moving sessions, the times when people are most deeply transported beyond the idea of being able to *do* anything to help anyone else. The facilitator is more like a recipient of Grace than any kind of giver. The room becomes infused with sacredness and divinity, like an intoxicating perfume in the spring.

No one seems to know how this works; in fact, it feels like a delight to let it remain a mystery. Nor does it seem important to understand who is surrendering and who is being surrendered to—whenever the problem state is released into the mystery, Grace happens. When we say that prayer works, we mean that every time the problem is laid completely at the feet of something greater than egoic control, and every time the utter incompetency of individuality to do anything at all is thoroughly acknowledged, the prayer is heard, and an answer comes. It may be in words or images in the session, or later in the course of life itself, perhaps in dreams or in the words of a friend. The resolution may not come as we expected, but things happen such that the problem can no longer be found.

When prayer is infused with awareness in this way, it is the purest, sweetest, most touching embodiment of humanity. Rather than offering case histories, as we have in previous chapters, here are some real quotes from people's responses in Step Five above:

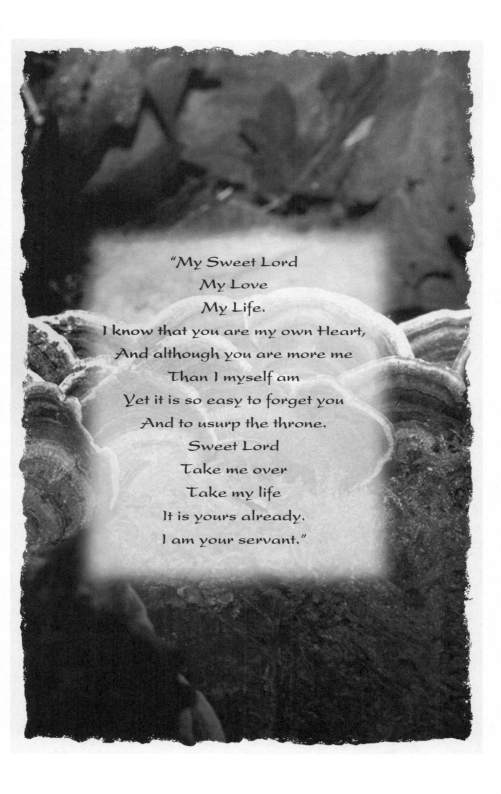

"My Sweet Lord
My Love
My Life.
I know that you are my own Heart,
And although you are more me
Than I myself am
Yet it is so easy to forget you
And to usurp the throne.
Sweet Lord
Take me over
Take my life
It is yours already.
I am your servant."

"Take these eyes
Take these ears
Take these legs
Take these feet
Take this mind
Take this tongue
Take this personality,
It is given freely.
I am yours,
You are all that is real
It is done."

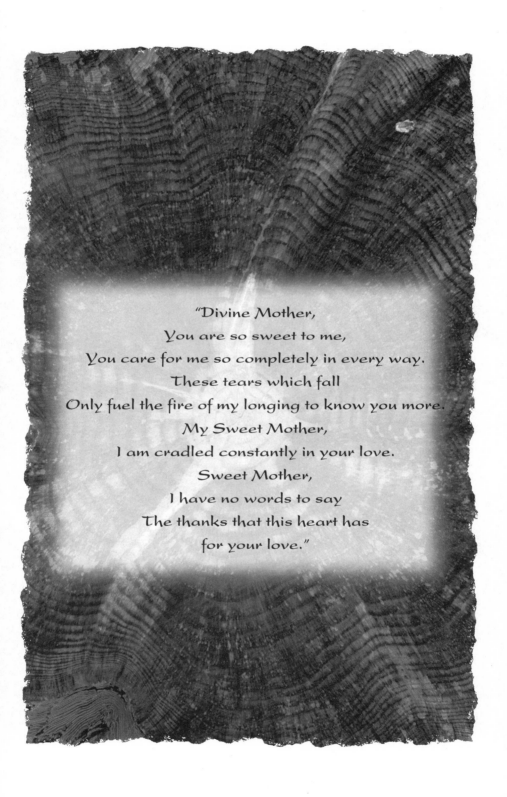

"Divine Mother,
You are so sweet to me,
You care for me so completely in every way.
These tears which fall
Only fuel the fire of my longing to know you more.
My Sweet Mother,
I am cradled constantly in your love.
Sweet Mother,
I have no words to say
The thanks that this heart has
for your love."

"Words given back to silence,
Form returned to formlessness,
Ideas returned to certainty,
Emotions dissolved into love,
All disslolved into perfection,
It is complete now…
In the only now that is."

"My Lord,
I feel you without feeling,
I hear you without sounds,
I know you without thinking.
You are more myself
Than these words which speak.
Take me,
For I am already consumed
From the beginning.
Touch me, for I am already melted,
Kill me sweetly, for only You are alive
My Lord, my Lord,
All is returned to you."

DEVOTION

We have described surrender in this chapter largely in terms of a recognition of the unseen hand of Benevolence that runs through all of life. There is another current to this recognition, which we have not yet explored and which is difficult to discuss in words, for it is completely outside the realm of the mind. When we fall into recognition of the hand of Benevolence, which is ultimately not separate from our own nature, there is not only a relaxation into trust, but also the birth of devotion and overwhelming love. All that I took myself to be now falls face-forward at the feet of that which I really am. Many are brought to tears of gratitude and awe at the recognition of the Divine.

There is a tradition in India of treating the teacher with utmost respect, in a way to which we are unaccustomed here in the West. It is an expected formality, rather like shaking hands, to prostrate yourself before the Guru. If done "properly," you are completely prone, with both legs, both arms, the whole body, and the forehead on the floor. Sometimes, particularly among Western devotees who are trying to do the Indian thing just right, this kind of prostration can become mechanical and contrived.

I remember one particular occasion at Poonjaji's house during the monsoon period. It was raining buckets outside, like nothing one ever sees in America. It seemed as if the ocean was falling out of the sky. I had been visiting him for tea, and it was time to go home for dinner. Outside the main door to the house, there was a covered passage only a few feet in length. Because of the force of the rain, the floor of this passage had become covered with almost an inch of water. As I stepped out beyond the porch, Poonjaji came outside and called out to me. I turned around and saw him offering me an umbrella to protect me from the deluge.

In that moment, with a bright moon shining overhead through the rain, our eyes met, and he looked back at me with his knowing grin. As I looked into his eyes, I saw the whole universe there, infinite in all directions, and I simultaneously saw that I was looking into myself. This was the most intimate moment of my entire life. I became so overwhelmed with the recognition that what I was actually seeing in his eyes was my own nature seeing itself that my body fell involuntarily to the ground at his feet, right there in the puddle! Tears streamed down my cheeks into the rain water for no reason. This was not a premeditated act but occurred spontaneously as a result of the recognition of no separation. He laughed, picked me up, and took me back into the house for dinner and fresh clothes.

This kind of devotion overwhelms the human heart from time to time; it arises in the absence of any otherness. There is no difference between the devotee and the object of devotion, or between one who surrenders and that to which one is surrendering, but merely love falling in love with itself.

Some say that this is the very purpose of creation—that the original vastness and creative force may come into recognition of its own beauty, otherwise unmanifest, and fall in love with itself. We are willing to go through the pain and confusion of separation from our true nature just so love itself may finally look into its own eyes and say, "Aha! This is who I am!" It is this recognition that makes everything else worthwhile.

The other day, while I was driving, I absent-mindedly switched on the radio and heard a beautiful song by Tracy Chapman that included these lyrics:

> *The things we won't do for love...*
> *I'd climb a mountain if I had to,*
> *And risk my life so I could have you*
> *You, you, you....*[32]

And k.d. lang, the high priestess of devotion and pure longing of our generation, sings these immortal words:

> *When the sun goes down here*
> *And darkness falls,*
> *The blanket of winter leaves no light at all.*
> *You search for shelter*
> *To calm the storm,*
> *Shaking with an instinct*
> *Just to stay warm....*
>
> *But I'd walk through the snow barefoot*
> *If you'd open up your door to me.*
> *I'd walk through the snow barefoot....*[33]

There are so many songs like this that give expression to the Heart's willingness to do anything for love. When love is in the air, you do not care what you have to go through for it. "Only if one knows the truth of love, which is the real nature of Self, will the strong entangled knot of life be untied," says Ramana. "Only if one attains the height of love will liberation be attained. Such is the heart of all religions.

The experience of Self is only love, which is seeing only love, hearing only love, feeling only love, tasting only love, and smelling only love, which is bliss."[34] When the heart is listened to, it doesn't matter what the consequences are. All is made whole in that recognition.

In one sense, awakening happens in a single moment out of time. The shift from seeing oneself as a limited person with desires and fears in time and space to being the Self—infinite, expanded in all directions, and the source of all things—happens in the space between one second and another. The embodiment of this shift, however, happens in time and is progressive and evolutionary. The deepening expansion of infinity into itself is eternal. How can there be an end to the deepening of love falling in love with love? Can there be a limit to love, to devotion, to rapture? Wherever you start and wherever you reach, you remain eternally a beginner at the foothills of peaks that endlessly beckon you deeper. This seduction of infinity into itself is at the core of every bhakti tradition, at the core of Rumi's poetry, and gives the endless journey its heart.

There is an immense difference between devotion in duality and devotion in non-separation. When there are two, devotion is between "me" and "my beloved," and hence creates a feeling of separation. "When you talk of love, there is duality, is there not—the person who loves and the entity called God who is loved?" say Ramana. "The individual is not separate from God. Hence love means one has love towards one's own Self."[35] Without otherness, devotion is the feeling of God recognizing Its own nature and falling in love with Itself. That which registers these words in this moment is constantly in the process of coming into recognition of its own infinite mysteries and falling in love with its own self. "Devotion is nothing more than knowing oneself,"[36] says Ramana.

This is the devotion without separation, which is endless.

CHAPTER 14

THE WISH
FULFILLING JEWEL

Love's power to restore
Broken fragments into one whole
Is the supreme attainment
Of the human soul.[1]

ANGELUS SELESIUS

I n the last chapter we saw how surrender and devotion are
spontaneous attributes of Clear Seeing. In this chapter we look in
the same way at compassion. Compassion, we will discover, is
both a pathway deeper into non-dual awareness and the spontaneous
and choiceless result of seeing that there is really no separation
anywhere in life, outside of the distortions of the mind.

We have seen that nothing need be done to create the natural state;
the Self is always already present, but is often overlooked because of
obscuring emotions and points of view. When we see the Self in all
beings, compassion is the inevitable result. It does not need to be
created or imitated; it is another facet of our natural state and will

shine forth on its own once obscuring tendencies have been recognized and dissolved.

Just as rigid points of view and false identities block the recognition of our true nature, so our ability to see the same divinity in others is blocked by our judgments. Whether positive or negative, judgment always obscures the natural state of the Heart.

WHEN THE HAIRS ON YOUR BODY STAND ON END

In Chapter One I described how most of the processes in this book came, like a fax out of nowhere, when I spent two unplanned weeks in Katmandu. During that same visit I also received another blessing, which has deeply influenced the development of this work.

At that time there lived in Katmandu an eminent Dzogchen teacher in the Tibetan Nyingma tradition by the name of Urgyen Tulku Rimpoche. After Dilgo Khyentse died in 1991, Urgyen Tulku, who had been a teacher to the Dalai Lama, was regarded by many as the most eminent Dzogchen teacher in the world. Without knowing much about the formalities of Dzogchen practice, I had visited Urgyen Tulku on a number of previous visits to Katmandu, and each time I had been delighted by his utter simplicity and innocence. Despite his reputation as a high lama, the title of his book reflects his self-effacing humility: *Repeating the Words of the Buddha.*

One morning during my two-week visit, which was in the monsoon season, I felt that I would love to see Urgyen Tulku again. I walked around the corner from my guest house to the monastery of his son, Chokyi Nyima Rimpoche, also a prominent Dzogchen teacher, to find out where Urgyen Tulku was residing. Once again, the mysterious force of benevolence guided the situation to its conclusion, for the first person I bumped into was Eric Pema Kunsang, a Dane who had been Urgyen Tulku's personal translator for more than 20 years. Since the old Rimpoche only spoke Tibetan, a good translator was essential to meet with him. Urgyen Tulku resided in a monastery several hours journey from Katmandu through the Nepalese national forest, and it happened that Eric was going there at eight o'clock the following morning. He invited me to accompany him.

Not only did this give me the opportunity to meet with the great teacher with his own translator, but it also allowed me a morning to talk with Eric, who had spent twenty years immersed in the Dzogchen teachings. The journey required an hour taxi ride to a remote village far up the valley, where even buses do not go and the villagers are all dressed in traditional Nepalese clothes. I felt that I was time traveling. We then began an uphill hike for several hours, through the forest into the steep hills surrounding the Katmandu valley. Each switchback in the trail offered an even more spectacular view of the valley below. Each turn produced a feeling of greater remoteness, until it seemed impossible that anyone could be living so far from civilization. The trail by now was completely ridden with pot-holes and would not allow any kind of vehicle to pass. Then, out of the blue, we came across the multicolored prayer flags flapping in the wind that announce a Tibetan gompa[2] or stupa.

Tibetan gompas are built something like a wedding cake. First a rectangular building is constructed, then a smaller rectangle is built on top of it, and finally, sitting above the whole thing like a fairy on a Christmas tree, is a small room, no bigger than ten feet square. It was in this small room, with windows on all sides, that Urgyen Tulku resided. Eric led me up through the main part of the building, past the sounds of gongs and boys with shaven heads chanting in harmony, past the mixed smells of incense, yak butter tea, and Tibetan food, to the roof of the building. After announcing our arrival, he led me in to meet with the Rimpoche.

Urgyen Tulku Rimpoche

I do not think I have ever met a more innocent human being in my life than Urgyen Tulku Rimpoche. He sat on his small bed cross-legged, fingering some prayer beads, and looked at me through his round glasses with a grin of recognition and humor. He seemed like a newborn baby and a wise seer all at once. Although we had met before, I was so overwhelmed by his beauty and loving heart that I started to cry uncontrollably. Through Eric's translation, the Rimpoche responded with his characteristic humility, "Poor fellow, who sheds tears at the sight of one who can neither help him nor harm him."

We talked for a long time, punctuated by Eric's lucid translation. The Tibetans have a sophisticated understanding and language for the subtle tendencies of mind that rise up to obscure consciousness. Making a useful distinction between "absolute truth" and "relative truth," they recognize that while the ultimate nature of things is empty and inherently perfect, the world of form and duality still exists, and awareness does become caught in obscuration. This understanding helps to take the pressure off our tendency to ignore or feel guilty about the old habits of the mind.

At one point we began to speak of what they call *rigpa*, the unborn nature of awareness, which is equivalent to what Ramana Maharshi calls the Self. When I asked Rimpoche a certain question for clarification, he responded with a smile and a wave of his hand, then closed his eyes and turned our attention to the One who is observing all events occurring. Although the words he used were familiar, they were accompanied by a "transmission" that is known in the Dzogchen tradition as the "pointing out instruction" or "mind to mind instruction," in which the Rimpoche uses his own realization of the primordial state to reawaken and deepen the realization of the student. Everything disappeared: no more Rimpoche, no more Arjuna, no more room, and no more Katmandu in the valley below us. Just infinite empty awareness.

We sat in the small room for an interval out of time, three bodies, one awareness. Perhaps a few minutes elapsed in silence. Then our eyes met again, and he raised an eyebrow in invitation to continue speaking. The strongest pull at such a time is to bask as that natural awareness, not to touch thought or form again. But there was also an impulse to ask him another question, and I am glad I did, because the answer has proven to be of enormous value. The words he spoke to me, although very simple, have remained etched in my heart.

I asked him more or less the same question one is always tempted to ask in the presence of a great teacher. "This realization of the unborn nature of mind is exquisite and perfect, and no question arises out of it. At the same time, I know that I will soon be returning to Katmandu, to the demands and pressures of life, to my family and all the responsibilities of life in the world. In these situations, the innate perfection of life can seem to be overshadowed."

With a smile Urgyen Tulku looked at me with eyes that revealed no hint of judgment or superiority. He did not seem to be responding to "my" predicament as a struggling Westerner, but to *our* predicament as embodiments of spirit in flesh. He gestured to the view from the panoramic window, to the chaos and pollution of the Katmandu valley far below, and quietly said these words, which were simultaneously translated by Eric.

"When the Heart is so overwhelmed with compassion, seeing the suffering of humanity, that the hairs on your arms stand on end and tears involuntarily flow down your cheeks, then you are in the natural state. And when you are so overwhelmed with devotion and love, seeing the beauty of all sentient beings, that the hairs on your arms stand on end and tears involuntarily flow down your cheeks, then you are in the natural state."

As I listened to the translation, allowing the words to penetrate the pin-drop silence, the hairs on my arms involuntarily stood on end and tears began to flow down my cheeks. I found I was resting in my true Heart, and obscuring thoughts and concepts had no foothold. The moment added another layer of depth to the endless journey Home. His words penetrated every corner of my life for many months to follow.

Urgyen Tulku went on to speak about other things and gave me his blessings and an exquisite gift before I took my leave to descend into the valley below, into the testing ground of human life. I saw him on one other occasion, which was equally moving, and heard a year later that he had left his body. He remains a gentle and compassionate presence in my heart.

Like a baby gorilla in the womb, it took about six months for Urgyen Tulku's words to fully gestate. The following November I was visiting Boston, teaching one of the first workshops utilizing the tools that are offered in this book and giving individual sessions. My wife and child had gone back to Bali, where we had been living, and I was in America alone. We had planned to reunite for Christmas, but the travel plans had not yet been finalized, and the prospect of spending Christmas without my family loomed over me like a ghost.

Boston in the winter is not a heart-warming place. It is cold and damp, and everyone seems to be doing their best to avoid each other. My loneliness and grief over the separation from my family was painting my whole world a dull gray. Because I was without a car during my short stay in Boston, I was obliged to use the local subway system, known as the "T," which was filled by people who looked as cold and lonely as I was feeling.

One day, when I was taking the T downtown to an appointment, I looked across the car and saw a man in his fifties; his gray hair was long and unkempt, and he had a few days of stubble on his face. He was wearing clothes that even a thrift store would have refused to carry. He had holes in a pair of sneakers that looked quite inadequate for the snow, his tattered pants were a few sizes too big, and his worn-out jacket was torn and revealed the lining. Finally our eyes met, and I saw that he was gently mumbling to himself, obviously lost in some dream world of his own.

When we see people in pain or down on their luck, we instinctively look away in an attempt to avoid the feelings that facing them might arouse. It is a reflex of self-protection that separates us from their plight and walls off our Heart. This time, however, as our eyes met, I recognized myself. The clothes, the body, and the mind were older and more ragged, but I saw my own pain and loneliness looking back at me, and my own mumbling, chaotic mind being reflected. Most important, underneath it all I saw the same ground of Being, unaffected, shining, looking back at me, back at itself.

Our eyes were locked in something like an embrace. The hairs on my arms stood on end, and tears came to my eyes and fell down my face. The man broke into an uneasy grin, and his eyes shone with the light of seeing and being seen. We sat on the T train out of time, out of story, and out of mind, resting together in the natural state of Self-perfection.

In that moment, I realized that there really is no separation anywhere, either at the ground of Being or at any dimension of our human experience. The pain I see around me is my pain. The joy I see in a new mother and child is my joy. The peace and wisdom I admire in Poonjaji or the Dalai Lama is my wisdom. And the violence I judge in Bosnia or Northern Ireland is my own disowned violence. The intimacy I share with close dharma friends is available with everyone, even this sad man on the Boston T. The key is the willingness to feel and allow pain without defending oneself against it in any way. Urgyen Tulku's teaching from that summer had borne fruit: the way to stabilize and deepen the view is in that capacity of the Heart to transcend judgment. It is through love.

NATURAL COMPASSION

Like surrender, compassion can be the spontaneous overflowing of the natural state, or it can be an imitated or cultivated quality. Poonjaji is fond of telling the story of his visit to a seminary in Spain where missionaries are trained how to exhibit compassion. They are taught how to speak and how to look with their eyes in a serious and mournful way. According to Poonjaji, who recounts the story tongue in cheek, they are even told to put a little piece of onion in their handkerchief so tears will flow when they put it to their eyes! He uses this story to illustrate how absurd cultivated compassion can be.

Cultivated compassion, as taught by many organized religions, is the attempt to feel or behave in a certain way in the belief that it is the right thing to do. The more we try to cultivate compassion, however, the more plastic and self-righteous it becomes, like an imitation of the real thing. As schoolboys we used to tell a joke about an enthusiastic vicar who walks into a hotel lobby and sees an old lady struggling with her suitcase halfway up the stairs. He promptly rushes up the stairs after her, grabs the case with a saintly grin, charges to the top of the stairs with it, and waits there for her, beaming with Anglican pride. The old lady mounts the stairs after him, raises her umbrella, and starts to beat him furiously.

"Stop, madam, I implore you," the vicar shouts in dismay. "Have I not performed a great Christian service by carrying your case for you? Why are you hitting me?"

"Fool!" cries the angry woman. "It took me half an hour to get it halfway down the stairs!"

Cultivated compassion uses the misfortunes of others to reinforce our own sense of righteousness.

As we discussed in Chapter Twelve, cultivated compassion will only create its opposite buried in the shadow. Sometimes a spirit of separation—and even cruelty—can be bred as its inevitable counterpart in consciousness. We hear stories of corruption and various kinds of abuse within the confines of large organized religions, because the so-called divine qualities we find there have been cultivated rather than being the spontaneous by-product of realization. "Do not pretend you love others as yourself. Unless you have realized them as one with yourself, you cannot love them," says Nisargadatta. "True love of others is the result of self-knowledge, not its cause. Without self-realization, no virtue is genuine. When you know, beyond all doubting, that the same life flows through all that is and you are that life, you will love all naturally and spontaneously. When you realize the depth and fullness of your love of yourself, you know that every living being and the entire universe are included in your affection. But when you look at anything as separate from you, you cannot love it, for you are afraid of it. Alienation causes fear, and fear deepens alienation. It is a vicious circle. Only Self-realization can break it. Go for it resolutely."[3]

Natural compassion is not an imitated quality; it is the spontaneous, inevitable, choiceless result of seeing that there is no other in the universe, that all the room has already been taken by your own infinity. It is all you. There is no other from whom pain can be inferred, in whom sadness can be felt. "Ultimate and unconditioned love can only be achieved through a realization of Voidness. Because there are no sentient beings to be pitied, Buddha has the greatest pity; because from the very beginning no sentient beings ever existed, Buddha 'came down' to earth to save sentient beings,"[4] says Chang Chen-chi. We are indivisible, I am you and you are me, not only in the silent, infinite, unborn ground of our Being, but also in our humanity. Your pain is my pain; your confusion is my confusion; your sadness is my sadness; your joy is my joy. "A genuine, not artificial, compassion, can only arise after we have discovered our own condition,"[5] says Namkhai Norbu.

Natural compassion involves the recognition that there is no dotted red line where I end and another begins, either in my original nature or in my incarnateness. All beings are suffering, their suffering is part of the incarnate condition, and all the suffering I see around me is my suffering. This realization cuts through spiritual pride, destroying the platform on which we feel "holier than thou" or more enlightened or more elite. Maybe today I am sitting in ecstasy, basking in my original nature, and someone else is living on the streets on the edge of madness. But isn't it just by coincidence and good fortune that I am here and he is there? I could so easily be in his place and he so easily be in mine if circumstances had unfolded differently. And is it not possible that tomorrow the situation could be reversed? "There but for the Grace of God go I," say the Christians. Life has a wonderful way of changing all the time.

Through this kind of compassion we see that there is only one Self, only one Heart, and only one mind. There is only one pain, one joy, one tendency to separate, and one longing to come home. There is only one suffering, and it is the suffering of the one Heart. We are not separate at source, nor are we separate in manifestation. "One is the Alone not by way of exclusion but by way of inclusion,"[6] says Douglas Harding. In this awakening to our original nature, the Heart is naturally enlivened, taking realization beyond the realm of understanding and recognition into the unfathomable depths of unconditional love. "In my world, love is the only law. I do not ask for love, I give it. Such is my nature,"[7] says Nisargadatta. In the dawning of the realization of Truth, love is enlivened and cries out for compassion; it is choiceless. In the degree to which it is resisted or allowed, there may be the appearance of choice. In this chapter we will see how, by responding to the call of the Heart, we can both deepen the realization of truth and manifest it more fully in our lives.

FOR ALL SENTIENT BEINGS

Almost every spiritual tradition has emphasized selfless service and compassion as an inevitable dimension of awakening to the truth of things. Why should this be so? Particularly since there are no others out there to serve anyway, why is such emphasis placed upon service? In Buddhism they speak of the *bodhisattva* vow, in which an adept dedicates this and every future life to the service of the awakening of all sentient beings and solemnly promises to keep returning to the world of form until all beings have been liberated.

Some see this emphasis as a device. As long as attention is fixed on personal liberation, there is still an obsession with a fictitious self, limited in time and space and needing to be liberated. This very self-obsession can become self-defeating. In fact, the awakened view is to see through the illusion of the separate person who follows a path or desires to be liberated. In the moment of Clear Seeing, there is only consciousness, which has always been free, and there are forms that are constantly shifting and changing and hence unliberatable.

One of the essential tenets of Buddha's teaching is that the yearning for liberation is not personal. It is not our own liberation we seek, but the liberation of all. "As a mother at the risk of her life watches over her only child, so let everyone cultivate a boundlessly compassionate mind toward all beings,"[8] says Gautama Buddha. Every practice performed in the Tibetan tradition begins with *bodhichitta*, dedication for the good of all sentient beings.

All paths and teachings of pure dharma have in some way emphasized service and compassion because it is only in this way that attention can be turned away from the needs of the individual self to the needs of all sentient beings, which are ultimately recognized to be the needs of who you really are. All liberation is your liberation, and the universe itself is your embodiment.

EXPANDING THE LIMITS OF A PERSONAL WORLD

We easily forget how indoctrinated we have become to an Aristotelian and Newtonian universe. Since Aristotle, the Western mind has come to see the human being as a separate entity among innumerable other entities. In a vast universe with innumerable components there is a piece of rock floating irrelevantly in space. On this piece of rock are billions of beings, one of which is me, a little person. The sense of being extraneous, irrelevant, and expendable can be overwhelming. In such a view the war in Ireland or Bosnia, the problems in the inner cities, even the neighbors fighting next door are all "out there," beyond the confines of my separate personal reality. The farthest we can extend in such a view is to feel our connection to a greater whole, but we are always simultaneously separate from it.

Plato, Aristotle's predecessor, lived in a very different universe. So did his teacher, Socrates, and most of the mystics cited in this book, like Ramana Maharshi and Padmasambhava. In the non-dual view, things are the other way around. Everything starts with knowing that I am the indivisible wholeness itself, and everything that arises is an expression of that wholeness. From the wholeness arises the thought "I," just a concept with no definition to it. As it seeks to define itself— "I am like this, I am like that"—"I" gives rise to what is called mind: a collection of definitions. Mind in turn solidifies as body, the manifestation of desires and fears, and this body of desire creates the universe in which to experience its own creations. Rumi puts it like this: "Wine got drunk with us, not the other way 'round. The body developed out of us, not we from it. We are bees, and our body is a honeycomb. We made the body, cell by cell we made it."[9]

The non-dual view is alien to traditional Western science, although the most recent advances in subatomic physics are coming to the same conclusions, both theoretically and through experiments in the effects of consciousness on subatomic particles.[10] The view accords with our immediate experience, however. When you wake up in the morning, stretch, and slowly open your eyes, do you have the feeling that the universe remained stable and scientifically predictable while you temporarily disappeared? Or do you have a relaxed confidence in your own continuity of existence while you welcome the return of an objective environment that had disappeared for a while? Don't answer this question now, as your answer will almost certainly be clouded by habits of thought. Instead, wait until you wake up tomorrow morning and check to see which is true.

As we reorient from the dualistic to the non-dual view through realization of our true nature, we expand who we take ourselves to be beyond the confines of this body to include more and more of our environment. The Earth becomes our body, the universe our business.

When you put your finger into the flame of a candle, there is a natural reflex to pull it out right away. You do not need to cultivate compassion towards the finger or pray that "all sentient fingers be free from suffering." It is a natural instinct, because you feel the pain and identify with it. The same is true when your child is sick. The impulse to alleviate the pain is immediate because you feel that you and your child are not separate. When my children were sick, particularly when they were infants, I felt that I would gladly cut off one of my limbs if it would alleviate their pain. The same could be true of anyone you love or feel close to, for example a pet or an old friend.

By contrast, we do not always feel this way towards a beggar on the street or someone else's child or pet because we have created lines of demarcation around what is within my world and what is outside it. When the lines are narrow, everything is someone else's problem, and we do not care about anything except our own immediate needs. We cut down old-growth forests for profit, we exploit cheap labor in Third World countries, we dump our waste into the ocean, because all those things are outside my small universe. This preoccupation with the small sense of self is known appropriately as selfishness.

When the lines of demarcation are removed through self-inquiry, you start to feel the pain of the planet as inseparable from your own condition. When you see the news reports about the slaughter of innocent people in Rwanda or the religious wars in Northern Ireland, there is a natural tendency to want to alleviate the situation, not out of some identification with being a good or politically correct person, but because you feel the pain as your own. Everything becomes my business, as there is no one else to whom to give it. We replace selfishness with *Self*-ish-ness, where the Self now knows no bounds.

Joanna Macy, who teaches at the California Institute of Integral Studies in San Francisco, has developed a wonderful integration, based on this view, of her Buddhist background and environmental activism. The Dalai Lama embodies the same spirit of spontaneous and natural concern. In such people you do not experience sentimentality or anguish, but a calm and authoritative willingness to own and be responsible for an arena of life much greater than the personal. "Unlike the lower forms of love, compassion is not an emotion," writes Aldous Huxley. "It begins as an act of the will and is consummated as a purely spiritual awareness, a unitive love-knowledge of the essence of its object."[11] Without this spirit of living participation, the awakened view becomes narrow and elitist.

Compassion is both the cause and the result of awakening to our true nature. The more the limited and fictitious sense of self gives way to the realization of vastness, the more the manifest universe with all its sentient beings is felt as our body and our responsibility. Simultaneously, the more that compassion is recognized and allowed, the more the attention shifts from this fictitious "I," and the deeper the awakening to vastness becomes. This capacity to feel another's pain as one's own and to recognize Oneness not just in silence but also in feeling and action is natural to consciousness; compassion is just another facet of our natural state.

RELEASING JUDGMENT

All that interferes with the natural flow of compassion is the tendency to separate this indivisible wholeness into self and other. Whatever we are unwilling to accept as our own embodiment, we have to project outward onto an "objective" universe, which is actually a creation of mind. Once it has been "othered" in this way, we judge it as good or bad, better than me or worse than me. It is primarily this habit of evaluating and judging that keeps an objective universe in place and inhibits compassion. To judge is to separate others' experience as essentially different from our own. To free the floodgates of compassion it is necessary to call back all judgment, for in the dissolving of judgment, otherness dissolves. Then there is the willingness to see that all manifestation, positive or negative, arises out of who I am.

Judgment does not only mean seeing the negative in others; we equally create separation through adulation. The qualities of wholeness we project outside ourselves and then judge in a positive way become the basis of idolatry. If we cannot own real authorship of our life, we have to create external figures of authority, which may lead to hero-worship and ultimately to a willingness to subject ourselves to tyranny. We see this demonstrated in the groups that have grown up around certain spiritual teachers in the past few decades, where an unwillingness to own one's own original state gives rise to the need to project it onto others, which then becomes the foundation for accepting political and spiritual hierarchies.

Our negative projections, on the other hand, have become the basis of cruelty and social inequality. If we are unwilling to feel what poverty, loneliness, and despair are like as a part of our human experience, we project those negative qualities outside of ourselves. In this way we subtly participate in the creation of the very things we may appear to be trying to eliminate—poverty, homelessness, and social ostracism. We see this demonstrated in the political attitudes of extreme right-wing governments and dictatorships and currently in the attitude of many politicians in the United States towards social inequality, drug use, and the AIDS crisis. A spirit of scapegoating and punishment may do more to perpetuate these problems than to end them.

Like points of view, judgments coexist on a spectrum. If you admire a certain quality, reject its opposite, and then project the polarity outside without owning it in yourself, you will inevitably judge others according to this polarity. For example, you may worship Kim Bassinger as beautiful and judge your wife as ugly because you don't own either your own ugliness or your own beauty. When we project a negative judgment and do not own the quality as an expression of self, we inevitably disown its opposite also and have to project it outwards. Judge another as stupid without acknowledging your own stupidity, and you will have to project wisdom outside yourself also. In this way we mortgage our wholeness and pay interest on what we already own.

Compassion is a natural consequence of the willingness to own any state of incarnation as our own. When we are willing to embody any of the myriad possibilities, there is no separation and therefore no need to project onto others, either positively or negatively. This willingness to bear the unbearable, as the Dalai Lama puts it, is the surrender of all judgment into compassion and the surrender of all the edges and demarcations that have been imposed through belief.

Think, for example, of a quality about which you have strong judgments, and recall a person who embodies this quality. Now let yourself experience how the judgment, the sense of separation and "not me," arises. When you are caught in the judgment, is it simultaneously possible to own the quality in yourself?

In our training and sessions we have discovered that whatever we judge in another we have been unwilling to accept as a dimension of our own wholeness. Of course, we can perceive certain qualities in another without also seeing the person as separate from ourselves. In other words, we can acknowledge what is objectively true without sacrificing the wholeness of consciousness. You might recognize with great compassion that another person has some issue they need to work through. Perhaps the person is overly conceptual or mental in his view of the world and gives little credence to feelings or intuitions. From a judgmental position you might say, "He's stuck in his head. He's too intellectual." From a place of compassion you might instead think, "Poor fellow, he is trying to find his way home through his mind. I know how frustrating that can be."

When you perceive a tendency from compassion, you recognize its underlying positive intention, and you see that it is just a tendency, not some fixed quality of the person himself. At the same time you feel the pain of the the person's separation from his true nature. In judgment you make the other person wrong and take a righteous position yourself. "He's so mental, he has no idea how to be open and loving and flowing *like I am.*" In compassion you see universal qualities in which we all get stuck from time to time. In compassion you "feel with" (*cum* and *patio* are the Latin roots for the word "compassion"); in judgment you refuse to feel at all.

We will explore a simple and graceful way of dissolving judgment and opening the floodgates to natural compassion by removing the feeling of not-me. In our training we call this "calling back judgment." The first step is to see the mutuality. If we perceive our own laziness when we become irritated with Jane's, we recognize that laziness is a universal quality, rather than something personal and unique to Jane. When we perceive the Dalai Lama's wisdom, we recognize it as the wisdom of wholeness itself, rather than something exclusively inside or outside of me. It's "ever-present everywhere," to borrow a phrase from Van Morrison. Once the mutuality is recognized, the quality is no longer stuck to a particular individual.

The second step is to accept every quality without judgment as having an underlying life-supportive intention. This acceptance is possible only after the judgment, the not-me-ness, has been removed. For example, once Jane's laziness is seen as our laziness, or universal laziness, we might notice that it is actually a form of relaxation, ease, or expansiveness. Without some relaxation or "laziness," we might become so tense that we would have a heart attack. Once the judgment disappears, we see that every quality, positive or negative, is just another aspect of our essential wholeness.

Session Outline:
Calling Back Judgement

Step 1:   Pre-Induction Talk.

Step 2:   Induce relaxation.

Step 3:   Evoke a memory or visualization.

Step 4:   Express judgment out loud.

Step 5:   Notice feelings in the body.

Step 6:   Dissolve the appearance of the other.

Step 7:   Build up the feeling in the body.

Step 8:   Project the quality outward.

Step 9:   Judge the subpersonality.

Step 10: Ask her to become the subpersonality.

Step 11: Dialogue between the two.

Step 12: Rename this part.

Step 13: Integrate the part back into wholeness.

Step 14: Recreate the other person.

Step 15: Dissolve both forms back into
             formlessness.

Step 16: Suggestions.

Step 17: Count back from five to one.

SESSION OUTLINE: CALLING BACK JUDGMENT

This session is useful when the mind has become obsessively caught by judgment, whether predominantly positive or negative. It helps to dissolve the tendency to make another wrong and oneself right, as well as the tendency to set up another as superior and oneself as unworthy. I have used this session quite often to dissolve the feeling of spiritual superiority, which occasionally follows a glimpse or taste of our true nature. When we become identified with being "enlightened," it's easy to start dividing humanity into those who have "got it" and those who are still struggling in darkness. This tendency is particularly prevalent when Westerners gather around non-dual teachings. Gangaji[12] describes how awareness comes to a recognition of its own nature outside the mind and then tries to recreate this recognition as an experience. When this "landing" occurs, a subtle (or not so subtle!) sense of individuality returns, which carries the label "awakened." Ironically, in the name of this newly awakened "I" can come more separation and judgment than ever occurred before the glimpse.

Step 1: Pre-Induction Talk.
Talk together about the person who is the target of judgment, and see if your friend can articulate the judgment clearly. Find out if this same judgment also exists about other people. You can ask if your friend is aware of these qualities in herself, but be careful not to say something like, "Oh, you are just projecting your own stuff!" Let this insight arise gently out of the session that follows.

Step 2: Induce Relaxation.

Step 3: Evoke a Memory or Visualization.
Ask your friend to imagine herself entering a situation with this other person where strong judgment arises.

Step 4: Express Judgment Out Loud.
Ask your friend to express all judgment aloud to the person imagined before her. Ask her to be as forthright and total as possible. She may hesitate in order to spare the other's feelings,

but you can remind her that the whole point of releasing judgment in a safe and conscious way is to ultimately spare the other's feelings!

Step 5: Notice Feelings in the Body.
As your friend continues to express judgment out loud, she will slowly start to feel the quality that is being judged, usually as a contraction or energy in her own body. For example, if she expresses the judgment "You are totally dishonest, untrustworthy, and lacking in integrity" with enough intensity, she will evoke the qualities of dishonesty, untrustworthiness, and lack of integrity as a resisted sensation or energy in her own body.

Step 6: Dissolve the Appearance of the Other.
Now ask your friend to stay with the energetic quality that has been evoked, forgetting about the other person. The easiest way for her to stay in touch with this feeling is to put a hand on the place in the body that resonates with the judgment.

Step 7: Build Up the Feeling in the Body.
Now ask her to use the breath to intensify and exaggerate the feeling in the body. Remember that since this is a quality that has been objectified and judged, it is also probably a quality that has not been accepted as a part of herself. For this reason you will need to be especially supportive in this step, providing reassurance and space for her to experience this disowned energy directly.

Step 8: Project the Quality Outward.
Now ask her to imagine this quality as a part of herself and to give that part, or subpersonality, an appearance. Ask her to imagine what this part of herself might look like. What is its name? Its age? Its gender? How is it dressed? Is it fat or thin? What color is its skin?

Step 9: Judge the Subpersonality.
Ask her to continue to express the judgments, but this time directing them towards the subpersonality.

Step 10: Ask Her to Become the Subpersonality.

Ask your friend to take a deep breath and *become* this part of herself. Ask her to notice how it feels energetically, emotionally, and physically. As the subpersonality, ask her to express out loud what her needs are and what is important to her as this part of herself.

Step 11: Dialogue Between the Two.

Now ask your friend to alternate between the habitual sense of identity and the part that has now been projected out in front of her. As she moves between the two, ask her to take a deep breath each time before she makes the shift. During the dialog she will naturally come to a deeper understanding of and sympathy for this part of herself and will recognize its underlying positive intentions. You might take as much as twenty minutes for this step.

Step 12: Rename This Part.

If this part has been given a derogatory name, like "lazy" or "power tripper," ask her to rename it in a more respectful way, like "restfulness" or "strength."

Step 13: Integrate the Part Back Into Wholeness.

Now that this part has been recognized and all judgment has been removed, ask her again to take a deep breath and feel herself embracing this part of herself until it is absorbed and dissolved back into the wholeness from which it was fragmented. Continue to do this until no sense of otherness remains.

Step 14: Recreate the Other Person.

Now ask her once again to imagine herself with the other person we discussed in Step One and evoked in Step Three. See if any sense of separation remains. Ask her to take a deep breath and become the other, as we did in Chapter Six. If there is still any feeling of separation, repeat Steps 4 to 13, perhaps this time discovering another fragmented part, until no separation remains.

Step 15: Dissolve Both Forms Back Into Formlessness.

On the in-breath, ask her to dissolve the image of the other, as well as the sense of herself as a separate person, back into formlessness, and invite her to rest as that for as long as she feels comfortable.

Step 16: Suggestions.
By now you may be getting quite adept at giving suggestions in a state of induced relaxation. Just in case you need additional inspiration, here are some suggestions I might use in this session:

> *And it is good to know*
> *Isn't it,*
> *That whenever judgment arises*
> *You can bring it back in this way*
> *And so discover*
> *Ever-expanding dimensions*
> *Of the infinite potentiality*
> *Which is your true nature.*
> *You are vast.*
> *You are formless.*
> *You are the origin of all named things.*
> *Out of this formlessness all things arise*
> *And all things must return.*
> *That's right*
> *The universe is your child,*
> *And you can rest,*
> *Undisturbed,*
> *As this Peace which includes all.*

Step 17: Count Back From Five to One.

CASE HISTORY: BRUCE

Bruce was a real estate agent in a small town. He had a good relationship with the other agents in his area, except for one man, Chuck, whom he hated with a vengeance. In our interview he told me that his obsession with Chuck would keep his mind busy for hours. It was made all the worse by the fact that his wife and most of his friends supported his perception. Chuck had actually been friendly to Bruce on a number of occasions, but Bruce remained adamant in his animosity.

We induced relaxation and imagined a situation where Bruce could meet Chuck on neutral territory. I encouraged Bruce to pour out all his judgments without censoring them in any way. He called out, "You are loud, you are insensitive, you are judgmental and opinionated, you are a bully, you are overwhelming." As he did this he became more and more upset.

Once he had exhausted his battery of judgments, I asked him to let go of the image of Chuck and stay with the feeling of upset in the body. It was easy for Bruce to imagine a subpersonality based on this charge, and he came to meet his own judging mind: loud, abrasive, and bullying. All the same judgments applied to this part of himself as he had applied to Chuck. It turned out that he resented this quality of his own mind much more than he resented Chuck.

The dialogue between Bruce and this subpersonality took quite a while, because his habit of splitting it off had become so deep. Slowly he came to recognize that this part had good intentions, which were to be unrepressed and authentic. He came to a deeper acceptance of this energy, which had always been there, and renamed it "big dog." As he petted and played with the large Labrador retriever that his subpersonality had become, he was able to integrate this energy back into wholeness.

When we came back to Chuck, the judgment had completely dissolved. This session took place as a demonstration in one of our professional training, and Bruce even invited Chuck to the graduation party at the end of the training.

CASE HISTORY: JANE

I did this session with Jane, a woman who had so much ongoing unresolved anger at her ex-husband that she could hardly speak to him, even though they shared the care of their child. He had come to represent everything she most abhorred about human beings, particularly men. She saw him as unfeeling, selfish, harsh, dishonest, and manipulative—all of which, incidentally, were qualities she considered the exact opposite of her own personality.

In the session Jane was able to face him and express her judgments. It quickly became clear that it was not really her ex-husband she was judging, but some quality of men in general. Soon we were able to allow her ex-husband to back out of the picture, and she could feel the strong energetic charge remaining in her body, which she projected out as a subpersonality. As she moved back and forth between being herself and being this part of her, she discovered that this part was the exact opposite of who she took herself to be, and represented all that she denied in herself. This part was selfish, whereas she saw herself as selfless. This part was manipulative, whereas she saw herself as direct and honest. This part was harsh, whereas she saw herself as sweet.

As she came to understand this part of herself more clearly, she could recognize it as the quality of self-preservation, the quality that knows how to take care of oneself and get one's needs met. It was a dimension of wholeness that she had completely banished from her life as a mother, wife, and doctor. Once she had appreciated this quality and welcomed it back into her life, she again created an image of her ex-husband and now just saw him as a multi-dimensional human being. "He's just like me!" she exclaimed. "He's not all devil, and he's not all saint!"

Later she told me that a few days after the session she and her ex-husband had talked on the phone concerning the mutual care of their child, and for the first time she had been able to meet him humanly. When he said he could not pick up their daughter on time because he was too busy, she noticed the same judgments stirring within her— that he was being selfish and irresponsible—but she was able to call back to the energy within herself. She was able to say "Well, I know how you feel because I feel the same way. I am also very busy," and so they could find a place for negotiation. In the dissolving of judgment they were able to meet in mutuality. They even went out for a meal together with their daughter, which began to heal a rift that had existed in the child's life for more than a decade.

BYRON KATIE

This chapter would not be complete without some mention of Byron Katie and "The Work" she teaches so tirelessly all over the world. To speak of the cultivation of compassion without mentioning Byron Katie would be like writing about great moments in rock and roll and leaving out Elvis. I imagine Katie would enjoy that analogy.

Byron Katie was a successful businesswoman in southern California; she raised a family, made plenty of money, and was the embodiment of success. In her forties, however, she developed symptoms usually associated with mental illness. She became extremely fearful and closed herself in the house for days or weeks at a time.

The moment of her transformation came one morning in the attic room of a halfway house. She felt a cockroach walking over her foot.

In that moment out of time she recognized that she and the cockroach and all of creation were one. The idea of a separate entity evaporated and revealed the one indivisible Self.

As she returned to her life as it had been, she saw that the recognition was completely at odds with the habits of the conditioned mind. Her old patterns served separation, while the awakening in the attic revealed that nothing exists outside of the One. Since the awakening twelve years ago, she has shared tools to systematically support other minds in awakening. She calls these tools "The Work."

With her permission, the steps of the Work are reproduced in the appendix. As you can see, they are similar to the session outline we have already described. The words in the appendix could never substitute for being with Byron Katie in person, which is easily available.[13] All are welcome to the Center for the Work in Barstow, California, where Katie and others share "The Work." She travels all over the world and facilitates this process with groups. Her presence is loving, compassionate, and, above all, delightfully simple and ordinary, and she is always willing to meet in mutuality.

UNIVERSAL RESPONSIBILITY

Another effect of practicing the session described here, and of cultivating compassion in general, is that we can become a conduit to release energy held in consciousness that may not appear to have anything to do with us as individuals at all. In a mysterious and invisible way, we can begin to liberate the untold suffering and confusion of humanity through our own incarnate form. "If you've opened your loving to God's love," says Rumi, "you're helping people you don't know and have never seen."[14] This help may not show up as overt social action; however, the willingness to feel pain fully can free it to be absorbed back into its source. Ramana Maharshi echoed this understanding. When asked, "Does my realization help others?" he replied, " Yes, certainly.... It is the best possible help. But there are no others to be helped. For a realised being sees only the Self, just like a goldsmith estimating the gold in various items of jewellery sees only gold. When you identify yourself with the body then only the forms and shapes are there. But when you transcend your body the others disappear along with your body consciousness."[15]

As the lines of demarcation dissolve and our identity expands to include all beings, our sense of responsibility naturally expands as well.

This does not mean that we feel personally guilty for a war on the other side of the world; rather, it means that we see all conflict, suffering, and discord, no matter where it is occurring, as arising out of the same one mind, which is, after all, our mind. Taking responsibility does not involve atoning for past mistakes or righting past wrongs. Instead, it means being willing to sit in the eye of the hurricane and welcome all the tumult and suffering as our own. We can't pass the proverbial buck because there is no one outside us to pass it to. The effect of "taking responsibility" in this way is all-pervasive, as Nisargadatta Maharaj suggests: "When more people come to know their real nature, their influence, however subtle, will prevail and the world's emotional atmosphere will sweeten up."[16]

As realization deepens and the imagined separation melts away, in both an absolute and a relative sense, this body, which is the projection of individual identity and desire, transforms into a body of compassion, which is motivated and fueled in a completely different way. The Buddhist tradition calls this the bodhisattva, whose life is dedicated to the liberation of others.

CHAPTER 15

THE END IS THE BEGINNING

We shall not end from exploration
And the end of all our exploring
Will be to arrive where we started
And know the place for the first time.[1]

T.S. ELIOT

More than two years passed between the completion of the first draft of this book in May of 1995 and its being printed in the fall of 1997. During this period I had the opportunity to refine and edit the manuscript a number of times and to add case histories from my practice as well as references to other works. One factor significantly delayed the completion of this book, one that has turned out to be germane to most of the students who have participated in our training and that may be relevant to you as well, as you integrate what you have read here.

When our attention turns to the vastness of the Truth, we inevitably feel inadequate to say anything about it. We are left in utter humility and awe. As I came close to completing this book, the question kept arising, "Who am I to speak about such things? The Truth is so vast and immaculate, so deep, mysterious, and unknowable; as an individual, I am only a tiny wave in this ocean. It has been described so many times in so many beautiful ways and with such depth, I am not remotely qualified to add a single word."

I mention this here because I have noticed the same shyness in many of the students who have taken our training. Through the processes they learn, they may come to a deep recognition of the essential emptiness of things, be brought into ecstatic states of rapture and dissolving of limitation and identification, and experience profound results in facilitating these sessions with others. But they may also often feel unworthy or inadequate, as I did, to express the Heart's song of Truth.

I have come to respect this feeling of unworthiness and inadequacy when I see it in our training, for it is the counterweight to the tendency to spiritual arrogance. It prevents the "landing" we referred to in Chapter Fourteen. It preserves the humility and honesty necessary to recognize that, while the truth is great and immeasurable, there is still this apparent individual, this person subject to the foibles and absurdities of a temporal life. It ensures that we do not take ourselves too seriously.

I have also noticed that those students who have the deepest sense of inadequacy seem to facilitate the most effective sessions. They are innocent and unknowing, like teenagers on a first date. Once they begin to feel confident and knowledgeable, they lose some of their innocence and start trying to make it happen, rather than letting it happen on its own. At the same time, if the sense of inadequacy and natural humility is allowed to dominate, a precious gift may be withheld. There is a middle ground between the arrogance of "I am awakened, and now I know" and the unworthiness of "I am full of darkness and illusion, and I know nothing." This duality is transcended when the focus on "me" and "my attainment" is replaced with a passion for the mystery itself.

This book is written from passion, not from attainment. I have fallen in love with the mystery. Sometimes the mystery falls in love with me too, and then only the mystery remains. Sometimes it hides from me, and I long for it with all my heart as I slide around in the muddy back garden of the mind. But whether it is hidden or present, my passion for the nameless is inexhaustible. I am a beginner, but like you, I have

seen the beauty of the view, and now I am intoxicated with its promise. It has eclipsed all else in my life, and my attention is fixated there.

It is often said that we teach what we most need to learn, and that
is certainly true of this book. The more we dedicate our lives to the
Truth and the more we share it through this form, the more integrated
it becomes as day-to-day experience. I encourage you to let your passion determine your activity and not to wait until you feel that you
have somehow reached a goal of your mind's imagining. You could
wait forever. I hope that in reading these pages you may feel inspired
in the same way to share what your Heart longs for and knows to be
true and forget about any concern with attainment.

Many who fall in love with the view hold back from sharing
because of some idea they have about a future state called "enlightenment." Although the Self has been revealed, they feel that their
realization is somehow incomplete because they still have human
tendencies and qualities. To maintain that "Because I still get angry, I
cannot be awareness itself" is like saying, "Because there are waves
today, the ocean is no longer wet." The tendencies that constitute
individuality may, and probably will, continue for the rest of this
lifetime. Ramana speaks of this *prarabda karma*[2] in this way: "The
potter's wheel goes on turning round even after the potter has ceased
to turn it when the pot is finished. In the same way, the electric fan
goes on revolving for some minutes after we switch off the current.
The *prarabdha karma* which created the body will make it go through
whatever activities it was meant for."[3]

I remember when Poonjaji first asked me to give Satsang in the
West. In characteristic fashion, he did not tell me directly at first, but
began to mention to his Indian guests, in Hindi, that I was returning
to America to do "great work." These rumors would filter back to me,
often embellished by their carrier into all kinds of fantastic imaginings.
Finally I asked him over tea what he had in mind, and he told me
directly that he wanted me to return to America and conduct Satsang.
I did not feel remotely prepared for this task, being fully aware of the
myriad ways that identification would still reoccur. I said to him "You
must be joking." "Yes, the Truth is the greatest joke," he responded,
"and you must share it with many people!"

For the next few days I felt agitated. Every feeling of unworthiness
and self-doubt passed through the mind, along with the familiar sense
of being in some way inauthentic. A few days later we were alone
together in his living room, drinking tea. He was reading the classified

ads in the *Lucknow Mail:* "Learn computer both hard and softwaring styles." "Triple your money in three months with Ajit investments." "Chatterji and Sons require boy for various official duties." I broached the subject of the assignment Papaji had given me.

"Papaji," I began.

"Mmmph," he grunted without looking up from his paper.

"You know you asked me to teach in the West."

"Yes, good, teach," he replied, again without taking his attention from the ads.

"Well, I do not feel ready to teach."

"You are ready," he muttered, still with the paper.

"I feel more like I am in a process of gradually awakening, rather than really being awake," I tried to explain.

He looked up from the paper directly into my eyes. I always freeze when he does that, like a mouse cornered by a cat.

"Do not ever speak or think in that way," he said, holding me with his gaze. "It is not about you. It is the Truth that is great, and it is the Truth that will speak. Do not worry."

I repeat these words here because they have relevance to so many of us. He was right. Satsang happens on its own, and each time there is the sense of the Self speaking through the apparent individual, rather than any sense of personal doing. The same thing occurs in private consultations and in our training. To share the Truth, to be a vehicle for the awakening that is occurring all over this planet, either in your own way or through the tools presented in this book, you do not need to be "enlightened," whatever that may mean. If you wait until there is nothing left to liberate, you could wait forever. It is enough to slip out of your own way and allow That which has already touched your Heart in its silent magnificence to do its work through you. This is the greatest blessing of the sacred life: to be used as a vehicle for the nameless and formless.

We talk about this frequently with the graduates of our training. Although they have repeatedly demonstrated to themselves that the gateways to vastness are open and that they have the capacity to help others enter them as well, the majority of our graduates hold back from sharing their understanding because of a feeling of incompleteness. In the moment of Clear Seeing, however, it is no longer *my* attainment or lack of it that has any importance, but the view itself. "Realization, non-realization, these are attitudes and viewpoints you hold. When you are really awake, this is as much a dreamland as any dream is,"[4] says Joe Miller. Sosan, the Third Zen patriarch, has the same advice: "Even to be attached to the idea of enlightenment is to go astray. Just let things be in their own way, and there will be neither coming nor going. Obey the nature of things (your own nature), and you will walk freely and undisturbed."[5]

When hiking in the Sierras or the foothills of the Himalayas, you may turn at a particular switchback and come across a stunningly beautiful vista. With respect to that view, you are now "enlightened"; you have seen the bigger picture, which is the valley below in its entirety. You might call out to a friend walking behind you, "Come and see this beautiful view," and you might marvel together at its splendor. But she would be missing the point if, instead of enjoying the panorama, she became fixated on your face or behavior: "Yes, I think you have seen it. I can see the reflection of the view in your eyes!" So often that is precisely how we treat the view described in this book—we are more interested in the one who has seen than in what has been seen or in seeing the same for ourselves.

Equally, on returning to the valley, things may seem different to you now because you have a broader perspective. But if someone down in the valley who had not yet seen the view were to ask, "If you've really seen the view, why do you still need to drive a car and walk about like the rest of us? Why do you still step out of the way when a big truck comes down the street, if you know now that it's just a tiny speck in a huge valley?" That too would be missing the point. The view is valid and real irrespective of its effects.

Who then, we might ask, is qualified to speak about these things? Based on my experience in training students over the years, I would say that while a doctorate in psychology may be necessary to treat mental illness, it is certainly not necessary to facilitate awakening from the dream of separation. Similarly, reading lengthy books about comparative religions may create an erudite mind, but it does not necessarily bring one closer to the Truth. While the practice of techniques and *sadhanas*[6] may create a fertile soil, it does not necessarily bear fruit. Watching so many people learning to work in this way, I have come to feel that there is only one qualification needed: a deep, sincere, and innocent passion for the Truth beyond the mind. With this passion, there is a natural willingness to hand over the process to the greater mystery. This passion, together with the humility to know that it is not the little me doing it at all, is all that is necessary for these sessions to flow smoothly.

334 RELAXING INTO CLEAR SEEING

The introduction to your original nature marks the end of a search in time, the end of the struggle to improve or evolve a limited personality. The futile attempts of the mind to improve itself or to look for fulfillment outside of its own nature can be brought to a complete stop right now, in the discovery that there is in fact no one seeking. Although the shift from content to context, from being a limited creature in time and space to being that in which time and space arise, may happen in a moment out of time, it can take the rest of one's life to fully integrate and embody what has been seen.

Although this shift marks the end of striving and confusion, it is the beginning of another journey, in some ways more demanding: the process of embodying the formless in the world of form. With a foot in two worlds, neither fully awake nor completely asleep, we stand at the beginning, the middle, and the end of the journey all at the same time. Whatever giddy heights we may reach today, looking down upon the magnificent view now revealed below, it pales in comparison to the uncharted peaks still to be explored. This recognition of simultaneously being at home and coming home, being at once complete and a beginner, is a contradiction to the mind, but a marvelous play to the Heart.

When I met Poonjaji in 1991 I felt in many ways like an adept. I had been meditating for more than twenty years and had studied with many teachers in different traditions. I thought I knew something. Now, six years later, I have become a beginner. I stand at the foot of the mountains, in awe of their majesty and mystery, and wonder how far I could ever penetrate their peaks. The Truth brings you to your knees; it knocks accumulated concepts and thoughts aside, grabs you by your shirt collar in an intensity that is completely sobering. I have come to delight in being a beginner again and again, in moving from the teacher seat to again putting my head on the block with a wink of consent to whoever is today's executioner of the false.

Each time I return to Lucknow to visit Poonjaji, he seems to reveal yet another dimension of the constantly unfolding mystery. Since those early days, many people have gone to live there, more or less permanently, and a community has grown up around him. Sometimes I yearn to be with him more in physical form, but I have also discovered that the Master who looked into my eyes six years ago and turned everything upside down is now omnipresent. He is within the Heart, and he is outside as everything, when it is seen with the respect one pays to the Truth. There is a perfect synchronicity to how the right teacher

repeatedly appears as a mirror for the Self. In this life, as well as appearing as Poonjaji, it has appeared as Byron Katie, whom I mentioned in Chapter Fourteen; as Urgyen Tulku; as friends; as unexpected events; and misfortune that cuts through the bonds of attachment.

Finally, through the willingness to share the Truth with others, the process of facilitating and teaching itself becomes the greatest teacher. Out of my own longing to marinate in the mystery and dissolve the boundaries in every aspect of life, this work has been born. Like everyone I work with, I have areas of my own life where the permeation is greater and areas where it is less. Those places where it is less have motivated me to create these tools and teach them to other people, and in the process to learn more deeply what I am teaching!

Once awareness has turned around and realized its original nature, this original nature begins to permeate every dimension of our incarnate existence. The process is endless, because the individual can always more fully reflect its source. Life is a demonstration of the source trying, again and again, to incarnate itself with more beauty and completeness. Now we are witnessing, perhaps for the first time, the democratization of this process, in which the permeation occurs through mutuality and friendship, rather than through hierarchy and organization.

This book is an encouragement to allow every aspect of your life to be infused with what the Heart already knows to be true. Dance your passion, live your passion, let your work reflect your passion, until your passion takes over your life.

In one sense, everything has always unfolded perfectly on its own, without the need for any individual effort. In another sense, things seem to be speeding up now. *The New York Times* bestseller list bears testimony to the fact that a passion for Truth, clarity, and presence is shared by more than an elitist subculture. Whether the cause is environmental degradation, a shift in the planets, UFOs floating in another dimension, or merely a natural maturation, millions of people throughout the world are tuning to the frequency of wakefulness. A collective lotus is ready to blossom, and the situation will no longer tolerate spiritual hierarchies, inaccessible teachers, or complicated, esoteric teachings.

I hope the tools and reflections offered in this book contribute to your own relaxation into the Clear Seeing of the obvious, and afford you an opportunity to participate in the midwifing of the glorious rebirth that is already unfolding.

Om
Shanti
Shanti
Shanti

Arjuna Nick Ardagh
Olema, California
April 1997

Postscript—September 1997.

Just as the last corrections were being typed into the manuscript, news came from Lucknow that Poonjaji had died. At first I felt tremendous shock and grief, for I was planning to be in Lucknow, with the completed manuscript in hand, only two weeks later.

As waves of sadness, regret, gratitude, and every other possibility passed on the screen, so the silence of His presence also deepened in me, and the unavoidable Truth revealed itself more and more clearly: there is no difference between the teacher, the Divine and the True Self. It is only a matter of knowing where to look.

Poonjaji has not gone, he has only changed his address, which for the health conscious might be seen to be good news. He no longer resides exclusively in Lucknow, India, but is to be found, as every true teacher is to be found, as the One who reads these words.

For this reason I have left the manuscript untouched, other than this brief postscript. It still seems perfectly appropriate to refer to Him in the present tense.

APPENDIX:
"THE WORK" OF BYRON KATIE

These are the steps of "The Work" referred to in Chapter Fourteen. For more information and detailed instructions call The Center for The Work at (760) 256 5653 or (760) 261-1828.

A. Write out what stresses you in the form of a statement. Pick one person, thing or situation. <u>Do not write about yourself</u>. Write as a child, judgmental and courageous. Don't be spiritual or kind. Write short, simple sentences.

(1) Who or what don't you like? Who irritates you? Who or what saddens or disappoints you?
I don't like or I am angry at (name _____ because _____
_____
_____

(2) How do you want them to change? What do you want them to do?
I want (name) _____ to _____
_____
_____

(3) What is it that they should or shouldn't do?
(Name)_____ should or shouldn't_____
_____
_____

(4) Do you need anything from them? What do they need to do to please you?
I need (name) _____to _____
_____
_____

(5) What do you think of them? Make a list.
(Name)_____ is / are _____
_____
_____

(6) What is it that you don't want to experience with that person, thing or situation again?
I don't ever want to_____
_____
_____

Turn Over /

B. This work is a meditation. Go back to your original statements (1-5) and apply the following process: With intention, go deep inside and ask yourself the following questions after each of the statements you wrote. (Take your time; go slowly. The thinking mind may want to speed past valuable information.) Be gentle and let the answers reveal themselves to you.

1. **Is it true?**
2. **Can I really know that it's true?**
3. **What's in it for me to hold that belief?**
4. **Who would I be without that belief?**

C. After doing the above inquiry, turn the subject and/or the object around to discover:
What was most true in that immediate experience? Or, what may be just as true?

Example:
For a statement like: "I don't like J because he doesn't understand me."
    Turned around: "I don't like me because I don't understand me."
          And: "I don't like me because I don't understand J."

For your statements at #6, the turn around is: "I'm willing to..." and "I look forward to..." because it may very well happen again, if only in your mind. Each distress we experience gives us another opportunity to do the work and get free.

Example:
For a statement like: "I don't ever want to trust J again."
    Turned around: "I am willing to trust J again."
          And: "I look forward to trusting J again."

You've just completed the ABC's of "The Work":

A: **Write down your distress.**
B: **Go inside to ask four questions.**
C: **Turn it around.**

Reproduced with kind permission of Byron Katie
and the Center for The Work, Barstow, California.

NOTES AND REFERENCES

Wherever possible the title, author, editor, translator and page reference have been noted. For more complete bibliographical information, refer to the recommended reading list which follows. Wherever appropriate, permission has been obtained from the relevant party.

CHAPTER ONE: THE ROAD TO HERE

1. Jelaluddin Rumi, from *Unseen Rain*, trans. by Coleman Barks, p. 75, reprinted with permission.

2. *Satsang:* literally to sit in association with the absolute truth. From the roots, *Sat*: absolute unchanging Truth, and *Sangha*: an association or group gathered together. Common usage is to sit with a teacher, or *Sat Guru*, whose presence provokes awakening.

3. *Samsara*: literally the web of illusion which keeps us lost in identification.

4. For information about the courses offered by the Living Essence Foundation, see page 357.

5. Padmasambhava, *Self Liberation through Seeing with Naked Awareness*, trans. by John Reynolds, p. 28. This and other quotations from this work are gratefully reprinted with permission of Station Hill Books.

6. See Chapter Eight for a more complete discussion of this.

7. Patrul Rimpoche, *Heart Treasures of the Enlightened Ones*, trans. by Padmakara translation group, p. 25. This and other quotations from this work are gratefully reprinted with permission of Shambhala Books.

8. Quoted by Matthieu Ricard, Dilgo Khyentse's secretary for many years, in a conversation in Katmandu in 1994.

CHAPTER TWO: THE VIEW

1. Ramana Maharshi, *Day by Day with Bhagavan*, ed. by D. Mudaliar, p. 155. Reprinted with permission of Sri Ramanasramam.

2. Padmasambhava, *Self Liberation...*, trans. by John Reynolds, p. 27.

3. Lao Tzu, *Tao Te Ching*, Section One, my translation, based on the translations by Gia-Fu Feng and by Stephen Mitchell.

4. Ludwig Wittgenstein, *Tractatus logico-philosophicus*, Section 6.522.

5. From *Open Secret, Versions of Rumi*, trans. by Coleman Barks and John Moyne, p. 50, gratefully quoted with permission of the translator.

6. Buddha, *The Diamond Sutra*, trans. by A.F. Price and Wong Mou-lam, p. 19.

7. Ramana Maharshi, from *Talks with Ramana Maharshi*, trans. by M. Venkataramiah, p. 178. Reprinted with permission of Sri Ramanasramam.

8. Padmasambhava: *Self Liberation...*, trans. by John Reynolds, p. 26.

9. Angelus Silesius, (Johann Scheffler), *The Cherubin Wanderer*, my translation, based on the translations by Maria Shrady and Frederick Frank.

10. Douglas Harding, *On Having No Head*, p. 2.

11. Shardza Gyaltsen, *Heart Drops of Dharmakaya*, p. 42.

12. The word "God" refers even in mainstream Christianity to an omnipresent and omnipotent Creator who has unconditional compassion for His creation. This same definition applies to the Self which is revealed beyond the mind.

13. Padmasambhava, *Self Liberation...*, trans. by John Reynolds, p. 22.

14. Lao Tzu, *Tao Te Ching*, Section 4, my translation, based on the translations by Gia-Fu Feng and by Stephen Mitchell.

15. Shunryu Suzuki, *Zen Mind, Beginner's Mind*, p. 21.

16. Lao Tzu, *Tao Te Ching*, Section 32, my translation, based on the translations by Gia-Fu Feng and by Stephen Mitchell.

17. Shardza Gyaltsen, *Heart Drops...*, p. 44.

18. Buddha, *Diamond Sutra*, trans. by A.F. Price and Wong Mou-lam, p. 43.

19. Ramana Maharshi, *Maharshi's Gospel*, ed. by T.N. Ventakaraman, p. 31. Reprinted with permission of Sri Ramanasramam.

20. From an unpublished Satsang in Lucknow, Dec. 30, 1991. Reprinted with Sri Poonjaji's permission.

21. Angelus Silesius, (Johann Scheffler), *Cherubin...*, my translation, based on the translations by Maria Shrady and Frederick Frank.

22. Huang Po, from *The Zen Teaching of Huang Po*, trans. by John Blofeld, p. 37.

23. Hakuin, "The Song of Zazen" in *A First Zen Reader*, trans. by Trevor Leggett, p. 67.

24. *Kena Upanisad*, my translation, based loosely on translations by S. Radakrishnan and also by W.B. Yeats with Purohit Swami.

25. Ramana Maharshi, *Day by Day...*, ed. by D. Mudaliar, p. 90.

26. Sosan, Third Zen Patriarch, *Hsin Hsin Ming*, trans. by Richard B. Clarke, p. 2.

27. This account is based on Joe Miller's essay, "The Sutra of Hui-Neng," in *Great Song, the Life and Teaching of Joe Miller*, pp. 117-124.

28. Wu Men, from *Gateless Gate*, trans. by Nyogen Senzaki and Saladin Reps, p. 66.

29. Sosan, *Hsin Hsin Ming*, trans. by Richard B. Clarke, p. 1.

30. Lao Tzu, *Tao Te Ching*, Section 29, my translation, based on the translations by Gia-Fu Feng and by Stephen Mitchell.
31. Shunryu Suzuki, *Zen Mind, Beginner's Mind*, p. 134.
32. Ramana Maharshi, *Day by Day...*, ed. by by D. Mudaliar, p. 155.
33. Transcript of a conversation in San Francisco with Dr. Golden in 1995.

CHAPTER THREE: RELAXATION

1. Namkhai Norbu, *Dzogchen the Self Perfected State*, p. 54.
2. See: *Mega Brain* by Michael J. Hutchinson and *Altered States of Consciousness* by Charles Tart, both in the bibliography.
3. The word "Heart," when used with a capital letter in this way, has a specific meaning in this book: it is used as a synonym for the True Self, in its capacity to feel and love. It does not refer to the pump which propels blood around the body. It also does not simply refer to the emptiness of the Self, but to its manifest quality as Love.
4. *Ashtavakra Gita*, adapted from the translation by Hari Prasad Shastri.
5. *Kaivalya Upanishad*, based on the translation by S. Radhakrishnan, verses 19-20.

CHAPTER FOUR: THE HEART MEDITATION

1. Shantideva (690-740) was an Indian Buddhist Master, and a teacher at the famous Nalanda University. He is the author of the famous Bodhicharyavatara. This passage is quoted in Dilgo Khyentse Rimpoche's *Enlightened Courage*, p. 28.
2. The bibliography contains several commentries on and editions of Atisha's *Seven Points of Mind Training: Enlightened Courage* by Dilgo Khyentse Rimpoche; Chapter 12 of Sogyal Rimpoche's *The Tibetan Book of Living and Dying*; and Bhagavan Shri Rajneesh's *Book of Wisdom*.
3. Dilgo Khyentse Rimpoche, *Enlightened Courage, An Explanation of Atisha's Seven Points of Mind Training*, p. 1.
4. For the commentary on these lines: *Ibid.*, p. 28-38.
5. Bhagavan Shri Rajneesh, *The Book of Wisdom*, Vol. I, p. 115.
6. *Ibid*, p. 117.
7. Sogyal Rimpoche, *The Tibetan Book of Living and Dying*, p. 205.
8. Namkhai Norbu, *The Crystal and the Way of Light*, p. 49.

CHAPTER FIVE: WHO AM I ?

1. D.E. Harding, quoted in *On Being One Self*, ed. by Anne Seward, p. 27.
2. Ramana Maharshi, *Crumbs From His Table*, ed. by R. Swarnagiri, pp. 25-6. Reprinted with permission of Sri Ramanasramam.
3. Paul Brunton, *A Search in Secret India*, pp. 156-157.

4. Ramana Maharshi, *Talks...*, ed. by M. Venkataraman, p. 571.
5. Padmasambhava, *Self Liberation...*, trans. by John Reynolds, p. 19.
6. Patrul Rimpoche, *Heart Treasures of the Enlightened Ones*, trans. by Padmakara Translation Group, p. 195.
7. Ghalib, from his *Diwan-e-Urdu*, translated for me by a chance acquaintance in India.
8. *Vigyana Bhairava Tantra*. This text has been handed down in oral traditions, and is probably about five thousand years old.
9. For Douglas Harding's books, see the bibliography for complete listing of his work.
10. This version of *Vigyana Bhairava Tantra* is from *Zen Flesh, Zen Bones*, ed. by Paul Reps, p. 161.
11. Shardza Gyaltsen, *Heart Drops...*, p. 37.
12. *Ibid*, p. 42.
13. *Ibid*, p. 46.
14. Lao Tzu, *Tao Te Ching*, Section 52, my translation, based on the translations by Gia-Fu Feng and by Stephen Mitchell.

CHAPTER SIX: THERE IS NO OTHER

1. Jelaluddin Rumi, from *The Essential Rumi*, trans. by Coleman Barks and John Moyne, p. 36. Gratefully used with permission of the translator.
2. Jiddu Krishnamurti, *The Only Revolution*, pp. 43-4.
3. *Bhihadaranyaka Upanishad*, from *The Ten Principal Upasishads*, trans. by W.B. Yeats and Sri Purohit Swami, p. 119.
4. Heraclitus, Fragments, #46 and #84.
5. Kabir, from *The Kabir Book*, trans. by Robert Bly.
6. Novalis, from *Philosophical Writings*, ed. by Magaret Mahony.
7. Angela of Foligno, from *Complete Works*, trans. by Paul Lachance, p. 133.
8. William Blake, "The Marriage of Heaven and Hell," in *Blake, Complete Poems*, p. 108.
9. Meister Eckhart, *Sermons and Treatises*, trans. by M.O. Walshe, p. 134.
10. Meister Eckhart, *Ibid*, p. 68.
11. Peter Sterry, *Select Writings*, ed. by N.I. Muter, p. 164.
12. Sosan, *Hsing Hsing Ming*, trans. by Richard B. Clarke, p. 6.
13. William Blake, "The Marriage of Heaven and Hell," in *Complete Poems*, p. 108.

CHAPTER SEVEN: THE PAST IS NOT NOW

1. H.W.L. Poonjaji, *The Truth Is*, p. 346. Reprinted with permission of Yudishtara, publisher.
2. Buddha, *The Dhammapada*, trans. by Irving Babbitt, p. 3, vv. 3 and 4.
3. J. Krishnamurti, *Freedom from the Known*, p. 35.
4. For a more detailed examination of how eye movement can be a clue as to whether the person in deep relaxation is actually remembering or imagining a memory, see Bandler and Grinder's book, *Trance-formations*.
5. For example: *Emotional Anatomy, the Structure of Experience*, by Stanley Keleman; *BodyMind* by Ken Dythwald; and an excellent small book, *You Can Heal your Life* by Louise Hay.
6. For more detailed training and information in how to conduct a Childhood Rescue Mission, I would refer you to David Quigley's excellent book, *The Alchemical Hypnotherapy Workbook*, which is in the bibliography.
7. This is the basis of the approach known as "Dehypnotherapy," developed by Jehru Kabbal.

CHAPTER EIGHT: THE BELOVED.

1. Attributed to Jelaluddin Rumi. Unpublished translation by Coleman Barks. Used with his permission.
2. Drunvalo Malchezadeck, in an interview with Aurora Jeanie, 1992.
3. The simplest and clearest explanation of these seven levels of resonance that I have found is in Ken Dythwald's *Bodymind*.
4. This story, which is certainly Sufi, is also sometimes told of Mulla Nasrudin.
5. Stephen and Ondrea Levine, *Embracing the Beloved*.

CHAPTER NINE: THE GURU IS IN

1. Jiddu Krishnamurti, *Freedom from the Known*, p. 11.
2. For example, P.D. Ouspensky, *In Search of the Miraculous*, in the biblography.
3. Examples of these kinds of violations of integrity are to be found in the article in *Common Boundary*, referred to in the next footnote.
4. *Common Boundary*, August 1994 edition. See also George Fernstein's excellent book *Holy Madness* and Joel Kramer's *The Guru Papers*.
5. Joe Miller, *Great Song…*, p. 62.
6. Douglas Harding, *The Trial…*, p. 203.

7. Tung-shan (807-869) from *The Record of Tung-shan*, trans. by William F. Powell.

8. Ramana Maharshi, *Maharshi's Gospel*, trans. by T.N. Venkataraman, pp. 36-7.

9. *Oxford Sanskrit-English Dictionary*, 1899, pp. 356 and 881.

10. C.G. Jung, from the foreword to *The Spiritual Teachings of Ramana Maharshi*, p. ix.

11. St Athanasius, quoted in Evelyn Underhill, *Mysticsm*, p. 419.

12. A beedie is a very inexpensive type of mini-cigar made by wrapping a tobacco leaf into a tight tube, and then tying a thread around it.

13. Quoted in *Zen Flesh, Zen Bones*, ed. by Paul Reps, p. 62.

14. Joe Miller, *Great Song...*, p. 75.

15. Ramana Maharshi, *Maharshi's Gospel*, ed. by T.N. Venkataraman, pp. 36-7.

16. Namkhai Norbu, *Dzogchen, the Self-Perfected State*, p. 7.

17. Yun Men, from *Original Teachings of Ch'an Buddhism*, trans. by Chang Chung-Yuan, p. 288.

18. Joe Miller, *Great Song...*, p. 63.

19. Ramana Maharshi, *Talks...*, p. 136.

20. *Ibid*, pp. 20-21.

21. Joe Miller, *Great Song...*, p. 64.

22. Quoted in *Zen Flesh, Zen Bones*, ed. by Paul Reps, p. 99.

23. Ramana Maharshi, from *Day by Day...*, ed. by Mudaliar, p. 145-6.

24. Namkai Norbu, *The Crystal and the Way of Light*, p. 35.

CHAPTER TEN: GREED TO GRATITUDE

1. Lao Tzu, *Tao Te Ching*, Section 44, my translation, based on the translations by Gia-Fu Feng, Raghavan Iyer and by Stephen Mitchell.

2. Joe Dominguez and Vicki Robin, *Your Money or Your Life*, Chapter 1.

3. *Directory of Intentional Community*, published by the Fellowship for Intentional Community.

4. Jack Lessinger, *Penturbia*. These five population movements are:
    i)   The arrival of the Pilgrim fathers in the early 17th century.
    ii) The population of the East Coast in the 18th century.
    iii) The spread West, finally to include the Gold Rush in California.
    iv) Suburbia, the movement out of the middle of the cities into the suburbs, post World War II.
    v)   Penturbia, the repopulation of specific smaller towns, starting in the '80s.

5. In a telephone interview in 1994.

6. *Guru Gita*, verse 50, trans. by Swami Narayananda, p. 18.

CHAPTER ELEVEN: DESIRE AND FEAR

1. Sosan, *Hsin Hsin Ming*, trans. by Richard B. Clarke, p. 1.
2. Basho, from *A Zen Wave, Basho's Haiku and Zen*, trans. by Robert Aitken, p. 37.
3. Quoted in *Zen Flesh, Zen Bones*, ed. by Paul Reps, p. 28.
4. Joe Miller, *Great Song...*, p. 43.
5. A number of examples of this are described in Philip Kapleau's *Three Pillars of Zen*.
6. Adapted from a Satsang in Lucknow with Sri Poonjaji on May 19th, 1992.
7. St. John of the Cross, quoted in Seward, *On Being One-Self*, p. 25.
8. *Samsara*: see footnote 3, Chapter 1.
9. Joe Miller, *Great Song...*, p. 85.
10. Simone Weil, *Waiting for God*, trans. by Emma Craufurd, quoted in *The Enlightened Mind*, ed. Stephen Mitchell, p. 204.
11. Padmasambhava, *Self Liberation...*, trans. by John Reynolds, p. 22.
12. This view of addiction as a signpost to our depth is elaborated upon in Philip Kavanaugh's *Magnificent Addiction*.
13. Joe Miller, *Great Song...*, p. 57.
14. The most useful model of personality type to explain these different ultimate fears might be the Enneagram of personality, a Sufi system brought to the West first by George Gurdjeiff and later by Arica founder Oscar Ichaso. The Enneagram describes nine core qualities which distinguish one person from another. One's worst fear would then represent the inability to express one's essential personality quality. For a "two," for example, being deprived of the opportunity to be of service might be a fate worse than death. For a "seven," the loss of the ability to be creative and free would be a fate worse than death. For a "five," exposure and loss of privacy would be worse than dying.

CHAPTER TWELVE: BEYOND BELIEF

1. Al Alawi, from *A Moslem Saint of the Twentieth Century*, p. 33.
2. Sosan, *Hsin Hsin Ming*, trans. by Richard B. Clarke, p. 2.
3. Hal Stone and Sidra Fieldman, *Embracing Ourselves*, pp. 10 -17.
4. Jean Piaget, *The Origins of Intelligence in Children*, trans. by Magaret Cook.
5. Hal Stone and Sidra Fieldman, *Embracing Ourselves*, Chapter I.
6 *The Six Vajra Verses*, trans. by Brian Beresford and John Shane, quoted in Namkhai Norbu's *Crystal....*

7 Rumi, from *The Essential Rumi*, trans. by Coleman Barks. Reprinted with permission.

8 Gregory Bateson, *Steps Towards an Ecology of Mind*, p. 271ff.

9 William Shakespeare, *Hamlet*, Act III, Scene i, lines 57 to 60.

10 Meister Eckhart, quoted in Aldous Huxley's *Perennial Philosophy*, p. 186.

11 Patrul Rimpoche, *Heart Treasures...*, p. 195.

12 Joe Miller, *Great Song...*, p. 99.

CHAPTER THIRTEEN: SWEET SURRENDER

1. Ramana Maharshi, *Talks...*, ed. by M. Venkataramiah, p. 175.

2. Quoted in Paul Reps, *Zen Flesh, Zen Bones*, p. 32.

3. Rolling Stones "You Can't Always Get What You Want" from the album *Let it Bleed*, Decca records.

4. Namkhai Norbu, *Crystal*, p. xv.

5. "Beautiful Boy," by John Lennon on the album *Double Fantasy*. Capitol records, 1980.

6. H.W.L. Poonjaji, from an unpublished Satsang in Lucknow, December 6th, 1991. Printed with his permission.

7. Suzanne Segal, *Collision with the Infinite*, p. 142.

8. Lao Tzu, *Tao Te Ching*, Section 23, my translation, based on the translations by Gia-Fu Feng, Raghavan Iyer and by Stephen Mitchell.

9. Dilgo Khyentse Rimpoche, *Heart Treasures...*, p. 189.

10. Joe Miller, *Great Song...*, p. 63.

11. Shardza Gyaltsen, *Heart Drops...*, p. 73.

12. Ramana Maharshi, quoting Patanjali in *Letters...*, ed. by S. Nagamma, p. 147.

13. Nisargadatta Maharaj, *I Am That*, Vol. II, p. 28.

14. Andrew Harvey, *The Way of Passion, A Celebration of Rumi*, p. 41.

15. Kabir, from *The Kabir Book*, ed. by Robert Bly, p. 70.

16. October Project, "Dark Times" from the album *Falling Further In*, Epic Records Group, 1995. Reprinted with permission of October Project Publishing.

17. k.d. lang, "Wash Me Clean," from the album *Ingénue*, Sire Records Company, 1992. Reprinted with permission of Bumstead Publishing Company.

18. Swami Vivekananda, in *Letters of Swami Vivekananda*, letter dated April 18, 1990, p. 423.

19. Ramana Maharshi, *Talks*, ed. by Venkataramiah, p. 285.

20. Lao Tzu, *Tao Te Ching*, sec. 74, my translation, based on the translations by Gia-Fu Feng, Raghavan Iyer and by Stephen Mitchell.

21. Fenelon, from Aldous Huxley's *The Perennial Philosophy*, p.132.

22. De Caussade, *The Sacrament of the Present Moment*, p. 69.

23 Atisha, from Dilgo Khyentse Rimpoche's *Enlightened Courage*, p. 1.

24. Meister Eckhart, from the collection by Franz Pfeiffer. Quoted in Douglas Harding's *Trial...*, p. 179.

25. Madame Guyon, *A Short Method of Prayer and Spiritual Torrents*, trans. by A.W. Marston.

26. Ramana Maharshi, from *Talks*, ed. by Venkataramiah, p. 175.

27. C.G. Jung, in the foreword to *The Spiritual Teachings of Ramana Maharshi*, p. ix.

28. Jelaluddin Rumi, quoted in Douglas Harding, *Trial...*, p. 30.

29. Ramana Maharshi, from *Day by Day...*, ed. by D. Mudaliar, p. 42.

30. Julian of Norwich, *Revelations of Divine Love*, ed. by Warrack, p.23.

31. Neale Donald Walsh, *Conversations with God, An Uncommon Dialogue*, pp. 3-4.

32. Tracy Chapman, "For You" from the album *Tracy Chapman*, Electra Records, 1988. Reprinted with permission of SBK April Music inc./ Purple Rabbit Music.

33. k.d. lang: "Barefoot" from her unplugged TV appearance, available on the album *The Unplugged Collection*, Volume One, Warner Bros, 1992. Reprinted with permission of Bumstead Publishing.

34. Ramana Maharshi, quoted. in Muruganar, *Guru Vachaka Vovai*, vv. 974, 652, 655. Reprinted with permission of Sri Ramanasramam.

35. Ramana Maharshi *Letters...*, ed. by S. Nagamma, p. 309.

36. Ramana Maharshi, *Talks...*, ed. by M. Venkataramiah, p. 176.

CHAPTER FOURTEEN:
THE WISH FULFILLING JEWEL

1. Angelus Silesius, my translation. Based on the translations by Frederick Frank and Maria Shrady.

2. A gompa is a Tibetan monastry, usually comprising a temple, living quarters for monks, and the seat of an abbot, or Rimpoche. A stupa was a monument built to enshrine the relics of a deceased Buddha, but has come to be a monument built to remind one of the supreme reality.

3. Nisargadatta Maharaj, *I Am That*, Vol. II, ed. by Maurice Friedman, p. 28.

4. Chang Chen-chi, quoted in Seward, *On Being One-Self*, p. 35.

5. Namkhai Norbu, *Dzogchen...*, p. 3.

6. D.E. Harding, quoted in Seward, *On Being One-Self*, p. 49.

7. Nisargadatta Maharaj, *I Am That*, Vol. II, ed. by Maurice Frydman, p. 34.

8. Gautama Buddha, quoted in *The Enlightened Mind*, ed. by Stephen Mitchell, p. 10.

9. Jelaluddin Rumi from *When Grapes Turn to Wine*, trans. by Robert Bly, p. 53.

10. The most famous of these was conducted by Werner Heisenberg in 1952, and is known as Heisenberg's Uncertainty Principle. He demonstrated that subatomic particles behave as waves until they are perceived. In the moment of being seen, of having consciousness shine on them, they "become" particles.

11. Aldous Huxley, *The Perennial Philosophy*, p. 100.

12. Gangaji, or Toni Varner, is also a student of Poonjaji's. She met him in Hardiwar in 1990, and now conducts Satsang in many parts of the world.

13. You can find out about Byron Katie's work and schedule through the Center for the Work, tel. (760) 256-5653.

14. Jelaluddin Rumi: *Open Secret: Versions of Rumi*, translated by Coleman Barks, p.69. Reprinted with permission of the translator.

15. Ramana Maharshi, *Talks...*, ed. by Venkataramiah, p. 6.

16. Nisargadatta Maharaj, *I Am That*, Vol II, ed. by Maurice Friedman, p. 73.

CHAPTER FIFTEEN:
THE END IS THE BEGINNING

1. T.S. Eliot: *The Four Quartets*, "Little Gidding," Section V, in *Collected Poems*, p. 222.

2. *Parabdha karma* means the predestined effects of actions performed in previous lives or earlier in this life, that must still complete themselves.

3. Ramana Maharshi: *Day by Day...*, ed. by D. Mudaliar, p. 189.

4. Joe Miller, *Great Song...*, p. 110.

5. Sosan, *Hsin Hsin Ming*, trans. by Richard B. Clarke, p. 3.

6. *Sadhana*: spiritual practices and austerities.

BIBLIOGRAPHY

These books have all in some way been influential on the creation of what you have read here. Many are quoted and referenced in the Notes section; others were influential in their understanding and inspiration, but are not quoted from directly. It is not recommended to read all of them at once; this may result in severe brain damage.

Adams, Robert. *The Silence of the Heart*. Canoga Park: Adams, 1992.

Aitken, Robert, ed. *A Zen Wave, Basho's Haiku and Zen*. New York: Weatherhill, 1978.

al-Bistami, Abu Yazid. *Translations of Eastern Poetry and Prose*. Ed. by Reynold A. Nicholson, Cambridge: Cambridge University Press, 1922.

Alawi, Al. *A Moslem Saint of the Twentieth Century*. London: George Allen and Unwin, 1961.

Almaas, A.H. *Essence*. York Beach, Maine: Samuel Weisner, Inc., 1986.

_____ *Diamond Heart Books 1-3*. Berkeley: Diamond Books, Almaas Publications, 1987-90.

_____ *The Pearl Beyond Price*. Berkeley: Diamond Books, Almaas Publications, 1988.

_____ *The Void*. York Beach, Maine: Samuel Weisner, Inc., 1986.

Andreas, Connirae. *Heart of the Mind*. Moab: Real People Press, 1989.

Assagioli, Roberto. *Psychosynthesis*. Wellingborough: Turnstone Press, 1965.

Bach, Richard. *Jonathan Livingston Seagull*. Indianapolis: MacMillan, 1970.

_____ *The Bridge Across Forever*. New York: Morrow, 1984.

Badrayana. *Brahma Sutras*. Ed. by Swami Vireswarananda. Calcutta: Advaita Ashrama, 1956.

Balsekar, Ramesh. *Pointers from Sri Nisargadatta Maharaj*. Bombay: Chetana, 1982.

Bandler, Richard and John Grinder. *Frogs into Princes*. Moab: Real People Press, 1979.

_____ *Reframing*. Moab: Real People Press, 1982.

_____ *The Structure of Magic*. Palo Alto: Science and Behaviour Books, 1975.

_____ *Tranceformations*. Moab: Real People Press, 1981.

Baron, Renee and Elizabeth Wagele. *The Enneagram Made Easy*. San Francisco: Harper-SanFrancisco, 1994.

Bateson, Gregory. *Steps Towards an Ecology of Mind*. New York: Ballantine Books, 1972.

Benoit, Hubert. *The Supreme Doctrine: Psychological Studies in Zen Thought*. UK: Sussex Academic Press, 1995.

Bentov, Itzhak. *Stalking the Wild Pendulum: On the Mechanics of Consciousness*. Vermont: Destiny Books, 1984.

Blake, William. *Collected Works*. London: Oxford University Press, 1971.

Bohm, David. *Quantum Theory*. London: Constable, 1951.

_____ *Wholeness and the Implicate Order*. London: Routledge, 1973.

Brunton, Paul. *A Search in Secret India*. Bombay: B. I. Publications, 1980.

Buck, Maurice. *Cosmic Consciousness*. New York: Dutton, 1946.

Buddha, Gautama. *The Teachings of the Compassionate Buddha*. Ed. by E.A. Burtt. New York: Mentor, 1955.

_____ *Dhammapada*. Trans. by S. Radhakrishnan. New York: Oxford University Press, 1936.

_____ *The Diamond Sutra & The Sutra of Hui-Heng*. Trans. by Wong Mou-lam and A.F. Price. Boston: Shambhala Publications, 1990.

Byrom, Thomas, ed. *The Heart of Awareness: Ashtavakra Gita*. Boston: Shambhala Publications, 1990.

Capra, Fritjof. *The Tao of Physics*. New York: Bantam, 1976.

Caussade, De. *The Sacrament of the Present Moment*. Trans. by Kitty Muggeridge. London: Collins, 1982.

Chang, Chu Chi. *The Buddhist Teaching of Totality*. University Park: Pennsylvania State University, 1971.

_____ *The Hundred Thousand Songs of Milarepa*. Trans. by C.C. Garma. New York: University Books, 1962.

Chuang Tzu. *The Complete Works of Chuang Tzu.* Ed. by Burton Watson. Columbia: Columbia University Press, 1968.

Chung-Yuan, Chang, trans. *Original Teachings of Ch'an Buddhism.* New York: Pantheon Books, 1969.

Dalai Lama. *A Flash of Lightning in the Dark of the Night: A Guide to the Bodhisattva's Way of Life.* Boston: Shambhala Publications, 1994.

_____ *A Policy of Kindness.* Ithaca: Snow Lion Publications, 1990.

_____ *Path to Bliss.* Ithaca: Snow Lion Publications, 1991.

Dattatreya. *Avadhuta Gita.* Trans. by Swami Ashokananda. Mylapore: Sri Ramakrishna Math, 1988.

Dominiguez, Joe and Robin, Vicki. *Your Money or Your Life.* New York: Penguin Books, 1992.

Dowman, Keith. *The Flight of the Garuda.* Boston: Wisdom Publications, 1984.

_____, ed. *Sky Dancer: the Secret Life and Songs of the Lady Tsogyel.* London: Routledge & Kegan Paul, 1984.

Druppa, Gyalwa Gendrum. *Training the Mind in the Great Way.* Ithaca: Snow Lion Publications, 1993.

Dytchwald, Ken. *Bodymind.* London: Wildwood House, 1978.

Eckhart, Meister. *Sermons and Treatises.* Trans. by M.O. Walshe. London: Watkins, 1981.

Eliot, T.S. *Collected Poems.* London: Faber and Faber, 1936.

Emerson, Ralph Waldo. *In Tune with the Infinite.* London: Mandala, 1965.

Erickson, Milton. *The Collected Papers of Milton H. Erickson on Hypnosis.* Ed. by E. Rossi. New York: Irvington, 1967-1980.

Feild, Reshad. *The Last Barrier.* New York: Harper and Row, 1976.

Fellowship for Intentional Community. *Directory of Intentional Community.* Langley: FIC, 1995.

Fernstein, George. *Holy Madness.* New York: Paragon House, 1990.

Foligno, Angela of. *Complete Works.* Trans. by Paul Lachance. New York: Paulist Press, 1993.

Foundation for Inner Peace. *The Course in Miracles.* Glen Ellen: Foundation for Inner Peace, 1975.

Gangaji. *You are That, Vols. I and II.* Boulder: Satsang Press, 1995-6.

Gawain, Shakti. *Creative Visualization.* Mill Valley: Whatever Publishing, 1979.

Geldin, E. *Focusing.* New York: Bantam, 1981.

Gibran, Kahlil. *The Prophet.* London: William Heinemann Ltd., 1924.

Golas, Thadeus. *The Lazy Man's Guide to Enlightenment.* New York: Bantam, 1983.

Goldstein, Joseph. *The Experience of Insight.* Boston: Shambhala Publications, 1987.

Goldstein, Joseph and Jack Kornfield. *Seeking the Heart of Wisdom: The Path of Insight Meditation.* Boston: Shambhala Publications, 1987.

Graham, A.C., trans. *The Book of Lieh Tzu.* London: John Murry, 1960.

Gray, John. *Men Are From Mars, Women Are from Venus.* New York: Harper Collins Publishers, Inc., 1992.

Grof, Stanislof. *Beyond the Brain.* Albany: SUNY Press, 1985.

Gurdjieff, George. *All and Everything.* New York: Dutton, 1950.

Guyon, Madame. *A Dazzling Darkness.* Trans. by Patrick Grant. Great Britain: Fount, 1985.

_____ *A Short Method of Prayer and Spiritual Torrents.* Trans. by A.W. Marston. London: Watkins, 1875.

Gyaltsen, Shardza Tashi. *Heart Drops Of Dharmakaya.* Ithaca: Snow Lion Publications, 1993.

Hahn, Thich Nhat. *Old Path White Clouds.* Berkeley: Parallax Press, 1991.

_____ *The Miracle of Mindfulness.* Boston: Beacon Press, 1976.

Hai, Hui. *The Zen Teaching of Hui Hai.* Ed. by John Blofeld. London: Rider & Co, 1969.

Harding, Douglas. *Head Off Stress.* London: Penguin Books, 1990.

_____ *On Having No Head.* London: Penguin Books, 1961.

_____ *The Little Book of Life and Death.* London: Penguin Books, 1989.

_____ *The Trial of the Man Who Said He Was God.* London: Arkana, 1992.

Hari Dass, Baba. *Silence Speaks.* Santa Cruz: Sri Rama Foundation, 1977.

Harvey, Andrew. *The Way of Passion: A Celebration of Rumi.* Berkeley: Frog, Ltd., 1994.
Hay, Louise. *You Can Heal Your Life.* Carlsbad: Hay House, 1984.
Heraclitus. *Fragments.* Chicago: Argonaut, 1969.
Herbert, Nick. *Quantum Reality, Beyond the New Physics.* New York: Anchor Press, 1985.
Hubbard, Barbara Marx. *Revelation: Our Crisis Is Our Birth.* Greenbrae: Foundation for Conscious Evolution, 1993.
_____ *The Hunger of Eve: A Woman's Odyssey Toward the Future.* Eastsound: WA, Sweet Forever Publishing, 1989.
Hutchinson, Michael. *Megabrain: New Tools and Techniques for Brain Growth and Mind Expansion.* New York: Beech Tree Books, 1986.
Huxley, Aldous. *The Perrenial Philosophy.* London: Chatto and Windus, 1969.
Ingram, Catherine. *Walking in the Footsteps of Gandhi.* Berkeley: Parallax Press, 1990.
Jampolsky, Jerry. *Love is Letting Go of Fear.* Millbrae, CA: Celestial Arts, 1979.
Johnson, Robert. *He.* New York: Harper, 1974.
_____ *She.* New York: Harper, 1976.
_____ *We.* New York: Harper, 1978.
Julian of Norwich. *Revelations of Divine Love.* Ed. by Grace Warrack. London: Methuen, 1949.
Kabir. *Songs of Kabir.* Maine: Samuel Weiser Inc., 1992.
_____ *The Kabir Book.* Trans. by Robert Bly. Boston: Beacon Press, 1971.
_____ *Try to Live to See This.* Trans. by Robert Bly. St. Paul: Ally Press, 1976.
Kalsang, Lama Thubten, et al. *Atisha, A Biography of the Renowned Buddhist Sage.* Bangkok: Social Science Association, 1974.
Kapleau, Philip. *The Three Pillars of Zen.* Boston: Beacon Press, 1965.
Kavanaugh, Philip K. *Magnificent Addiction: Discovering Addiction as a Pathway to Healing.* Alpharetta, GA: Aslan Publishers, 1992.
Keleman, Stanley. *Emotional Anatomy, The Structure of Experience.* Berkeley: Centol, 1985.
Keyes, Ken. *A Conscious Person's Guide to Relationships.* St. Mary: Living Love Publications, 1979.
_____ *The Hundredth Monkey.* St. Mary: Vision Books, 1981.
Khyentse, Dilgo. *Enlightened Courage.* Delhi: Sechen Publications, 1992.
_____ *The Heart Treasures of the Enlightened Ones.* Trans. by Padmakara Translation Group. Boston: Shambhala Publications, 1992.
_____ *The Wish Fulfilling Jewel: The Practice of Guru Yoga According to the Longchen Nyingthig Tradition.* Boston: Shambhala Publications, 1988.
Klein, Jean. *Who Am I.* Ed. by Emma Edwards. Shaftesbury: Element Books, 1988.
Kohn, Sherab Chödzin. *The Awakened One: The Life of the Buddha.* Boston: Shambhala Publications, 1994.
Kornfield, Jack. *Path With a Heart; A Practical Guide to the Perils and Promises of Spiritual Life.* New York: Bantam, 1993.
_____ *Seeking the Heart of Wisdom: The Path of Insight Meditation.* Boston: Shambhala Publications, 1987.
Kramer, Joel and Diana Alstadt. *The Guru Papers: Masks of Authoritarian Power.* Berkeley: Frog, 1993.
Krishnamurti, J. *Commentaries on Living.* New York: Harper & Bros., 1956.
_____ *Freedom from the Known.* Ed. by Mary Luytens. New York: Harper & Row, 1969.
_____ *Krishnamurti to Himself, His Last Journal.* San Francisco: Harper & Row, 1987.
_____ *The Awakening of Intelligence.* London: Ebenezer Baylis & Son, 1973.
_____ *The First and Last Freedom.* London: Victor Gollanz, 1954.
_____ *The Only Revolution.* London: Gollanz, 1970.
_____ *The Penguin Krishnamurti Reader.* Ed. by Mary Luytens. Harmondsworth: Penguin Books, 1970.
_____ *The Second Penguin Krishnamurti Reader.* Ed. by Mary Luytens. Harmondsworth: Penguin Books, 1974.
_____ *Think on These Things.* New York: Harper & Bros., 1958.
Kunju, Swami. *Reminiscences.* Tiruvannamalai: Sri Ramanasramam, 1992.

Kurtz, Ron and Prestera, Hector. *The Body Reveals*. San Francisco: Harper, 1976.

Lama Surya Das. *Awakening the Buddha Within, Eight Steps to Enlightenment*. New York: Broadway, 1997.

_____ *Snow Lion's Turquoise Mane: Wisdom Tales from Tibet*. San Francisco: HarperSanFrancisco, 1992.

Lang, R.D. *The Politics of Experience*. London: Penguin Books, 1973.

Lao, Tzu. *Tao Te Ching*. Trans. by Raghavan Iyer. London: Concorn Grove Press, 1983.

_____ *Tao Te Ching*. Trans. by Stephen Mitchell. New York: HarperPerennial, 1988.

_____ *Tao Te Ching*. Trans. by Gia-Fu Feng with Jane English. London: Wildwood House, 1973.

Leggett, Trevor, ed. *A First Zen Reader*. Rutland, VT: Charles Tuttle Co., 1960.

Lessinger, Jack. *Penturbia: Where Real Estate Will Boom After the Crash of Suburbia*. Seattle: SocioEconomics, 1991.

Levine, Stephen. *A Gradual Awakening*. New York: Anchor Press, 1979.

Levine, Stephen and Ondrea. *Embracing the Beloved: Relationship as a Path of Awakening*. New York: Doubleday, 1996.

Long, Barry. *Only Fear Dies*. London: Barry Long Foundation, 1984.

_____ *Stillness is the Way*. London: Barry Long Foundation, 1969.

McGill, Ormond. *Hypnotism and Meditation*. Los Angeles: Westwood Publishing, 1981.

_____ *Hypnotism and Mysticm in India*. Los Angeles: Westwood Publishing, 1979.

McLaughlin, Corinne and Davidson, Gordon. *Builders of the Dawn*. Walpole: Stillpoint, 1985.

Miller, Joe. *Great Song: The Life and Teachings of Joe Miller*. Ed. by Richard Power. Athens, GA: Maypop, 1993.

Milton, Erickson and Davidson, Gordon. *My Voice Will Go With You: The Teaching Tales of Milton H. Erickson*. Ed. by Sidney Rosen. New York: Norton, 1982.

Mitchell, Stephen. *The Enlightened Heart, An Anthology of Sacred Poetry*. New York: HarperPerrenial, 1989.

_____ *The Enlightened Mind, An Anthology of Sacred Prose*. New York: HarperPerennial, 1991.

Muktananda, Swami. *Play of Consciousness*. South Fallsburg: SYDA, 1971.

Muni, G. *Sri Ramana Gita*. Tiruvannamalai: Sri Ramanasramam, 1977.

Naimy, Mikhail. *The Book of Mirdad*. London: Clear Press, 1962.

Narayanananda, Swami, ed. and trans. *Sri Guru Gita*, Rishikesh: Divine Life Society, 1991.

Nisargadatta, Sri Maharaj. *I Am That, Vols. I & II*. Ed. by Maurice Frydman. Bombay: Chetana, 1973.

_____ *Prior to Consciousness*. Ed. by Jean Dunn. Durham: The Acorn Press, 1985.

Norbu, Namkhai. *Dzogchen, The Self Perfected State*. Ed. by John Shane and Adriano Clemente. London: Arkana, 1989.

_____ *The Crystal and the Way of Light*. London: Routledge & Kegan Paul, 1986.

_____ *The Mirror*. Ed. by Adriano Clemente. Barrytown: Station Hill Press, 1983.

Novalis. *Spiritual Saturnalia*. Trans. by John Ritter. New York: Exposition Press, 1971.

Nyima, Chokyi Rinpoche. *The Union of Mahamudra and Dzogchen*. Trans. by Kunsang Erik Pema and Ed. by Marcia Schmidt. Hong Kong: Rangjung Yeshe, 1994.

Om, Swami. *Guru Vachaka Kovai*. New Delhi: Sri Ramana Kendra, 1980.

Osborne, Arthur. *Ramana Maharshi and the Path of Self Knowledge*. Bombay: B.I. Publications, 1954.

Ouspensky, P.D. *In Search of the Miraculous: In Search of an Unknown Teaching*. New York: Harcourt Brace, 1949.

_____ *Tertium Organum: The Third Cannon of Thought: A Key to the Enigma of the World*. Ed. by Nicholas Bessaraboff. New York: Knopf, 1922.

Oxford University Press, *Oxford Sanskrit-English Dictionary*. Oxford: Oxford University Press, 1899.

Padmasambhava. *Self Liberation Through Seeing with Naked Awareness*. Trans. by John Reynolds. Barrytown: Station Hill Press, 1989.

_____ *The Tibetan Book of the Dead*. Trans. by Francessca Freemantle. Boston: Shambhala Publications, 1975.

Patanjali. *How to Know God: The Yoga Sutras of Patanjali*. Trans. by Christopher Isherwood and Swami Prabhavananda. California: New American Library, 1953.

Perls, Fritz. *Gestalt Therapy Verbatim*. Moab: Real People Press, 1969.

Piaget, Jean. *The Origins of Intelligence in Children*. Trans. by Margaret Cook. New York: International University Press, 1952.

Plato. *The Collected Dialogues of Plato*. Trans. and Ed. by R.M. Hare & D.A. Russell. London: Sphere, 1970.

Po, Huang. *The Zen Teachings of Huang Po*. Trans. by John Blofeld. New York: Grove Press, 1958.

Po, Li. *Banished Immortal: Visions of Li T'ai -Po*. Trans. by Sam Hamill. New York: White Pine Press, 1987.

Poonjaji, H.W.L. *Papaji: Interviews*. Ed. by David Godman. Boulder: Avadhuta Foundation, 1993.

_____ *The Truth Is*. Ed. by Prashanti and Vidya. Los Angeles: Yudishtara, 1995.

_____ *Wake Up and Roar, Vols. 1 & 2*. Ed. by Eli Jaxon Bear. Kula: Pacific Center Press, 1992-3.

Prabhavananda, Swami and Frederick Manchester. *The Upanishads*. Los Angeles: Vedanta Society of Southern California, 1948.

Quigley, David. *Alchemical Hypnotherapy*. Readway, CA: Lost Coast Press, 1984.

_____ *The Alchemical Hypnotherapy Workbook*. Santa Rosa: Alchemical Hypnotherapy Institute, 1985-1997.

Radhakrishnan, S., Ed. and Trans. *The Principal Upanisads*. New York: Harper, 1953.

Rajneesh, Bhagwan Shri. *The Book of Wisdom, Vols. I & II*. Poona: India, Rajneesh Foundation, 1976.

Ram Dass. *Be Here Now*. San Cristobal, NM: Lama Foundation, 1975.

_____ *Grist for the Mill*. Santa Cruz: Unity Press, 1976.

_____ *Journey of Awakening*. New York: Bantam, 1978.

_____ *The Only Dance There Is*. New York: Anchor Press, 1974.

Ramamoorthy, H. Dr., trans. *The Ribhu Gita*. Santa Cruz: SAT, 1995.

Ramana Maharshi. *Be As You Are: The Teachings of Sri Ramana Maharshi*. Ed. by David Godman. London: Arkana, 1985.

_____ *Crumbs from His Table*. Ed. by R. Swarnagiri. Tiruvannamalai: Sri Ramanasramam, 1981.

_____ *Day by Day with Bhagavan*. Ed. by Devaraja Mudaliar. Tiruvannamalai: Sri Ramanasramam, 1977.

_____ *Forty Verses on Reality*. Ed. by S.S. Cohen. London: Watkins, 1978.

_____ *Letters from Sri Ramanasramam*. Ed. by Suri Nagamma. Tiruvannamalai: Sri Ramanasramam, 1970.

_____ *Maharshi's Gospel*. Ed. by T.N. Venkataraman. Tiruvannamalai: Sri Ramanasramam,1979.

_____ *Moments Remembered*. Ed. by V. Ganesan. Tiruvannamalai: Sri Ramanasramam, 1990.

_____ *Self Realization, The Life and Teachings of Ramana Maharshi*. Ed. by S.S. Cohen and Swami B.V. Narasimha. Tiruvannamalai: T.N. Venkataraman, 1985.

_____ *Spiritual Stories*. Tiruvannamalai: T.N. Venkataraman, 1980.

_____ *Talks with Sri Ramana Maharshi*. Ed. by Munagala Venkataramiah. Tiruvannamalai: Sri Ramanasramam, 1978.

_____ *The Collected Works of Sri Ramana Maharshi*. Ed. by Arthur Osborne. London: Rider and Company, 1970.

_____ *The Maharshi's Way*. Ed. by D.M. Sastri. Tiruvannamalai: Sri Ramanasramam, 1989.

_____ *The Spiritual Teachings of Ramana Maharshi*. Boston: Shambhala Publications, 1972.

_____ *The Teachings of Ramana Maharshi*. Ed. by Arthur Osborne. Tiruvannamalai: Sri Ramanasramam, 1988.

_____ *Who*. Tiruvannamalai: T.N. Venkataraman, 1931.

Reps, Paul. *Zen Flesh, Zen Bones*. Garden City: Doubleday, 1957.

Roman, Sanaya. *Creating Money: Keys to Abundance*. Tiburon, CA: H.J. Kramer, 1988.

Rossi, Ernest. *The Psychobiology of Mind Body Healing*. New York: Norton, 1986.

Rumi, Jelaluddin. *These Branching Moments*. Trans. by Coleman Barks and John Moyne. Providence, RI: Copper Beach Press, 1988.

_____ *Delicious Laughter*. Trans. by Coleman Barks. Athens, GA: Maypop, 1990.

_____ *Like This*. Trans. by Coleman Barks. Athens, GA: Maypop, 1990.

_____ *Open Secret: Versions of Rumi*. Trans. by Coleman Barks and John Moyne. Putney: Threshold Books, 1984.

_____ *The Essential Rumi*. Trans. by Coleman Barks. San Francisco: HarperSanFrancisco, 1995.

_____ *This Longing*. Trans. by Coleman Barks. Putney: Threshold Books, 1988.

_____ *Unseen Rain: Quatrains of Rumi*. Trans. by Coleman Barks and John Moyne. Putney: Threshold Books, 1986.

_____ *We are Three: New Rumi Poems*. Trans. by Coleman Barks. Athens, GA: Maypop, 1987.

_____ *When Grapes Turn to Wine*. Trans. by Robert Bly. San Diego: Firefly Press, 1983.

Saraswathi, Ramamanda, trans. *Tripura Rahasya*. Tiruvannamalai: T.N. Venkataraman, 1980.

Segal, Suzanne. *Collision With the Infinite: A Life Beyond the Personal Life*. San Diego: Blue Dove Press, 1996.

Senzaki, Nyogen and Saladin Reps, Eds. *The Gateless Gate*. Los Angeles: John Murray, 1934.

Seward, Anne, ed. *On Being One-Self*. Ipswich: Sholland Publications, 1991.

Shakespeare, William. *Complete Works*. Baltimore: Penguin Books, 1969.

Shantideva. *The Way of the Bodhisattva: A Translation of the Bodhicharyavatara*. Trans. by Padmakara Translation Group. Boston: Shambhala Publications, 1997.

Shastri, Hari Prasad. *Ashtavakra Gita*. London: Shanti Sagar, 1972.

Silesius, Angelus. *The Book of Angelus Silesius*. Ed. and trans. by Frederick Franck. Santa Fe: NM, Bear and Co., 1976.

_____ *The Cherubinic Wanderer*. Trans. by Maria Shrady. New York: Paulist Press, 1986.

Sinetar, Marsha. *Do What You Want and the Money Will Follow: Discovering Your Right Livelihood*. New York: Dell, 1987.

Sinkler, Lorraine. *The Spiritual Journey of Joel S. Goldsmith*. Valor: Valor Foundation, 1992.

Small, Jacquelyn. *Becoming Naturally Therapeutic*. Austin: Eupsychian Press, 1981.

_____ *Embodying Spirit*. San Francisco: Hazelden, 1994.

_____ *Rising to the Call*. Marina Del Ray: Devorss & Co., 1997.

_____ *Transformers, The Therapists of the Future*. Marina Del Ray: Devorss & Co., 1982.

Sogyal Rimpoche. *The Tibetan Book of Living and Dying*. Ed. by Andrew Harvey. San Francisco: HarperSanFrancisco, 1992.

Sosan, The Third Zen Patriarch. *Hsin Hsin Ming*. Trans. by Richard B. Clark. Buffalo, NY: White Pine Press, 1970.

Sterry, Peter. *Select Writings*. Ed. by N.I. Muter. New York: University of Kansas Humanistic Studies, 1994.

Stone, Hal and Sidra Fieldman. *Embracing Ourselves*. Marina Del Ray: Devorss & Co., 1985.

Sunyata. *Sunyata*. Ed. by Betty Camhi. Berkeley: North Atlantic Books, 1990.

Suzuki, P.T. *Zen Buddhism*. New York: Doubleday, 1956.

Suzuki, Shunryu. *Zen Mind, Beginner's Mind*. San Francisco: San Francisco Zen Center, 1970.

Tagore, Rabagrindath. *Gitanjali*. London: Macmillan and Company, 1924.

Talbot, Michael. *Mysticism and the New Physics*. New York: Bantam, 1981.

_____ *The Holographic Universe*. New York: Harper Collins, 1991.

Tapasyananda, Swami, ed. *Srimad Bhagavad Gita*. Mylapore: Sri Ramakrishna Math, 1970.

Tart, Charles. *Altered States of Consciousness*. New York: Wiley, 1969.

_____ *Living the Mindful Life*. Berkeley: Shambhala Publications, 1994.

_____ *Waking Up: Overcoming the Obstacles to Human Potential*. Boston: New Science Library, 1986.

Titmuss, Christopher. *Freedom of the Spirit: More Voices of Hope for a World in Crisis*. UK: Greenprint, 1992.

_____ *Spirit of Change: Voices of Hope for a Better World*. UK: Greenprint, 1990.

Titmuss, Christopher(cont.). *The Profound and the Profane: An Inquiry Into Spiritual Awakening.* UK: Buddhist Publications, 1995.

Trumpa, Chogyum. *Journey Without a Goal.* Boston: Shambhala Publications, 1981.

_____ *Cutting through Spiritual Materialism.* Ed. by John Baker. Berkeley: Shambhala Publications, 1973.

_____ *Shambhala.* Boston: Shambhala Publications, 1984.

_____ *The Myth of Freedom.* Ed. by John Baker. Boulder: Shambhala Publications, 1976.

Tsogyal, Yeshe. *The Lotus Born, the Life Story of Padmasambhava.* Boston: Shambhala Publications, 1993.

Tulku, Tarthang. *Knowledge of Time and Space.* Oakland: Dharma Publishing, 1990.

_____ *Time Space and Knowledge: A New Vision of Reality.* Oakland: Dharma Publishing, 1977.

Tung-shan. *The Record of Tung-shan.* Honolulu: University of Hawaii Press, 1986. Ed. by William F. Powell.

Tweedie, Irina. *The Chasm of Fire.* Longmead, UK: Element Books, 1979.

Underhill, Evelyn. *Mysticism: The Nature and Development of Spiritual Consciousness.* New York: Dutton, 1961.

Vasistha. *Yoga Vasistha Sara.* Trans. by Swami Sureshananda. Tiruvannamalai: Sri Ramanasramam, 1973.

_____ *The Supreme Yoga: the Yoga Vasistha.* Freemantle: The Chiltern Yoga Trust, 1976. Ed. by Swami Venkatesananda.

Vivekananda, Swami. *Letters of Swami Vivekananda.* Calcutta: Advaita Ashrama, 1976.

Walsch, Neale Donald. *Conversations With God, An Uncommon Dialogue.* Charlottesville, VA: Hampton Roads, 1995.

Watts, Alan. *Psychotherapy East and West.* London: Random, 1975.

_____ *The Book on the Taboo Against Knowing Who You Are.* London: Random, 1989.

_____ *The Joyous Cosmology.* London: Random, 1968.

_____ *The Supreme Identity.* London: Random, 1972.

_____ *The Wisdom of Insecurity.* London: Random, 1975.

Wei Wu Wei. *The Tenth Man.* Hong Kong: Hong Kong University Press, 1971.

Weil, Simone. *Waiting for God.* New York: Putnam, 1951. Ed. and Trans. by Emma Crawford.

Welwood, John. *Journey of the Heart.* New York: Harper Collins, 1990.

Whitman, Walt. *Leaves of Grass.* New York: Grosset and Dunlap, 1931.

Wilber, Ken. *A Brief History of Everything.* Boston: Shambhala Publications, 1996.

_____ *Eye of Spirit: An Integral Vision for a World Gone Slightly Mad.* Berkeley: Shambhala Publications, 1997.

_____ *No Boundary: Eastern and Western Approaches to Personal Growth.* Boulder: New Science Library, 1981.

_____ *Quantum Questions.* Boston: New Science Library, 1984.

_____ *Sex, Ecology, Spirituality.* Boston: Shambhala Publications, 1995.

_____ *The Spectrum of Consciousness.* Wheaton, Ill: Quest, 1977.

Wittgenstein, Ludwig. *Tractatus-Logico-Philosophicus.* London: Routledge & Kegan Paul, 1981.

Wolinsky, Stephen. *Quantum Consciousness: The Discovery of the Birth of Quantum Psychology.* Connecticut: Bramble, 1992.

Wolinsky, Stephen. *Trances People Live.* Connecticut: Bramble, 1991.

Yeats W.B. & Shree Purohit Swami, trans. *The Ten Principal Upanisads.* London: Faber and Faber, 1937.

Zukav, Gary. *The Dancing Wu Li Masters: An Overview of the New Physics.* New York: Bantam, 1984.

ABOUT THE LIVING ESSENCE FOUNDATION

The Living Essence Foundation operates on a not-for-profit basis, and at the time of writing is applying for 501(C)3 status. Our offices are located in San Rafael, California.

We offer individual sessions, evening events, weekend seminars and a professional training utilizing the principles described in this book.

To arrange for Arjuna or another practitioner to bring this work to your area, you can contact us at the address below.

Individual sessions are available with practitioners in many locations in the US and also in Europe. Contact us for a referral in your area.

We offer five different weekend seminars as an introduction to this work. Each seminar starts on Friday evening, and finishes on Sunday evening. Seminars include sessions of deep relaxation and inquiry as a group, partnered exercises, periods of meditation, stretching and movement, and plenty of time for questions and discussion. Facilitators are available to travel to your area to conduct seminars.

Our professional training comprises six levels, each of which is a 50-hour module. We offer courses both on weekends and as residential retreats. Levels 1 to 3 include many of the sessions described in this book. Levels 4 and above cover more advanced material. The training includes exercises and meditations done as a group or with a partner, demonstrations, movement, as well as discussion and practice time. Although many people take our training for their own personal enhancement, Levels 3 and beyond lead to certification as a hypnotherapist, and our courses are recognized by the American Council of Hypnotist Examiners.

For more information contact:
Living Essence Foundation
454 Las Gallinas Avenue, #308
San Rafael, CA 94903
within the San Francisco Bay area: (415) 492-1186
outside the SF Bay area: 1-800-VASTNESS
fax: (415) 491-1085
e-mail: info@livingessence.com
Web address:
www.livingessence.com

THE LIVING ESSENCE
TAPE SERIES

The Living Essence Tape Series allows you to experience the sessions described in this book on your own. On side A of each tape, Arjuna guides you through one of the sessions, accompanied by music composed specifically to enhance deepening and wakefulness. Side B features the same music used on Side A without voice so that you can guide yourself through the process after you have used Side A a few times.

Titles currently available:
Tape 1: Who Am I? (described in Chapter 5).
Tape 2: There Is No Other (described in Chapter 6).
Tape 3: The Heart Meditation (described in Chapter 4).
Tape 4: Deeper and Deeper (described in Chapter 3).
Tape 5: The Beloved (described in Chapter 8).
Tape 6: The Guru Is In (described in Chapter 9).

Other titles will become available during 1998.

Each tape costs $10.98.
CA residents add 80¢ per tape sales tax.
Shipping: $2.50 first tape, $1.50 each additional tape in the U.S.

For a brochure describing the tapes which are currently available, or to order tapes, write to us at:

Self X Press Publications
4340 Redwood Highway, Suite F218
San Rafael, California 94903
USA

You can also call us at 1-800-VASTNESS
(415) 492-1186 within the San Francisco Bay area
Extension 2.

e-mail: books@livingessence.com

Visit us on the Web at
www.livingessence.com/tapes

THE AUTHOR AND FRIENDS

Arjuna Nick Ardagh operated the Macintosh computer used to write this book, and so gets to have his name on the cover. The real author remains a mystery. After graduating with a Master's degree from Cambridge University in England in 1979, Arjuna trained in a variety of styles of hypnotherapy and bodywork. He has been practicing and teaching since then, and is an examiner for the American Council of Hypnotist Examiners. He founded the Alchemical Hypnotherapy Institute of Seattle in 1988, and created the *Alchemical Journeys* tape series.

Arjuna has maintained an unbroken passion for spiritual awakening since 1971, and has lived and studied with teachers from a number of different traditions and backgrounds. In 1991 he met his true Teacher, H.W.L. Poonjaji, who pointed Arjuna's attention back to the immediate availability of the Self in this very moment. Arjuna lived with his Teacher for a year, and returned to the West to teach in 1992, at Poonjaji's request.

Arjuna is the founding director of the Living Essence Foundation, and the creator of the Living Essence tapes series, and the Living Essence training. He conducts Satsang, weekend seminars and the Living Essence training in many locations both in the U.S. and elsewhere. He maintains a private practice in Marin County, California, where he lives with his wife and two sons, who perform regular earlobe elongation therapy on him.

Stephan Bodian, MFCC, edited the manuscript. He was editor of *Yoga Journal* for ten years, and is the author of *Timeless Visions, Healing Voices*. He maintains a psychotherapy practice in San Rafael, and works as a freelance editor and writer.

Trinette Reed took the cover photograph. She is a freelance photographer living in San Anslemo, California. Contact her at (415) 457-2267, or see more of her work at www.sirius.com/~trinette.

Jaclyne Scardova created the illustrations. She is a freelance illustrator living in Fairfax, California.

ACKNOWLEDGEMENTS

Many hands have brought this into reality over the last three years. If I forgot you please forgive me, and know that I am grateful for your help.

For editorial comments and encouragement I want to thank Jack Kornfield, Stephan Bodian, Hanuman Justin Golden, Juliette Anthony, Brian Mayne, David Quigley, and Catherine Ingram.

For providing refuge from the slings and arrows of outrageous fortune, I want to thank Swami Prabuddhananda and the endlessly generous community at the Vedanta Retreat in Olema.

For generous financial support I want to thank Juliana Navarra.

For typing and transcribing my wild ravings I thank David Webb, Elloddee Cloninger and Mary Bibighaus.

For painstakingly reading the manuscript and spotting all my dyslexic errors I thank Juliette Anthony, Renee Stark, Jeanne Messer, Jane Ferris, Kamala Austin, Richard Shapiro, Karen La Puma, and Subhadra Ardagh. And for not only spotting record numbers of bloomers, but also correcting them all, way beyond the call of duty, I thank the book's official guardian angel, Becky Brudniak.

Thanks to Gaelyn and Braum Larrick and their staff at Lightbourne Images for creating the cover. Thanks to Evan Naylor at Inhouse Design for performing Cinderella-like transformations on my photographs in Photoshop.

Thanks to Simon Warwick Smith for introducing me to the giddy world of publishing, and holding my hand through the labor pains.

I thank Wendy and Serge Feder in London, Muckti and Veda Marcom in Boston, Roger and Heidi Day in Seattle, Jocelyn Olivier and her staff in Marin, Vajra Matusow in Marin, Renee and Rich Stark in Denver, Trisha Mitchell, Hugh Kuzara and Illeen Haykus in Pagosa Springs, Donna Hamilton in Reno, Judy Ward in Spokane, Debra Evans at the Whole Life Expo, and Gil Boyne at the American Council of Hypnotist Examiners for the willingness and courage to take a chance on something new, and to sponsor my workshops and trainings.

I thank Peter Devries, Catrina Roesch, Susan Justice, Maxine Steingold, George Monoson, Bill Swahlen, Jai Conley, Swarna Wendy Wilkins, Kamala Austin, Jen Klarfeld, Jaclyne Scardova, Karen La Puma, Jane Ferris, Donna Hamilton, Patricia Krown, Richard Shapiro, Robin Fett and Kathlyn Pihl for offering themselves as guinea pigs for these tools, and assisting me in the presentation and teaching of the training. I also thank all my students and clients for support and patience during the birthing of this new approach.

And above all I want to thank my friend and wife, Subhadra and my two sons, Abhi and Shuba, for the patience to tolerate the disruption to normal family life while I retreated away with my laptop Mac for days on end.

INDEX

ORDERING INFORMATION

You can purchase more copies of this book from your local book-store, or directly from Self X Press Publishing.

Additional Copies cost $18.95 each.
Discounts are available for purchases in quantity.
Bookstores order from all major wholesalers.

Sales Tax:
California Residents please add 7.25%
Ohio residents ordering by phone with credit card
please add 6%.

Shipping:
For 4th class book rate in the U.S. please add $4.00 for the
first book, and $2.00 for each additional book.
For priority mail in the U.S. please add $6.00.
For overnight delivery please add $18.00
For surface mail overseas, please add $4.00.
For air mail overseas, please add: Canada and Mexico:
$7; Europe or Australia: $12.00

By telephone: Call 1-888-32-BOOKS. (24 hours).
Have your Mastercard, Visa, Discover or
American Express card ready.

By Mail: Send your order with payment to:
Self X Press Publications
4340 Redwood Highway Suite F218
San Rafael, CA 94903
USA.

For wholesale rates please call (415) 492-1186 Extension 3.
Or fax us at (415) 491-1085.

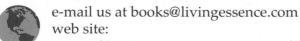

e-mail us at books@livingessence.com
web site:
www.livingessence.com/books